Britain and Barbary, 1589–1689

Florida A&M University, Tallahassee
Florida Atlantic University, Boca Raton
Florida Gulf Coast University, Ft. Myers
Florida International University, Miami
Florida State University, Tallahassee
University of Central Florida, Orlando
University of Florida, Gainesville
University of North Florida, Jacksonville
University of South Florida, Tampa
University of West Florida, Pensacola

Britain and Barbary, 1589–1689

Nabil Matar

University Press of Florida
Gainesville · Tallahassee · Tampa · Boca Raton
Pensacola · Orlando · Miami · Jacksonville · Ft. Myers

First Paperback Printing, 2006

A record of cataloging-in-publication data is available from
the Library of Congress.
ISBN 0-8130-2871-X; ISBN 0-8130-3076-5 (pbk.)

The University Press of Florida is the scholarly publishing agency
for the State University System of Florida, comprising Florida A&M
University, Florida Atlantic University, Florida Gulf Coast University,
Florida International University, Florida State University, University of
Central Florida, University of Florida, University of North Florida,
University of South Florida, and University of West Florida.

University Press of Florida
15 Northwest 15th Street
Gainesville, FL 32611-2079
http://www.upf.com

For Rudy,
friend and colleague

Contents

Preface and Acknowledgments

This book is the final installment in my trilogy about Britain and the Islamic world, and my excursion into captivity writings. In particular, I turn to the direct impact of the Barbary region on the culture and history of Britain and focus on specific case studies. Barbary was the region in the Muslim world that had the widest-ranging relations with Britain—more so than the Ottoman Levant or Central Asia. It was a region that played an important role in the nation formation (Richard Helgerson's phrase) of early modern Britons.

The English victory over the Spanish Armada in 1588 inaugurated diplomatic and military coordination between the monarchs of England and Morocco, Queen Elizabeth I and Mulay Ahmad al-Mansur. This cooperation brought to London Moroccan ambassadors, who inspired the complex and disturbing figure of the Moor in Elizabethan drama, starting with George Peele's *The Battle of Alcazar* (1589) and ending with Shakespeare's *Othello* (ca. 1602) and Thomas Heywood's *The Fair Maid of the West, Part I* (ca. 1600–1603). From the death of Queen Elizabeth on, relations between Britain and Barbary swung between cooperation and conflict, trade and piracy, and were often determined by the crisis of captivity that dominated the policies—if there were any—of the Jacobean, Caroline, Interregnum, and Restoration administrations (those of James I and II, and Charles I and II). The captivity of thousands of Britons—men, women and children—and the inability or unwillingness of the monarchs to liberate them, drove numerous members of Parliament to join in an opposition to King Charles I that, along with other issues, finally led to the Civil Wars. Meanwhile, the crisis of captivity was effecting an important change in the social roles of women: the first political movement of women (mostly wives) in early modern England came into being as a result of the Barbary captivity of male breadwinners. Women organized themselves as petitioners and approached both king and Parliament with their "wifely" appeals for ransoming their kinsmen. Other women were themselves taken captive in Barbary and subjugated and enslaved. For the first time in the history of Britain, change was forced on its political and social culture by the world of Islam.

The evolution in British naval and commercial power in the early years of the Interregnum enabled Britons to expand their slave trade from the Atlantic to the Mediterranean, and to expand from capturing and selling sub-Saharan Africans to trading in Libyans, Tunisians, Algerians and Moroccans—the "Moors" (in Arabic, the Magharibi). Britons were not only captives, as Linda Colley has shown in *Captives* (2002); they themselves were captors of North Africans. Meanwhile, the occupation of Tangier in 1662 brought Britons their first colonial challenge in the lands of Islam. Having had some experience in North America, Britons found themselves having to forge a different colonial strategy, and to change and modulate it in light of financial, military and administrative expediency. The vast literature on Tangier shows how the challenges of Barbary were not successfully met and ended in the defeat of 1684 and the desertion of the bastion.

By the time the last Moor play was staged, John Dryden's *Don Sebastian* (1689), British stockholders and military strategists had realized that it was better to dominate not territory and people but the venues of commercial activity—the maritime routes of the Mediterranean and the Atlantic. The expansion of the navy from the middle of the century on brought to an end the military challenge of Barbary, after which the Moors disappeared from Britain's political and literary imagination. They became so unreal and unthreatening that when Jonathan Swift thought of Lilliputians in 1726, he thought them "Alcoran"-reading Muslims. The period between 1589 and 1689 marks the rise and fall of the role of the Moor in the making of the British identity.

*   *   *

Some of the material in this book has been taken from my earlier publications: "Moroccan Captives in Early Modern England," in *Actes du 1er Congrès International sur le Grande Bretagne et le Maghreb: Etat de recherche et contacts culturels* (Zaghouane, Tunisia, 2001), 141–51; "The Barbary Corsairs, King Charles I and the Civil War," *The Seventeenth Century* 16 (2001): 239–59; and "Wives, Captive Husbands and Turks: The First Women Petitioners in Caroline England," *Explorations in Renaissance Culture* 23 (1997): 111–29. I am grateful for permission from the publishers to use some of the material.

Part of chapter 1 was presented as the Sam Wanamaker Fellowship Lecture at Shakespeare's Globe Theatre in London on 7 April 2004. I am grateful to Patrick Spottiswoode, director of Globe Education, for inviting me to deliver this lecture, and for his warm companionship throughout the week I was in London. I am also grateful to Professor Jack D'Amico of Canisius College for initially putting forward my name, and to H.E. Mr. Mohammed Belmahi, Moroccan ambassador to the United Kingdom, who shared with me his private collection of documents and illustrations and graciously responded to many of my queries. I also wish to thank Andrew Marr for inviting me to his *Start of the Week* show on the BBC, where I had occasion to present my work on Britain and Barbary.

I wish to thank Jean–Raymond Frontain for inviting me to present "Contextualizing the Elizabethan Moor: Three Case Studies" at the University of Central Arkansas (3 October 2003); Lynn Dahmen for inviting me to present "Moroccan-European Encounters" at al-Akhawayn University, Ifrane, Morocco (16 June 2003); and Khalid Bekkaoui for exposing me to a most energetic and wonderful group of students at the University of Sidi Mohammed Ben Abdallah in Fez, where I presented "British Captives in Morocco" (18 June 2003). Both Lynn and Khalid made my trip to Morocco memorable. Many thanks are also due Kenneth Parker for inviting me to give one of the plenary presentations at the University of London, 5 December 2002, and to Matthew Birchwood and Matthew Dimmock for their help and cooperation. Thanks are also due Mihoko Suzuki for inviting me to present "Women Captives in the Early Modern Mediterranean" at Miami University (7 November 2002). I am grateful to the participants in the Ninth International Conference on the Seventeenth Century, Durham University, where I presented "English Women Captives in the Barbary Coast" (15 July 2001), and to Richard Maber, who always brings together a wonderful assembly of researchers; and to the participants in the conference on "From Strangers to Citizens," London, where I presented "The First Muslims in England" (5–7 April 2000).

Many friends and colleagues have shared with me their thoughts and works-in-progress. I want to thank Bindu Malieckal of St. Anselm College, Gerald MacLean of Wayne State University (also for giving me the opportunity to read his insightful *The Rise of Oriental Travel* in galleys), Mark Netzloff of the University of Wisconsin, Milwaukee, and John Tolan of the University de Nantes, all of whom were kind enough to send me many of their publications. Professors Mohammad Shaheen (University of Jordan) and Muhammad Asfour (University of Sharjah) responded to many of my queries with their usual dedication and perspicacity, while Anouar Majid (University of New England), in very trying times, remained my inspiring guide on Moroccan history. Also, I wish to thank the three readers to whom this typescript was sent. Their corrections and suggestions helped me greatly. I also want to recognize fellow travelers on the road, whose friendship and work have been inspiring: Jerry Brotton and William Dalrymple; and from my Cambridge days, my friend of over thirty years, David Brooks, and my supervisor and first mentor, Dominic Baker-Smith. To Alex Baramki, who always reads and comments carefully, I extend my gratitude for sparing me many an embarrassing slip.

I also wish to thank Carolyn Russ, copy editor for the University Press of Florida, for her meticulous work in ensuring the accuracy and consistency of the typescript. Any errors that remain are mine.

From Florida Tech, I wish to thank my new dean, Mary Beth Kenkel, for approving funds to cover the finalization of this book; and my previous dean, Gordon Nelson, whose encouragement of humanities research has been invaluable to me over the past years; Alan Rosiene, who is ever helpful with his detailed knowledge of medieval comparative literature and history; Jane Tolbert for discussing French seventeenth-century history with me; Tina Christodouleas for helping me with Spanish material; and as always, my former department head, Professor Jane Patrick, whose soul shines with light and who gave me the start that made everything possible.

I am also grateful to the secretaries at the Humanities and Communication

Department: Marilyn Goravitch, Suanne Powell and Delilah Caballero. Without them, I would not have had the protection that is needed for research, and without their efficiency and reliability, I would have met with many departmental misfortunes.

The staff of many libraries made this project possible: the Houghton Library, Harvard University; the library of UCLA; the Public Record Office, London; the Bodleian Library, Oxford; the University Library, Cambridge; the British Library, London; the Devon Public Record Office, Exeter; the Bibliothèque Nationale, Rabat; the Bibliothèque Royale, Rabat; and the Bibliothèque Nationale, Tunis. I wish to thank very much Victoria Smith of the Interlibrary Loan Services at Florida Institute of Technology for her continued and unfailing dedication during the course of the years. Finally, every Wednesday, I worked in a soundproof room at the library of Sebastian River High School: I am thankful to Dr. P. Jones, the principal, and to the library staff for their cooperation and assistance.

✳   ✳   ✳

Unless otherwise indicated, all translations are mine. I have remained as close to the original as possible. I have used "England" for the period before 1603, and "Britain" thereafter.

✳   ✳   ✳

This book is dedicated to Rudolph Stoeckel. For nearly two decades, he has been part of my life in a way that few friends can be, but then he is a man who has been in the lives of many, ranging from friends in the U.S. Marine Corps to undergraduate and graduate classmates, students, academic colleagues and boon companions. I am fortunate that I have been one of the many. Since the late 1980s, we have been friends, through thick and thin; we have agreed and disagreed, shouted and debated, argued and listened to music. In the process, I have learned much from him, about both seventeenth-century English drama and the culture of America (Rudy wrote his dissertation on John Ford). It is to Rudy that I have turned with my questions about America—its codes, buzzwords, anxieties and conundrums, which the immigrant can never understand and must carefully learn. Through him, I have been able to enter more richly into the life of my adopted society. He has always been a voice of rationality and individuality, and even in the most tense of times, he has retained his breadth and courage. Never, in all the years I have known him, did he not uphold his intellectual fierceness.

But the greatest mark that Rudy makes is on his students. As a professor, none has been admired and liked more than he. Whenever I mention his name to students during their exit interview, their faces beam and their eyes light up. He has had the ability to enter into their world, and with his extensive reading and incisive memory, his musical ear and travel knowledge, to engage them passionately and critically. Even as he struggled with pain and cancer, he never missed his classes, ever inscribing himself on the minds and hearts of his students. Once, as we were having a bagel at a coffee shop in Melbourne, a student came up to him and said, "You don't remember me, but years ago, you taught me to identify the material of the handle on Telemachos' bedroom door. I have never forgotten it." Rudy is a master of detail, in reading poetry as in analyzing rhyme and meter, in selecting wines and delving into words and frescoes, as in exploring his native Montreal and the alleys of Trastevere.

As Rudy approaches retirement, he will remain the dearest of friends. May he, with his wife Camilla beside him, ever be the inspiration for young and old, a mind burning with a passion for beauty and truth.

Introduction

Studies on the making of Britain's imperial identity have been appearing on a regular basis. In an excellent group of essays collected by Nicholas Canny, *The Oxford History of the British Empire: The Origins of Empire, British Overseas Enterprise to the Close of the Seventeenth Century* (1998), the authors examined Britain's imperial venture, from the modest but brutal beginnings in Ireland to the conquest and creation of Virginia and New England. In another impressive collection, by Martin Daunton and Rick Halpern, *Empire and Others* (1999), the editors maintained that the colonization of America dramatically and deeply influenced British identity. In their survey of the historiographical evidence, the authors focused on the relationship between the making of national identity and the expansion of the imperial borders in the eighteenth and nineteenth centuries.

In these and other studies, the making of the English (and later British) identity has been associated with two forces: Protestantism and colonization. Britons, both men and women, it has been argued, gradually articulated their sense of self in light of their adherence to Protestant theology (with explicit opposition to Catholicism) and their colonial thrusts into Ireland and North America—thrusts that later transformed into imperial realization. In *Colonial Writing and the New World, 1583–1671* (1999), Thomas Scanlan identified the year 1583 as a convenient date for the beginning of the articulation of that identity because in that year, Las Casas' *Brevísima relación* was published in an English translation. The text combined a description of the Spanish conquest of America with an indictment of Catholic violence against the Native Americans. To its English readers, the book served to alert them to the vast opportunities on that rich continent, and at the same time to denounce Catholicism and set the readers apart from the Papacy and its Inquisition. The "colonial project," Scanlan stated, "became one of the primary ways that the English used to articulate and define their own emerging sense of nationhood."[1]

But the "colonial project" was more in English imagination than English deeds, as Mary Fuller, Gerald MacLean, Kenneth Parker, Jeffrey Knapp, David Armitage and others have shown. It is difficult to speak of a "language of empire" in Elizabethan England in the manner that that language informed Spanish literature of the Golden Age, as Anthony Pagden has shown.[2] After all, when England declared itself an "empire" in the Act of Restraint of Appeals in 1535, the term simply meant, according to Willy Maley, that it was a "sovereign territorial state which was completely independent of the pope and all foreign princes," and when Henry VIII declared himself king of Ireland in 1541, he merely turned "empire" into "an imperial monarchy."[3] Even a century later, England had very few possessions beyond the British Isles—in contrast to the vast regions claimed by Spain. It was John Dee who first used the phrase "British Empire," as Joyce Youings has observed, a phrase that had "a decidedly Welsh flavour, incorporating for example the legend of Prince Madoc, who allegedly began the colonization of Dee's *Atlantis* (viz America) in the twelfth century."[4] The British Empire was a construct of literary imagination and nationalist exuberance; it did not reflect a contemporary reality. Queen Elizabeth admitted to her unwillingness to support imperial expansion, as a speech given at the closing of Parliament in April 1593 shows:

> It may be thought simplicity in me that all this time of my reign I have not sought to advance my territories and enlarge my dominions, for both opportunity hath served me to do it, and my strength was able to have done it. I acknowledge my womanhood and weakness in that respect, but it hath been fear to obtain or doubt how to keep the things so obtained that hath withholden me from these attempts; only, my mind was never to invade my neighbors, nor to usurp upon any, only contented to reign over my own and to rule as a just prince.[5]

Notwithstanding the possible posturing on the part of the queen, especially in regard to her "womanhood" to which she often alluded when she sought to explain her actions or inactions, her words confirm Molly Greene's argument that Fernand Braudel's thesis about the European "Northern invasion" is not valid before the second half of the seventeenth century. Greene argued that lucrative trade and exchange continued to take place among the various peoples of the Mediterranean "throughout the seventeenth century, only giving way to English and French dominations towards its end," more specifically in the case of England, after 1650.[6] Indeed, if the English emphasis on trade delayed the fulfillment of the colonial goal, as Youings and Armitage have argued, it may well be that the availability of large amounts of resources in North Africa and the openness of the Muslim markets also played a role in delaying the westward colonial venture. As long as there was profitable trade with the Barbary region, there was no need to sail far and wide in dangerous search of colonial conquest and settlement.[7]

The English imaginary imperialism, or the "empire nowhere," to use Jeffrey Knapp's title of his seminal study,[8] does not, of course, diminish the role of Protestantism and colonization in the formation of England's and Britain's national identity. English readers, after all, were being encouraged to "rule the waves" and were told that they should set their goals at gaining more land and wealth in the Americas than the Spanish or Portuguese imperialists.[9] But what has been ignored in all the above studies—and in novels, too[10]—is geographic inclusiveness. Literary critics, historians and cultural historians have all focused their attention on England's thrust into Ireland and later into America, without mentioning anything about England's trade, diplomacy and treatises with the Barbary States.

Although Linda Colley, in her *Captives*, alerted readers to the importance of England's involvement in Tangier (and much earlier, E. M. G. Routh, too, in her study on *Tangier: England's Lost Atlantic Outpost*), she focused predominantly on the seizure of British captives. But "Barbary" presented to England more than just a crisis of captives: long before English sailors and settlers crossed the ocean to North America to conquer and settle, they had sailed down the Spanish coast to the northern coast of the African Mediterranean or to the western Atlantic coast of Morocco to trade, pillage or simply "discover." If Elizabethan England wondered where its economic future was going to lie, "in Europe or overseas," as Pamela Neville-Sington asked,[11] then the overseas focus was first of all on Barbary.[12]

The term "Barbary" was not used in the North African Arabic or Turkish languages, but to English writers it referred to the Ottoman regencies of Libya (Tripolitania), Tunisia and Algeria, and the kingdom of Morocco. The Barbary States constituted distinct geopolitical entities. They differed in that Morocco was independent of Ottoman rule, while Algeria, Tunisia, and Libya had both Ottoman pashas who oversaw their affairs and Ottoman troops with their designated military commanders (*agha*s). The states were similar in their jurisprudential traditions as well as in their regional identity. Thousands of English and Scottish traders, soldiers, sailors and travelers repeatedly met with the peoples of those states and learned of their distinct form of Islam and distinct ethnolinguistic characters. There were "Moors," "Turks," "Arabs" (by which they meant the Bedouins of the mountain zones), Moriscos, Jews, Armenians and European "renegades." The languages of the region varied between Arabic, Turkish, the lingua franca and, after the expulsion of the Moriscos to North Africa, Spanish as well. Religiously, the whole Barbary region appeared monolithically Muslim, although some astute European observers noted the difference between the Ottoman (Hanafi) and the native Magharibi (Maliki) schools and courts of jurisprudence. Meanwhile, Magharibi traders and envoys traveled to England to conduct business, to negotiate or to spy. Others were hauled to Portsmouth or Exeter or London as captives and slaves, to languish in jails, to stand trial in southwestern courts, to beg for succor or to disappear into the underworld of the growing metropolis. The Moors of the Barbary States, with their fearsome pirates and dignified ambassadors, rich resources and multireligious society, became a defining region for British soldiers, sea captains, merchants, and craftsmen in the Mediterranean and Atlantic. Against these Moors, who tolerated the Protestant Christianity of England more than the Catholicism of France or Spain, and who employed English and Scottish ships for their business and religious travel—against those peoples, many British men (and some women) found that they had to reevaluate their beliefs, convictions and identity.

An anonymous record in 1665 of the list of "Agents. Amdors" (ambassadors) in "Barbarie" shows the long legacy of commercial trade and diplomatic exchange: "1577 Edmond Hogan received lett'r & a Com[missio]n from Q. Elizabeth for an Ambassy to Abdelmalik ye son of Mahomet Xeg Imbark'd at Plymouth May 6 arriv'd at Saphia ye 21 entred Marocco June 1 returns with Letter."[13]

The list then continues with references to numerous agents who went to Morocco throughout the period. Simultaneously, many travelers and traders to the Levant discovered firsthand the danger of captivity in those regions; others realized how crucial it was to revictual in one of the Barbary ports—Tripoli, Tunis, Algiers or Tetuan—before continuing their journeys to the Levant. Despite the distance from the British Isles, encounter with the Barbary States was unavoidable and frequent. Particularly after Antwerp was closed to English trade, merchants had to look for new consumers with hard cash to pay for their national products: after Morocco's 1591 invasion of the Sudan and the subsequent annual arrival of massive amounts of gold to Marrakesh, the English gravitated to the kingdom of Morocco, eagerly taking with them their two most prominent exports, woolen cloth and cannons. In return, they bought currants, silk, sweet oils, sugar, spices, carpets, wines and saltpeter.

Notwithstanding the ongoing trade with Istanbul, Smyrna, Aleppo, Beirut and Cairo, there was far more British commercial, maritime, and political interaction with the Barbary States than with any place else in the Islamic world. That is why, perhaps, various Moors strutted on the Shakespearean stage, but not a single Turk. After all, more envoys and ambassadors visited England from the Barbary States than from the Levant. Britons realized that despite the hegemony of the Ottomans, the regencies and kingdom of Morocco were not unwilling to explore venues for independent relations and individual treaties. Moroccan rulers were actually fighting off, both diplomatically and militarily, Ottoman and Spanish hegemony, and were eager to negotiate alliances with European countries hostile to the two superpowers of the Mediterranean. An undated letter from the Moroccan ruler Muhammad al-Mutawakkil (reg. 1574–76) to Queen Elizabeth states how he had received the "Christian ambassador of the great one among her people, and the one who is well-liked by us and the one eager to know and communicate with us, the tyrant regnant of the English (*taghiyat al-injleez al-rayina*)." She was a "tyrant," ruling outside the principles of the Islamic polity, but he could still cooperate with her because she was a Christian, one of the People of the Book—as he could cooperate with her subjects. His letter shows the desire on his part, and presumably of the English ambassador in Morocco as well, to encourage travel between the two countries and to ensure the safety and proper treatment of visitors:

> He who came to our Porte, protected by God and by God preserved, sent by her and seeking peace—he asked for a truce which I also desire in order to continue in our communication, good relations, polite exchange and amicable protection for the traveler and the resident, incoming and outgoing, the pious and the profligate *(al-fajir)*, the buyer and the merchant.

[We propose the following:]

. . .

Every Muslim [Moroccan] who wants to trade in their country [England] and in any of their regions should not be overburdened by taxes. He should be given all due respect.

Every Christian [English] merchant in the lands of Islam that are obedient to us and belong to our blessed rule, and which are preserved by God, should not be overburdened by taxes and should not be asked except for the tithe that is the duty which cannot be avoided or ignored.[14]

Al-Mutawakkil wanted England to be a trading partner and a place where his subjects could conduct business affairs, at the same time that the English could trade in his own dominions. Mutual commercial benefits and realpolitik marginalized religious difference. After all, quite a few Britons were wandering into Morocco and not necessarily leading a devout life, but enjoying the profligacy of the expatriate.

In his study *The Ideological Origins of the British Empire* (2000), David Armitage incisively showed that the English and later the Britons were driven toward navigation and discovery, not by the spirit of Protestant imperialism but by commercial need and greed. This thesis receives ample proof in the British enterprise in North Africa, where Britons arrived as merchants, peddlers and roamers, and where traders and settlers and other English, Welsh, Scottish and Irish men worked and lived. What was unique about the British experience in Islamic Barbary was the dangerous encounter with the religious Other—the Muslim, who threatened Christian belief by enticing hundreds of men and women to Islam and making them renounce their allegiance to God and monarch. In the Barbary Coast, Protestantism, and the pride in its English expression, Anglicanism, came to be forcefully challenged. That Protestantism made the invention of England possible, as Colley maintains,[15] is accurate, but only if we recognize that it was nothing other than an "invention," which was frequently forced. For there was an English identity that was deeply (but not exclusively) molded by the commercial experience in the Islamic world. There was a complex articulation of the sense of English/British self that had to take into account not just the Protestant conquest in Ireland and afterward in America, but the obsequious entry into the Islamic markets and the Muslim triumph over Britons as well. Before there was America and its imperial legacy in the formation of British identity, there was trade and employment in the Barbary States.

At the same time that Britons peddled and bartered, they were serving as high officials in the courts of Algiers, appearing as eunuchs in English plays, or laboring as slaves and concubines in the harems of Morocco and Algiers. One example will suffice to show the complex impact of Barbary on early English identity.

"Assan Aga . . . the sonne of Fran[cis] Rowlie of Bristow merchant, taken in Swalow" exhibits the challenge to Englishness and Protestantism. Assan (Hassan) was the treasurer to the pasha in Algiers. He had converted to Islam, had lost his original name and had been castrated in the process. He had risen to a position of such power that the English factor, William Harborne, had to plead with him for assistance in ransoming some English captives. What is striking about the 1584 letter to Assan that has survived, and that was published by Richard Hakluyt, is the common identity that Harborne desperately tried to assume with his addressee. Harborne did not accept Assan's conversion to Islam, assured him how much he still saw him as a Christian, and therefore addressed him as a fellow Englishman. What more Assan had to do to assure Harborne that he had indeed deserted both Christianity and Englishness was not clear: after all, Assan was not lamenting his condition but was luxuriating in his powerful position, as the surviving oil painting of him shows. But, to Harborne, Algerian eunuch that Assan was, and "notwithstanding your body be subject to Turkish thraldom, yet your vertuous mind [remains] free from those vices, next under God addict to ye good service of your liege Lady & soveraigne princes, her most excellent majesty."[16]

What had completely shaken Harborne was meeting an Englishman who had become a Muslim. Assan still spoke English, still remembered his family of Bristol, seemed to admire the queen, but he had become a Muslim, a "Turk." Harborne could not cope with this new Mediterranean reality and insisted on seeing the Englishman under the turban, and the Christian in the eunuch. For Harborne, Englishness was in the blood, and changing religion did not change national commitment; for Assan, national identity and religion were both matters of choice, not birth. It was perhaps this flexibility in national self-fashioning in the world of Islam that completely perplexed Harborne—and enticed his compatriots to North Africa and the Levant.

Despite seeing in the renegades a different religion, different nomenclature, different clothes, and sometimes even a different manhood (or the lack thereof), Harborne wanted to believe that there was something quintessentially English that no amount of physical or spiritual mutilation could eradicate. But the English identity in the Muslim person lay, in reality, only in the confused and desperate eyes of the beholder; and so, when his English compatriots (or Scottish or Welsh) renounced their Protestantism, their compatriots (but no longer their coreligionists) refused to believe that they had abandoned Englishness or Scottishness or Welshness. When Robert Daborne wrote a play about the notorious Tunisian pirate John Ward in 1611, A Christian Turn'd Turk, he still dealt with Ward as if he were an Englishman. Despite the fact that Ward had converted to Islam (out of expediency if nothing else) and had adopted an Arabic name, Wardiyya, Daborne could not but see and present him as English—so much so that at the end of the play, but not his life (which extended to 1621), Ward dies while confirming his undying and unchanged allegiance to England and Christendom.[17]

Such a desperate suspension of belief repeatedly appeared in Elizabethan, Jacobean and Caroline writings. Travelers and captives tried to see Englishmen or
Irishmen in the "renegades" only to discover that the most bigoted Muslims were
exactly those men whom they had thought their compatriots. Such converts projected North Africa's power in attracting Christians to Islam: for the "renegades," as they were derisively called, enjoyed the support of the Ottoman superpower that had been engaged in fighting Christendom for centuries, and
which was in possession of formidable sea and land warfare technology. The
Ottoman reconquest of Tunis in 1574 and the Moroccan victory at Wadi al-
Makhazin in 1578 (against a Portuguese invasion that included a contingent of
English soldiers) had shown the might of both Ottoman and Moroccan Islam,
and the danger that Turks and Moors could pose to assured Protestants and
aspiring conquerors. It is not surprising therefore that as soon as English traders
and pirates arrived in the North African harbors, they realized that "Barbary"
was not New England or Ireland with populations that were defeated and pushed
back; nor was the region easy for colonization.[18] Rather, they found large urban
centers with well-run military organizations, often led by English- or French-
speaking converts, thousands of European slaves, and an attractive market for
trade and profit. As Britons left cities and hamlets that were swollen by a growing
population, they sought opportunity in the Mediterranean. Of course, not all
found it: some fell victim to North African pirates and privateers and were sold
in the slave markets of Salé and Tunis, but others renounced their faith and
"turned Turk," and prospered. There were others who settled to merchandizing
and trade, or joined the Barbary corsairs in an Islamic world that tolerated
strangers from among the People of the Book. Others became pirates and took
part in a slave trade that profited from the captivity of Moors and Turks. While
in sub-Saharan Africa, the Caribbean or New England Britons acted with military and religious superiority, in North Africa they found themselves living and
working among Muslims, often having to explain their actions to potentates in
Fez or Tunis or Santa Cruz in order to protect their lives and livelihoods. At all
times, immigrants and captives, traders and sailors and pirates could not but be
aware of the impact of Barbary on Britain.

In *Shakespeare and the Geography of Difference* (1994), John Gillies analyzed the "paradigm-shift in the discursive construction of otherness between the
beginning and the end of the seventeenth century," between Othello and Oronooko. Gillies pointed out how Othello represented the "hard" side of a dangerous exoticism, while Oronooko was "soft," actually displaying a nonthreatening
and a "romantically off-European appearance."[19] Gillies' analysis is similar to
Karen Newman's observation that the image of the "blacks" had changed from
men playing "exotic, and mythic ideological roles" to "slaves situated in a capitalist economy."[20] Gillies contextualized some of Shakespeare's protagonists
within the geographical and cartographic culture of early modern England, but
his (as well as Newman's) contrast between a Moor and an American slave (de-

spite their repeated conflation in English writings) is misleading, which is why the distinction between the "hard" and the "soft" is not adequate to explain the shift in British perception of Barbary in the early modern period.

The shift I prefer to examine is that between the representation of the Moor in Peele's *The Battle of Alcazar* (1589) and Dryden's *Don Sebastian* (1689), two plays dealing with the same events: the encounter between Europeans and North African Moors during and after the 1578 battle of Alcazar (also known as the battle of Wadi al-Makhazin). As I propose to show, the plays reveal a shift in the perception and representation of Moors that had its causes in the transformation of British power on the high seas. Peele's play, written soon after the arrival of the first official Moroccan delegation to London, is the first to present Moors on the London stage and to present them within a historical context. The Moors were victorious and intimidating, but not much was known about them beyond the sources on which Peele drew. Along with his friend Shakespeare in their coauthored *Titus Andronicus* (ca. 1589–91), Peele was the first playwright to introduce Moors to London audiences—and no playwright afterward was able to avoid the stereotypes created through Mahamet, Seth and Aaron. Under James I and Charles I, relations deteriorated between Britain and Barbary, and only a few envoys and ambassadors traveled to London—which may well explain the paucity of Moors on the English stage.

Within a hundred years of Peele, John Dryden wrote *Don Sebastian,* revealing a drastic change in the representation of the Barbary world. In that century, Britain underwent a change of global magnitude that can be studied in two time periods. The first extends from 1588 and the victory over the Spanish Armada to the Interregnum, when Cromwell undertook the expansion of the navy. In this period, Britons were fearful of the Moors. Unlike the colonial making of the English identity in Ireland and New England, the encounter with the Moors of Islam was precarious and dangerous: this was an encounter where the Other prevailed and where English captives and slaves, along with their wives, children, parish neighbors, merchants who went bankrupt and ransomers who were outmaneuvered, tricked or ignored had to rethink what it meant to be English or British. Every time Britons sailed the Mediterranean or ventured out across the Atlantic or spotted a Turkish or Algerian man-of-war off their coasts, they learned how the course of domestic economy and foreign policy was challenged and even changed by the power of Barbary rulers and the large numbers of their own compatriots, grinding at the mills of slavery.

With the rise in the number of captives seized and taken to North Africa, the impact of the Barbary States became not only religiously but also politically destabilizing. One of the many causes of the Civil Wars lay in the slave ports of Salé and Tunis, Algiers and Tetuan. Although ecclesiastical, financial and national issues polarized Parliament against the monarch, the matter of captives proved instrumental in heightening that polarization. It was King Charles's misfortune that throughout his reign, he did not, or could not, pay enough attention to the captives in Barbary. But the captives precipitated a social crisis that was felt by their wives and families, who, left destitute after the seizure of their husbands and breadwinners, petitioned the king, the Parliament, the Privy Council and anybody else in power for assistance toward ransoming the captives. It was also felt by women (by far fewer in number) who were themselves taken captive by the Barbary corsairs and were either ransomed and taken back to their communities, or remained in North Africa. During the Jacobean and Caroline periods, captivity constituted the chief foreign affairs crisis between Britain and the Barbary region.

Where in America Britons colonized Indian lands and successfully replaced the native population, in the Barbary region, it was only from the middle of the seventeenth century on that Britons were able to begin imposing their commercial and military will. The turning point in Britain's position vis-à-vis Barbary began in the Interregnum when, between 1649 and 1651, the navy was doubled in size and Oliver Cromwell set his goals to "expand England's commercial and colonial horizons."[21] In this second period, the British trader was no longer to see himself as a peddler at the mercy of the North African buyer, but as a salesman with military and diplomatic strategy—and supported by a powerful fleet to implement that strategy. After the passing of the Acts of Navigation (1650 and 1651 and confirmed by Charles II in 1661), a new ideology and a new naval technology were introduced, including the long-range and lighter-weight cannons that enabled ships to carry more firepower on board.[22] The development of "battleships designed for launching explosive shells at sea" was also instrumental in the naval superiority over the North Africans.[23] These changes gave Britons (and the French) the upper hand commercially; they also enabled Britons to capture Moors and enslave them. In need of money that could be won by the sale of Moorish captives, Britons entered the Mediterranean slave market with a vengeance, buying and selling Moors in ports stretching from Cadiz to Genoa. The beginning of the British Empire was effected on the backs of thousands of not only Britons who were seized by the Barbary corsairs, as Linda Colley correctly argued,[24] but more numerically, Moors and Turks who were seized by Britons and sold into slavery—thereby enriching the coffers of investors and stockholders, who proceeded to build more ships to capture and transport and sell more slaves. By 1670, Britons dominated both the sub-Saharan and North African slave trade.[25]

Morocco, Algeria and Tunisia had thriving populations that, despite numerous bouts of the plague, did not dwindle as did the Indian population in North America that was subsequently transferred or destroyed. As a result, Britons adopted the diplomacy of the gunboat. If there is a date for the beginning of Britain's gunboat diplomacy in the Mediterranean, it is during the Cromwellian and the Restoration periods; and if there is a specific location, it is North Africa, where British naval power burned Barbary fleets, destroyed ports and devastated native trade, commerce and enterprise. By the third quarter of the seventeenth century, Britons were becoming the most formidable power in the western Mediterranean: "We are still conquerors," declared the clergyman Henry Teonge, as he sailed on Britain's invincible Mediterranean fleet in the mid-1670s.[26]

Such power influenced the British imagination, which in the Elizabethan period had produced dramas of literary and psychological intensity about Barbary but in the Restoration period lost interest in the complexity of the region and its people. When Britons feared the Moors, they invented them in Othello-like heroic and dangerous terms; when they no longer feared them, they turned them into dull natives or noble savages—stereotypes to entertain but not to threaten, as *Don Sebastian* shows. The play is the best of the few Moor plays that appeared in the second half of the seventeenth century; but its lustful and corrupt Moors are a far cry from the multifaceted, sometimes humorous but also intimidating figures of the Elizabethan stage. As Dryden approached the project of describing the Moors, he simply invented and fantasized. While Peele had had to contend with actual Moorish representatives on the streets of London who were treated with respect and fear, Dryden lived in a Britain that enjoyed naval and imperial might. Dryden used that sense of power to remove the culture and people of North Africa from history into his personal world of dramatic manipulation and transformation. Now that the British were dominating the Mediterranean shores of North Africa, they lost not only their curiosity about the inhabitants but also whatever capacity they had had to integrate themselves into that world of non-Christians. In the play, Dryden failed to communicate ("translate") to his audience the Moorish "source" culture.[27] Even the captives in the second half of the seventeenth century give the impression in their published and unpublished accounts that they had lost the sense of anxiety at being seized by "Mahometans": as John Whitehead shows (appendix 2), captivity became an adventure, a journey into unknown regions that the unshakable Christian Briton would later describe for the commercial benefit and social entertainment of his compatriots.

It is important to study Anglo-Barbary relations chronologically and not synchronically because the decisive change in military and naval power that occurred in mid-seventeenth-century England completely changed the nature of those relations with, and representations of, the Moors. The change specifically transformed the way in which the British responded or reacted to Barbary and to the making of their own national image. Historians who have analyzed the making of the British identity in the context of encounter with the colonies, and specifically with the world of Islam, have been remiss in ignoring important period differences: the impact that Moors or Turks left on the English differed drastically between Moors who were powerful and rich, and much invoked by Queen Elizabeth, and Moors who were wandering haplessly on the streets of London under an indifferent George I. The balance of power between Morocco and England in the Elizabethan period was quite different from the imbalance during the Restoration. And a play about Moors written under Elizabeth or a ship seized by the corsairs at a time when England was still a "little England," as

Thomas Kyd stated in *The Spanish Tragedy*, reflected, and in turn produced, very different anxieties among the English public than at a time when the British fleet ruled the Mediterranean waves and when writers were proclaiming a British empire. By the same token, the impact of the "Turks" on the making of Britons changed too between those Turks whose navies were invoked against Spain by a fearful Elizabeth and who were instrumental in the defense of the English Channel against the Dutch in 1666,[28] and the Turks who had been pushed back from Vienna less than twenty years later, and who would sign one treaty of capitulation after another relinquishing their role and influence in Western Europe.

Historians such as Jerry Brotton and Daniel Goffman have shown how fallacious it is to isolate the Ottomans from "Renaissance Europe" and how global and intertwined relations were between Islamdom and Christendom during the early modern period.[29] In similar fashion, it would be fallacious to separate the early modern history and literature of Britain from the collusions and captivities, trade and piracy, alliance and military confrontation with the Barbary States. Britain and Barbary were intertwined in the making of their national histories. This book will examine chronologically the historical context of the "paradigm shift" between 1589 and 1689, and identify the causes and the effects that shift had on English imagination and British political and social self-identity.

I

The Moor on the Elizabethan Stage

At no other period in early modern English history did more plays include Moorish characters than in the second half of the Elizabethan period: *The Battle of Alcazar*, *Titus Andronicus*, *The Play of Stucley*, *The Merchant of Venice*, *Lust's Dominion*, *Othello* and the *Fair Maid of the West, Part I*.[1] These plays constitute some of the finest in the Elizabethan repertoire, and important early studies by Eldred Jones, Anthony Gerard Barthelemy, Jack D'Amico and others examined the image of the Moor and its literary derivation. After G. K. Hunter's "Othello and Colour Prejudice" in 1967, historicist and postcolonial critics started treating the Moor from within the racial and cultural legacy of European exclusion and separateness. With the rise of interest in Islam, critics have moved beyond the racial to situate, or rather attempt to situate, the Elizabethan Moor within the context of Islamic-Christian relations and rivalries.

In his seminal study *The Moor in English Renaissance Drama* (1991), Jack D'Amico drew attention to the importance of historical context in many of the "Moor" plays and masques. The commercial and diplomatic connections between England and Morocco, he argued, help explain why English playwrights became interested in Moors during the reign of Elizabeth. Also, the different skin color of the Moors made their appearance on stage quite attractive: "They were literally spectacular," Alden T. Vaughan and Virginia Mason Vaughan stated.[2] But, as Emily Bartels has shown, Hakluyt's opus had alerted English readers to the variety of peoples and races outside the English range of experience,[3] and as Robert Ralston Cawley showed in his detailed study of *The Voyagers and Elizabethan Drama* (which included references not just to Elizabethan but also to seventeenth-century works), London was full of travelers, sailors, diplomats, merchants and wandering entertainers whose stories about distant lands and different peoples were told and retold on the streets as in the court, in sermon as in sonnet, in love poetry as in theological diatribe.[4] Londoners interested in news about the world found much to satisfy them in "gossip, rumour and private letters. There can be no question that the oral transmission of news was rife in late Elizabethan London."[5] The Moors were not the only people about whom the English were informed.

Given the currency of international news in London and the information available about other peoples, religions and regions, the following question can be raised: Why were there so many plays written about Moors but not, for instance, about Native Americans, Muscovites, or other peoples described in Hakluyt, whose skin color and cultural habits were also different from the English? The answer lies in the dates of the Elizabethan Moor plays, insofar as those dates are known. All the plays appeared soon after the arrival in England of delegations from Morocco: Moors on the streets of London in 1589, 1595 and 1600 led to Moors on the stage. Indeed, two edicts by the queen to expel "Blackamoors" from her dominions also appeared subsequent to the visits of Moors—in 1596 and 1601. Moors on the Elizabethan stage were not, therefore, just a product of literary invention, the European legacy of race discrimination, or biblical denunciations of the sons of Ham: they were a direct result of England's diplomatic initiative into Islamic affairs and of the negotiations and collusions that took place between Queen Elizabeth and Mulay Ahmad al-Mansur.

George Peele, *The Battle of Alcazar*

Upon acceding to the Moroccan throne in August 1578 after victory in the battle of Wadi al-Makhazin, Mulay Ahmad al-Mansur did not pay Queen Elizabeth any special attention. Actually, he may have looked askance at her after an English and Irish contingent of Catholic soldiers joined King Sebastian and fought against him in battle. Furthermore, English capitalists such as Sir John Gresham had established good relations with his rival and predecessor, Muhammad al-Mutawakkil (al-Maslukh, "the flayed"), who had been killed in the battle, and with whom Gresham had reached an agreement on the monopoly of the sugar trade. He had actually paid the Moroccan ruler sixty thousand pounds to control that trade. Upon the death of al-Maslukh and the accession of al-Mansur to the throne, Gresham tried to retrieve his money or resecure his monopoly, only to find al-Mansur canceling all agreements and debts. As Augustine Lane wrote on 9 September 1579, al-Mansur showed his "satisfaction in woordes, but nothinge in deedes."[6] But in fact, as Thomas Heywood wrote in his 1606 play *If You Know Not Me You Know No Body*, al-Mansur sent Gresham a dagger and "a paire of flippers" as a consolation present.[7] Meanwhile, the queen's coffers were not as full as they needed to be to make England a power to reckon with. When the English ambassador arrived in Marrakesh to congratulate al-Mansur on his victory and accession to the throne, he brought presents with him that were seen to be so insignificant that, unlike the gifts of the French, Spanish and Turks, they were not recorded by the Moroccan court scribe, Abu Faris Abd al-Aziz al-Fishtali.

It was England's victory over the Spanish Armada, ten years later, that made al-Mansur seriously view the queen as a potential military and diplomatic ally. A year before, Queen Elizabeth had sent Matias Becudo to Morocco, a capable Portuguese who had served under Don Juan of Austria and had been trained in international affairs. He told al-Mansur that the queen needed a well-protected harbor as a base for transporting merchandise to England—although in effect, she wanted a Moroccan port from where her ships would try to deflect the Spanish fleet preparing to invade her island. Al-Mansur did not agree to the request: he told Becudo that the English were already using Safi and the beach of Sus, and he feared if English ships started attacking the Spanish fleet from other Moroccan ports, the Spanish would retaliate by occupying those ports.[8] Al-Mansur was not yet sure either about English intentions or English naval capability. He was going to wait to see how European affairs developed and who was going to be the winner in the ongoing hostilities between England and Spain.

The winner was England after it defeated the Spanish Armada in the summer of 1588. News about the English victory reached al-Mansur by means of the English merchants in Marrakesh, and he promptly gave them permission to celebrate. They built "Bone-fires," as George Wilkins reported, and then went outside the city, where they organized themselves into a "gallant order" after which they came "backe into the Citty, in a triumphant and ciuill manner, to doe honour to their Country."[9] Anti-Spanish sentiment was running so high in the city that an exultant mob of French, Dutch and Moroccan men joined the English group and marched at the house of the Spanish representative/interpreter, intent on breaking into it. Later, forty jubilant English merchants in Marrakesh took to the streets, shouting and drinking and carrying with them a large banner on which they had painted Queen Elizabeth triumphant over King Philip II. The Moroccans not only shared in European news, they also saw, possibly for the very first time ever, a picture of the English queen with her adversary under her feet.[10] For them, European affairs had become matters of local representation and celebration.

Mulay al-Mansur realized that relations with England and her queen had to be improved, and he decided to send her an ambassador. On 12 January 1589, "Marzuq Rais," as he came to be known (his actual name was Ahmad Bilqasim), arrived in London and was met by the Barbary Company "merchants of London with 200 horsemen."[11] He was suave, articulate and, being a Morisco, spoke Spanish fluently. Although he planned to discuss commercial relations with the queen, there were other pressing diplomatic and military matters to negotiate: supplies and financial support to the queen in her attempt to reinstate Don Antonio, the claimant to the Portuguese throne, in return for logistical and naval support to al-Mansur in his hope to conquer the Andalus. The Moroccan ruler knew that the queen, having taken up the cause of the Portuguese contender after Spain's seizure of Portugal in 1580, had pitted herself against the ire of the Catholic monarch. Morocco, located across the strait from Spain, could play an important role in providing natural resources and personnel for any military action that England might undertake.

The ambassador submitted to Queen Elizabeth the conditions on which al-Mansur would be willing to support her. He could not have arrived at a more opportune time. The queen's finances were extremely tight, and her plans to attack Portugal had been delayed because of meager resources, so much so that she thought of turning to her Dutch allies for help.[12] In the ambassador's memorandum, al-Mansur promised Elizabeth "men, money, vyctualls, and the use of his poortes, [and] also his owne person" in return for "a sownde and perfect leage of amytye betwen them."[13] That "amytye" would entail using some of her ships and mariners, and buying oars for his galleys in order to strengthen his naval capacity and carry out his invasion of Spain and the liberation of the Andalus.[14] Furthermore, and in light of his desire to improve the Moroccan fleet, al-Mansur would be permitted to hire "carpenters and shipwrights" to build "certain foystes and fregates, in tymes of warre."[15] Should the queen agree to turn England into a marketplace for Moroccans where they could buy English naval products and hire English labor, he would underwrite the military expenses of an operation against Philip—150,000 ducats. But he would only pay the money once the queen sent her troops to Morocco to join his own troops and begin an invasion of Spain from Spanish-held Tangier. As far as he was concerned, any battle conducted from his terrain had to be under his authority.

It was as these political and financial negotiations were underway that Peele wrote his play *The Battle of Alcazar*, the first on the English stage to present Moorish characters. Before the play, Moors had appeared in London pageants and sometimes in miracle plays. In 1585, Peele introduced a man "appareled like a Moore" in his *The Device of the Pageant Borne before Wolstan Dixi*, and in 1587, Christopher Marlowe included the kings of Fez, Morocco and Argier in *Tamburlaine*.[16] All three kings had been tributaries of the Ottoman sultan, and all were defeated in battle and replaced by Tamburlaine's Persian followers. But Marlowe knew next to nothing about the North African region except what he saw in Ortelius's atlas and what he had heard or read about the "cruel pirates of Argier" (3.3.55).

Peele's *The Battle of Alcazar* is the only play in the whole Elizabethan repertoire to portray the Christian-Islamic conflict in North Africa with historical accuracy. Samuel Chew, however, was disappointed in it, "so clumsy that not even dumb-shows and a 'presenter' or expositor clarify the situations."[17] But in his study of the play, A. R. Braunmuller focused on what he believed to be its central theme: the question of royal succession. He argued that viewers of the play would recognize in the struggle for the throne of Morocco the struggle that bedeviled England and that had recently led to the execution of Mary, Queen of Scots. Peele's uses of "rightfull" and "lawfull," as well as other politically evocative terms, Braunmuller continued, "were familiar to English audiences and would become even more familiar as the queen aged and adamantly refused to name her successor."[18] Alternatively, Peter Hyland argued that Peele's main concern in the play was the "complex of competing religious and political positions centred on the figure of Sebastian," and the uncertainty about Portugal's future under the Spanish Crown.[19] The play described the rivalry between Spain and England in regard to the status of Portugal.

While anxiety about succession and about Spanish control of Portugal was deeply felt by the audience, Peele addressed another more immediate and pressing anxiety by dramatizing from a Euro-Christian perspective the build-up to, and consequences of, the famous but disastrous battle. Although it is not known when exactly Peele wrote the play, John Yoklavich has argued that it must have been written sometime in the period between July 1588 and 18 April 1589.[20] There was in this nine-month period such excitement about Moors that for the first time since 1551, the London Lord Mayor's Pageant included a number of Moors among its assemblage of characters.[21] Peele rode the Moorish wave, and in writing a play about Moroccans and their relations with Europeans ten or more years after the actual events he described, he presented in his play not so much the anxiety about succession as excitement over the arrival of the Moroccan delegation from Mulay al-Mansur. After all, this was the first time in living memory that such non-Europeans, and presumably for the uninformed mobs, "pagans," had walked in their city not like frightened and "salvage" sub-Saharan or American Indian slaves who had been brought to entertain viewers, but with elegance, decorum and pomp.

Upon the arrival of the delegation, Peele turned to John Polemon's translation of battle histories in "sundrie languages," *The Second part of the booke of Battailes* (1587), and with an eye to the Moors in negotiation with his queen, he wrote his play as a "popular pot-boiler."[22] He opened the play with a "dumb shew" in which the Moor, Muly Mahamet, murders his brothers: the Christian presenter, the "portingall," speaks to the audience directly, showing them the violence of the Moors against their own kind and, thereby, the violence they did not hesitate to inflict on Christians. The portingall then warns how, ten years earlier, that same Moor, "Blacke in his looke, and bloudie in his deeds" (1.1.16), deceived the "honorable and couragious king" Sebastian, who had undertaken "a dangerous dreadfull warre, / And aid[ed] with Christian armes the barbarous Moore" (1.1.5–6). Later in the play, in act 2, scene 3, Peele has one of the Moorish attendants and then Muly Mahamet's son boast of Muly's duplicity. Subsequently Muly Mahamet confirms the evil he has in store for the Christians:

Now have I set these Portugals aworke,
To hew a way for me unto the crowne,
Or with your weapons here to dig your
graves. (4.2.1133–35)

As a result of the duplicity of Mahamet, the decisive battle on 4 August 1578 ended with the victory of the Moorish-Turkish force and the death of Sebastian, and the assumption to the throne of "Muly Mahamet Seth" of the play—the Ahmad al-Mansur whose delegation was knocking on the doors of the queen's royal palaces.

Despite the positive image of the uncle of Muly Mahamet, Abdelmelec, in Peele's play and in Polemon's translation, the dominant Moors are the evil Muly

Mahamet and the dangerous Muly Mahamet Seth, the latter still alive and plotting from his Marrakesh palace.[23] Peele uses the material from Polemon selectively: while the latter does not show great admiration for Sebastian, Peele turns the Portuguese into a heroic defender of Christianity; and while Polemon does not emphasize the role of Muly Seth, Peele ends his play with Muly Seth/Ahmad al-Mansur standing victoriously over the body of Sebastian. The spectacle of Moorish fratricide and the triumph of Moorish deception signal the danger of the Moroccans in London: what happened ten years earlier to the Christian king could well happen to the Christian monarch of England, and the same kind of deception that was practiced by Muly Mahamet on Sebastian could well be intended by Mulay al-Mansur's delegation to the queen.

Act 2, scene 4 introduces the "Moores, those men of Barbarie" on stage as "Embassadors" (2.4.570, 622) who entice Sebastian into invading Morocco—like the Moors in London enticing Elizabeth to cooperate with their master in invading Spain. As Sebastian was intent on helping Muly Mahamet "reobtaine his roiall seate, / And place his fortunes in their former height" (2.4.579–80), so is Mulay Ahmad al-Mansur eager to conquer the Andalus and regain the throne of Spain. After all, Seth/al-Mansur was asking for ships and munitions from England in the same manner that "the Moore" of the play asked from Sebastian. "Lo," warns the Christian "Presenter," with an eye to the Moroccan demands,

> thus into a lake of bloud and gore,
> The brave couragious king of Portugall
> Hath drencht himself, and now prepares amaine
> With sailes and oares to crosse the swelling seas,
> With men and ships, courage and canon shot,
> To plant this cursed Moor in fatall houre. (3.737–74)

In the mouth of Arged Zareo, Abdelmelec's servant, Peele puts another warning for Christians: "So will they [Christians] be advisde another time, / How they doo touch the shore of Barbarie" (4.1.1043–44).

To bring further home the danger of political and military entanglement with Moors, Peele shows that the Christians who were killed by the swords of Mahamet Seth/al-Mansur and his armies were not just continental Christians, but English soldiers under the leadership of Tom Stuckley. The English contingent that had joined in the battle was so insignificant that contemporary Moroccan sources did not bother to mention it; nor had Polemon, who mentioned nothing at all about English military participation. But to a London audience that had grown to admire Stuckley and had actually built legends about him,[24] Peele confirmed the heroism of the soldiers in the invasion of Morocco and praised Stuckley as a true-born Englishman who had not hesitated from going to battle for "Saint George for England" (2.4.734) and who, along with other Englishmen—and the word "Englishmen" is repeated emphatically in the play—had paid with their lives. Stuckley was an English hero who, along with about eight hundred English, Irish and Italian Catholic soldiers, had been killed side by side with thousands of other Christians from Portugal and Spain. Despite the Christian cause they had been pursuing, the Sebastian-led invasion failed, after which Portugal was annexed to Spain. The battle of Alcazar, Peele concluded, had served the Moors' purpose, while proving a "great dishonour . . . to Christendom."

The queen was quite alert to the danger of which Peele was warning and prevaricated about agreeing to al-Mansur's proposal for an alliance. In February 1589, she wrote to him informing him of her desire to keep the Moroccan ambassador in England as long as possible so she could show her appreciation for al-Mansur.[25] The real reason for keeping the ambassador, however, became clear a few weeks later when she wrote to thank al-Mansur for offering to assist Don Antonio and to request that her fleet, soon on its way to Spain under Drake, be able to victual in Moroccan "portes and havens" and that her subjects who "resort" into al-Mansur's dominions be "curteously and favorably used."[26] Sir Roger Williams also hoped that he would agree to "retrench our army to do other exploits as our numbers and Generals will permit."[27] So close appeared the cooperation between England and Morocco that on 9 May 1589 the Spanish spy in London, Manuel de Andrada (known as "David"), reported (wrongly) that the money and powder sent by al-Mansur had reached London and were to be used in the invasion of Portugal.[28] Even in Brussels, the informant of the Fugger moneylenders confirmed that Morocco had joined the European anti-Spanish alliance.[29] Soon after, Francis Drake sailed with Don Antonio (and with the returning Moroccan ambassador on board the same ship) against Lisbon.

Despite turning down the offer of a league with al-Mansur, Elizabeth still expected the Moroccan ruler to help her fleet and to continue his support of Don Antonio. But as a man who felt himself a pivot in the anti-Spanish coalition and who could set his own terms for European cooperation and alliance, al-Mansur refrained from action; no help was extended ("none came")[30] as a result of which the English fleet returned to England after having suffered heavy losses. The English blamed the failure on al-Mansur, who, they complained, had reneged on his promise and had not sent them the supplies he had promised. Don Antonio too felt betrayed and wrote demanding that al-Mansur send the money he had promised him (and for which he had sent his son as hostage). But as the Spanish spy reported, the Portuguese in Morocco, close to al-Mansur's court, were quite certain that the Moroccan ruler was not going to send any money before receiving assurance of a league.[31] In August 1589, al-Mansur sent a letter to "captains" Francis Drake and John Norris stating the following:

> Know that this envoy of ours whom you mention left our noble presence before your fleet had sailed and before we had heard about [your plans]; and only after he reached your country did your fleet sail. How then can you say and claim that we had promised you anything while we knew

nothing. If, however, his promise to you is in regard to future assistance, know that all your requests would be met, God willing, because of the *mahabba* [love] whose foundations have been established between you and us.[32]

Actually, having noted the queen's prevarication in regard to his request for an alliance, and as the English fleet sailed against Lisbon blithely expecting support from al-Mansur,[33] al-Mansur seized the opportunity to propose to Philip II that the Spaniard buy his noncooperation with the English and Portuguese by returning to him the city of Asila in northern Morocco—which Philip did on 13 September 1589. While delaying on a decision regarding the alliance, Elizabeth was unaware that al-Mansur had been pursuing other options—options that could and did negatively affect her military goals. Al-Mansur showed that neither Drake, that great English icon of heroism, nor the queen was a match for his political acumen.[34]

In recognizing the danger posed by Moors and "Seth," Peele was not alone. News about the negotiations with al-Mansur was so widespread in the city that David, the Spanish spy in London, reported in July 1589 how he had heard about Don Antonio's fruitless pleading with al-Mansur to send him money; Edward Prynne had also told him that al-Mansur was not going to cooperate with the Portuguese pretender.[35] Political matters were being discussed on the streets as they were being dramatized on stage: spies, envoys, playwrights and audiences were sharing rumors and information throughout the metropolis. Soon after, in October, John de Cardenas, envoy of Don Antonio to al-Mansur, warned Walsingham of exactly the same danger. In order to get a better understanding of whether al-Mansur would really become "party in the present action against the King of Spayne," Cardenas traveled to Marrakesh and requested an audience with al-Mansur. He was kept waiting for nearly two months before he was granted audience, whereupon he asked al-Mansur bluntly whether he would support Don Antonio. He met with evasion, which convinced him that the "Moore doth not purpose the perfourmaunce of his promis." Cardenas warned that the "Moores drift was only to drawe her [the queen] by such incouragement the more willingly to enter into open warre against the King of Spayne (whom he exceedingly feareth . .) and then to leave her to herself: knowing that the warre once begunne cannot so soone be endid, though he put not to his helping hand, and that, in the meane while, himself shall lyve quiety at home."[36]

Throughout the report, Cardenas never referred to al-Mansur except as "the Moore"—very much like Peele, who had reserved the title "the Moore" for "Muly Hamet the villain" in the play.[37] Had Cardenas watched Peele's play? What Cardenas reported to Walsingham, Peele's players were performing before a London audience: the duplicity that Cardenas described about al-Mansur mirrored the duplicity of Peele's "Moor Mahamet." The anxiety about al-Mansur resonated with the London audiences, who responded favorably to the play.

Possibly under the title of *Muly Molocco,* the play was performed again and again—fourteen times at the Rose theater from 20 February 1592 to 20 January 1593.

Peele's Muly Mahamet is the formative Moor in English dramatic imagination: Negroid, evil, anti-Christian and ruthless. Muly Seth is not as evil and is not black, but he is an ally of the Turks: his women actually "erect a statue made of beaten gold, / And sing to Amurath songs of lasting praise" (2.315–16). And it had been none other than the alliance between the Moors and the Turks that had brought about "Sebastians tragedie in this tragicke warre" (2.328). While the first Moor was inherently evil, his successor, who was sending his delegation to London, was militarily formidable and dangerously associated with the Turks—those same Turks whose fearsomeness Marlowe, Greene and Peele had already presented on stage. For Peele and his audience, the strangely dressed men from Barbary were dangerous—which is why they appeared against the backdrop of dumb "shews" of murder and ghosts howling on stage, and of the three Furies with their "whipp," "blody torch" and "Chopping knife." The queen should beware.

William Shakespeare, *The Merchant of Venice*

Despite the uncertainty between Queen Elizabeth and Mulay al-Mansur, commercial, military and diplomatic cooperation continued to flourish between their countries. After all, the queen was in need of help and wanted to strengthen her naval forces and man them with the best available fighters—at the same time that al-Mansur needed England's naval and military technology. In this respect, a difference prevailed between the queen's position regarding cooperation with the Moors and the vox populi: if the theater was the press of the period, then it conveyed a strong reaction against cooperation and engagement with the Moors. But the queen did not, of course, go by the vox populi, especially the voice that came from south of the Thames. Instead, looking at the larger political picture and the need of the nation to confront a formidable adversary across the Channel, Queen Elizabeth maintained her policy of cooperation with the Moors. While Peele and, soon after, Shakespeare in *Titus Andronicus,* showed on stage the danger and duplicity of the Moors, the queen was pushing her political vision for the country into the international arena, determining alliances not on the basis of religion or skin color but on national priorities. So widely known was her reputation for religious expediency that in 1591, a Muslim petitioned to join her fleet as a sailor. Having been released from Spanish captivity, "Hamett a poore miserable and distrest Turke" (obviously somebody had written the English petition for him) felt confident enough to ask to join her "Majesty's service against the Spaniard." Importantly, he saw himself as a mercenary and not as a convert, who was to fight with English sailors against their mutual enemy. Equally important, he was aware that such a possibility—of a Muslim serving in the Protestant fleet—was not impossible. For he concluded his petition by swearing allegiance to the Christian queen on his Muslim faith: "I vowe by the fayth of a turke to do you most true and faythfull service." Since the queen had not been eurocentric enough to reject cooperation with Muslim potentates, from Marrakesh to Istanbul, neither was the Muslim islamocentric enough not to seek employment and service under the Cross. Even under James I, there were other "Turks" like Hamett who, after serving in England, were given passes to return to their countries: on 10 October 1622, "A pass for Allen [Ali] and Hasson, Turkes, to returne into their countrie and to take with them necessaries, not prohibitied"; on 14 April 1623, "Another passe for ten Turkes to returne into their country, by special order from the Boarde."[38]

In May 1595, Edward Holmden wrote from Barbary describing the members of a Moroccan delegation that was to be sent to England. The delegation consisted of an ambassador, Ahmad bin Adel, two alcaids and a retinue "of twentye five or thirtye persones."[39] The delegation was to negotiate with the queen the request that she had passed on to al-Mansur via the Ottoman sultan for her ships to use the Atlantic port of Santa Cruz, and for permission to build a fort there (in order to sail against the Spanish gold fleet). Although al-Mansur had sent a negative reply to the queen, he assured her of Moroccan cooperation in regard to England's imminent attack on Cadiz. No reference to this delegation appears in the English diplomatic records,[40] but an important presence of Moors appears in Shakespeare's *The Merchant of Venice*, written after the English attack on Cadiz in June 1596 when the looting of the city led to the capture of the Spanish vice admiral's ship, the *St. Andrew* (to which there is a reference in the play).[41] The success of the attack had depended on the cooperation of the Moroccan ruler, who had sent soldiers and ships to help the English. Indeed, reports circulating on the continent confirmed that Barbary ships took part in the attack: the Fugger informant stated that al-Mansur had sent "five galleys from Barbary" to assist the English and had also given permission to the English fleet "to put into Barbary and obtain provisions and other military stores."[42] Another report added an exaggerated reference to six thousand Barbary soldiers with Don Antonio.[43] Actually, Mulay al-Mansur had sent three galleys with supplies. Al-Fishtali, the court scribe in Marrakesh, confirmed that al-Mansur, "may God be with him, [had] prepared for jihad against the enemy of religion [Philip II] to punish him for what he had done to Islam."[44] In order to divert Spanish resistance, al-Mansur had also sent some ships against the Eternal Islands (the Canaries).[45] England and Morocco were joined in jihad against Spain.

A decisive Moorish contribution to the victory was undertaken by one of the captives on board the Spanish ship *St. Philip*. As soon as the English fleet commenced operations, a "Moorish Slave" set "fire to the Gunpowder [aboard the *St. Philip,* which caused it to blow up and] destroyed two or three other ships that lay near."[46] In recognition of Moroccan cooperation, the English assisted the Moors who had been held galley slaves on Spanish ships:

While the Lordes Generalls weare at Cadiz, there came to them certain
poor wretches, Turkes [Moors] to the number of 38, that had beene a longe
tyme galley slaves and, ether at the very tyme of the fight by sea or ells
immediatelie thereuppon, taiking their opportunitie, did then make their
escape and swimme to land, yielding themselves to the mercie of their honorable Lordshippes. It pleased them with all speede to apparrell them and
to furnishe them with money and all other necessaries, and to bestowe on
them a barke and pilot, and so to have them freelie conveyed into Barbery.[47]

Some of these former captives were taken by two English ships to the Moroccan
ships that sailed back to North Africa. Others, both Moroccans and sub-
Saharans, boarded the English ships but sailed to England. Soon after their arrival and dispersal in London, there was a public outcry against their presence so
much so that the queen had to intervene and, on 11 July 1596, issue a proclamation to the lord mayor demanding the expulsion of the "divers blacmoores
brought into this realme, of which kinde of people there are already here to
manie."[48] Moorish ambassadors and delegations were welcome, but not vaga-
bond "blacmoores."

In *The Merchant of Venice*, Shakespeare gave prominence to the Moroccan
prince because of the Moroccan role in domestic as well as international diplomacy. After all, nothing in the sources of the play which he had consulted included a Moor. Since the early 1590s, the Moroccans had been assuming an
important role within Mediterranean military and political affairs: the kingdom
had become a superpower after the transformation of the country into an
eldorado of gold. In 1591, Mulay al-Mansur had sent his troops into the sub-
Saharan region of modern-day Niger, defeated the Songhay king and seized his
gold mines. As part of the capitulation, the defeated king started sending an
annual tribute of gold that arrived in such vast quantities that in August 1594, a
letter sent from Marrakesh to London reported "mules laden with gold" that had
reached the Moroccan city from the conquered Sudan.[49] None of the countries of
the other suitors in the play—the French, the Germans, the English and the Ital-
ians—could boast the same wealth and affluence. It is not surprising, therefore,
that from among all the other suitors, only the Prince of Morocco appeared on
stage—twice—and once on his heels, Aragon.

The Prince of Morocco was not an Aaron-like fiend, coming out of nowhere
and dreaming of retreating to a cabin in some wilderness. By coming on the
"pilgrimage" to propose to Portia, all difficulties for the geographical crossing
into Christendom seem to have been overcome. If he succeeded in his suit, and
there would be no reason why he should not, he would settle down in Christendom to become lord of an Italian household of Christians and a Jewess turned
Christian. To Portia and the rest of Belmont society, he was as acceptable or
unacceptable as the comical Spaniard: "Yourself, renowned Prince, then stood as
fair / As any comer I have looked on yet / For my affection" (2.1.20–22). In this

respect, he was, as Anthony Barthelemy noted, the first "non-villainous" Moor in English drama.[50] Such a Moor was new to the English but not to the Spanish stage or imagination, which had presented various images of heroic Moors in its literature of Maurophilia. In this play, Shakespeare is not exactly an English Maurophile, although he presents the first Moor on stage who had fought with his "scimitar" against the fearsome enemies of Christendom, the Persians: he was the first Moor whose heart lay in Christendom, or at least whose enemies were the enemies of Christendom. Perhaps that is why there is no mention of the religion of the Moor, as Jack D'Amico carefully observes: although he goes to a "temple" to pray before the test of the caskets, he projects neither Christian nor Islamic zeal.[51]

The prince was also the first Moor on the Elizabethan stage who knew something about England—thus the precise reference to its coinage: "They have in England / A coin that bears the figure of an angel / Stampèd in gold" (2.7.55–57). This reference to gold had an implication for Anglo-Moroccan cooperation that the prince invoked. The fact that a Moor referred to English coinage, presumably used in North Africa, corroborated the role that Queen Elizabeth had desired—that the coinage of England become internationally used. The queen had prohibited her trading companies from using Spanish coinage in the East Indies or anywhere else, arguing that only silver and gold with her effigy on one side should be used: only thus would she become known to the rest of the world as a great monarch equal in financial stature to the king of Spain. Meanwhile, Morocco had itself become a country of gold, representing the new "world money" that was not coming from Spain, which had monopolized that money since the conquest of America.[52] Indeed, Mulay Ahmad al-Mansur had come to be known around the Mediterranean as "the Golden," al-dhahabi, in recognition of the magnitude of his coffers. Eager to show England's superiority, Shakespeare had the Moroccan prince praise Elizabeth's coinage—and fail in the casket test. Given the fabulous wealth of Morocco, it was important that England and her queen not be overshadowed.

Shakespeare confronted through the Prince of Morocco the destabilization he saw in the Mediterranean Moors—a destabilization he had gruesomely shown in the Aaron of Titus Andronicus.[53] In The Merchant of Venice, and given the favorable change of political climate between England and Morocco, he presented a benign Moor, but still, a Moor who could not be accommodated in the European polis: the only way in which Shakespeare could bring about stability to Belmont was by sending the Prince of Morocco and his retinue back to where they came from. He could overcome and integrate the Jews by converting them to Christianity; after all, as in the case of Jessica, she was "fair" and therefore not physically different from the Belmont community into which she would integrate.[54] The Moors, though, were dark in skin—which is why the only way to overcome them was by sending them away, not converted or culturally defeated; simply sent back to the regions beyond the Mediterranean frontier, to a life of sterility and loneliness. As there had been no place in London for the Moors brought by English ships, so would the case be in Belmont. By admitting the Moors into Europe and then sending them out, Shakespeare showed that there was space for a royal Moroccan delegation to visit and perhaps negotiate a treaty; but there was no welcome for Moors to settle in the city, as some had already tried to do. Perhaps such Moors inspired the other Moor in the play, who is made pregnant by Launcelot, a "clown" and a "servant," and who provides the opportunity for some gratuitous quibbling on the word "Moor." The prince was at the Mediterranean frontier of Europe, and although he had succeeded in breaking through that frontier, he could not stay on European soil.

A year after Cadiz, the Fugger scribe in Brussels wrote that the English were preparing to equip two hundred thousand Moors from Barbary and "descend upon Spain."[55] Although no such equipping was taking place, the Moors, and their cousins the Moriscos, were anxious for anti-Spanish action. After the 1596 treaty of Greenwich in which England, France and Holland united against Spain, the Moriscos of Aragon tried to negotiate an alliance with Henri IV of France, while Moriscos in al-Andalus sought an alliance with England and Holland.[56] In February 1597, the Venetian ambassador in Spain reported that the Moors, in cahoots with the queen of England, were preparing to land in Spain.[57] By May of that year, Queen Elizabeth was still believed to be supporting a large army of Moors against Spain,[58] and in June, Spain prepared against a joint attack by "English and Moors."[59] Later that year, an anonymous memo addressed to Robert Cecil expressed the hope that the "King of Maroko" would send "som of his Mores to burne and spoyle the Spaniards corne adjoyning to their fortts and garisons in Barbarie."[60] From Spain to Venice and in the rest of the Mediterranean, monarchs and their courtiers were speculating feverishly about Anglo-Moroccan coordination. With the Ottomans having been militarily marginalized after Lepanto, despite the activities of the regency pirates, the Morocco of Ahmad al-Mansur al-Dhahabi was emerging as the new cornerstone for alliances and collusions in the western Mediterranean. And England was on top of the list for such collusions.

William Shakespeare, *Othello*

The climax of such collusions occurred in the summer of 1599, when a secret conversation took place between Jasper Tomson, an English trader and spy in Barbary, and one of al-Mansur's chamberlains, al-Caid Azouz. The latter asked him, as Tomson reported in a letter of 4 July 1599, whether the queen would be willing to invade Spain with twenty thousand of her own men and twenty thousand "horses and men from Barbarie." It is unlikely that Azouz would have broached such a topic without his master's approval, especially since Tomson was known to be in direct contact with the queen. Tomson stated that he did not know his queen's will, but that if al-Mansur was serious about the invasion, he should send an ambassador to England to discuss the matter. Azouz insisted on more commitment, and so Tomson passed on the information to London: Even if the queen was not interested in the offer, he wrote, her secretary Robert Cecil and her lord admiral, Charles Howard, should know "about this motion." Tomson was sure that the "motion" was too outrageous and would be a matter to "lawgh at"—but still he needed to convey al-Mansur's ambitious scheme.[61]

Al-Mansur's motion did not seem to generate much laughter since the queen gave permission for a Moroccan ambassador to travel to England. There was, after all, the important trade with Morocco and the need for continued cooperation against Spanish intrusion and piracy. Also, the wealth of Morocco was irresistible, and if there was any way of tapping into it, she would try. Tomson had ended his letter with a further report about the return of the military commander who had invaded the Sudan with "thirtie camels, laden with tyber, which ys unrefyned gold (yet the difference ys but six shillinges in an ownce weight betwene yt and duccattes)." John Pory, who had translated and was just about to publish an account about Africa by Leo Africanus, confirmed how the revenues of the "Xeriffo" "haue beene augmented of alte yeeres by mightie sums of gold, which he fetcheth from Tombuto and Gao in the lande of Negros; which gold (according to the report of some) may yeerely amount to three millions of ducates."[62] Al-Mansur had become a world power with whom the English queen could not afford not to negotiate. "Of Barbary rich, and has Moors" (1.2.17), Thomas Dekker wrote in *Lust's Dominion* (ca. 1600), confirming the impression that Londoners must have had of North Africans at the turn of the seventeenth century.[63]

The Moroccan ambassador arrived in Dover on 8 August and a week later was in London; on 22 August he presented his credentials at Nonsuch. Abd al-Wahid bin Masoud bin Muhammad al-Annuri, accompanied by fourteen other Moroccans, carried with him two letters from al-Mansur to Elizabeth, along with the Flemish captives for whom the queen had asked. In the surviving copy of the first letter (27 March 1600), al-Mansur explained that his ambassador was going to Aleppo but was stopping by England to deliver the Flemish captives, "for the *mahabba* [love] and friendship between you and us."[64] In the second letter (15 June 1600), al-Mansur stated that the ambassador would convey, orally and face-to-face *("mushafahatan . . . wa muwajahatan")* the real purpose of his visit:[65] "Wee giue you to understande and knowe," the translation reads, "that wee haue sent him touching that matter unto you; & haue enioyned him to shew you our meaneinge, yf you please to heare that wch wee haue commaunded him to deliuer."[66] Al-Mansur treated Elizabeth to the highest honorific titles that Arabic could devise: in the letter that the ambassador presented, she was addressed as the *"asala* which enjoys such high renown in Christian lands, who has status and majestic glory, firmness and stability, a rank which all her co-religionists, far and near, recognize, the sultana Isabel whose status among the Christian peoples continues to be mighty and elevated."[67]

What is known about "that matter" appears in the memorandum prepared in London and showing that al-Mansur wanted to discuss a possible alliance between England and Morocco against the Spanish-held possessions in North Africa and in America. Al-Mansur was also eager for Elizabeth to join him in an attack on Spain itself in order to fulfill his age-old dream of liberating the Andalus.[68] But there was another part to the "matter," too dangerous to put into writing, that al-Annuri conveyed, *mushafahatan wa muwajahatan*: coordination for an attack on Ottoman-held Algiers. Algiers had been Morocco's nemesis since even before al-Mansur ascended to the throne.[69] Actually, during the battle of Wadi al-Makhazin, as al-Fisthali reported, the Turks of Algiers had tried to assassinate al-Mansur.[70] That is why, a few years later, in 1582, al-Mansur "sent ambassadors into king Philip to demande him ayde against the Turks,"[71] seeking a joint invasion of Algeria to dislodge the Turks.[72] Such anti-Turkishness on the part of the Moors was well known in England: Hakluyt included an account by Laurence Aldersey, who had seen in 1586 "a prince of the Moors prisoner . . . [who was to be presented] to the Turk,"[73] while Thomas Kyd showed in his *The Tragedye of Soliman and Perseda* (1592) a Turk boasting of having "staind / With blood of Moores . . . the desert plaines of Affricke" (1.3.56–57).[74] In June 1599, Jasper Tomson reported that al-Mansur was happy to "heare that the Turkes afaires succeded not well."[75] In *Lust's Dominion*, Eleazar the Moor fought with Christians against Turks, while John Pory described the Turks "abas[ing] and bring[ing] to extreme miserie the Christians and Moores their subiects."[76] The "and" may have suggested to English readers not only the solidarity of the two groups against the Muslim Turks but a possible commonality in religion as well.

The queen listened to al-Annuri unfold al-Mansur's schemes, but she had ideas of her own. A letter has survived in Arabic by Mulay al-Mansur (23 Shaaban 1009/1 May 1601) responding to Elizabeth after al-Annuri's return from England. From this letter, preserved in the National Library in Rabat, it is possible to reconstruct what further took place during the negotiations. Evidently, the queen refused to commit herself to an alliance with al-Mansur; instead, she decided to try and outmaneuver him. Having seen that the ambassador was a Morisco, as his painting confirms, she decided to co-opt him into her service. The Moriscos of Morocco were the elite fighting force and were known to be restive. Al-Mansur's uncertainty about their commitment to him was such that he had sent them away, as George Tomson, Jasper's brother, reported to Robert Cecil, to fight the Christian forces in the presidio of Mazagan: "The Kinge hath noe trust in the Spaniardes [Moriscos]," he wrote.[77] In a treatise about Morocco dedicated to Philip III and written in the first years of the seventeenth century, the Spaniard Jorge de Henin also confirmed that "some of the Moriscos had become disruptive and untrustworthy" in the eyes of al-Mansur.[78]

Alert to this Moroccan instability, the queen proposed to al-Annuri that the Moriscos join her and become part of her fighting force in the battles against

Spain. Seeing that Moriscos deeply hated Spaniards, and seeing that they were the elite force in the Moroccan army, the queen believed that al-Annuri, along with other Moriscos, would not look unfavorably on this scheme. There was, after all, a precedent: the 1596 *Play of Stucley* had mentioned the presence of "three thousand mercenary Spanish moors" in a Christian army.[79] The ambassador promised to relay the request to his ruler, but then some Morisco members in his delegation decided to act on their own. The offer of serving in England and fighting the Spaniards was not to be missed, especially as it came from a queen whom they praised for her "estate and bountie."[80] The leader of this revolt was Hajj Musa, who had been initially designated to lead the delegation but had fallen foul of al-Mansur, who then replaced him with al-Annuri. Supporting him in the revolt was another Morisco, "Andalouz," who, as a report of 1 July 1600 had stated, was the "trudgman or interpretor."[81] This was Abdullah Dudar, knowledgeable about weapons because he had served in Italy as a soldier and had learned about European military technology.[82] Perhaps it was at this time in the "revolt" against the ambassador that he started using Italian in his communication with the queen: although he knew Spanish, he did not want al-Annuri to understand what he said to her, since al-Annuri could speak some Spanish but no Italian.[83] Al-Annuri now found himself with a crisis on his hands. How he handled it is not stated anywhere, but soon after January 1601, rumors started circulating in London that the ambassador and his advisers had "poysoned their interpretor, being borne in Granado . . . [and also] their revernd aged pilgrime [Hajj Musa]."[84] Like all ambassadors, al-Annuri had authority of life and death over members of his delegation. Did he crush the revolt by committing murder? If so, were the corpses of the Muslims buried outside the city limits, as perhaps Thomas Heywood recalled in *A Fair Maid of the West, Part I,* when he mentioned how infidels and heretics were buried, "Confin'ed unto the fields" (4.4.142–43)?

Upon learning about the queen's plot from al-Annuri, al-Mansur wrote to let her know that he had discovered her plans: "So-and-so, the Andalusian [the Arabic term for Morisco], came before our high Porte and relayed to us all your intentions and plans which you had discussed with him and conveyed to him. We listened with attentive ears until we understood them all, and became alert to all that you had plotted." We shall not send them over, he continued, "because we fear that they may be swayed [against us] by the enemy. The enemy will find occasion and then they will be exposed to danger. We do not want to put them in danger, because they are not alone in this matter."[85] Then al-Mansur turned to remind her that such plots were counterproductive to her traders and merchants residing in his territories. He informed her that his forces had arrested an Englishman who had been spying, a merchant "who had been inquisitive and acted in a manner different from other [English] merchants. He had been found inquiring about matters that did not concern him. We hereby inform you about him."

Al-Mansur was angry at the queen's plotting with the Moriscos; but he also wanted to keep the possibility of cooperation open even if she did not want to fight the Turks. He hoped she would at least be willing to fight the Spaniards in America. He explained that the campaign would require a big build-up of troops, "not less than a hundred thousand horses and fighting men." If she would be willing to cooperate, he would declare a jihad that would attract all the Berbers and the Arabs of the Maghrib. But, he continued, only if the Muslims know that upon conquering the lands, those lands would remain in their hands, would they be willing to fight; otherwise, if they were to conquer and then leave, the jurists would oppose the expenditure and loss of life. Al-Mansur repeated this point twice: he was willing to spend all that was needed only if conquest led to possession. Finally, he concluded, he was really not in need of military hardware from her, only "six ships, the largest of their kind." If she agreed to send those ships, he would dispatch six naval commanders, *riyyas*, along with their servants—all of whom would be paid by him and not cost the queen anything. These *riyyas* would buy what was needed, and would learn to use what was new and innovative. By agreeing to this, the queen would prove her *mahabba* and support for the enterprise.

Did Elizabeth's collusion with the Morisco ambassador and his retinue influence the making of Othello the Moor?[86] Although al-Mansur's letter to the queen does not exist in an English translation, and therefore must not have been known generally, the proposition the queen made to the Moriscos coincided with Shakespeare's reading of Cinthio's *Hecatommithi* and his subsequent composition of *Othello*. In *Hecatommithi*, Shakespeare found the story of a Moor serving in a Christian army. But Cinthio mentioned nothing about Turks or Mediterranean battles and sieges: his story described a domestic affair. Only in the first lines of his tale did he mention the service of the Moor to the state. In *Othello*, Shakespeare retained the domestic tragedy but moved it into the vast and confrontational world of the Mediterranean, where Venetian Christians employed Moors to fight the Ottoman Turks. Shakespeare was careful about his use of the terms "Turks" and "Moors": they were not politically or religiously interchangeable. "Turk" had two meanings: first, it meant an "Ottoman" preparing to invade a Christian island in the Mediterranean. The Ottomans (Ottomites) were geographically specific, representing imperial cunning as they sailed to Rhodes with the intent of attacking Cyprus; they also were brutal and aggressive as they berated Venetians in Aleppo. The Venetians used interchangeably the terms "Turk" and "Ottoman" in the play—without exhibiting either invective or racial bigotry, only anxiety about the formidable military power. The second meaning was used by Iago, for whom "Turk" was synonymous with liar or deceiver: "I am a Turk" (2.1.114). Soon after, Othello used it in a similar manner: "Are we turned Turks, and to ourselves do that / Which Heaven hath forbid the Ottomites?" (2.3.161–62). The "Turk" was the Muslim, the moral enemy at the frontiers of Mediterranean Christendom. Meanwhile, the term "Moor" described an African

with distinct racial and psychological features and with unquestionable trustwor-
thiness in defending the borders of Christendom ("straight employ you," 1.3.47).
The Moor was heaven's agent against the "general enemy Ottoman" (1.3.48)—
those Ottomans who were enemies of both Venetians and Moors.

Did Shakespeare model Othello on al-Annuri, the Moor who was to coordinate war against the Turks by joining the English army? It may well be that since
the queen had had no problem receiving a "Moor" in her court and had shown
no reaction to his "Moorishness," neither did the duke in the play react to a
Moorish admiral of his fleet. When Othello declared: "I do agnize / A natural and
prompt alacrity / I find in hardness and do undertake / This present wars against
the Ottomites" (1.3.231–34), he represented the Moorish willingness to fight for
Christians against Ottomans—which is what al-Annuri was invited to do. It is
important to note how Shakespeare presented Othello in a strikingly different
manner from contemporary representations of Moors on the English stage—
especially Eleazar in *Lust's Dominion*. At the outset of the play, Othello is the
seduced rather than the seducer, and as Iago sets his trap for him, he becomes the
victim rather than the victimizer. Further, the love affair with Desdemona was
quite unusual in English and indeed European literature, because it reversed the
expected stereotypes. Instead of being a lascivious Moor, Othello was restrained
and polite; and instead of the European woman fearing the Moor, as she always
did in the plays of Cervantes and de Vega, the Venetian fell in love with the Moor.
Instead of being the "maiden never bold," Desdemona thrust herself on Othello
with passionate kisses—or sighs (as in the alternative reading). It may well be that
the aloofness of the Moroccan ambassador, which his painting clearly conveys,
projected itself into Shakespeare's depiction of the Moor of Venice.

In this context of cooperation between Moor and Venetian and polarization
between Ottoman and Venetian, the question that has bedeviled much of *Othello*
criticism raises its head: what is the religion of the Moor? The fact that Othello
is a Moor need not translate into Muslim since, as Kim Hall has shown, to the
Elizabethan audience "Moor" could mean Muslim, Native American, Indian,
white North African or Jew.[87] Still, some critics have declared that in *Othello*,
and in the other representations of the Moor in early modern English drama,
"religious difference [is] more powerfully felt than racial difference,"[88] while
others have maintained that Islam and not blackness is the specter that haunts
early modern Europe.[89] The alleged Islam of Othello was first suggested in 1693
by Thomas Rymer, who followed the precepts of French Neoclassical criticism
and denounced Shakespeare for presenting unreal and implausible characters.[90]
He calculated that Othello was a Muslim after a Muslim ambassador from Morocco visited London in 1682 (see chapter five). Seeing the Muslim Moor in the
city, along with members of his retinue one of whom married an English woman,
Rymer concluded that Othello the Moor was a Muslim, too. Three hundred years
later, critics have revived Rymer's conclusion.[91] But the evidence for the Muslim

Moor is unconvincing: one writer has argued for Othello's Islam based on the Moor's use of the phrase "merciful and cruel God," which, rather strangely, reminded the critic of the "merciful and compassionate" God of the Qur'an. How Othello's "cruel" could recall the Qur'an's "compassionate," and how Shakespeare would have known of the "merciful and compassionate" Allah at a time when there was still no English translation of the Qur'an, and no easily available Latin version either, are left unexplained.[92] Also left unexplained are the Christian, rather than Islamic, references in the play: in Act 5 alone, Othello made thirteen allusions to biblical and liturgical sources—sources the echoes of which the audience could not have missed.

How much Shakespeare knew about Islam is not clear. If he knew anything, he knew Islam not as a theology but as an Ottoman empire with its peculiar political and social culture. That is why he mentioned "Mahomet," for instance, only once in his whole work (in *1 Henry VI*) and "Alcoran" never: contrast that with Cervantes or Marlowe or Kyd—Marlowe having over a score of references to "Alcaron" and two score to "Mahomet." Shakespeare was, of course, aware of a dangerous Turkish or Ottoman empire, although how precise his knowledge was is not clear. He referred to Sultan Suleyman (who had died in 1566) fighting the Persians (*Merchant of Venice*, 2.1.26)—although much closer to his time, Sultan Murad III had fought against them, too. He referred to eunuchs serving among the Turks and to the lust of the Turk and the "tributes" he collected; to the despotic court in Constantinople over which the Turk presided, and to the enmity the Turk had for the Christian and his cross.[93] All these allusions Shakespeare could have picked up from plays about Turks that had appeared on the London stage or from sources on which he and other playwrights drew (especially William Painter's *The Palace of Pleasure*, 1575). Shakespeare presented no information about Islam beyond what London audiences had seen on stage.

Actually, while Shakespeare kept Othello's religious past unclear,[94] he made it very clear that Othello was a Christian Moor, the first ever on the Elizabethan stage. No previous Moor on stage had ever been presented as anything other than pagan or areligious: from Muly Hamet to Aaron to the Prince of Morocco and Eleazar, the Moors belonged to a Senecan dramatic convention where they predominantly invoked classical deities, regardless of what their religion was or was not. The first reference to the Christianity of Othello appeared in Iago's confirmation of Othello's baptism. Othello had accepted baptism, Iago urged, but Desdemona wielded so much power over him (she was the "captain's captain," 2.1.74) that she could unbaptize him, whereupon he would revert to the damned condition before his "redemption thence" (1.3.138):

And then for her
To win the Moor; were't to renounce his baptism,
All Seals and symbols of redeemed sin,

His soul is so enfettered to her love
That she may make, unmake, do what she list. (2.3.333–37)

Christian as Othello was, his Christianity was questionable since he could be induced to renounce it; it was a Christianity that could be subverted. Perhaps Iago felt that with Othello now in Cyprus, geographically nearer to the lands of the Turks or Muslims than he had been in Venice, it might just be possible to unmake the Moor's baptism. Iago set himself the task of unbaptizing Othello, making him renounce his Christianity and commit what would surely disqualify him from Venetian service. Then he, Iago, would take his position.

This doubtfulness about Othello's Christianity is sustained until the end of the play. Soon after landing in Cyprus, and in a moment of brawling drunkenness, Cassio proclaims that "there be souls must be saved, and there be souls must not be saved" (2.3.96–98). Talking to Iago, and loosened by the alcohol he had consumed, Cassio adds: "For mine own part, no offence to the general, nor any man of quality, I hope to be saved" (2.3.100–101). Although Othello cannot hear him, Cassio does not want to offend his general, a man whom he admires for his "quality"; but by referring to his general immediately after asserting that "some" will not be saved, he points to the uncertainty of Othello's salvation—a salvation dependent on the Christian "God" whom he repeatedly invokes in lines 60–105—and whom Othello never does in the whole course of the play. Later, after Othello accuses Desdemona of being a "strumpet" (4.2.83), she answers:

No, as I am a Christian!
If to preserve this vessel for my lord
From any other foul unlawful touch
Be not to be a strumpet, I am none. (4.2.84–87)

Although "as I am a Christian" was a commonly used assertion in Shakespearean England, it must have made its mark on Othello and on the London audience since it is followed by a conflation of biblical images of the "weaker vessel" that is to be honored by the husband (1 Pet. 3:7) and the vessel that is to be "sancti-fied, and meet for the master's use" (2 Tim. 2:21). Desdemona upholds to her Moorish husband the New Testament image of the wife as an honorable vessel to her husband/master. This is the only time where Othello is confronted with an assertion of Christianity: in marrying him, Desdemona is telling him, she entered into a Christian framework of matrimony that she trusts him to uphold.

The flaw in Othello lies in his inability to see the "Turk" near him, intent on unbaptizing him, and instead sees Cassio and Desdemona intent on deceiving him. While he is formidable in confronting the Ottoman Turks in battle and has proved himself the fearless warrior, he fails to see through Iago the Turk. When he is about to kill himself, he admits that the Turk, whom he had always defeated, both in Aleppo and elsewhere in the Mediterranean, has defeated him. For before him, fully exposed, stands Iago the Turk. Only at the end does Othello see the Turk who has deceived him. While the earlier deception of the Turks in sailing to Rhodes but aiming at Cyprus had been discovered by the Venetians who subsequently dispatched Othello to Cyprus, the deception of Iago in focusing on Cassio and Desdemona but aiming at Othello was not discovered by the non-Venetian general dispatched to fight the Turks. It is significant that only in Cyprus did Othello make any allusion in all the play to the geography of the dominions of the Turks. Perhaps with an Ortelian map before him, Shakespeare could see how near Cyprus was to the East Mediterranean coast: looking at the Turk Iago, Othello imagined that he saw the Aleppo where he once had killed a Turk, and the Arabian tree, and the "Iudean" (Folio)—all in the land of the "enemy" Turk, east of Cyprus. Othello killed himself in order to kill the Turk Iago within him, with whom he had bonded in a "sacred vow" (3.3.458) while admitting defeat before the Turks/Ottomans whose lands he could envisage.

To underscore the anti-Turkish motif, Shakespeare ensured that nothing Turkish or Islamic characterized Othello. The reference to the turban and the circumcision in Othello's last speech characterizes the enemy Ottoman or "Turk"—and therefore is not the Moor's. Indeed, the reference to circumcision calls into question the claim that Othello had been a Muslim at all, as Samuel Chew noted long ago.[95] As for the turban, and although it is not known how Othello was dressed on stage, he could not have worn a turban, nor did any of the great Othello actors wear one—from Edmund Kean to Orson Welles to Laurence Olivier.[96] For the turban was the most obvious and decisive signifier of a Muslim in early modern England; converts to Islam were summarily denounced for having "donned the turban."[97] The Moor of Venice who was defending Christendom against the turbaned Turks would not have worn one.

Shakespeare did not explore in Othello the "Islam" of the Moor, but rather his color. Although many writers—Hakluyt and Pory/Africanus most importantly—distinguished the "white" from the "tawny" from the "black" Moors of North and sub-Saharan Africa, the Elizabethan playwrights completely ignored the distinctions and created black and dangerous figures. Michael Neill has noted that Purchas united the Europeans through a common whiteness, while all other colors were associated in "a common non-Europeanness."[98] Shakespeare, the playwright with the greatest number of Moors on the Elizabethan stage, was not satisfied with nonwhiteness: he proceeded to blacken and racialize the Moors. But the Moors who had arrived in London, and particularly the delegation leaders, were all Moriscos with features that did not much differ from those of other Spaniards, nor perhaps from those of the Mediterranean/Italian Iago with the Spanish name. The surviving painting of al-Annuri confirms the non-Negroid features of a sharp-eyed and haughtily intimidating man. Indeed, so unnoted were the racial features and skin color of the visiting Moors that a report about them in October 1600 denounced them as "infidels" but mentioned nothing about their color.[99] Another report, written after the Moroccans' departure in

January 1601, told how the delegation members had visited Hampton Court and street markets in London and had gone to Whitehall to attend Queen Elizabeth's Coronation Day celebration, observing and asking questions to the point that they aroused suspicion and provoked anger and anxiety.[100] Furthermore, when official announcements for the expulsion of Moors were made in 1596 and 1601, there was emphasis on religious rather than racial differences. The "Negras and Blakamoors, which (as she [the queen] is informed) are crept into this realm" from Spain "are infidels, having no understanding of Christ or his Gospel."[101] The reaction against them was based on their ignorance of Christianity.

While Shakespeare and all Elizabethan dramatists were interested in the race of the Moors, the government was concerned about their religious identity—an understandable concern in a monarchy that equated loyalty to the monarch with Anglican conformity. This difference between the royal or government reaction and the stage reactions to Moors prevailed throughout the Elizabethan period. It may well be that political anxiety about Moors in London drove playwrights to blacken them, with all the historical and theological associations that blackness evoked in the imagination of a white community. The Moors became Negroid because such blackening was necessary for stabilizing politico-diplomatic fears and neutralizing national concern. After all, the Moroccans on the London streets represented power, gold and anti-Spanish and anti-Turkish support. Such power militated against their being framed in the English discourse of colonial domination. To the Elizabethan groundling or the courtier, especially the latter, the Moors on the stage and the street did not represent subdued natives but rather men of stealth, ambition and triumph. It was because of their fearsomeness that Elizabethan playwrights racially excoriated the Moors on stage: Aaron is demonized for his blackness (despite his defense of his son), the Prince of Morocco is embarrassed by his skin color, and Othello is berated for his Barbary features, while Mullisheg, in *The Fair Maid of the West, Part I*, is racially ridiculed. To English playwrights whose country had not yet colonized one inch of Africa, the Moroccans were not defeated subalterns and kidnapped savages—as other non-Europeans and non-Christians were. That is why playwrights blackened them into sons of the cursed Ham with thick lips and rolling eyes, fearful "to look on" (*Othello*, 1.3.98). Even as a Christian, the Moor was problematic, unsettling and dangerous.

Thomas Heywood, *The Fair Maid of the West, Part I*

At the same time that *Othello* was being written, Thomas Heywood prepared *The Fair Maid of the West, Part I* to celebrate the success of his monarch in dealing with Mulay al-Mansur.[102] Heywood wrote a sea romance about a sailor and his beloved, Spencer and Bess, and the difficulties of commitment in the lives of seamen. But in act 4, he diverted the action toward the Anglo-Spanish conflict and the role that Morocco played in supporting England against Spain. The

Moroccan material in the play shows some familiarity with, as well as confusion about, the history of the North African region.[103] It could well be that upon the arrival of al-Annuri and his delegation in London, and with the negotiations ending without a firm commitment on the part of the queen, Heywood realized that there was a place for an entertaining Moorish subplot in his play.

Heywood was relatively accurate in describing Anglo-Moroccan relations. Where he derived the name of Mullisheg is unclear: it is close to Mulay al-Sheikh,[104] one of the sons of Mulay al-Mansur, but the references to Mullisheg's relations with the English more accurately apply to Mulay al-Mansur than to his son al-Sheikh, who colluded with Spain. Still, the "intestine broils" to which Mullisheg refers recall the Alcazar battle that finally resolved the matter of succession in Morocco: "now at last establish'd in the throne / Of our great ancestors, and reign King / Of Fez and great Morocco" (4.3.3–5). The reference to the "Alkedavy, the great palace" is one of the earliest references in English to the famous palace of al-Badee' that had been finished by Mulay al-Mansur in 1593 and was a marvel of design, as well as the seat of Moroccan power, "Where Mullisheg now deigns to keep his court" (4.3.34).[105] Heywood also stated how the English were exposed to Spanish attacks and how they found the Moroccans willing to protect them in the pirate port of "Mamorah" (4.5.162)—a port that was notoriously known, both in England and in the rest of Europe, to swarm with English pirates working in cooperation with local pirates. Heywood showed Florentine, Italian, French and other Christian merchants and captives in Marrakesh turning to the English Bess for help with the Moroccan ruler, in the same manner that, in the real world, they turned to Queen Elizabeth—in May 1599, the Dutch States General had asked the queen to try to effect the release of Dutch captives held by al-Mansur.[106] Finally, and like Shakespeare, Heywood alluded to the legendary gold of Barbary, "the gold / Coin'd in rich Barbary" (5.1.81–82), while at the same time proudly showing how valuable and widely used in Morocco English coinage ("angels") was (5.2.147).

Heywood dramatized the relation between the English queen and al-Mansur through the figure of Bess (Elizabeth Bridges) who arrived at the court of the king of Fez. As soon as Mullisheg saw her, he declared his love for her and for the country from where she had come: Bess was the first English woman he had ever seen. "The English earth may well be term'd a heaven, / That breeds such divine beauties" (5.1.43–44). In the "pro-English universe" of this play,[107] Heywood presented Bess as the Virgin Queen: the Spanish captives thought Bess "Famous Elizabeth" (4.4.122), as did Mullisheg, "maid of England, like a queen" (5.2.7). Heywood then continued with a fantasy of assurance and ethno-religious pride: Bess demanded a treaty from Mullisheg to ensure "safe conduct to and from her ship," "to be free from all violence either by the king or any of his people," and to permit "mariners fresh victuals aboard" (5.1.50–56). Such a treaty echoed the demands that Queen Elizabeth and her court had repeatedly made to Mulay al-Mansur—and which the latter prevaricated over in the hope of a military alliance. The treaty to which Bess agreed reflected the hopes of the seamen and traders in the audience: to be safe and to be able to revictual in Morocco, without having to make national or religious concessions to the Moors.

A sense of English assuredness enabled Bess to keep her distance from the Moor despite his willingness to offer half his kingdom to the "beauteous English virgin." Only after he agreed to the treaty with her did she deign to offer him a labial kiss in conformity with English custom of "first greeting" (5.1.63). Although Moors could well have been kissed by Christian women on the English stage before (Desdemona and Othello kissed on stage, and Maria and Eleazar, as perhaps did Tamora and Aaron), Bess's kiss was the first by an Englishwoman to a Moor.[108] Evidently Heywood had no anxiety about such incipient miscegenation, especially that the kiss opened up venues for English ascendancy in the Moroccan court. Bess was able to assume authority in Fez and to intercede on behalf of "Christians" whom she saved from the galleys. More kissing took place on stage as Mullisheg's "black face" smooched Bess's "white lips"—for the cause of Bess's English queen, her trading coreligionists, and her lover, Spencer. Heywood ended the play with Mullisheg magnanimously giving his blessing to the wedding of Spencer and Bess. The latter had succeeded in evoking in the Muslim potentate a sense of chivalric honor: "You have waken'd in me an heroic spirit; / Lust shall not conquer virtue.—Till this hour / We grac'd thee for thy beauty, English woman" (5.2.118–20).[109]

Whether Bess and Spencer would return to England after the play is over is not made clear, but Heywood could not but have been aware, as were many of his audience, that large numbers of his compatriots were settled in Barbary and were acquiring both wealth and status. For Bess and Spencer to be thinking of staying and serving Mullisheg was not outlandish—which is why Spencer declared to the Moroccan king at the very end of the play, "We are your highness' servants" (5.2.146). With relations prospering between the English queen and the Moroccan ruler, despite the absence of official treaties, Heywood projected a happy and promising picture of mutually beneficial cooperation.

At no time did Heywood construct the Moor as "a religious threat to England," as Jean E. Howard has carefully noted.[110] This religiously nondangerous Moor is significant because Heywood was the first Elizabethan playwright to link the figure of the Moor to Islam. No previous playwright had associated the racial difference of the Moors with the religion of Islam. The Moors in Christopher Marlowe's *Tamburlaine, II* are "coal-black" who swear by "Jove" (1.4.14–15), and Peele, despite using Polemon's text, did not include any reference to Islam in his play. Rather, his Moors swear by the "gods" and by Jove, and invoke Pluto and the Three Sisters. As Peele did not use religion to characterize the Moor, neither did his coauthor Shakespeare in the Roman world of *Titus Andronicus*. Like Peele's Mahamet, Aaron is not distinguished by religion but by race: he is the Negroid man of moral degeneracy, danger and motiveless evil. In *Lust's Dominion*, Eleazar swears by "Indian gods."[111] As Shakespeare was the first playwright to present a Christian Moor, so was Heywood the first English playwright to put Islamic words in the mouths of his Moors, to have them swear by "the mighty prophet," and to repeat vague generalizations about Islam: Islam as a religion of pleasure (4.3.39), propounded by a prophet from Mecca (4.3.40), whom Muslims "adored" (5.1.26). To the London audience, this was the first occasion when a Moor openly associated himself on stage with the "worshippers" or followers of the Prophet from Mecca—as the Turk had long done on stage.[112]

After Heywood, English drama about North Africa either made clear the Christianity of the Moors, or openly associated them with Islam. In *The Triumphs of Truth*, which was dramatized in 1613, Thomas Middleton captured that clash of color with religion: the Moorish king who appeared on stage saw "amazement" on the faces of his English hosts because his "black" skin revealed to them how far he was from "the true religion" of Christian "sanctity." Because they saw "darkness" and "error" in his face, he hastened to assure them that he had been led to the "true Christian faith" by "English merchants, factors, travelers."[113] A few years later, in *The Knight of Malta* (ca. 1618), Beaumont and Fletcher confirmed the link between Moorishness and "the prophet that you worship," while the Dane Norandine declaimed against the "sleepy prophet" and the "silver crescents" of Islam.[114] In *All's Lost by Lust* (1619), Middleton and Rowley associated the Moors with "the lustfull lawes of Mahomet" (2.6.45).[115] In *The Fair Maid of the West, Part I*, Heywood established the Islam of the Moor.

*   *   *

The death of Queen Elizabeth and the beginning of a civil war in Morocco in 1603 brought an end to England's cooperation with Morocco—and an end to the Moors on stage. A year after James I acceded to the throne, in 1604, a Spanish delegation walked the streets of London, signaling the end of the politico-dramatic importance of the Moors. Under King James, England/Britain separated itself politically and imaginatively from Barbary. Although *Othello* was performed before the king in the Christmas season of that year, interest in the Moors declined except for the devastating women Moors—bawds, evil, black, fearsome—who appeared in later plays. In *The Tempest*, there was the never-seen Moorish king of Tunis, to whom Christian women were sent against their will as wives (just as captured Christian women were sold into the harems of North African rulers). And, of course, there was the half-Moor Caliban, whose mother was from Algiers, "an African of some kind," probably "a (negro) slave."[116] Perhaps the son whom Aaron had, and who was nurtured on roots and in a cave (*Titus* 4.2.178–80), emerged in Shakespeare's imagination nearly two decades later as the cave-dwelling and root-eating "thing of darkness."

In *The Tempest*, Shakespeare expresses the various levels of anxiety caused by the shifting commercial and dynastic borders of the Mediterranean frontier.[117] Caliban is not taken back to Europe because, for Shakespeare, he belongs to that savage world of the non-European frontier about which many travelers had written—the frontier beyond which were "the Cannibals, that each other eat; / The Anthropophagi, and men whose heads / Do grow beneath their shoulders" (*Othello* 1.3.143–45). By leaving the son of the Algerine sorceress behind, Shakespeare showed that the space for exchange, encounter and interculturation that Fernand Braudel invoked for the multireligious and multiracial Mediterranean of Philip II, Elizabeth I, Mulay Ahmad al-Mansur and Sultans Murad III, Mehmed III and Ahmad I was now closed. A new age was about to begin marked by the death of the architects of détente between Britain and Barbary: Queen Elizabeth I and Mulay Ahmad al-Mansur. It was the age of the corsairs.

2

"Imperialism," Captivity and the Civil Wars

Anthony Pagden and Barbara Fuchs have pointed to the Spanish model of, and sources for, the development of the British overseas imagination.[1] In the same way that Spain colonized North Africa while it was colonizing South America, so did some British writers conceive of colonizing not only North America but also the Barbary region. Notwithstanding the protection of the Mediterranean by the Ottomans, the sea battle of Lepanto in 1571, which ended with the defeat of the Ottoman fleet, ensured that west of the Rome-Tunis axis, the region was open to reconfigurations of alliances and military aspirations. Travelers and captives, diplomats and geographers started to learn about the differences in the ethnography, culture, languages and geography of Barbary: they ranged in their imagination from one country to another, plotting against an Atlantic port in Morocco and in the same breath describing the wealth of Algiers. Whether it was the coast of Virginia or of Barbary, the entrepreneurs dreamed of swift wealth, lordly manors and subdued natives. As a result, a "mimesis" of imperial imagery and ideas, to use Barbara Fuchs's term, was applied to the two regions of the Atlantic.

But as this chapter shows, the imperial desire remained confined to English imagination. Although writings urging the occupation of North African regions appeared as of the early 1600s, the seizure by the Barbary corsairs of captives from all over the British Isles circumvented the fulfillment of that desire, as a result of which, and until the middle of the century, British involvement in the Islamic Mediterranean remained confined to trade, negotiations, freeing of captives and, only once, a successful naval campaign (against Salé). The North Africans fought back against the intrusion of British (and French) merchant fleets by capturing sailors, travelers and traders, men, women and children—thereby projecting to the home communities, from London to Edinburgh, an image of a fearful and dangerous region. By so doing, they subverted the imperial dream while inadvertently playing a crucial role in destabilizing England's internal politics and aggravating the conflict between the king and Parliament.[2]

During the reign of Charles I, a crisis developed around the captives seized by the Barbary corsairs that added another cause to the constitutional and ecclesiastical conflicts that culminated in the Civil Wars. Although K. R. Andrews has argued that the captives and their "clamorous" relatives had a "small influence" on the course of events leading up to the Civil Wars, and although other historians have completely ignored the crisis of captivity,[3] the seizure and enslavement of Britons in Barbary cities played an important role in compounding the conflict between King Charles and members of the parliamentary opposition, many of whom were closely associated with the Levant and East India Companies whose sailors and merchants were the target of Barbary attacks. These companies lost hundreds of employees and scores of ships to the corsairs and blamed the king for not spending the monies raised through customs, tonnage and poundage, forced loans and Ship Money (which had been intended to improve the fleet and extend British sovereignty over the seas) on maritime security. Similarly, seamen's wives and their families blamed the king and his ministers for the failure to ransom their kin. By not acting decisively to resolve this foreign policy challenge, and by ignoring the numerous petitions that were presented to him by kinsmen and employers of the captives, King Charles allowed Parliament to take the initiative in helping, or appearing to help, the captives, and in adding one more cause to the Civil Wars. The captives not only impeded British imperial strategy but also played a role in changing the course of Britain's domestic history.

Imperial Desire

The establishment of the East Levant/Turkey Company in 1580 and of the Barbary Company in 1585 confirmed the Elizabethan commercial interest in the Mediterranean, while Hakluyt's 1589 and 1599 *Navigations* included numerous writings by English travelers about the wealth and opportunity in the Islamic Levant and North Africa. Even captives discovered that their accounts about their ordeals in Barbary could provide their countrymen with useful information. In 1595, Richard Hasleton described his captivity in Algeria and drew his readers' attention to the "pure metals, as gold, silver, and lead; and good iron and steel" and "among the dross of the iron, very perfect gold," which the natives did not recognize.[4] John Pory's 1600 translation of Leo Africanus's account about Barbary provided an extensive description in English of the regions with their differing religions, peoples and cultures. The book also alerted the readers to Spain's numerous possessions in North Africa—Oran, Ceuta, Tangier, Melilla, Pennon and Mazagan—and the danger to English trade in the Mediterranean from such strategically located presidios. *The Worlde, or An historicall description of the most famous kingdoms and common-weales therein*, which appeared a year later, included a substantial section on "the Xeriffe," the sultan of Morocco, a powerful monarch ruling a powerful monarchy that was "excellent well peopled." So attractive was the kingdom of Fez and Morocco for traders and fortune seekers that "greate store of Englishmen and Frenchmen resort[ed]" there, carrying "thither armor and other wares of Europe, which they barter[ed] for sugar and other commodities."[5] The author pointed to the employment opportunity for Europeans in North Africa—particularly if they had experience in land and naval warfare. The Barbary region offered temporary work for the unemployed among Britain's growing population, long-term residence, immigration and dreams of wealth. In some men, it also planted the seed of imperial desire.

In April 1603, immediately upon the death of Queen Elizabeth, the first "imperial" call for conquering Barbary was sounded. The English agent in Morocco between 1585 and 1589, Henry Roberts, wrote to the new king, James I, to inform him about the "new" lands of Barbary that needed to be conquered for king and Christ. Roberts told the king that he had kept his ideas secret for the past fifteen years, until after the death of Queen Elizabeth. He urged the king to recognize the value of the conquest of a region that was by far less difficult to reach than North America and that was rich in "comodities." There were "verie great and riche [lands]" the possession of which would not only bring glory to Christianity but also "profite and increase of your Maties demynions, trafique or marchantes, ymployments of navies and people." Roberts listed what the country yielded—in a manner similar to listings that had appeared during the Elizabethan period about North America: he described terrain, fauna and flora, minerals and other exploitable natural resources. "The soile," wrote Roberts, was "verie fertile [producing] Wheate, barley and pease, aboundance and very good anniseeds and sugar, verie good dates, annecles, wynes, oyles, raisons, hides, goatskinnes, waxe, honye and rawe silke. Saltpeeter more plenty and better then in any countrey." Roberts continued with separate listings of beasts, fowls and fruit. The country was rich, and its acquisition could prove profitable to the new king. The fact that there were already people, armies and royal authorities in these lands did not seem to bother him very much: he assured King James that the fighting forces of Morocco were weak and that upon the arrival of the invading British troops, many of the inhabitants would convert to Christianity, and even those who did not would realize how much better it was for them to be ruled by a "Christian government" than by the cruel "Mahometans." Others would flee to the mountains, but Roberts was confident that the majority would come around to their new Christian king, for they were "very unstable and changeable in their mynde, and will be drawne with faire wordes and good promises." The conquest of Morocco would be a gateway to the conquest of the sub-Saharan Niger, "very rich both of goulde and other great riches comodities," would "annoy" the Turks and would challenge the Spaniards in a region into which they were continuing to expand.[6]

Roberts was the first English writer to propose an imperial thrust into North Africa. He was familiar with a few regions of Morocco in which he had traded, but his imperialist imagination would have applied better to North America, with its traumatized native populations, than to North Africa, where Ahmad al-Mansur commanded a standing army of, according to Roberts himself, not only "fortie thowsand" soldiers of different ethnic backgrounds, but another forty thousand who reported directly to him, and two hundred thousand more bedouins, "Larbies." How British soldiers were to defeat such a massive force was not explained by Roberts, and what King James thought of this proposal is not known. But in his letter, Roberts anticipated the emergent dream of English and British imperialism: after all, his countrymen (and their European counterparts) were eagerly buying the popular and beautifully colored atlases of Ortelius and Mercator and leafing through them, speculating about the vastness of the terra firma and the possibilities of new markets, factories and possessions. In 1601, 1603 and 1606, English translations of the *Theatrum Orbis Terrarum* listed the abundance in Morocco, the "many vineyeards, large gardens of palme-trees and other fruites, goodly cornefields most fertile and well manured."[7]

Paradoxically, the strength of the Moroccan army about which Roberts wrote lay in its employment of British (and other European) mercenaries so much so that King James was concerned that his subjects, both soldiers and sailors, were deserting their country to fight, sail, pillage and sometimes die with the Moors. So many of his subjects found more opportunity in North Africa than in England that in 1609, George Wilkins published (having written it around 1604–5) a description of the disastrous conditions of Barbary: *Three Miseries of Barbary: Plague. Famine. Civill warre.* Although Wilkins praised the country, "abundant in riches, flowing with Arts and trafficke with all Nations," he also showed how the internecine conflict had depleted it of its riches. The impression that he created about Barbary was that it was rich but devastated—something, he warned, that could happen to England as well. Barbary provided a model for a country on which God had poured his wrath; it was a place to learn from rather than to occupy.[8] But such a damper of disasters did not reduce the importance of Morocco: after all, it was much nearer than Virginia, Japan or the Spice Islands, and was assured of gold (from the Niger), which had eluded the English settlers of America. Although in North America the colonists would, in the absence of gold, turn to commodify land as their main source of wealth, in North Africa, gold could still be had in an area that was not separated by oceans with dangerous "hurricans."

In 1613, Samuel Purchas produced his first edition of *Pvrchas his Pilgrimage. Or Relations of the World,* with four chapters on the kingdoms of Tunis, Tripoli, Algiers, Fez and Morocco. (In that year, Jorge de Henin, adviser to Mulay Zaidan in Morocco, also finished a detailed history of Morocco the purpose of which was to motivate King Philip III to invade and take possession of the country.)[9] Two years later, in 1615, the translation by Edward Grimstone of *The Estates, Empires & Principallities of the World* was published, providing descriptions of "contemporary" Morocco with details about the abundance of "oyles, honie, wax, sugar, cotton, goats haire . . . and mines of gold" and about the social life of the community, "the ciuilitie of them of Fez, their goodline stoues, innes, trafficke of mills, distinct dwellings for mechanicke arts."[10] "Barbarie" was clearly a rich and enticing region—a view that was confirmed by an anonymous writer in 1618 who listed the "Oranges, Dates, Oliues, Figges, and certaine kinde of Goate, whose haire doth make a stuffe as fine as silke . . . [and] gold"[11] as part of the resources of the land. John Speed repeated those words, and added a reference to the death site of Thomas Stuckley, perhaps to remind his readers of the first English venture into that region.[12] Evidently, the colonists-to-be in North Africa thought they would find a land without a people, a "Barbary" without "Barbarians," where they would be at leisure to exploit natural resources and start another New England. Purchas, Speed and others were cautioning their readers about "imperial" dreams: while North America was for colonization, North Africa was for trade and commerce.

Upon the death of King James and the accession of his son, the English agent in Morocco, John Harrison, wrote a proposal to the commander of the fleet in the Mediterranean about the possibilities for intervention and conquest. Harrison, who worked for the Barbary Company, was eager to promote British trade in, and possible occupation of, parts of the region.[13] Having seen how the Spaniards and the Portuguese operated, Harrison thought that British policy should follow in the same direction: seizure of territory as a means of securing trade. What Harrison believed was encouraging about such a direction was the population he had met in Morocco and other parts of the region. Interacting chiefly with Europeanized Muslims or Moriscos who were hostile to the central government in Marrakesh, Harrison believed that those "Moores and Jewes"— the former having been expelled from Spain just over a decade earlier—would be willing to cooperate with the English against the Spaniards. The vast majority of the Moriscos whom he met had been expelled from Spain between 1609 and 1614. Upon arriving in North Africa, they had not found the open welcome they had hoped for because the local populations feared them as Islamicized Christians. As a result, they separated themselves into socially and culturally exclusive enclaves, and it was not long before they started thinking of separating themselves politically as well. The Moriscos were also very anti-Catholic, just like Harrison himself, and were not unwilling to join forces with any Christian power that opposed the Spaniards and promised them help against their persecutors. Harrison believed that they would be willing to cooperate with the Protestant King Charles: after all, he asserted, they were eager to read "Calvin and other bookes of our religion" and were generally well disposed "towardes our nation, and even to Christian religion." Passionately, Harrison invoked the commander through the mouth of the Lord ("o noble English! March valiantlie, as in tymes past") to conquer Ceuta: it was, he explained on a more sober note, an important port for British traders in the Mediterranean and which "a small garison would mayntaine." Harrison also urged the seizing of Gibraltar and Mamoura whereupon England's enemies, were they in Spain, Portugal or other regions of "Barbary," would "flee away (as God commandeth) out of Babylon." From Roberts' conversion-cum-profit conquest, Harrison's goal had changed not in quality but in quantity: conversion was still desired, but the conquest was now of ports rather than of the whole region.[14]

Harrison was proposing a new direction for the British fleet in the Mediterranean: not the conquest, or attempted conquest, of whole countries, but the control and safety of the means of transportation—which necessitated the possession of select harbors. In the Mediterranean, where the populations were hostile and powerful, wealth would follow trade, not conquest. Two years later, he wrote a proposal to King Charles I about the limited conquest of the Spanish presidio of Ceuta. Ignoring his country's weakened navy and the emptied royal coffers, Harrison turned to rouse the king by writing an account of the natural resources and the abundance of commodities in North Africa and, given the piety of the king, by the possibility of spreading the Christian religion there. Numerous changes, he reported, had occurred in the quasi-independent republic of Salé, populated by Morisco exiles from the Hornacho region in Spain: these Saletians, he reported to the king and his Privy Council in September 1627, had seceded from the central authority in Marrakesh and were seeking military help to hasten the "tyme of their restauration into Spaine." They had informed Harrison that they would "put themselves wholly under" the English king's protections and help the English seize the ports of Mamoura and al-Araish (which were in Spanish hands). After receiving weapons and ammunition from the king, they wanted to join the Protestant faith, thereby rejecting "that idolatrous Roman religion" and the "Mahometanisme under which now they groane." Harrison urged the king to take up their cause not only because the Saletians would support British trade and cut out the Spaniards and other European rivals, but also because "they be Christians in heart, all these Andaluzes."[15]

Although no attempt was made by King Charles to undertake such conquests, sea commanders recognized the need for seizing some bases in the Mediterranean, just as Harrison had suggested. After all, they were worried about the French attempts to colonize Morocco: the Chevalier de Razilly, Isaac, was intent on placing Morocco under French suzerainty as the "plan" presented by Razilly "de colonizer l'Afrique" showed.[16] After the capture of La Rochelle in 1628, Razilly was instructed by Cardinal Richelieu to install a French garrison in Mogador on the Atlantic coast of Morocco. Although he did not succeed, his plans remained a danger that the British could not afford to ignore, especially after the French promised to allow the Moroccan ruler to purchase "Navires et Munitions" that could strengthen his maritime capability and threaten British shipping.[17] The Dutch had also established cordial relations with Mulay al-Mansur's successor, Mulay Zaidan, and had sold him ships and founded factories on the Atlantic coast of the country. If Britons did not move quickly to establish military and commercial ties with the region, other European powers would cut them off from the lucrative markets; and with the Thirty Years War devastating the continent and reducing trade, they could not afford to lose another venue for their products.

In 1635, Peter Heylyn published his *Cosmographie, In Four Bookes* with an extensive history of Tunisia, Algeria and Morocco, from the earliest Roman records, passing through the sixteenth-century Ottoman-Spanish rivalry, until 1632 when the English carried out a naval attack to release captives (an episode to which Heylyn frequently refers). He praised the beauty of Algiers, with its "pub-lick Innes, Bathes, and Mosques, exceeding sumptuous," and listed the natural resources in Morocco, "Grain and Pulse, plentiful of Oyl, Honey and Sugar, liberally furnished with Dates, Grapes, Figs, Apples, Pears . . . Cattel" and the rich gold mines of the Sus region in the south of the country. He also included a description of Mulay al-Mansur's al-Badee' palace (taken from Speed), with its "three Globes made of pure Gold." The repeated allusions to the Sa'dian palace in English writings reflected not only the opulent splendor of the palace but also the amazement of the English writers: they clearly had seen nothing like it in their own country. But alongside the wealth and fertility that Heylyn described were the references to Morocco's military power, consisting of "60000 Horse" that had in the past defeated the Portuguese and their allies. The North African coast, he was warning his readers, was not an easy target. Still, Heylyn recognized that the region was vulnerable: because the North African army lived "on daily allow-ance," when the ruler's provisions run out, the army "dissolve and scatter."[18] There was might that protected the land and its riches, but a weakness was beginning to appear in the fabric of its polity: while the regencies were too strongly protected by their Ottoman ruler, Morocco, which had gone through a civil war, could well be targeted for European possession. Two years later, King Charles stepped forward to help the Moroccan ruler, Muhammad al-Sheikh al-Asghar, against rebels in the port city of Salé. He sent his fleet to support the besieged forces of the ruler, thereby securing the release of captives, who returned with the Moroccan ambassador to London in a celebration of Anglo-Moroccan cooperation. Despite the pomp and circumstance of the ambassador, with his black slaves and Barbary horses, it was now recognized in England that the North African region, mighty as it was in cavalry and footmen, lacked naval vessels and munitions—and that a fleet armed with the latest war technology could overcome coastal defenses.

In September 1641, Robert Blake, a member of the king's Privy Chamber and the Fleet Commander in the Mediterranean, proposed the conquest of Salé (which Harrison had also suggested in 1627 and which was in the same Atlantic region as Mogador). By controlling the port of Salé, he explained, the English not only would secure their trade in "all the coasts of Barbary with those natives," but would also cut out French and Dutch traders. Alongside the "honour which [would] redound to His Majestie and this nation" there would be numerous "benefittes": by "driving out the inhabitants," it would be possible to develop a salt industry there that would supply all the kingdom's need. There were also tin mines nearby, he continued, that could yield large profits. These mines were richer and produced better quality tin than the mines of Cornwall, and, by put-ting the natives to work, the British would be able to control the amount of tin imported into Holland, France and Turkey, and "soe keepe upp its price."[19] For Blake, the conquest of Salé did not just entail the acquisition of a presidio but also the enslavement of the population, the expropriation of resources and the domination of trade. Aware that England's trade with North Africa and the Levant was still by far higher, more lucrative and more economically crucial than trade with any other part of the world,[20] Blake was eager to begin the age of African imperialism and follow the model of the Spanish exploitation of Peru and Bolivia. Britain would do in North Africa what it was unable to do in North America.

Barbary was instrumental in forming and transforming British ideology from trade to conquest. Under Elizabeth, trade had been the Englishmen's sole goal: Barbary was a market and a source of natural imports. But with the advent of King James, and with royal intervention into the policies and politics of the chartered companies, a change occurred that slowly moved British ideals closer to the Spanish model. The Spaniards and the Portuguese had always viewed conquest as the roadway to the control of natural resources and of subsequent trade. As the transition from Harrison to Blake shows, Britons slowly moved toward the Spanish model: although trade remained their dominant goal, they started to associate the success of trade with the conquest of land. But North Africa was not North America, and conquest of North Africa was more easily said than done. As a result, and instead of total conquest and settlement with conquistadors flooding the conquered territories, Britons conceived of the seizure and occupation of strategic locations that would enable them to control trade and, by Blake's time, control the natural resources in those locations.

Captivity and the Civil Wars

But only after the mid-seventeenth century would it be possible to attempt such control. From the beginning of the Jacobean period and well into the first years of the Cromwellian period, whatever imperialism there was, was mere talk, for the facts on the Barbary ground and at sea presented a completely different and often grim and unpromising picture. Most destabilizing was the captivity of Britons in the Barbary States. In the coastal towns and sea ports of England and Ireland, on the high seas of the Mediterranean or the Atlantic, and in other parts of the Islamic world, Britons encountered a persistently unconventional religious and military adversary—pirates and privateers who seized ships and sold the passengers and crew as slaves in slave markets ranging from Salé to Algiers and Tunis. Against these pirates and privateers, the infamous "Barbary corsairs," little could be done to protect the sailors and the investors. Much as Harrison and Blake thought of conquest, and much as Heylyn realized that Britain's modernizing technology would secure naval victory over the corsairs, they all soon realized that the Barbary regions were able to fight back in a very effective manner. If the purpose of venturing into North Africa was to pursue trade and profit, and if Britain was to use its naval power to enforce such trade, the Barbary populations could retaliate not with their less powerful fleets, which the British navy could overcome, but by a much-tried way: piracy. They would attack the small trading ships, capture the merchants and their cargos, enslave the sailors and entice them into their society—thereby depleting British naval manpower, forcing negotiations and ransom, and ultimately generating handsome incomes to their coffers.

This dangerous strategy of the corsairs was confirmed in numerous publications and plays that reflected public anxiety about Barbary. In *The Knight of the Burning Pestle* (1607), Francis Beaumont described a barber with the ominous name of Barbaroso (recalling the famous corsair in Algiers of the first half of the sixteenth century) who holds men and women captive—and treats them in the same manner as captives in North Africa described their ordeals: "This bread and water hath our diet been," wails a captive woman, "Together with a rib cut from a neck / of burned mutton; hard hath been our fare" (3.4.147–50).[21] This description coincided with the ongoing seizure of women and men, sailors and mariners who were taken on the high seas or abducted from their coastal Welsh and English villages—and subsequently languished in the hope of benevolence from their monarchs or collections from their parishes to effect their release. Perhaps that is why Beaumont sarcastically introduced a quixotic figure who liberates the captives, since King James neither advanced nor secured the safety of merchants and their employees in the Mediterranean. A few years later, *The Tempest* (1611) also reflected the conditions of captivity in North Africa: Caliban carried wood and labored under the cruelty of Prospero, as did Ferdinand, whose neck and feet were manacled together and who, like Caliban, drank seawater and ate roots and husks (1.2.465–66). Such description of Ferdinand's captivity is similar to numerous accounts in English and Spanish that reported on the dire conditions of captives in the Mediterranean.

To add to the danger of captivity, and throughout the Jacobean period, merchants believed that the navy was doing nothing to prevent the attacks of the Barbary pirates.[22] Between 1609 and 1616, North African privateers captured hundreds of English and Scottish ships in the Mediterranean and the Atlantic, and in 1616, a "Turkish pirat" entered the Thames and reached Leigh in Essex, just a few miles above Southland; by 1618, Lord Carew informed Sir Thomas Roe that the "Turkish pirates do great harm to our ships in the Mediterranean; if they are not destroyed, the Levant trade will be at an end; they also damage the coast of Spain much."[23] In 1621, Sir Henry Mainwaring, who had been a pirate with the Tunisians before returning to serve in the English navy, reported that a battle had taken place between Turkish and English ships in which six English ships were lost. In that same year, the English fleet unsuccessfully tried to attack Algiers in order to free the captives. Not only had the Barbary corsairs grown stronger, but the naval forces of England (and other European countries) had grown weaker—a fact that the seventeenth-century Tunisian historian Ibn Abi Dinar confirmed: European Christians of the early seventeenth century, he wrote, did not send out large ships, as a result of which the Muslim privateers who sailed in frigates were able to capture much booty.[24]

In 1622, Nathaniel Butter published the first original account by a Jacobean sailor of his captivity among the Muslims: John Rawlins' *The Famous and Wonderfull recoverie of a Ship of Bristoll, called the Exchange, from the Turkish pirates of Argier*. The account was written by Rawlins himself, as the dedication states, "an unpolished worke of a poore Sailer."[25] Rawlins told a story of captivity and escape that was carried out not with any governmental help, but by his heroic English determination and his reliance on a God who helped Christians. Rawlins dedicated the account to the Duke of Buckingham, but after adumbrating the necessary platitudes of loyalty to king and love of (Christian) God, he ended his opening address with a jolt:

> For though you [Duke of Buckingham] haue greater persons, and more brauing spirits to lie ouer our heads, and hold inferiours in subiection; yet are we the men that must pull the ropes, weigh up the anchors, toile in the night, endure the stormes, sweat at the Helme, watch the Biticle, attend the Compasse, guard the Ordnance, keepe the night houres, and be ready for all impositions: If then, you vouchsafe to entertaine it, I haue my desire. For, according to the oath of Iurors, it is the truth, and the very truth: If otherwise you suppose it triuiall, it is only the prostitution of my seruice, and wisdome is not bought in the market.[26]

These were bold and angry words. For they suggested that Buckingham did not care for the "small" sailors who manned the English fleet. While Buckingham was clearly a man of power and status (Rawlins included all of the duke's titles and functions, taking up twelve lines), he was not a man of the sea and did not seem to know or care about what sailors endured on their journeys. Rawlins hoped that his account would enlighten the duke about how defenseless England's poorly paid sailors were against the Barbary corsairs in the absence of government protection at sea.

There can be little doubt that such a dedication, along with the subsequent account, which shows how captives had to rely solely on themselves (and God) but not on their country's fleet, was written to alert the uncaring admiralty to the plight of sailors. Rawlins was joining other writers who were also complaining about the inefficacy of the fleet and the growing danger of the corsairs. In October 1621, the Venetian ambassador in London reported "wide lamentation at the news of the severe losses inflicted by the Barbary pirates upon the Scots in the capture of fifty trading and fishing ships and of some 2,000 men." And then in cipher, he continued: "Such, exclaim the people, are the fruits of the fleet which has been kept at sea at such great expense to guard the coasts of Spain," and not of England.[27] In 1622, four men from Bristol fought off Algerian pirates and returned to indifference from the admiralty but a heroic welcome from members of their community. In the publication that appeared describing their feat, *A Relation Strange and True*, there was sourness at the difference between the way these poor seamen were received and the way commanding officers and wealthy nobility would have been celebrated:

> Had Iohn Cooke beene some Collonell, Captaine, or Commander, or William Ling, some nauigating Lord, or Dauid Iones some gentleman of land and riches, or had Robert Tuckey beene one of fortunes minions, to haue had more mony then wit, or more wealth then valour, oh what a triumphing had heere beene then, what rare Muses would haue toyld like Mules, to haue gallopt with their flattering encomiums, beyond the 32 points of the compasse; whilst these 4 rich caskets of home-spun valour and courage, haue no pen to publish their deserued commendations, no inuention to emblazon their saltwater honour, but the poore lines of a freshwater Poet.[28]

In this account, the bitterness expressed by Rawlins had turned into a blunt declamation against hierarchy and social division.

A similar appeal for royal intervention on behalf of sailors and captives was made from the other Levant: in April 1622, Sir Thomas Roe, the English ambassador in Istanbul, pleaded with the king to ransom his subjects. In Istanbul, he wrote,

> are diuers poore men your Majesties subiects in captiuity to the Grand Signor, and to other men, which might be redeemed for money. . . . I have obserued in England many collections made for particular men in churches, by licenses of grace from your Majestie, which I feare, haue bene abused; therefore, if your Majestie were pleased to speake with my lord keeper therein, that no priuate letters patents might be granted; but that your Majestie would vouchsafe to take order with him, that a warrant under the great seale might be giuen to some honest and elect men of the Spanish and Turkish companyes, as tresures for the poore captiues, to make a monethly collection in the parishes of London and Middlesex, to receiue the charity of compassionat and well affected men.[29]

Evidently, money was being collected but was not being used for ransoming the captives. Where it was being diverted was not stated; but it was clear to Roe that the money was being fraudulently taken and was not being used to help the "poore captiues." The weakness of the fleet, the unwillingness of the king to exert himself on behalf of the captives, and the brutal hierarchical division that resulted in better treatment for untrained officers than for seasoned sailors all added to the dangers of the Mediterranean and to the subsequent captivity of Britons at the hands of the Barbary corsairs.

At the same time that plays and captivity accounts exposed the monarchy's failure to help the captives, they also heightened awareness about the danger of North Africa. It was a telling difference that while, under James I and Charles I, a severe censorship of the press prevented the publication of material describing the danger of going to North America and of captivity by the Indians, no censorship was implemented in regard to North Africa. The reason for this difference in strategy is not difficult to find: with its inadequately armed and sickness-prone "natives," North America was vanquishable—as South and Central American had already been vanquished by the Spaniards and the Portuguese. Thus promotional material was permitted off the press to encourage emigration and conquest. No similar conquest was foreseen, much as it was desired, in the dangerous lands of the Moors, and therefore no attempt was made to hide the danger. While trade was crucial, sailors and seamen, shipowners and investors sought to learn about risks and consequences. From the 1580s until the 1620s, captivity accounts were repeatedly printed in London about North Africa—but nothing about North America, where there had also been suffering, despair, abduction and loss. But then had captivity narratives among the Indians been published, the flow of immigrants would have come to a halt. There was a concerted policy in England to advertise the horrors of Barbary captivity to the English reading public—and ignore or suppress those of North America.

It was unfortunate for Charles I that his accession to the throne coincided with the spring season of the year when the weather in the Mediterranean and the Atlantic allowed the corsairs to range far and wide. In May 1625, the Privy Council learned from St. Ives that thirty ships from Salé were near the coast: the inhabitants were afraid that the corsairs would land "by night among us," especially because there were no ships from the king's fleet to "fear them."[30] In August, the mayor of Poole urged the Privy Council to "take it into [your] consideration the [protection of] Newfoundland fleet, being about two hundred and fiftye saile of shippe . . . haueng some foure or fiue thousand men belonging to the westerne parte."[31] The mayor was afraid that "within this two yeares They [the corsairs] will not leaue his most excellent Majesty saylors to man his ffleet." Again in that month, the grand jury of Devon wrote to Sir Richard Hutton, "praying him to make known to the King or the Council" the danger of corsair depredation.[32] Meanwhile, the August debates in the Commons decried the failure of protection at sea. One speaker declared "that the Kinge's shipps doe nothinge, goeinge up and downe feastinge in every good porte; which was confirmd by Mr. Shervill. Burgess for Plimmothe." Another stated that "there was a barge taken in the sight of Sir Fra[ncis] Steward, and the Kinge's shipps, which they let alone, sayinge they had no instructions to goe upon the coasts of Fraunce."[33] From the common sailor to the member of Parliament, there was criticism of the Lord Admiral and his poor administration of the navy.

The Barbary corsairs threatened British ships in the mouths of the English Channel, the Bristol Channel and the waterways between Ireland and England. By spreading themselves from Poole around Land's End to the island of Lundy, they endangered all shipping to and from the major western ports of England and Wales.[34] In this respect, the corsairs were a serious cause of commercial and maritime destabilization.[35] Aware of the magnitude of the crisis inherited from his father, and within weeks of assuming power, King Charles sent a letter to the

Moroccan ruler, Mulay Zaidan, on behalf of the "many poore Christians made captives in your contry, both Engelishe and Frenche." In his first foray into Mediterranean foreign policy, King Charles reminded his addressee of the close relation between England and Morocco and confirmed the appointment of John Harrison as his representative.[36] Armed with that letter, John Harrison addressed in turn a "generall letter to the Moores" in which he expressed his hope "that Englishmen may no more be made captives as enemies, contrarie to those ancient priviledges in tymes past, but be released and set free."[37] The letter seems to have had the desired effect: on 30 July 1625, Harrison sent a letter to the commander of the English fleet in the Mediterranean in which he mentioned that a proclamation had been made by the *muqaddam* (military commander) of Tetuan that "noe Englishman hereafter should bee bought or sould, as hearetofore, by the Turkes, or made captives, but freelie trade."[38] To expedite matters with Zaidan, Charles told Harrison to take "8 Moores" who had been captured and brought to England with him back to Morocco.[39] Still, by the end of the year, there were thirty-four English captives in Tetuan. More money was needed, for which Harrison pleaded, and which the king did not seem eager to dispense.[40]

Two factors prevented the king from successfully realizing his goal of freeing all his captured subjects. First, there was the rampant favoritism surrounding the ransoming, or more often, the nonransoming of captives—something that had likewise been common during his father's reign. His father had authorized the following process for the ransoming of captives: after money was collected from the friends, neighbors and parish members of the captives, it was given to a representative of the monarchy, specifically, the archbishop of Canterbury, "the receaver generall of the said contribucions" for the redeeming of captives.[41] The archbishop took advice from members of the Privy Council, including a number of bishops, and, in light of that advice, authorized payments to agents to ransom specific captives. Ransom money was thus distributed with the exclusive authority of the archbishop, the Privy Council and, most decisively before the Civil Wars, the king himself. Although the money came from the private pockets of captives' friends, relatives and parishes, its distribution was determined by royal decision—if it survived the embezzling pockets of intermediaries and agents.[42] Such royal supervision ensured that the captives who were ransomed were men of whom the king and his council approved: not the agent, but the council that paid the agent held the strings of freedom. The result of such control was that men with connections to the court and the trading companies were promptly ransomed, while the "small" captives were either delayed or completely ignored.

Second, although the king could negotiate with Mulay Zaidan of Morocco, there still remained the danger of the Atlantic seaports of Morocco not under the control of Zaidan (specifically Salé), along with the Ottoman regencies of Tunisia and Algeria. There were also English sea captains and pirates who did not obey their king's orders and attacked North African ships as a result of which the North Africans retaliated by seizing English and Scottish ships. The Algerian ambassador to London, Jaafar Agha, complained on 10 August 1625 about the "inconveniencys" that Britons carried out against Muslim traders, contrary to the accords that had been agreed upon in Constantinople.[43] Given the frequent breaking of treaties by British privateers, reprisal from the North African corsairs was inevitable. Caught between the financial needs of the Barbary rulers, on the one hand, and the wide-ranging piracy of English and other British sailors, on the other, King Charles resisted spending the vast amounts of money needed to ransom his hapless subjects. Not only were payments not securing the seas, but also the number of captives was so high that ransoming them all would require a fortune. In May 1626 it was reported that there were three thousand captives in Algiers and fifteen hundred in Salé: and although these numbers may have been exaggerated, they pointed to the vast sums that would be needed by the Crown to bring the captives home.[44]

Public disaffection with the king's procrastination and failure to bring back captives coincided with the ongoing attempt to impeach the Duke of Buckingham for failing to guard the seas, which had become "ignominiously infested by pirates."[45] There were many reasons for the public dislike of the duke, but the danger by the pirates to merchants and sailors was an effective rallying cry for his opponents. The duke was well aware of public anger when, in June 1626, he stated: "And for the pirates of Sallie, and those parts, he [the Duke] saith, it is but very lately that they found the way unto our coasts, where, by surprize, they might easily do hurt; but there hath been that provision taken by his maj. not without the care of the duke, both by force and treaty, to repress them for the time to come."[46]

Such ingenuousness angered the Commons and produced a vitriolic rebuttal from the lord high admiral, Sir Robert Mansell.[47] In a post facto effort to support the duke, in 1626 the king sent Francis Vernon to the king of "Barbarie" to "deale for the releasing of those his said subjects."[48] Without a naval force that could confront the pirates (especially after the duke's unsuccessful expeditions against Cadiz and Rhee), and with a treasury that could not afford the large sums needed for ransom (especially after the coinage shortage and the depression in the early 1620s),[49] Charles had very limited options for resolving the danger to traders and sailors alike. Despite the forced loan he imposed to raise money for war (in support of King Christian of Denmark),[50] the Cadiz expedition of 1627 had resulted in thousands of deaths and nearly half a million pounds of debt. The king's only option was thus to try to bribe the Barbary States into some "treaty," as the duke had mentioned. The envoy, John Harrison, took with him a number of Moroccan captives who were being held in England, along with "four brass and two iron cannons, with ammunitions, & c."[51] On May 1627, it was reported that the Moroccan rebel al-Ayyashi had been provided, against Mulay Zaidan's wishes, with six pieces of artillery by none other than John Harrison.[52] Eager to develop all possible alliances, Harrison was not unwilling to cooperate with rebels in defiance of the central government in Marrakesh.

Notwithstanding the king's bribery and diplomacy, piratical attacks increased so much that by April 1628, the number of captives in Algiers alone was reported to be fifteen thousand—an impossible number, but a number showing continued public anxiety at the extent of piracy and insecurity on the high seas.[53] Edward Kellet and Henry Byam preached two sermons on the return of a captive to England and to Christianity—highlighting thereby the religious danger sailors and the rest of their countrymen faced in the Mediterranean.[54] Such anxiety was widely felt as families and parishioners were never quite sure whether the returning captive returned with Islam in his heart or marked on his body. Actually, Byam instructed the communities to check on the returning captives and to make sure that they had not been circumcised, while other returning captives sought certificates from village magistrates or justices of the peace attesting to their Christian commitment.[55] Captivity by the Barbary corsairs did not end with ransom; its implications continued well after the captive was reunited with his family and reestablished in his community. On 22 June 1633, Francis Blith presented to the Committee of Trade a statement emphatically proving that he had been redeemed, "as a Christian," by the charitable contribution of the consul Nathaniel Bradley.[56] Upon returning home, neither the captives nor their communities could forget the danger of conversion to Islam.

Pressured to act on behalf of the captives in Salé, the House of Lords appointed on 29 May 1628 a committee to oversee the distribution of ransom money that had been collected as far back as 1624 but had not been used. Earlier, on 14 April 1628, the archbishop of Canterbury declared that money had been collected "upon a brief granted upon that order, which brief is dated 29th of June in the same year [1624], for redemption of the English captives at Algeirs." The sum of nearly three thousand pounds, however, had not been used for the Algiers captives; although the bishop of London, who had control of the money, had been ordered to pay the sum on 15 May 1626, he evidently had not. The reason had been that the ransoming of the captives was to be kept firmly in the hands of the authorities, and not of the trading companies or the families. As in the days of James, so in the days of Charles: the money came from private pockets, but its distribution was dependent on royal decision. That is why the new committee was to "take accounts of the monies" and then use them for the captives. In the following month, on 23 June 1628, the committee turned to the bishop of Bristol, who still had money that had been "collected in the time of the late infection" (the plague of 1625) in order to use it for ransoming the husband of Margaret Praulfe, a prisoner of the Turks.[57] Again, money had been donated by parishes and communities but not disbursed, and captives with court connection enjoyed priority in the ransoming process. Royal supervision ensured that the captives who were ransomed were men of whom the king and his council approved.

The insecurity at sea and the growing number of unransomed captives precipitated a general malaise among traders, sailors and investors. One speaker in the Commons lamented on 3 June 1628 the state of affairs—the "Exchequer . . . is empty. . . . The ancient lands are sold, the jewels pawned."[58] In the recapitulation of Parliament's grievances to the king after the Petition of Right (June 1628), Sir John Eliot alerted the king to the "Turkish" dangers that beset the kingdom. Witness, he called on the king, "the Turks—witness the Dunkirkers—witness all. What losses we have sustained, how we are impaired in munition, in ships, in men! It is beyond contradiction, that we were never so much weakened, nor ever had less hope how to be restored."[59] Events soon after vindicated Eliot's fear that his countrymen would not be "restored": the Franco-Algerian treaty of September 1628 turned the corsairs away from the French and against British shipping.[60] After the king's dissolution of Parliament in 1629, Eliot wrote in his *Negotium Posterorum* about "twelve hundred christians, the loss of whom causd great lamentation wth their frinds."[61] In that same year, James Wadsworth published an account about his experiences among continental Catholics—which included a chapter about his captivity in Morocco. He elaborated on the suffering of captives, describing the sodomy committed on young men, the chores he himself had had to complete, the rough diet he was given, the chains and the lice and the fleas. "And it chanced on a time that I hauing not performed my ordinary taske, was beaten by my master so cruelly, that for a long time after I lost the vse of my left arme, which hee [the master] perceiuing said, at most it was but the losse of a Christian dogge." Fortunately, however, Wadsworth was ransomed by his uncle, the English consul in St. Lucas.[62] As with many other ransomed captives, it was his connection that saved him and not the intervention of the king.

Perhaps it was because Britons were not faring well in the Mediterranean and the ideals of empire were being replaced by the traumas of captivity that theater stepped in with its panacea of entertainment. In 1630–31, Thomas Heywood's sequel, *The Fair Maid of the West, Part II*, was presented at court, and then published with *Part I*. Heywood realized that he could not present any criticism of royal policy (or the lack thereof) in regard to Mediterranean affairs, especially if the play was to be performed by the Queen's Majesty Comedians or Queen Henrietta's Men: thus the praise for the English "royal . . . princes" by the Moroccan queen (3.3.74). Heywood, therefore, picked up where the first part had ended and showed how, after Bess and Spencer were married in Morocco and had gone into the service of Mullisheg, they fell victim to his lust as well as that of his consort. The image of a cooperative and benign Moroccan potentate, which had been acceptable and credible under Elizabeth, was no longer possible now: relations had changed between London and Marrakesh, and the situation in Morocco had become unstable after years of civil strife and after pirates from the two countries had grown more active in the seizure of ships and captives. In the play, Heywood showed Bess and Spencer, along with the English ship company of the "Negro," facing numerous dangers: but they successfully fought off the Moors while maintaining their dignity and projecting the noblest image of their culture and religion. They held together at the same time that they held onto their honor: even when promised bribes, Goodlack and Roughman, serving Spencer and Bess, would not deceive their superiors, and adhered to "Honor and virtue." And it was this seeming social classlessness of the English and the commitment to each other that brought wealth to Bess, Spencer and the sailors: at the end of the play, they all left Morocco, with the full blessing of a reconciled Mullisheg, who gave them a rich and "ample dower," around "half a million" (4.1.143).

Heywood created an entertaining fiction showing how in the Barbary region, an English woman could prevail—and acquire riches and honor. Of course, in England, a woman such as his heroine Bess was a nonentity; but in Morocco, she was shown to assume authority and command—just because of her Englishness. Heywood wanted to show how trade and travel opened up possibilities for social and financial mobility. The play was to motivate English men and women to sail, barter, gain wealth, and ultimately return to king and country. It also showed the importance of commitment and honor: under the direst conditions, such as those of Spencer or Bess, the English retained their Christian courage and then escaped from the Moors—even won them over. While sailors, shipowners and stockholders were clamoring for more money to protect their trade in the Barbary seas, and while thousands were languishing in the bagnios of Tunis, Algiers or Salé, Heywood showed that it was not money that was needed to ensure safety and bring captives home, but English "honor, faith, and . . . / The reputation of a Christian" (3.2.101–2). Completely oblivious to the conditions of captives in Barbary, and seemingly indifferent to the dangers and terrors they encountered, as communicated in letters, depositions and captivity accounts, Heywood created a fiction for the court that may have further alienated the king from his subjects: while his subjects endured hardships in the Mediterranean with little help from him, he was being assured that morality and heroic faith were the qualities needed for seafaring success. Heywood concluded the play by praising the "Great King," certain that his royal audience would be pleased at having no mention made of responsibility to his subjects overseas, or to the families in the docks.

In November 1630, King Charles ordered John Harrison to take with him to Morocco two pieces of iron and ordnance with powder, and use them to liberate captives; a month later, he told him to redeem captives, "our poore subjects," not by buying their freedom, but by exchanging them with Moors "who are allsoe prisoners with us . . . in this our realme of England."[63] The king clearly did not want to spend money and was not unwilling to stoop to any means to liberate his subjects without dipping into his coffers. Unfortunately, soon after this feeble show of concern for the captives, disaster struck. In June 1631, Algerian corsairs attacked Baltimore in Ireland and seized 120 men, women and children.[64] Not only were the corsairs dangerous in the Mediterranean, they were now growing dangerous in the British seas, too, and compromising the safety of the realm: not only sailors but also villagers were being seized. Two months later, in August 1631, James Frizell, consul in Algiers, mentioned that there were 390 captives in the city, including "89 of them [who] are Women & Children taken lately from

Baltamore."[65] In October 1631, a license was issued "for a Collection through-out England and Wales, towards the redeeming of a number of poore English men Captives under Muley Abdawelly [Mulay al-Walid, r. 1631–36] King of Morocco." From all over Wales, England and Scotland, there were captives lan-guishing in bagnios without effective royal action on their behalf. People were having to assume financial responsibility for the captives by going around par-ishes collecting charity and donations—from people who were often as poor as they were. The danger of the Barbary corsairs, together with the king's hesitancy about action and the financial strain of ransoming the captives, did not augur well for English domination of the seas—or the conquest of some North African outposts, as Harrison had urged. What was needed was money to bring the captives home and to protect the mainland.

In February 1632, a petition "of many poore woemen declaring yt more then 500 of theyr husbands, sonns and friends were Lately taken and kept in bondage by the Turks and Moors of Algier and Tunis" was presented to King Charles. Unlike earlier petitions, this petition created a stir, and numerous assessments of the situation were generated in the immediate months after. On 20 April 1632, a response to the petition was presented to the king in the form of proposals deal-ing with the pirates of Algiers.[66] Significantly, these proposals were made not by men who had been, like Harrison, on the Moroccan ground and had witnessed the actual causes of Barbary attacks, but by London-based administrators who did not hesitate to pontificate on maritime matters in the Mediterranean. The first proposal stated that since no treaty would be honored by Algiers, Tunis or Salé, there was no point in pursuing such agreements. Completely ignorant of, or ignoring English piracy in the Mediterranean and the destabilization it caused, they blamed the North Africans rather than their own people for the collapse of the agreements. The second proposal urged the king to use force and to show the grand sultan that he was "resolved to right his Subiects"; the king could send four ships to the Mediterranean, two of 500 tons and two of 300 to "weaken" the enemy. About fifteen thousand pounds sterling would be needed annually to maintain the men on these ships and provide them with wages, clothes, ammuni-tion and victual. Because of the large expense that would be incurred, however, the author viewed this proposal as "impossible." He therefore urged that the king grant a commission to the joint stock company to send its ships only to ports and cities where trade was safe and profit was assured. The commission was also to seize Algerian, Tunisian and Saletian ships, attack North African ports indis-criminately, and "waste burne & spoyle, to take women and children and to doe unto them as they have done unto us."

The idea that the British fleet should become involved in naval warfare, ab-duction, slave trading and pillaging could not have appealed to a king who was eager to maintain commercial links and profits in the Islamic Mediterranean. Furthermore, King Charles was well aware that the North African regencies had attained some autonomy from the Ottoman sultan: attacking Istanbul did not necessarily help in neutralizing Algiers. The king thus turned the petition of the desperate women to Sir Sidney Montague, who passed it on to a commission that had been appointed to examine the matter.[67] The "humble" opinion of the anonymous author of the commission report explained that the number of captives from "the western Parts" was more than a "1000. at least" and that the cost of ransoming them would exceed "40000 (the Exchange and Collection borne)." Realistically, the author continued, the sum was impossible to raise through charitable collections, and even if two years were to be spent, only one-twentieth of that sum might be raised. The author urged the king not to pay the ransom demanded by the pirates because such payment would encourage them to seize more sailors after they find that the "Bodys of your Majties subjects [have] become so good merchandize." Therefore, the writer proposed to present to the king three ways to deal with the "Pyrates": a "Treaty of Peace," "War," or the temporary but complete suppression of trade with the Ottoman sultan. The king should also grant letters of marque, royal authorization for naval reprisal, so that English privateers could do what the Barbary pirates had been doing. Instead of the king's fleet, let privateers do the dirty work.

The author was fully aware that such drastic measures would meet with heavy resistance from the merchants. He thus turned to anticipate the three objections to his "opinion" and refute them. To the objection that the king's income from customs would be diminished, he replied that unless piracy was stopped, trade and fishing in the west of England would come to a halt and cause as "great a loss and more durable both to yor Matie and your whole Kingdome, as the forebearance of yor Customes one yeare." To the objection that such a drastic step would cause the "stop of Trade and Vendinge of Cloth," he replied that "trade may faynte but never dye." Actually, what the merchants of "the Company of Turky, East India, and Eastland" should do was to change the destination of their cloth trade and turn it away from the Ottoman cities to Ragusa, Leghorn, Messina and other places. Meanwhile, those traders who exported their cloth to Aleppo where it was purchased in "ye greatest quantity" by "the Ajams" (Persians)—these traders should send their products with the East India merchants to the Persian Sea. Losses from such diversion of trade for a year or two would be less than the losses incurred at the hands of the pirates. Such a strategy, concluded the author, would enable the traders to reestablish their trade in Constantinople and to endure the safety of the seas.[68]

The crisis of captivity was generating extensive and dissonant debate. Royalists, parliamentarians and members of the Privy Council were all finding themselves getting involved in affairs taking place thousands of miles away, while traders were thinking of strategies to reduce their losses and, importantly, to urge the king to formulate some policy or initiate some action. And while there was a general conviction (and pride) that Britain had the might to confront the corsairs, the reality at sea was both dangerous and complex. Furthermore, there was a clear division between the merchants and the king—which is why the "business" discussed in the report failed. The report had articulated the opinions of non-merchants whose goal was to find a solution for piracy by avoiding financial drains on the king. The report had confirmed the position of the king, which was not at all helpful to merchants: that responsibility for the safety of sailors and ships lay with the merchant companies and not with him. It was merchants and sailors who needed to be circumspect and reduce risks, while looking for alternative markets; it was they who needed to find new routes for their ships, and new ports in which to trade. And it was they who had to protect themselves. Meanwhile, all that the king was expected to do was recall the English ambassador from Constantinople and issue letters of marque—which would further place responsibility for naval warfare and prize taking not on his fleet but on the merchant fleet. The merchants were not unwilling to assume some of the responsibility if the king would issue letters of marque; but the king would not do so since attacks by the merchants on North African or Turkish shipping could seriously jeopardize his diplomatic relations in the Mediterranean. The king also feared that if he let loose his privateers on the open seas, they would not hesitate to attack European ships, creating thereby diplomatic tension that could precipitate conflict.

Already, a divergence was growing between the king's policy and the merchants' need: court and city were beginning the separation that would eventually polarize them on the battlefield. And while the proposals were discussed and debated, little was being done to ransom captives and reduce the danger to sailors and ships. Families and parishes thus reverted to the only action available to them to ransom their breadwinners from "Turkish thralldom": collecting charity even without government approval. So widespread did such collections become that on 21 March 1633, there was a royal "Proclamation against the making Collections without Licence vnder the Great Seale." The growing number of captives was pushing relatives to desperate measures and causing serious problems to shipowners and merchants whose seamen were refusing to sail out to what could be certain captivity. In about 1634, a petition was addressed to the king (which he again passed on, to Sir Thomas Roe, Sir Kenelm Digby and Sir Peter Pindar for consideration) on behalf of the captives that was quite blunt in its demand: that assurance be given to mariners that should they be captured, there would be "a course . . . for theyr present redemption with money."[69] Having seen the plight of seamen who had languished in North African slavery for years, sailors were no longer willing to risk their lives unless they knew that the monarch had money to spend in ransoming them. But what they saw around them was not promising: in March 1634, donations were received from Sir Nicolas Raynton and Sir George Sands amounting to 942 pounds, 14 shillings and 4 pence—which sum was spent on buying "4 Mares" from Rotterdam, pikes and iron chests from Amsterdam, "2 helmets . . . 2 paire of pistolls" and covering the expenses of transporting the mares to England.[70] All these items were to be sent as presents to Morocco in order to facilitate the ransoming of captives. It was not the king but the merchants who were trying their best to bring back captives. It is not surprising that seamen, growing anxious about their conditions, started leaving England and seeking employment elsewhere in the Mediterranean. So many left the country that the king was forced to issue a proclamation on 5 May 1634 "commanding all Our Subjects, being Sea-men and Ship-wrights . . . to returne home within a certaine time." [71] While the Great Migration sent Britons to North America, there was another migration sending them to North Africa in quest of employment and security.

So serious did the complaints of the seamen—and their employers, the merchants—grow that King Charles decided he would need a source of revenue that could be used for ransoming his subjects. In order to raise the needed money, he extended Ship Money from the sea towns to all the realm, and in October 1634, he announced that it would be used for fighting pirates, "certain thieves, pirates, and robbers of the sea, as well Turks, enemies of the Christian name, as others, being gathered together, wickedly taking by force and spoiling the ships, and goods, and merchandises . . . delivering the men in the same into miserable captivity." [72]

Unfortunately, Ship Money did not increase maritime security, and a year later, in September 1635, the mayor of Dartmouth wrote to the Privy Council about the numerous seamen who had been taken into "miserable captiuitie to increase the number of our westerne captiues there." [73] "Unless the Lords use speedy means for protection" of trade, the mayor of Plymouth had written to the council six days earlier, on 20 September, "many thousands in those parts will be utterly undone." [74] Soon after, a request was made for a ship to take the above-listed presents to Morocco in order to return some captives home, and "to provide for the safetie both of their persons & ships and goods from being taken hereafter wherein the great love and compassion of his Matie toward his poore & distressed subjects" would be shown. [75] The king was trying to help but was hampered by his limited resources. More complaints were lodged about the danger of sea travel, [76] and in July 1636, the Privy Council received a letter from Plymouth stating that "we haue already suffered more this sumer then wee did these many yeares last past" and that the Salé corsairs were so devastating that "two hundred Christians [were] brought into Sally in April the last in [just] one day." [77] By March 1637, seventy-three ships and 1,473 persons had been seized to Algiers since 1629, [78] while in October 1637, James Frizell reported from Morocco that in the last four years, sixty-four ships had been taken with 1,524 Englishmen "sould for slaves." [79] The continued failure to protect maritime trade, not only in the Mediterranean but also in the Atlantic, resulted in the beginnings of a "principled opposition" as people recognized that Ship Money was being imposed by the king not as an extraordinary levy but as a regular tax—that produced no results. [80]

No voice captured the discontent and growing hostility to the king and his failed policy better than the preacher Charles FitzGeffry in his sermon of October

1636 in Plymouth, a port city that saw hundreds of seamen sail away and never return. While the king and his court enjoyed their masques and plays, along with fantasies about happy seas and heroic seamen, thousands of hard-working and miserable captives were lying helpless in North Africa. In his address to "The Christian Reader," FitzGeffry turned to the court: "How much hathe beene lavishly expended in Pompes, in Playes, in Sibariticall-feasts, in Cameleon sutes, and Proteus-fashions, besides other vanities, and yet there is no complaining of want? How many soules might have beene ransommed from that Hell on Earth, Barbarie, with halfe these expences?"[81]

Whether it was under the pressure of such sermons (FitzGeffry's description [46] of the capture of the English and Cornish residents from Baltimore was particularly moving), or because he received a request from the Moroccan ruler, Mulay al-Sheikh al-Asghar, for naval assistance against rebels in Salé,[82] Charles realized that he could not ignore the captives any longer, and he began preparations for an attack on the Atlantic harbor. Salé was an ideal target: its pirates had repeatedly attacked English ships and were holding hundreds of British captives; furthermore, the Moroccan city was divided between two factions, one to the south of the Bou Regreg river (Rabat) that supported the weak central government of Mulay al-Sheikh al-Asghar, and another to the north of the river that opposed him and that was controlled by exiles from Hornachos in Spain who had turned the harbor into a formidable pirate republic.

In 1637, Charles sent his fleet to fight with the Old Saletians (in Rabat) against the New Saletians (in Salé). In order to coordinate military action, he signed a peace treaty with Muhammad al-Ayyashi in May 1637,[83] so that al-Ayyashi, a legendary fighter against Spanish occupation, would besiege the Saletians by land and the king by sea. As a result of this cooperation, the English–Old Saletian alliance won, and all the captives were released. The commander of the expedition, Captain Rainsborough, reported after the victory that he had redeemed "the poore captives" and secured "His Majesties subjects for the tyme to come."[84] On 31 July and 1 August, some "400" captives were transferred to four ships that sailed out of Salé toward Cadiz, while two other ships headed toward Safi to pick up presents sent from the Moroccan king to Charles.[85] Soon after, the Moroccan ambassador, Alkaid Jaudar Bin Abdalla, arrived in England with "302, English, Scottish, and Irish" captives who had been released through the subvention of the Moroccan ruler—showing thereby "his exceeding Love to our King, and Country- men."[86] Upon reaching London, captives who had been released through Rainsborough's intervention were paraded behind the ambassador to exhibit the extent of royal concern and authority. The captives came from all over Britain and Ireland, and even included twenty-four French, eight Dutch and five Spanish captives—a demonstration of the king's care for Christians from all the European dominions. The author of the pamphlet describing the arrival of the ambassador praised the Moroccan potentate for his "Princely Bounty" and then urged the redeemed captives to praise King Charles, too: "We and they are all bound to love, honour, and obey Our most Gracious King, whose piety and pitty was so great, as to take the Affliction of his poore Subiects so farre into his most Princely consideration, as to send his Ships under such wise and able Commanders for their Redemption."[87]

Both the return of the captives and the reception of the ambassador served as a much-needed publicity victory for King Charles, who could not but have felt that his scheme of using Ship Money to redeem captives was vindicated.[88] The procession of the captives was the first on record in England: while in European capitals such processions were common, in England they were not because they would have been embarrassing to the monarch, who did not always exert himself to ransom captives. In Paris or Madrid, the redemptionist orders, working in cooperation with the monarchy, were in charge of ransoms, and relatives of captives recognized the commitment of the priests in these orders and the financial support of the Crown.[89] A procession of returning captives demonstrated the effectiveness and responsibility of the Church and the Crown. In England, no such processions took place because the king was never directly responsible for the redemption of captives. Rather, the money came from charity, and the agents came from the trading companies. It was only because the 1637 redemption had been effected by the king's fleet and by the king's financial contribution that a procession of captives appeared on the streets of London. In August, the Venetian ambassador informed his doge and senate that people in England "rejoice greatly on the score of reputation" and that the king and his council "hope that the people will support the burden of the contributions more patiently than they have done hitherto, when they see that there is some advantage in being compelled to support the fleet."[90] In September, Sir Nicholas Slanning mentioned the return of the English and Irish captives and how their return would "much forward his Majesty's service"; in October, the Privy Council assured the Mayor of London (Edward Broomfield) and the London merchants that the fleet the king had sent to Salé had been able to provide protection "from those sea enemies of Christianity."[91]

The success of the operation against Salé demonstrated that King Charles was actively involved in the defense of his enterprising subjects.[92] Toward the end of December of that year, William D'Avenant presented a celebration masque of *Britannia Triumphans* in which the hero of the masque, Britanocles, representing King Charles I, appears on stage: "the glory of the western world hath by his wisdom, valour, and piety, not only vindicated his own, but far distant seas infested with pirates and reduc'd the land, by his example, to a real knowledge of all good acts and sciences." D'Avenant then showed captives lying "bound" under the figure of a woman "holding the rudder of a ship, and in the other a little winged figure with a branch of palm, and a garland: this woman represented Naval Victory." In the course of the masque, the Muslim enemy was mentioned by a figure appropriately called "Imposture": "They beat my Grandsire Mahomet's / Divinity"; he says, "who doth allow the good, a handsome girl / On earth, the valiant, two in Paradise."[93] Having defeated the "Mahometan" pirates of Salé, it was important to show that Muhammad too was beaten by King Charles. The victory had been both naval and religious.

Unfortunately, the impact of the Salé victory was short-lived. For soon after the release of the captives, the Moroccans realized that Robert Blake had deceived them. In a blunt letter sent to King Charles in Arabic, the Moroccan ruler, Mulay al-Sheikh al-Asghar, described Blake as a liar. The latter had claimed to have left horses in Safi as part of the exchange, but he had "lied to you because of his infamy." Blake arrived with the intent of trading, and

[showed us] service and offered us advice and mentioned that you wanted a truce with us. . . . [He also promised] that should the truce be established, [English] traders who are now going to enemy ports, such as Salé and Tetuan, and providing the enemy with munitions and materiel, will discontinue such trade. To prove that we wanted this truce, we gathered all the English slaves in our country and sent them to you. We did that and gathered all the captives in our country, those under our roof, as well as those in the possession of our subjects and those in Salé, and we sent them all in the company of our noble *mamluk* [slave] Basha Jaudar, who delivered them to you and returned with a letter stating your acceptance of the truce. . . . [Later] we sent you our capable servant al-Caid Muhammad bin Askar to confirm what we had written to you in regard to the materiel and munitions that we need.

It is at that point that Blake deceived the Moroccans. He insisted on being paid fifteen hundred *gharara* (a measure of weight) of wheat for freighting the material, which he was given, despite the fact that after inquiring of some local English merchants, the ruler learned that half that amount would have been a fair price. Blake then sailed away without delivering the freight, leaving behind him all the promissory letters that he had sent to the ruler.[94]

The dispute was resolved by making a payment to Mulay al-Sheikh, after which, in September 1637, King Charles signed another treaty with him in which he pledged not to allow his subjects to provide arms to the rebels in the south of the country. Otherwise, as item 9 of the treaty read, "If any [British] ship bee found soe trading the aforesaide enemies, that the ships belonging to the kingdoms of Barbary may take both ships, persons and goods, as if they weare theire enemies."[95] Meanwhile, eager to increase his revenue from trade with Morocco and reward Blake for his feat, the king issued letters patent to a group of merchants, who included "Robert Blake junior," to establish a company to "trade and traffique to and from all and singuler regions, territories, countries, dominions, continents, sea-coastes . . . belonging to the said King of Barbary" (Mulay al-Sheikh). The group was to have monopoly over trade with Morocco, to pay King Charles his dues in customs, and have the right to seize any British ship that defied the monopoly. In return, the king promised to provide maritime protection and to defend them against any "wrong or injury" committed by "any foreigne king, prince or potentate."[96]

If the imperial dream was about to begin, with a commercial treaty rather than an occupation, it soon collapsed. The tumult in Scotland that would lead to the Bishops' Wars jolted King Charles to the realization that he needed Parliament in order to raise money to support the military campaign against the Scots. The meeting with the Scots at Berwick had forced him to make peace with them. On 13 April 1640, the king convened Parliament, and a week later Sir Henry Vane delivered a message from him that included a reaffirmation of the reasons for "shipping-writs"—much despised by the Commons. The king still wanted to impress on Parliament and the people that he was doing all he could to secure the seas against the pirates—but again, with money taken not from his coffers but from taxes: "That those of Algiers are grown to that insolency, that they are provided of a fleet of 60 sail of ships, and have taken divers English ships, particularly one, called the Rebecca of London (well known to the merchants upon the Exchange) taken upon the coasts of Spain, worth at least 260,000 £ and therefore, the writs having gone out upon those weighty reasons, before it was possible the parliament could give any Supply to provide for those things, his maj. cannot this year forbear it; but he doth expect your concurrence in the levying of it for the future."[97]

Among the many reasons for Ship Money, there was still, in the king's mind, the danger of the Barbary corsairs. The king was eager to show both merchants and sailors who were losing ships, lives and freedom that he was willing to protect their interests—if the Commons cooperated. But the Commons refused to "concur" unless the king addressed their grievances about church discipline, property and parliamentary liberty. On 5 May the king dissolved Parliament and explained to his subjects how Parliament had not supported him in his desire to raise the money he needed to put an end to "the insolencies committed by those of Algiers, with the store of ships they had in readiness."[98]

The king sought to put the blame for the nonransoming of the captives and the insecurity of the seas on his opponents—and indeed sent some of them to the Tower, including the Earl of Warwick, who was a fierce opponent of Ship Money and the idol of the seamen. Apprentices and sailors immediately took to the streets, enflamed by the recent "failure of the fleet to protect the Channel"[99] after Barbary corsairs had landed in Penzance and seized men, women and children. In the midst of this confusion, Francis Knight published *A Relation of Seaven Yeares Slaverie vnder the Turkes of Argeire, suffered by an English Captive Merchant*, with a grim frontispiece of a turbaned Turk whipping a prostrate captive. The account so captured the reading public's imagination that, a few months later, it was printed again. *A Relation* was the first in England to provide an eyewitness description of Barbary slavery since Hasleton's in 1595 and Wadsworth's single chapter in 1629. The account, however, did not just focus on the individual experience of the captive, but described the movements of the Algerian fleet—the battles it fought, the European ports it attacked, the captives it seized, including nuns and bishops, and its numerous successes against Christian ships and convoys. Knight was eager to write not only a personal memoir but also a geographic and military document. The picture that he drew was of a dangerous Turkish power that ranged far and wide in the Mediterranean and met with only one formidable adversary: not England, but England's maritime rival, France. Enviously, Knight described the forcefulness the French used in their dealings with the Turks of Algiers. They threatened and confronted, and most importantly, they did everything in their power to liberate the hundreds of French captives, sometimes by paying off the required ransom sums, at other times by exchanging Muslims with French captives. Knight described how he had endured seven years of captivity, along with numerous other Englishmen, and had seen the conversion of many of his compatriots and coreligionists to Islam because of temptation or duress. Indeed, to him, the worst part of captivity was witnessing, with his own eyes, as he emphasized, the renunciation of Christianity by so many captives and the inability of his king or government to do anything about it. That is why he ended the first part of his treatise lamenting the condition of the hapless captives, "left in those torments, many of whom I love most deare, doe end this discourse, desuing [?] God to send them libertie."[100] As far as Knight was concerned, the captives had none other than God to turn to. Neither from the king nor from the fleet were they receiving help.

Knight continued with a "Second Booke" in which he furnished a description of Algiers. By so doing, Knight initiated a new direction in captivity writing— where authors not only described their tribulations and the spiritual and physical dangers they encountered, but also used their experiences to provide information about the dangerous world of the captors. No previous captive had described the world of his captivity with the detail that Knight showed; indeed, no prior English captive had been interested in the world of the "Mahumetans," and none had ever bothered to document the names of his captors, or anything about their political and military roles. Knight, perhaps because he was an educated man— at least he seemed to know some Latin—realized that there would be value for his readers in learning not only about Mediterranean piracy but also about Algerian society and organization. In this respect, the captive became a geographer, a historian, an ethnographer and an informant. Realizing the need for reliable information about Algerian sea captains and the "Government, the particular denomination of its Governors, its Revinewes, its Forces by Sea and Land, its Victories, its Inhabitants, its Lands, Territories, and Riches,"[101] Knight presented the first accurate description of Algeria by an English writer.

Knight also warned about the power of the Algerians and pointed to their military weaknesses: there was danger in Algiers, he confirmed, but there were riches that could be reaped. Even in captivity, he wanted to keep the dream of English trade and possible conquest alive. To his London readers, merchants as well as mariners and most importantly members of Parliament, Knight underlined the need for a policy to confront the dangers in the Mediterranean. He reiterated that English pirates were often to blame for the retaliation of the Moors. "I am certaine that the last peace was broken by the English, by whom those of Argere received many injuries and long suffered them before they sought the least revenge."[102] In that revenge, the Algerians had captured English sailors, whom Knight prayed the king would ransom. He advised the king to send an agent to Algiers, "moderated, methodicall, and sufficient," while the Algerians would be asked to send their own agent to London, so that peace could be maintained and trade safeguarded. For Knight, it was clear that England and Algiers should exchange ambassadors or factors and open up their diplomatic channels. Algiers should have a presence in London in the same manner as other countries. After finishing his description of the land, Knight returned to the plight of captives and invoked the king to assume his responsibility of ransoming them since individual ransom efforts could never prove sufficient. Knight sought to embarrass both king and Parliament by praising them and urging them to negotiate with the Moors, who viewed them as the "most wisest and most virtuous Prince, and Councellors in the Universe."[103] The Mediterranean trade was lucrative and the English could dominate it, but only if the king took a more active role both in ransoming captives and in establishing sound commercial and diplomatic relations with the Algerians. Knight the captive had turned political adviser.

The presence of English pirates in the Mediterranean, whom Knight mentioned, always complicated the situation for both the king and the merchants who wanted him to address this matter, especially after the *Hopewell* affair. The *Hopewell* had been carrying merchandise to Moroccan rebels against Mulay al-Sheikh when it was seized by the latter's navy. A diplomatic crisis ensued as Mulay al-Sheikh accused King Charles of breaking the terms of the treaty to which both of them had agreed. Members of the Barbary Company were also angry with the king, who had neither prevented Britons from dealing with the rebels nor had protected their own ship. John Coke lamented that the days when a monarch such as Queen Elizabeth could keep her enemies at bay while increasing trade and improving correspondence with "Turkie and Barbarie" were gone. The king had failed in his responsibility to prevent "his subjects to trade with that Kings rebels" thereby putting Parliament in an awkward position, for the Moroccans would hold Parliament to blame for breaching the treaty. Not only was the king failing in his duty, he was jeopardizing the international standing of Parliament, undermining the parliamentary attempts to "redeeme our captives and to renue the ancient correspondence in those parts," and justifying Moroccan attacks on British ships.[104] There was a treaty between England and Morocco, Coke continued, and the Commons were eager that the English not be seen to break that treaty and that Parliament not be viewed as giving "countenance to the breach of anie treatie, to the disparagement of publique faith."[105] The failure of the king was translating into a negative image of the English and their political representatives.[106]

On 3 October, a petition of three thousand captives held in Algiers was presented to the king, describing the "unchristianlike works" of the captors and alerting the king to the conversion of many of the captives to Islam.[107] The petition was intended to apply pressure on the king and to show his ineffectiveness. The king could do nothing for these captives without money, and so a month later, he called another parliament, and within a month, on 10 December 1640, the Commons had formed a "Committee for Argiers" to receive petitions on behalf of prisoners and captives in Algiers and Tunis "or elsewhere, under the Turks Dominions."[108] The establishment of the committee was clearly intended by the Commons to demonstrate to sailors, families and the City investors their concern for the captives and for the safety of maritime trade. The committee consisted of men who had either had some experience in the Mediterranean, such as Sir Thomas Roe and Captain Rainsborough, or of parliamentary leaders who were leading the opposition to the king, such as John Pym, or of representatives of the sea towns and ports that were exposed to piracy. By forming the committee, the Parliament showed that it had assumed full responsibility for the captives from the king.

On 1 March 1641, news reached London that there were between four and five thousand captives in Algiers and Tunis, that the pirates were preparing to launch massive attacks, and that the policy of ransoming captives was counterproductive. The anxiety generated by this information coincided with anxiety over the general failure of the performance of the fleet, from its unsuccessful attack on the Isle of Rhee, wrote Sir John Suckling to the lower house of Parliament, to the "messe" in Algiers.[109] As a result, the Commons hastened to their first reading of the bill that would come to be known as "An Act for the releife of the Captives taken by Turkish Moorish and other Pirates and to prevent the taking of others in time to come"—an act that would go through many revisions before it passed. The first version, presented on 1 May 1641 and recorded in the journals of the House of Lords, had a completely different political goal than the version passed later on by the Commons. The Lords' version recognized the negative impact of piracy on national trade, and the "miserable bondages" under which captives labor. It proposed that "all his Maiesties Subiectes shall have free liberty without anie Letters of Marke, or Reprisall or other Warrant whatsoever to take and surprize by all meanes whatsoever all Turkish Moorish and other Pyrates whatsoever, their Shipps goodes prizes and persons, And to convert & freelie to dispose to their best advantage and profitt, all the said Turkish, Moorish & other Pyrates theire Shipps Goods and prizes without payeing anie duetie whatsoever to his Maiestie."

The act assured that Britons who seized Turkish and Moorish ships would not have to pay "anie dutie whatsoever [on the booty], to his Maiestie his heirs or Successors, or to the Lord Admirall for the time being." The only proviso the act imposed was that after sea captains seized ships, "a Christian Magistrate" should notarize "the tyme of takeing the kindes of Shipps, Goodes and persons and the value and prizes for which they were sould." There was need to keep strict record of who was attacked and how much was seized by the privateers. Furthermore, any person who was going to "sett fourth a Man of War" should "give Bondes in five thousand poundes" that neither the captains, the masters nor the officers of that ship would attack "any of the Kinges Subiectes his Friends or Allyes."[110] It was necessary that privateers not become indiscriminate in their attacks, thereby endangering national alliances and interests. The thrust of the act was clearly to lay the burden of fighting the pirates on the shoulders of merchant companies and not on the king. The king would give the merchants-turned-privateers free rein at sea if they could relieve him of the responsibility of securing the safety of the seas and of liberating the captives.

Such a strategy could not have appealed to the Commons. They felt that with the Ship Money, the fleet should assume responsibility, and on 21 May 1641 they resolved that "a Fleet of Twenty Ships and Pinnaces be sent to Algiers, to assail the Town, and their Ships, if the Captives be not delivered, upon the Demand of them."[111] Although no action ensued, Parliament was eager to demonstrate that it would act to subdue the Algerians—and not leave it to individual traders and merchants. On 30 October 1641, the act was read *la vice*.[112] It was read again on 2 November and committed to the Committee for Argiers. Three days later, and in order to raise the money necessary for the implementation of the terms of the act, a bill was drawn "for appropriating 70,000 £ or 80,000 £ of the Customs, per annum, to be employed against the Algerine pirates."[113] On 10 November, the "Committee for the Bill touching the Pyrates of Argiers" was summoned to meet on the following morning to go over the wording of the act and to examine proposed amendments. Two and a half weeks later, discussion of the amendments took place, and by 1 December, the "additions and amendments ... were assented unto and upon the question voted bee ingrossed"—written out in the large letters of legislative bills.[114] On that same day, Parliament presented to the king "The Grand Remonstrance" in which were listed 204 grievances. Significantly, in one of the first grievances, the MPs reminded him of the Ship Money he had taken for the purpose of subduing the "Turkish pirates"—which he had failed to do: "[No.] 20. ... a new unheard-of tax of ship-money was devised, and upon the same pretence, by both which there was charged upon the subject near £ 700,000 some years, and yet the merchants have been left so naked to the violence of the Turkish pirates, that many great ships of value and thousands of His Majesty's subjects have been taken by them, and do still remain in miserable captivity."[115]

Two days later, on 3 December, the final discussion of the act took place. As Simonds D'Ewes reported, "Divers spake for and against it,"[116] but at the end of the debate, the act was passed.

The passing of the act was a watershed in the history of Britain's relations with the Barbary region. For the first time, there was an admission of "defeat" at the hands of the "Barbary pirates": Britons were being taken captive, were not being liberated and, most dangerously, were being converted to Islam and deserting their king, country and family. Numerous petitions had often warned that Britons in captivity were either converting to Islam or were under great temptation or duress to do so; sermons about returning "renegadoes" had also alerted the congregations to the high number of converts.[117] It must have soon become clear to petitioners and parishioners alike that many of their kinsmen had converted to Islam and had settled among the Muslims because they had not been ransomed. The act is the first official document in England to refer openly to the "thousands" of Britons who had converted to Islam—especially seamen and sailors who were known to be serving among the Muslims. The danger to trade, the act was saying, partly consisted in not ransoming the captives: had they been ransomed, they would not have joined the Turks against their king and countrymen.

The act shows that the main concern of Parliament was the protection and improvement of trade. The Mediterranean was an important source of revenue for the trading companies that were represented in Parliament. That is why the act bluntly blamed the king for failing to protect very much needed sailors and seamen whose absence had adversely affected the national economy—and the profit of the companies:

> And diverse of those your subjects kept in bondage (being expert and skilfull Mariners) are usualy imployed at Sea against others your good subjects and prove [very[118]] prejudiciall to them and hurtfull to the trade and merchandise of your Majesties Dominions And whereas aswell your Majesties subjects as Strangers exporting or importing theire goods and merchandize into this Kingdome have ever sithence your Majesties accesse unto this Crowne beene charged with the payment of great sums of money under the name of Custom and that without consent of Parliament which had they beene legally taken ought to have been chiefly imployed to the safeguard of the Seas and preservation of your good subjects in theire trade of merchandize from the spoile of Pirats and other Sea Robbers.[119]

Aside from blaming the king for a weakened economy, the act established for the first time in England a national mechanism for raising money to ransom captives and to fight the corsairs. Throughout the years of crisis over the captives, the chief problem had centered on the financial responsibility for ransoming them: who should pay for their release, the monarchy, the company investors or the families? King Charles believed that his duty was to strengthen the fleet and confront or bribe the pirates—concern himself with the large military and political picture—and not, necessarily, to spend his limited financial resources on individual captives. After all, the sailors and seamen were employees of the trading companies and were not really in his service since the English commercial enterprise of the Levant Company and the East India Company was completely in private, not government, hands. As early as 1621, Thomas Mun had shown how the East India Company and not government took care of sailors and their families: many "poore Widdowes, Wiues and children of Blacke-well, Lime-house, Ratckuffem Shadwell, and Wapping" were relieved with "whole Hogsheads of good Biefe and Porke, Bisket and doales of ready money."[120] But twenty years and repeated levies of Ship Money later, the trading companies insisted that the responsibility for security and ransom lay with the king, who collected tonnage and poundage and other taxes expressly for that purpose. Although the king had not become like the French or Spanish kings, directly invested in the companies, he had become a player who should now assume full responsibility.

By initiating and pushing the act through Parliament, the City merchants and their supporters succeeded in placing the responsibility for the captives on shoulders other than their own: the act ensured that captive Britons would no longer have to seek help from the Privy Council, their impoverished relatives and communities, or the unwilling trading companies, but would receive help from a willing Parliament that had turned the ransoming of captives from parochial charity to national policy. Although the captives had been seized while pursuing a private enterprise, their ransom was to depend on state finance. The parliamentarian supporters of the act recognized that the presence of thousands of captives in Barbary was not a matter that could be relegated to foreign policy, as the king believed. Actually, they were aware that the captives were causing a domestic crisis on which they could capitalize in their opposition to him. That is why the act indicted the failed policy of the king and his "junta" (as Von Ranke called them[121]), and firmly established a confrontational policy toward the pirates: the indifference or limitedness of the king's actions was to be replaced by what the Speaker of the Commons described as "the destroying of the Turkish and Moorish Pyrates."[122] The act showed that Parliament, and not the king, had pushed for the establishment of a government mechanism to ransom the captives and confront the pirates—a mechanism that neither the king nor his father had ever instituted. The act was perhaps the first demonstration that the Commons Council, consisting of parliamentarians involved "in the new trades or the colonies," was in effect, running the "government of the City"—to the exclusion of the king who would soon after abandon it.[123]

Before leaving the city, on 15 January 1642, the king gave his royal assent for the passing of what came to be known as the Bill of Algiers.[124] It must have been a difficult act for the king to sign, given the harsh language in it against his "evil Ministers." But the king was unable to confront the Commons any longer: only two weeks before, on 3 January, he had unsuccessfully attempted to have five parliamentary leaders arrested, and on 6 January, London citizens had taken up arms and closed the gates of the City. Apprehensive, the king left London. Nine days after the king's assent, on 24 January, Parliament revived "the former committee for Algiers" and appointed eighteen members to assist "the lords concerning Algiers captives."[125] Among those who joined the Algiers committee were the following MPs: William Cage (Ipswich); Sir Henry Heyman (Hythe); John Blackiston (Newcastle-on-Tyne); Thomas Barrington (Colchester); Dennis Bond

(Dorchester); John Lisle (Winchester); John More (Liverpool); William Spurstow (Shrewsbury); Richard King (Weymouth and Melcombe Regis); Alexander Carew (Cornwall); Walter Long (Ludgershall); Giles Green (Corfe Castle, Dorset); Roger Matthew (Dartmouth); John Percival (King's Lynn); and John Waddon (Plymouth). The committee also included Robert Greville, Lord Brooke; Robert Rich, the Earl of Warwick; the bishops of London, Winchester and Rochester; Philip Herbert, Earl of Pembroke; Lord Henry Spencer; Edward Montague, Lord Kimbolton; and Algernon Percy, the lord admiral.

It is not difficult to see why many of the above became members of the committee: they represented cities and ports that were exposed to North African piracy and had suffered in trade and in the capture and enslavement of their residents. Some had also commanded Levant Company ships and had traveled the East India routes. But what is also significant is the ideological position: Cage, Heyman, Blackiston and Barrington, a "militant MP," as Robert Brenner described him, were in the war-party wing of Parliament.[126] Others on the committee were known for antiroyalist sentiments: Bond was a "war-party militant";[127] Lisle would become a "radical political Independent";[128] More became a regicide; Spurstow had been hostile to the king ever since he refused to pay the Forced Loan of 1626;[129] and both Lord Brooke and the Earl of Warwick had been arrested soon after the convening of the Short Parliament for opposing the king's demand of a loan from the City, after which, in August, the king declared them guilty of high treason.[130] The committee included a strong antiroyalist faction from Parliament.

Although opposition to the act in the Commons had been outvoted, there was still resistance to it from some trading sectors. A month after the royal assent, on 21 February, a petition from the Merchant Adventurers trading in French wine was presented to Parliament stating that instead of the 1 percent that was to be collected, the amount had been increased to 6 percent.[131] A new committee was therefore appointed—which included some of the Algiers committee along with "all the Burgesses of the Port Towns"—to "consider the Grievances pretended to be occasioned by the Bill for the Relief of the Captives of Algiers; and to receive Petitions concerning these Grievances."[132] Another petition was presented a few days later, on 24 February, by the Merchant Adventurers trading in cloth: they "were so oppressed by this new bill for the relief of the captives of Algiers that if they were not some way eased, they must of necessity give over trading."[133] These and other merchants were so unhappy with this new financial burden that one Henry Robinson presented a treatise "to the serious Consideration of the Honourable Court of Parliament" in which he urged that England wage war against Turkey in order to end the threat to trade and the continuing captivity of Britons. Speaking on behalf of the merchants, he argued that paying ransom would "encourage and enable those Pyrates to take them slaves againe." He recommended that the English fleet, with some forty ships, lay siege to Constantinople, whereupon the city would be starved into submission; he also recommended that the English merchants withdraw their investments in Turkey, which were just above "300 thousand pounds."[134] For Robinson, the Levant trade would not become lucrative unless the pirates and the Grand Turk were intimidated into cooperation. In the absence of such a forced cooperation, the best alternative was to discontinue trade, cut off commercial and financial ties, and declare war. But while the author was encouraging war against the Turks, the king, eager for international support, was writing to the Ottoman sultan, Murad IV (r. 1623–40), complaining about the "dangerous troubles" he was facing in "London and many other principall parts of Our Kingdome" and assuring him of the eagerness of his subjects to maintain the "entercourse of Trade."[135] Unable to secure the seas for his merchants, the king thought that if he cooperated with the Ottoman sultan, as earlier he had cooperated with the Moroccan ruler, the Muslim potentate would in turn curb the pirates and protect British sea merchants. Robinson's call for war with the Turks was not an option that either Parliament or the king could pursue.

In August 1642, Parliament renewed the act for three more years, since both piracy against British ships and enslavement of Britons continued to rise. Indeed, in September 1642, it was reported from La Rochelle that the Turks had taken "some sixty ships, and daily carry off English and Scots like cattle."[136] In November, a worse piece of information was published: two Algerian "Turks men of Warre" were taken near the coast, while another two were discovered to be smuggling arms (and "Irish Friars") to the Royalist party in Ireland.[137] As English traders had supported Moroccan rebels, Muslim traders were now supporting royalist "rebels." The growing military expenditure of Parliament disabled it from ransoming captives and providing effective protection of the seas, especially after the limited success of collecting the tax of 1 percent as a result of opposition by non-Levant merchants.[138] In October 1644, the Commons thus reduced the 1 percent to one-quarter.[139] Although this tax (over and above tonnage and poundage) was causing anger among merchants and traders, there was no alternative for raising ransom money except through this means. Three months later, on 28 January 1645, the Lords and Commons met and renewed the ordinance "for the Raising of Moneys for Redemption of Distressed Captives" (and printed the ordinance two days later). Again, they confirmed its reduction to one-fourth of 1 percent "to the Encouragement of Merchants in their Trade."[140] And again, the Lords and Commons urged that the money be collected more efficiently and spent appropriately. They appointed the chamberlain of the City of London and his deputies to "receive all such sums of Money" and to ensure that the money was spent for "the Redemption of the said distressed Captives."[141]

On 18 March 1645, the Committee for the Navy and Customs discussed the redemption of captives before the Lords and the Commons and noted that "divers Merchants have not paid in the summes due on the Bonds by them entred into for the said duty."[142] The merchants had not paid the duty that had been imposed on them by the Ordinance of 24 October 1644; the committee demanded payment within thirty days and threatened to take action against them in light of the ordinance. Evidently, the merchants had resisted paying the customs on all imports to England and Wales, and urged that the money collected should "be issued, imployed, disposed and payed . . . for and towards the Redemption of the said distressed Captives"[143]—clearly implying that money had been diverted for other purposes. The October ordinance was renewed on 5 July 1645, whereupon Parliament reiterated that the customs duty was the only means available for ransoming captives—which would not be possible "without continuance of the said duty."[144] The apologetic tone that informed the ordinance reflected the numerous grievances and complaints that had been made by merchants, especially those who found that various traders were cheating the government out of the duty by fraudulent registration of ships. Four days later, another ordinance was passed in which authority was given to a parliamentary committee to oversee the payment of the overdue sums.[145] Notwithstanding the best of intentions, Parliament was facing tremendous organizational difficulty in coordinating the collection and use of ransom money.

Apprehensive of the cacophony of criticism, and aware of the need to produce results with the money raised through the "Argiers tax," Parliament appointed Edmond Cason in August 1645 as its negotiating agent in Algiers. With the military victory of Naseby securely behind it (14 June), Parliament sought to show that the money it had been collecting for years in customs would serve the intended purpose of ransoming Barbary captives. After all, in that month "Seven Barbary ships" carried off "goods and prisoners, including about 200 women" from Cornwall.[146] Parliament needed a publicity victory and quickly dispatched Cason to North Africa to ransom captives. It also sent another representative to Constantinople to ensure the cooperation of the sultan in restraining the corsairs. There was a triangle within which British diplomacy had to work, linking London to Algiers (and Tunis) and then to Constantinople. The letter of commission issued by the Committee for the Navy and Customs stated that the envoy should "represent Unto ye Grand Sig: or Grand Vizier ye State of ye English in Argier & Tunnis [and ask them to ensure that Algerians observe] ye peace of ye English for ye future & that there be noe more Acts of Hostility done but yt ye English Nation may be treated as in ye other parts of ye Grand Sigs domynions."[147]

In the account that was later published about Cason's mission, *A Relation of the whole proceedings concerning the Redemption of the Captives in Argier and Tunis* (1647), Cason explained that at the end of 1645, he had sailed to Algiers with a large sum of money intended for the captives, but his ship sank and the money was lost. Parliament sent him again in 1646 whereupon he was able to effect the release of 242 captives: that more Britons had not been ransomed, he added, was because they had "turned Turks" and had subsequently been carried "to Alexandria, and other parts to the Eastwards."[148] Cason concluded his account by listing the names of all the captives who had been ransomed, their place of origin and the exact sum of money (recorded "both in Dobles and peeces of eight") paid for each. This meticulousness may not have been just a personal trait in Cason but a necessary assurance: there is a defensive tone in his *Relation* that suggests that questions had been asked about money and that Parliament needed to show precisely how much money had been spent on ransoming British captives. Cason further showed that Parliament and not the king was being viewed by foreign powers as the ruler of England: that is why he included a copy of the letter from the Algerian pasha that was openly addressed not to the king of England but to "the High Court of PARLIAMENT of ENGLAND."[149] Indeed, Cason emphasized how Parliament had always been concerned about the captives: although the captives were in "a forein State, so remote as Africa" and although there was "the storme" of war at home,[150] Parliament had not forgotten its responsibility.

Such emphasis on Parliament was double-edged. By offering strong support to the captives, Parliament showed that it was advocating the cause of the merchants—whom the king had ignored. But such assistance brought criticism on it from the left wing in the army, the Levellers, who championed the cause of prisoners for debt. The Levellers petitioned Parliament to do something about the "men, born free, Christians" who were languishing in jails without any assistance except the charity of passersby. What particularly angered the Levellers was the unconcern of Parliament for the "multitudes of poor distressed prisoners for debt" while at the same time it was actively raising money for captives in Barbary: "Your zeal makes a noise as far as Algiers, to deliver those captived Christians at the charge of others, but those whom your own unjust laws hold captive in your own prisons; these are too near you to think of."[151] Such discrimination was objectionable to a party that did not have as much of a voice in Parliament as the merchants had—and that was speaking on behalf of Englishmen who had been heavily burdened by Parliament's war taxes. The Leveller criticism, however, did not deter Parliament from passing ordinances in November 1646 and April 1647 to continue the act.

The efforts of Parliament on behalf of the captives soon paid off. Thomas Sweet and Richard Robinson, two captives in Algiers, wrote a letter showing how Parliament, and not the king, was now being seen as the deliverer of the captives. The two men had not been able to raise money for their own ransom because of the high price placed on them by their captors. As a result, on 29 September 1646, they wrote to their friends in England for assistance. Most significant in their moving appeal was the following statement: "There is now a part[y] in England renowned over the Christian world for their Piety this way [in redeeming captives]."[152]

Even in Algiers, the two men had heard about the "part[y]" in Parliament that was working toward the release of captives. Two months later, on 26 November, the captives wrote again: "Sithence our last sent you in September, Master Cason the Parliaments Agent, and the Basha have concluded a Peace, and it is agreed, that all English Captives (not turn'd Renegadoes) shall be redeemed."[153]

Parliament was so pleased with the praise in the letters that it authorized their publication in April 1647, not long after it had authorized the publication of Cason's *Relation*. Where the king, who had been handed over by the Scots to parliamentary representatives at the end of January 1647, had failed, now Parliament could show, both nationally and internationally, that it was succeeding. At the bottom of the publication, a short paragraph was added revealing the concern toward the captives by Richard Prise, baronet, along with seven others, "Members of the Honorable House of Commons" who had learned about the two men as a result of the "Testimony and recommendation of divers godly Ministers of the Assembly" of Divines in Parliament.[154] Not a single Briton was to be forgotten by a Parliament that prided itself on the successful ransoming of the captives.

A few months after the execution of King Charles in January 1649, another "Act for the Redemption of Captives" was passed on 26 March 1650. The reiteration of the act was a strong attempt on the part of the new administration to show that it was concerned about captives—and, by extension, trade. The ransoming of captives and the security of trade were the hallmarks of the new regime. Cromwell recognized that the main reason for the success of "Turkish" attacks on English commercial shipping and the subsequent enslavement of Britons was the absence of naval protection on the high seas. As a result, a massive ship-building project was undertaken, not for large "First Rate" ships as had been built under Charles I (such as the *Sovereign of the Sea*, built in 1638 with 102 guns), but for small "Third Rate" and "Fifth Rate" ships with a range of twenty to sixty guns. Because these were smaller ships and therefore less expensive to build than the First Rates, it was possible to build more of them and to provide a convoy for the merchant ships both in the Straits of Gibraltar and in the Channel—the areas where piratical attacks were frequent. Cromwell turned the national navy into a regular force of government and used it, in part, for the protection of the trade routes. "For the first time," wrote Julian S. Corbett, "the protection of the mercantile marine came to be regarded almost as the chief end for which the regular navy existed."[155] By October 1650, an act was passed in Parliament to use 15 percent of the customs revenue to defray the cost of building and manning regular men-of-war that would serve as convoys to merchant ships.[156] The English navy had started building what soon would become the most formidable war machine in the Mediterranean. A new era in the relations between Britain and Barbary was about to commence.

*   *   *

The crisis of the captives occurred at a time when the Barbary corsairs were strong and daring—while England, Scotland and Ireland were preoccupied with the Wars of the Three Kingdoms. The failure to pursue the imperial goals as advocated by a few writers and factors stemmed from a unique combination of internal political unrest and Mediterranean and Atlantic danger. Repeatedly, the

Barbary corsairs forced foreign affairs to dominate domestic policies. By seizing on English or Welsh, Irish or Scottish merchants and travelers, the Moors and the Turks produced an image of a dangerous "Mahumetan" world in the minds of the British reading, traveling, trading and sailing public. As a result, and instead of viewing themselves as rulers of the waves, Britons were forced to compromise with Muslims, and to negotiate and bargain, plead and appeal—even to submit to the forceful might of the corsairs.

Although the captives were a continent away, they precipitated a serious domestic crisis. In the absence of their breadwinners, wives and the families of the captives sank into poverty, and after exhausting parish charities, they moved to London and presented petitions on behalf of themselves and their captive kinsmen. King Charles I failed to realize that no similar number of Britons held captive overseas, whether civilian or military, had ever been recorded; and that those Britons were not soldiers who might get killed in foreign lands and be forgotten, but were sailors and seamen who were much needed by the trading companies and shipowners, and who were constantly communicating and pleading with their families and relatives from Hull to Devon, and Edinburgh to London and Portsmouth. King Charles was not unconcerned about them, but unlike his contemporary French counterpart, Louis XIII, he did not have the Trinitarian and Mercedarian orders to help bring captives home; and while King Charles had a restive and dissatisfied Parliament on his hands, King Louis had Richelieu in steely charge of affairs; and while the French king had enjoyed gazing as a child at redeemed captives so much that a tradition developed of parading ransomed captives before him (and continued with Louis XIV and XV), King Charles was not interested in such parades. Furthermore, Charles did not have the revenue to support a fleet, nor the willingness to send it against a foreign adversary, especially after the beginning of the Bishops' War. Repeatedly, he sought advice on how to help his captured subjects—and was told to send his navy into the Mediterranean centers of piracy, even as far east as Alexandria, and attack, pillage, capture and destroy.[157] The king listened but did not act.

King Charles failed to recognize that any foreign crisis would in turn cause an internal crisis.[158] By this failure, he opened the door for the opposition in Parliament to seize the initiative toward the captives and mobilize popular support against royal inefficiency and indifference. The Bill of Algiers presented the first official admission by the monarchy about the plight of thousands of subjects in North Africa and about the danger of their conversion to Islam; it also blamed the king's corrupt administration for failing to act effectively on behalf of the captives and their starving and parish-burdening families. More importantly, however, the bill changed the ransom process that Britons had been used to for decades: instead of depending exclusively on the arbitrary decision of the king and his Privy Council, ransom money became a matter of national responsibility administered by a parliamentary committee. Parliament succeeded in demonstrating to thousands of seamen, their kinsmen and their City employers that

Parliament, and not the king, provided the financial mechanism whereby funds could be raised to ransom the captives and bring them home. It also demonstrated that the king was both incompetent and incapable, and that he was not spending all the revenues he generated to help merchants, shipowners and destitute families of unransomed captives. Such lack of support for the victims of piracy added to the danger that was already engrained in the people's minds about the Barbary region and its fearsome captors. Much as Britons sought trade with Barbary, they realized that in the absence of royal support and protection, they would face the danger of captivity, enslavement and bankruptcy on their own. There is little doubt that as the king climbed the scaffold, there were those in the crowd who believed that he deserved his punishment for never doing enough for their kinsmen in the hands of "Turks" and "Moors."

3

Barbary and British Women

The political impact of the Barbary States on Britain led to a dramatic change in the role of women, both within Britain and overseas. Although the captivity of seamen and sailors was chiefly felt among shipowners and trading companies, it was also felt at the family and parochial levels. For, in the absence of their breadwinning men, British women were forced to fend for themselves and their children and to devise means for social agitation and expression. They organized themselves into quasi-political movements and began petitioning the monarch, the Privy Council and the houses of Parliament (when and if such houses were in session). The lives of women were changed as a result of the captivity of their kinsmen in the Barbary region: women had to acquire agency in order to conduct affairs independently of patriarchal authority.

Meanwhile, other women (by far fewer in number) were themselves taken captive and enslaved in Barbary. Because fewer records survive about women than about men, it is difficult to determine the number of women captives in this period. Some women were captured from their homes on the coasts of England, Wales and Ireland; others were seized while making the Atlantic crossing, or sailing from London along the southern coast of England and Wales, before ships launched off to the Americas. Travelers repeatedly mentioned how captains and sailors took their wives with them as they sailed out of London and then dropped them off in the last ports before the ocean. If such ships were captured by the Barbary corsairs, as they sometimes were, the corsairs found not only seamen and travelers but wives, mistresses and children as well. Husbands and kinsmen had now to confront the realization that their womenfolk would be slaves in Barbary and might never return home.

After the second half of the seventeenth century, as trading companies established and expanded their factories, and as more employees were sent to North Africa to man these commercial outposts, women went as wives, consorts, servants and menials of the emergent trading colonies. These women too felt the impact of the Moors, not like the captives, who were restricted in their movements, but as Europeans who assumed public roles in the metropolitan centers of trade, administration and negotiation. Tangier boasted two hundred wives of soldiers and traders, and seventy widows and single women,[1] not all of whom were gentle ladies. One woman was expelled from the garrison in 1664 for incitement to mutiny, while another, Elizabeth Harrold, was lashed for breaking her husband's head.[2] Other women, including the wife of the governor, were accosted by local Moors: on 29 December 1672, Moors affronted Lady Middleton's chair in Tangier, but nothing serious seems to have happened.[3] Women such as Lady Middleton did not, of course, experience the pressures that the captives did, and lived normal lives—as normal as possible within a male-dominated garrison.

There were also English wives of converts to Islam who seem to have lived peaceably in their husbands' new Muslim community. After the death of their husbands, they had the liberty to choose whether to remain in Barbary or to return to England. In 1682, after the convert James Rowlands died in Tangier, his wife "obtained leave to . . . return for England."[4] By the beginning of the eighteenth century, women had become so assertive within the expatriate communities of the Barbary region that they provoked both anger and embarrassment. On 7 July 1713, Samuel Thomson reported from Algiers to the Earl of Dartmouth the following action: "By order of the Bashaw there is one Mrs. Deivis that was Housekeeper to Consull Cole was this day sent on board the Mitford man of war, a person of a most infamous character and has been troublesome to the Bashaw that purely for his own quiet he ordered his Chiause's to see her put into the boat. . . . Her impudence here has been a scandall to the nation."[5]

What this housekeeper had done to deserve expulsion is not mentioned. But it is significant that she was seen to be "infamous" with all the immoral connotations of that word; it is also interesting that she had been troublesome to the pasha, indicating that her misconduct and range of activities had not been confined to her house or the English community but had extended to the Muslim population as well and had caught the attention of the ruler. Indeed, the pasha himself became so furious and frustrated with her that he mentioned her months later in his December 1713 letter to Queen Anne. Mrs. Deivis had obviously been unforgettable: "We have sent on board the ship that brought the new consul, a woman yt has been very troublesome to us, we bore a great deal with her in respect to the late Consuls age & infirmitie, but doe nott think it fitt she should remaine any longer."[6]

Whether they were behaving immodestly, or petitioning in London, or living in the harems of Meknes or Algiers, or serving in the houses of British factors, early modern British women were forced to confront and engage, physically and psychologically, the Muslims of the Barbary Mediterranean. In these respects, the Moors played a role in the "re-birthing" of English/British "identity,"[7] not only as it applied to men but to women as well.

Women Petitioners

The beginning of the Bishops' Wars in 1638 and of the Civil Wars a few years later has traditionally been seen as a liberating moment in British history. Movements and ideas that had been banned under the Laudian Anglican establishment, after Archbishop Laud imposed strict control over religious practice in the

English Church, flourished in books and on the streets and changed the political landscape of England and the rest of Britain. Literary and social historians such as Patricia Higgins, Simon Shepherd, Lawrence Stone, Margaret George, Keith Thomas and others have therefore assumed that it was these wars that mobilized the first female petitioners in England. In their view, the women who petitioned the Long Parliament on 31 January and 4 February 1642 were the first women ever to use petitions for social and political protest—and they did so because of the social disorder and "liberty" that the wars produced. "The women's petitions of the sixteen-forties," wrote Shepherd, "seem to be a sudden manifestation of [Civil War] feminism."[8] Before the Civil War, wrote Thomas, "recourse to prophecy [was] the only means by which most women could hope to disseminate their opinions on public events."[9] For Thomas, as for Higgins and others, pre–Civil War actions on the part of women exclusively came "out of religion":[10] "The exercise of female conscience," Patricia Crawford concurred, "was central to a fundamental issue of English political life before the Civil Wars."[11] The Civil War took women beyond prophecy and turned them into political and social petitioners.

But, over a decade before the first of the Bishops' Wars broke out, wives of husbands captured by the Turks and Moors (as the petitions always stated) of North Africa had organized themselves into a group of "distressed wives" and had presented petitions to King Charles I, to Parliament, to the Lords and to others in authority.[12] These wives made political appeals based not on "prophecy" or individual religious conscience, but rather on their destitution and their status as husbandless wives. It was not conscience but poverty brought about by the Barbary corsairs that compelled these wives, well before the 1642 petitioners, to undertake the first "wifely" petitioning in England. As they repeatedly explained, their poverty was caused by none other than the Moors and Turks who held their husbands captive, and who threatened to convert their husbands to Islam and thereby take them away from their Christian families and dependents.

Although the wives, in the absence of their husbands, were financially and socially devastated, and lacked political or legal clout, they chose to act—and to act in a manner that was unprecedented for women in England: they presented petitions directly to the highest authorities in the land.[13] At a time in England, before the Civil Wars, when a woman's voice was rarely if ever heard in the public forum[14]—when any publicity for women was seen to be "transgressive because not confined within the home"[15]—and when the "strain in gender relations" had resulted in extensive misogynist literature,[16] these women undertook an action that had largely been "a male prerogative."[17] Perhaps because they were of the lower classes where wives were more economically desperate and dependent than those in the upper and upper middle classes,[18] they came together in groups whose bond was both economically based and gender defined. Ranging between small groups of ten at one time to groups of more than fifteen hundred, these masterless wives presented petitions on behalf of their husbands in what must have been the first political rally of impoverished women in the metropolis.[19] Where these women assembled is not indicated, but it is quite likely that they met in the neighborhoods with "the thickest population of merchant seamen": Thames-side parishes east of London Bridge, St. Katherine's, Wapping, Ratcliffe, Limehouse and Rotherhithe.[20] But, as the list of ransomed captives showed, seamen migrated to the outskirts of London from all over Britain, extending from Penzance to Edinburgh. Among the petitioning women, therefore, were not only Londoners but also wives and relatives who gravitated to the city in the hope of effecting their kinsmen's release.

Wives thought of making their voices heard by the king and Parliament by means of petitions only after they realized that little was being done by the authorities to ransom their breadwinners. A broadside printed in 1624 depicted the precarious condition of captives. *The Algerian Slaves Releasement or, The Unchangeable Boat-Swain* was presumably written by a captive to assure his "dear love" that he was still true to her and that her commitment to him sustained him in his dire captivity:

All the tedious long Night
 In close Prison I lye,
But methinks I behold
 My dear love lying by:
In the midst of my pains,
 This doth still give me ease,
That is pleasant to me
 Which some call a Disease.

At a time when there was defection to Islam, there was need to assure the women left behind that their men were still in love with them and eager to return to their arms. The ballad may have also served to shame the captives who might think of converting to Islam and renouncing their families. Although common knowledge confirmed that the longer captives remained in captivity in North Africa, the more chances there were that they would be tempted into Islam, the ballad refuted such fears and emphasized, both to the women and to the sailors who might be captured in the future, that love would and should keep them focused on their country and community. The ballad prominently omitted any reference to ransom or government-sponsored liberation. The captive should rely on love to keep him committed, and then hope to return to "Betty" not by means of the king's power, money or intervention but by an act of God:

And now, through Providence
 I am return'd
By Shipwrack I scap'd
 for our Ship it was burn'd
No torment like mine was

when I was a Slave,
For the want of my Betty
was worse than a Grave.

It was necessary for women to help God in freeing their captured menfolk.

Poverty must have been a decisive factor in pushing women to act because petitioning was not an option previously utilized by women. They must have become desperate enough—and sufficiently emboldened—not to acquiesce to social restrictions and to undertake such an action. After all, by choosing to petition, the women risked being rebuked by a male establishment that was made anxious by the "mannish women" who were challenging social codes in London and who had been denounced for their insolence by King James.[21] Still, the wives of the captives went ahead, careful that the image that they projected in their petitions was not that of rebelliousness and destabilization but one that confirmed the idealized portrait of the submissive and dependent female. The petitions showed women as loyal, caring and impoverished, nurturing the memory and the cause of their husbands while trying their hardest to support themselves and their children. In this respect, the wives may have helped refute the antifeminist and misogynist writers of the 1610s and 1620s[22] because they were living proof of persevering, honest and "wifely" women: they were women who confirmed the ideals of patriarchy. No wonder that while later women's activities and petitions drew the ire of the male establishment,[23] there is nothing to show that these petitioners were ever viewed as being defiant or disobedient to the social order. These women made no social or political demands in regard to their status: all they wanted was the return of their husbands so they could be wives again. And given the abduction of children that was ongoing throughout the period[24]— children who ended up on ships that sailed into the Mediterranean and could be captured—the women also wanted to be mothers again.

The women realized that their trump card was to remind their addressees of the Muslim danger. Their case was unique because their husbands, unlike other prisoners of war in the usual European theaters of conflict, were threatened by forcible conversion to a powerful religion. The captured men could become apostates and renounce allegiance to the Crown; they could become "Turks" and "renegadoes"—terms that projected into the public mind images of anti-Christianity and "the present terrour of the world." The women were confident that their addressees sympathized with their demands because the public good and the safety of the realm were at stake. The women may have felt so "safe" in their cause that they did not feel presumptuous to importune the monarch personally in order to remind him of their plight. In 1623, the "wives, kindred, and frends" of captives "do so importune his Majestie at all turnes, that he is forced somtimes to geve them hard usage both in wordes and worse."[25] In September 1624, "many poore women whose husbandes and sonnes and servantes are detayned captives in Algier and other portes of Barbary" petitioned the Privy Council to permit Nicholas Leat(e), deputy governor of the Levant Company, who was on his way to Algiers, to use his own money to effect the release of their relatives, and upon his return, to be repaid from the sums collected from private charity and parishes.[26] A year later, it was reported how the "poor women that follow the King are many of them in great misery and want and likewise in the western parts";[27] and in 1633, the Privy Council issued an order for women not to implore the council any more.[28] Despite these rebuffs, physical as well as administrative, there is no documented evidence of legal prosecution of the women.

The first of the women's petitions that has survived was presented in March 1626 on behalf of two thousand wives. It was a petition in a sequence of petitions that had been "exhibited" to the king to which he had not given "yet any one answer." After repeatedly petitioning the king, the "distressed wives of almost 2,000 poor mariners remaining most miserable captives in Sallee" gave up on the monarch and turned to the king's friend, Lord Buckingham, who was also lord admiral of the fleet. Aware of the powerful position that Buckingham had at court, the wives hoped that he would intercede with the king on their behalf.[29] The wives also petitioned Parliament (19 March):

> The humble petition of the distressed wifes of neere 2000 poore marriers nowe remaining in most wofull and miserable captives in Sally in Barbary.
>
> In all humble manner, shewing that your poore peticioners said husbands have for a longe tyme contynued in most wofull, miserable and lamentable captivitie and slavery in Sally in aforesaide, undergoing most unspeakable torments and want of foode through the merciles crueltie of their manifolds masters, and which is the worst of all, the extreame want of the spirituall foode of their soules.
>
> And besides your peticioners with a many of poore smale children and infantes are almost reddie to perrish and starve for wante of meanes and food, the which throughe the industrie of the poore captives they have usually had, and unless the said poore and miserable captives bee by some meanes redeemed, they are like utterlie to perrishe, but your poore peticioners are noe waie able to redeeme them, the ransomes demanded are soe greate.
>
> Wherefore they most humblie beseech Your Honours, even for Christ Jesus sake, to commiserate the most wofull, lamentable and distressed estate of the said poore captives, your peticioners and theire poore children and infantes, and that you wilbe pleased, out of your pious and Christian charritie towardes the poore members of Christs mistical bodie, to bee a meanse to the Kings Most Excellent Majestie that hee would bee graciously pleased to send some convenient messenger unto the Kinge of Morocoe and Governor of Sally aforesaide, for the redemption of the saide poore distressed captives owt of their extreame tormentes and miserie, and they, your peticioners and their children, shall for ever (as alreadie they are

bounde) pray for Your Honours and Worships happines both in this worlde and in the worlde to come.[30]

A similar petition was presented to the Lords a few days later, on 24 March. Unfortunately, there is no account of how this petition on behalf of the wives was prepared. The few Caroline records that list the names and places of origin of ransomed Britons reveal a wide geographical area in England and the rest of the British Isles from which seamen hailed: from Dundee to Plymouth, and from Hull to Dartmouth and from Edinburgh to Poole. The wives of the captives had found each other near the docks in London, which throughout the early seventeenth century attracted the unemployed and, as in the case of these wives, the destitute.[31] By putting together a petition, the wives had formed an informal grassroots movement—the first in Renaissance England to be based on marital and not professional status.

Whether in response to petitions or to other pressures, in May 1626, the king advised Buckingham through the Privy Council, and "out of his royall care of his distressed subjectes who are helde in captivity by the Moores," to send Francis Vernon to Barbary "to treate and deale for the releasing of those his said subjectes."[32] Although there is no evidence that Britons were subsequently released from North Africa, there was a flurry of activity in Whitehall and among members of the Privy Council. But King Charles was not willing to spend the enormous amount of money needed to ransom the captives: the only action that thus ensued was an exchange between Muslim captives in England and British captives in Algiers. Unfortunately, there were too many Britons and too few "Turks": the Britons therefore who were freed must have been those with connections and power, for in the following year, 1627, one Marie Blundill complained that she had petitioned frequently for the ransoming of her husband, Richard Blundill, but that "others have recived the benefitt therof in haveing theire husbands and frends released of captivitie."[33] As always in matters of ransom, favoritism played a big role.

In 1632, *The Lawes Resolutions of Womens Rights* was published for the purpose of bringing together in one tome all the laws in the realm that concerned women. Evidently, as women were growing more active in publishing their appeals and defending their roles in society, and as writers such as Rachel Speght, Constantia Munda, Ester Sowernam and others were entering the polemical sphere, the "patriarchial" institution felt the need to remind them of their exact legal status. One of the sections explained to women (and men) their status during the captivity of their spouses. Although the section is directed at both husbands and wives, there is little doubt that it was of chief importance to women:

Captiuitie or Long absence of one which is married.
  It falleth out not seldome, the one of them which are married to be taken captiue, or otherwise so deteined, that it is uncertaine if he liue or no.

Therefore because it is in some sort dangerous to expect long the incertaine returne of an absent yoake fellow, here the Civill Law did ordaine, that after a husband had beene gone fiue yeares, and nothing knowne whether he liued or no, the wife might marry again, and so might the husband, that had expected his wife, &c. But the common Law commandeth simply to forbeare Marriage till the death of him or her that is missing be certainely knowne.[34]

Not only were women expected to wait five years (in dire poverty and uncertainty) before they could resume normal lives with new husbands and protectors, but they were to recognize that the common practice of the realm discouraged such a resumption of normalcy even after five years. For the wives, such a law must have caused deep concern; unless their husbands were ransomed, they could spend an indefinite time in uncertainty and social limbo. As long as the husbands were alive, the women had to wait for them; if the husbands were not speedily ransomed, they could remain in captivity for years and decades—with their wives and children remaining without support for that entire time.

The next petition on behalf of captive men was presented on 12 November 1635 by an unspecified number of women to "the Lords Commissioners for the Admiralty of England" on behalf of "husbands and ffathers, [who] are now in Slavery in Argeir and Sally."[35] The petition shows that the problem with the redemption of captives in the Caroline period lay not only in the unavailability of money or in favoritism but also in political decision—or the lack thereof. A certain Captain William Bushell, the petition indicated, was ready to bring back the "distressed persons" whose freedom had been purchased by the charity of their friends, but he needed the permission of the lords of the Privy Council—a permission that had not been granted. To the petitioners, it was evident that not only were those in authority unwilling to help in the ransoming of the king's subjects, they were also hindering the process. Soon after in that same year, another petition was presented on behalf of fifteen hundred women. Nine years after the first petition on behalf of a large group of women, this petition attested to the continued impact of the Barbary corsairs on London's social and political scene:

The humble petition of Clara Bowyer, Margarett Hall, Elizabeth Ensam, Elizabeth Newland wth a thousand poore women more and upwardes.

In all humble manner unto your most excellent ma[jes]tie that yor poore subiects and husbands being all Seafayring men, and are in number about 1500, and being all on the Seae following their lawfull calling, were att severall times taken by the Sally men of Warre, and carried to Sally in Barbary, where they now are & have beene some of them 3 yeares some more, some less in most miserable lamentable, & woefull slavery & captivitie, enduring hard, & extreame laboure, want of sustenance, and greevious torments, Throughe the merciless crueltie of theire manifold M[oors] and which is the greatest of all the want of the spirituall foode of their soules, but of wch miserable & woefull estate & toerments. Yor highnes said subiects & husbands cannot bee redeemed or deliuered, but by deathe, or extraordinary ransoms unless yor ma[jes]tie bee pleased to send to the kinge of Moorocoe, whoe as the saide subiects haue been informed will deliver them all out of captivitie if yor ma[jes]tie send an Embassador, or yor highnes letter.[36]

Their petition shows that the wives had access to the 1626 petition, since numerous phrases and sentences were copied verbatim from the earlier one. Obviously, the political vocabulary at the disposal of these wives was limited, and they (or whoever wrote the petition on their behalf) must have concluded that since the earlier petition had produced some results, then its tone and demeanor was appropriate. The women were hindered by a language dominated by patriarchal conventions and tropes, and in some respect they had to contrive different images and emphases if they were to effect some change in their conditions. But the women were also aware that however they framed their petitions, they would not be able to present themselves except within the available political and cultural institutions: these women, like others elsewhere in the realm, could not afford to challenge or attack the "institutions grounding their subjection."[37] Rather, these wives had to show their complete obedience to the institutions— since only those male-dominated institutions could effect the release of their husbands and breadwinners.

Notwithstanding the reliance on precedent, the 1635 petition shows some important differences. The wives assertively included their names: they were not just faceless women among the masses of wives and children, but were recognizable individuals, perhaps even leaders, within the movement agitating for the captives. These women also wanted to convey a change of tone in their petition: they therefore completely dropped biblical allusions and references. While the first petition had been imbued with biblical images and had appealed to the Mystical Body of Christ and the practice of Christian charity, this petition emphasized that the husbands, lying in miserable captivity, were hardworking and lawfully employed seamen—not pirates or rovers. In this respect, the wives were changing the discourse about their husbands and their redemption: they wanted redemption to be an act of royal responsibility and not merely an expression of Christian charity. The king was reminded of his duty for his subjects and not just his sentiment as a pious Christian who should help the needy and the helpless. That is the reason why the authors reiterated to the king the suffering of their enslaved husbands and the professions their husbands practiced: the captives were honest, breadwinning Englishmen who served their king and country. Having become more politically articulate and astute, the wives implored King

Charles to act out of his duty as monarch and his responsibility as protector of his subjects.

As in the earlier petition, the wives showed the king that they had acquired some inside information about the demands of the Moroccan ruler for returning the captives: either an enormous amount of money had to be paid or diplomatic representation between England and Morocco had to be raised to an ambassadorial level. Women were forced to familiarize themselves with international affairs through travel literature, traders' reports and other sources of information about the lands and regions where their kinsmen might be. Significantly, the request that the wives made to the king came a month before a letter sent by Captain Bradshaw, a merchant resident in Morocco. In December 1635, Bradshaw proposed to the king that "there be some persons of quality sent from His Majesty to the Kinge of Morocco";[38] three months later, in March 1636, the Privy Council also urged the king to send "a fitt person . . . to treate with the said Emperour."[39] It is quite possible that Bradshaw was listening to the women since they were the first people to get news from traders returning from Morocco about the condition of their kin, and therefore they would have been the first in the city to have learned about the Moroccan king's demand. The women may have set in motion the policy that Bradshaw and others urged on the king in dealing with the Moroccan ruler.

These wives, just like the wives of 1626, realized that the petition constituted an effective means to influence public policy. Significantly, the women did not seem to fear any consequences of their action: had "a thousand" men presented a petition, they would doubtlessly have evoked anxiety in the city. But these women were not seen as posing a challenge to the status quo: they were women who wanted to be wives again, thereby confirming the image of women as helpless without their husbands and "masters." As the mayor of Dartmouth wrote to the Privy Council in September of that year about problems he too was having with such women, "the wives and children are becoming an intolerable burthen."[40] There was no political danger in the women, only the problem of having to feed them and their broods. The London petitioners described themselves simply as "wives": they were destitute and wanted to be seen as spouses, not as a labor bloc—as was the case with the women weavers who petitioned the justices of the peace in Sadbury in 1631 or the "Gentlewomen and Tradesmens-Wives" who petitioned in 1642.[41]

After the 1637 attack on Salé, John Dunton, who wrote an account of that campaign, published the names of the men who were freed (which interestingly included one Robert Bowyear: was he the husband of Clara Boyer whose name had prominently appeared on the petition?). A few months later, the Moroccan ambassador, Alkaid Jaudar bin Abdalla, arrived in London, bringing with him the freed captives. The account of the welcome given to him in the city mentions thousands of people who stood and hailed his entry: it is not unlikely that many of the wives who had petitioned the king stood among the cheering crowds, pleased that their petition had borne fruit.[42] But the agitation of the wives was not over. On 31 May 1638, a petition was presented to the king by the wives of captives in Algiers. Although peace had been established with Morocco, confrontations continued between England and the regencies under Ottoman rule.

> To the kings most excellent Ma[jes]tie:
> The humble Peticon of diuers poore women in behalf of their husbands now in Captiuitie in Argeire.
> Most humbly Shewing unto yor sacred Ma[jes]tie: That yor peticioners and their many children are in great & extreame wantes, besides the insupportable miseries indured by their poore husbands in cruell bondage under the Turkes in Argere who were lately taken in a Shipp called the Mary of London bound to the Southwarde wherein were 12 more taken: Tho some of whose miseries and afflicions doth much torment your peticioners hauing nothing at all towards their ransome nor their owne lively hoods: but (upon their earnest request to the Merchants who set forth the saide Shipp)(though they haue lost the Shipp & goods to a great Gallen) the saide Merchants are (notwithstanding) content to contribute one hundred pounds towards the redeeming of them, which will cost about 800 £ in all.
> Mai it therefore please yor gratious Ma[jes]ty in yor [illegible] and pittie, to graunt your peticioners your gracious Letters patente by way of Breif for such places as your Ma[jes]ty shall think fitt, where by to collect the almes of well disposed Christianes, which (together with what the Merchants shall giue) maie ransome their husbands from their intolerable seruitude; In which (unless your Ma[jes]ty affords them this grace and fauour) they must there end their daies in Turkish slavery, and wee hard in miserable penury.[43]

Again, the wives were taking the initiative of suggesting solutions. They needed money. The merchant company was willing to provide part of it, but they also needed money from the king. And they were not going to let the matter rest: perhaps aware that the king was unlikely to help them financially, they prepared to shoulder the responsibility and go around parishes collecting charity for their kinsmen. Without institutions similar to those in Spain and France that specialized in collecting money, women had to take charge.

A similar petition (with nearly the same wording) was presented to the Privy Council on that same day.[44] The wives had also approached the owners of the *Mary* and asked them to petition, too. The merchants complied with the wives' request by presenting a petition to the king on the same day. They repeated the same information about the ransom, but they added that the ship had been taken after a sea battle with "three Great Turkes men of warr," and then they listed the names of the captives and a reference to the "Maister" of the ship as a "skillfull man & well experienced."[45] While the wives had emphasized their plight in their petition, the merchants' petition focused on the captured men. The merchants viewed the captives as lost employees, at a time when such seamen were in high demand in a country that was losing its expert sailors to slavery at an alarming rate. The merchants thus presented the captives as heroic English seamen who had fought against the "Turks" in the hope that the king would reward them with assistance. But both merchants and wives knew that, at a time when the king's attention was turning to the crisis in the North and to imminent invasion by the Scottish army, they could not expect him to focus on trade or extend financial assistance. No wonder there was despair in the wives' tone. The only hope for ending their dire "penury" and the "cruell bondage" of their husbands lay in a royal permission to collect charities. "To a woman of Yarmouth and a captain's wife," an entry in the Records of the Dissolved Corporation of Dunwich in 1638 states, "both whose husbands were in Turkey, 6d. and 1s."[46] People were charitable, but charity could never be enough to pay off the captors.

Another petition was presented on 31 May 1638 by wives to the members of the Privy Council on behalf of "many Marriners, prisoners in Argere and Tunis." This petition was a sequel to an earlier one (of which there is no record) that had been presented to the council. Evidently, the members of the council had responded to the wives' appeal in the earlier petition and had appointed one Captain Leate to ransom the captives. The money that was to be used for ransom was to come from the sums that were collected around England for that purpose. Unfortunately, the petition continues, the council members, the "Lords," had since "ordered ye contrary, and a staie is made" in that proceeding so much so that the petitioners were "still enforced to trouble yor honors for [th]eir reliefe." The petition concludes with a reminder of the "distresse and sorrow" of the women and their "poore husbands" and a plea to the council "to appoint some speedy order for redempson."[47]

What must have motivated the wives to petition was the treaty signed that month (18 May 1638) between Charles I and Muhammad al-Sheikh al-Asghar of Morocco in which it was agreed that no more captives should be held in either country.[48] Unfortunately for the women, this treaty did not extend to Algiers or Tunis, which were still attacking and capturing British ships. In their desperation, the women seem to have lost sight of the national differences among the captors. Because the petition did not produce any results, one of those wives, Bennett Wright, decided to present a petition on her own on behalf of her husband, "A most miserable distressed Prisoner under the tyranie of the divlish turkes." This petition confirms the favoritism that wives were facing in their attempts to secure the assistance of the Privy Council. Wright reminded her addressees that her husband had been a captive since May 1636 and that neither she nor his friends were able to pay his (quite high) ransom of ninety pounds (the average was sixty-five pounds). She then proceeded to remind them that in an earlier petition, she had "desired that her husband might be reansomed wth the ransome of some of those Turkes wch then lay in Winchester gaole." Unfortunately, "one Mr. Newland of ye Isle of Wight" had "bought" the prisoners: presumably, he sought to exchange the Turks with important British captives in Algiers. No wonder that Bennett Wright could only end her "poore" petition with a plea for a "worke of piety" by the council for "the reliefe and ransom of her poore husband."[49]

By now, the wives were turning their poverty into organized mass action, doing what no women in Renaissance England had done before. They were petitioning as a gender-defined group, but without ideological overtones—and with the passage of time, learning about strategy and maneuver. In the first petitions, the wives alluded to their suffering but derived the legitimacy of their petitions from the men on whose behalf they were acting. They also appealed to biblical motifs and reminded the monarch and all those in authority of the Christian duty to the poor and the distressed. A decade later as English society became desensitized to the suffering of the captives because of their high numbers and the inability of the royal coffers and the parish collections to ransom them, the petitioning wives drew attention to their husbands' plight but also focused on their own neglected conditions; they wanted to emphasize that they, too, had a cause to pursue. And it was a cause in the interest of the public good: if their husbands remained in North Africa, converted to Islam and renounced their families, the latter would then sink into poverty and drain parish charities. The ransoming of the captives was important not only because it brought subjects back to Christendom but also because it brought back breadwinners to destitute wives and children who otherwise would require public relief. Intelligently, the women treated petitioning not as an unusual or odd action for them to undertake, but as a serious option that benefited both the captives and the community.

The wives of the 1630s showed more political acumen than their predecessors had a decade earlier. Still, they always presented themselves as "distressed" wives so that they would not be seen to constitute a political danger. For they were deeply aware that the political establishment was uncomfortable with the gathering of poor women.[50] The appearance in 1641 of a short pamphlet denouncing women preachers and the gatherings of "bibbing Gossips" around them could not but have confirmed the danger women faced when they challenged biblical codes (the pamphlet opened with quotations from 1 Corinthians 14:34, 35 about the prohibition for women "to speake, but they are commanded to be under obedience").[51] Carefully, the wives of captives projected themselves as "wifely" petitioners on behalf of themselves, their captive masters and, indirectly, their parishes. It was an index "of the intensity of the crisis in English affairs," wrote Brian Manning, "that it spurred women to act in politics independently of men"[52]—and in this case, in the absence of men and well before 1642 and the first female petition to Parliament. Unfortunately, because they had acted independently, the women never got their petitions published: they could not appeal to patrons for support, nor did they have any financial resources to subsidize print. The nonpublication of the petitions on behalf of captives attests to the "domestic" and "wifely" manner in which the actions of these women were seen—and why they were not given an answer. None of the petitions elicited a direct reply; at least none exists in print.

By contrast, the 1642 petition by "Gentlewomen" was printed (and reprinted), unlike all the other earlier (and later) petitions presented by wives of captives. As the title shows, *A True Copy of the petition of the Gentlewomen and Tradesmen–Wives, in and about the City of London, delivered to the honourable Knights, Citizens, and Burgesses of the House of Commons, assembled in Parliament, on February the Fourth, 1641; together with their several Reasons, why their Sex ought thus to petition, as well as Men* was socially and politically unsubversive.[53] It was addressed by "Gentlewomen" to the "honourable" House of Commons, where, presumably, some of the husbands were. There was Mrs. "Anne Stage a Gentlewoman and a Brewer's wife, and many others with her, of like Rank and Quality." In presenting the petition, the women were very careful to invoke the example of the women of Tekoa (who had been asked by Joab to pretend to be mourners as they approached the king and implored him for help, 2 Sam. 14:1–4); they were not demanding but imploring, "with all thankful Humility, acknowledging the unwearied Pains, Care, and great Charge" that the house hazards. Like the wives of the captives, these women were alert to international affairs, in this case, the impact of the war in Germany on their kinsmen; and like the first women petitioners, they couched their worries in theological language. They were afraid that doctrinal novelties could taint their husbands and sons should they be sent to fight in continental wars. Because the danger was theological and not economic, as was the case of the captives' wives, these women did not expect to see immediate results. Theirs was a gesture to the patriarchy of the house: not a precise demand, but a gentle reminder by gentlewomen. That is why the answer given to them by Pym was deemed sufficient to send them happily and contentedly home: "Good Women, your Petition and the Reasons have been read in the House, and is thankfully accepted of, and is come in a seasonable Time. . . . We intreat you to repair to your Houses, and turn Your Petition, which you have delivered here, into Prayers at Home for us; for we have been, are, and shall be, to our utmost Power, ready to relieve you your Husbands and Children." As Mihoko Suzuki points out, Pym's reply denied "the legitimacy of their [women's] political intervention and remind[ed] them to limit both their activity and speech to the private and domestic sphere."[54]

After putting forth their petition, these middle-class women disappeared and never repetitioned. They had had no specific cause, and as they had themselves admitted, they had acted within the "Example of the Men." But the wives of captives had a very serious cause and therefore continued to petition for their husbands—and to get more and more involved in the ongoing parliamentary conflict. In June 1642, the House of Commons "ordered, That the Monies collected from the Members, for coming late to Prayers, be distributed among the poor Women that daily attend the House, whose Husbands are Captives in

Algiers."[55] But such charity was not what the wives wanted because they knew that it would never generate enough money to bring the captives home. Less than a year later, in April 1643, they presented a petition that was not coaddressed to the king or to his Privy Council, as had been the case before, but to Parliamen, which had at least offered them some financial assistance and which was now being viewed as the sole savior of the captives. It must have been an embarrassing petition for Parliament to receive. The Bill of Algiers had promised to protect traders and to ransom captives, but the war in Ireland had drawn away resources that Parliament might have used for an attack on the Algerians. Faced with the petition of the women, Parliament had no choice but to revert to the same old method for ransoming captives—raising money by public collections:

> The Petitioners humbly implore the Aid of the Parliament; as by the said Petition may appear: And whereas the Parliament did heretofore take course for the setting forth of a Fleet of Ships, for the suppressing of those Pirates, and Deliverance of those poor Captives. . . . It is therefore thought fit, and so Ordered, by the Lords and Commons in Parliament, that Collections be made in the several Churches within the Cities of London and Westminster, and the Borough of Southwark, and Suburbs, and Liberties of the said Cities, of the charitable Benevolences of well-disposed Christians, for and towards the Relief of the said Captives: And the Monies then collected to be returned and paid, by the Churchwardens and Collectors, into the Hands of the Commissioners of the Navy, appointed by both Houses of Parliament; who are to take care of the Distribution and Employment thereof, for and towards the Redemption of the said Captives.[56]

At least Parliament was promising that no longer would evil ministers be handling the money: new (and honest) navy commissioners would handle the money. Furthermore, the failure of Parliament, the "State," was due not to indifference but to "Pressures" that did not permit them to offer "any other Relief." On 25 April, four days after the petition had been received, the "Ordinance for Collections to be made for relief of Captives in Algiers" was issued—again emphasizing that money would be spent appropriately.[57]

Although Britons were ransomed in the next few years, the Civil War was taking its toll on the resources that could be diverted from the national conflict to foreign affairs. On 4 August 1648, a petition was presented by Sara Baugh, acting on behalf of the wives of twenty-seven Englishmen who had been shipwrecked and captured in Morocco in 1644 and had not yet been ransomed. Unfortunately for these women, the Moroccan ruler, Mulay al-Sheikh, did not want any money for the ransom of the captives—only a letter of cooperation from the then imprisoned King Charles (on the Isle of Wight).[58] Not fully informed about the plight of the king, the Moroccan ruler still believed him in control and in a position to respond. Sara Baugh requested permission to go and meet the king in order to get the letter from him personally. The women would do anything in order to free their husbands because in their absence, they "and theire children are undone and readie to perish here through want of maintenance."[59] It is unlikely, however, that the women were able to get a letter from the beleaguered king. The war in the three kingdoms was now focusing all efforts on the military and ideological fronts. Barbary was too far away.

The execution of King Charles in January 1649 did not make a difference to the wives who continued to petition on behalf of their captured kinsmen and providers. But times were changing: the age of "independent female prophecy" was coming to an end,[60] combined with the heightening of the "criminalization of women in England and throughout Europe."[61] Activities that brought women to the public eye were no longer tolerated and became rather dangerous. Still, desperate women with captured kinsmen could not but act. On 16 May 1653, a petition was presented "To his Excen:cie the Lord Genll Cromwell & the Honb'le Councell. The humble petition of diverse poore women whose husbands and children are slaues in Tripoly & c . . . ."[62] The women reported that for two years, money had been available for redemption, but because of the conflict with "the Hollanders," the ship *Worcester*, which was supposed to take the money for redemption, had remained in the Downs and was subsequently diverted for military purposes. The women reminded Cromwell that the duty of 1 percent, which was raised through customs, was still in place and was intended for the "Redemption" of captives from "Turkish thraldome." The women seemed quite familiar with the operations (or lack thereof) of the government, for they implored their addressees to "take some course by the way of Leghorn" where there was an English agent who could effect "the speedy releasment of those poore Soules and yor poore petitioners." Fully aware that they had no power to force action, they remained humble and beseeching—"take this charitable worke into your pious consideration"—but determined to propose solutions to a not-too-helpful council of state.

Sadly, and much as these wives were keeping themselves informed about government operations, they did not know the true reason behind the failure to ransom their husbands. In their naiveté, they thought that the reason their husbands had not been ransomed was the diversion of the money for military purposes. But a more accurate explanation can be found in the referral of the petition a few weeks later by the Coucil of State to the "Irish and Scotch Committee." The captives were not English, and therefore they were not deserving of the same immediate attention Englishmen received.[63] London was not concerned about subjects from two of the kingdoms its armies had defeated. At the end of July 1653, the Council of State ordered action on another petition presented by "several women and children" for their kinsmen in Morocco.[64] Those captives, however, were English. Similar petitions were presented in the next few months by women on behalf of their captured husbands (7 September 1653; 31 December 1653): the response of the Council of State was repeatedly to urge the ransoming of (English) captives because money had been generated by the "Custom House" for that purpose. The commonwealth was eager to show itself as the defender of the merchants and the ransomer of the captured Englishmen.

The beginning of female political and social petitioning in England, therefore, occurred before the beginning of the Civil Wars and among "distressed" wives driven by poverty and penury rather than by religious and prophetic goals. And it was the Barbary corsairs, thousands of miles away, from Tunis to Santa Cruz, who forced them into social and political action that continued well into the following century. In May 1717, letters and petitions were presented to the secretary of state from "Severall poor Women, the Wives and Relations of His Majesty's Subjects in Mecknass" asking for help in ransoming captives.[65]

Women Captives

The above women almost certainly never met Moors or Turks in their lives—and may only have caught a glimpse of the traders and ambassadors from the Barbary States as they went to Whitehall on official visits. The impact of Muslims on their lives was indirect but deeply felt. Meanwhile, other British women not only met Muslims but lived with and among them. These were women who were captured while traveling toward an American or inter-Britannic destination, or were simply wandering around their coastal homes when they were abducted and taken to Algiers or Tunis or Salé. Many of these women spent months or years before they were ransomed and returned to their homes; others were never ransomed and actually may not have wanted to be ransomed, as they attained status and power by marrying high in the North African ruling elite. As men found opportunity among the Muslims and were willing to convert and remain in North Africa, so did a few women. Curiously, the surviving evidence shows that many such women remained "English" in their identity. Although they renounced their Christian religion, they maintained their commitment to their native land and compatriots. Even after a lifetime in the harem of Mulay Ismail, one woman was still "English," as her trading compatriots confirmed by addressing her as "a Native of England." Although the experience of enslavement was terrifying, a few women were able to acquire agency through their captivity and to achieve status and wealth.

What did captivity mean to a British woman—to find herself suddenly enslaved among a people of different religion, ethnicity and language? Which British women were likely to be captured and enslaved? How did social status determine the outcome of captivity? Was there a difference in the ransom expectation between a male and a female captive? How were women seen and treated—once, and if, they returned to their communities? All these and other questions are important in any assessment of the changing role of women during England's age of encounter with the Islamic Mediterranean.

If "European women were at a premium in Asia" because they were desirable but scarce, as R. J. Barendse wrote in his survey of the Arabian Seas in the seventeenth century,[66] so were British women in North Africa—desirable but more available because of the wide-ranging activity of the Barbary corsairs.[67] When the first women were taken captive is not known, but it is quite likely that their captivity began in the second quarter of the seventeenth century—the period that coincided with the expansion of the North African pirate/privateer fleet, and with the English emigration to America. What Thomas Heywood said in his *The Fair Maid of the West, Part I*, that the "King of Fez, . . . ne'er before had English lady seen," may well have been true (4.5.14–15). But, a quarter of a century later, Massinger described in *The Renegado* Englishwomen arriving in North Africa as prostitutes in the company of sailors (1.1.50); and by the time Heywood wrote the second part of *The Fair Maid*, Englishwomen were more popular (or so at least Heywood liked to think) among the Moors than Venetians, Persians, French, Spanish, Turkish and Ethiopic women. None could "kiss with half that art / These English can," declared the Moorish potentate (3.3.13–17). Still, English (and other European) women captives were by far less numerous than men. This is why, as Elizabeth Crisp reported in the eighteenth century, when she entered Salé as a captive, the local women welcomed her with "a great noise . . . a Testimony of Joy on the arrival of a Female Captive."[68]

In regard to the condition of women in captivity, Heywood evidently did not have much of a clue when he created the fantastic portrait of Bess. His stage fiction was quite different from Mediterranean reality. Captured women from Britain and the rest of Christendom were confined in the boudoirs of Muslim rulers, husbands and masters and were not, à la Bess, dominating the courts and hearts of Moorish kings. Although Cervantes was not averse to exaggeration, his description of captivity conditions in one of the earliest plays he wrote after his return from Algerian slavery in 1580, *El trato de Argel*, was not inaccurate. His description of the trauma of sale and separation, the helplessness of the women (and the men), the farewell between mother and child, and the pressure by Yusuf the Pasha on Silvia to succumb to him all demonstrated the desperateness of women captives and their subjugation. Such stark and brutal reality may explain why in the whole corpus of English dramatic literature of the early modern period, there is not a single play about an Englishwoman captive in North Africa. No English writer could address a situation where the compatriots he described would be captives rather than captors. Neither were there fantasy plays like those written in the Golden Age of Spanish drama by Cervantes and Lope de Vega, describing Christian women captives who overpowered their lustful Muslim captors and escaped with their honor and chastity intact. Many of Cervantes' and De Vega's plays set in North Africa included captured Spanish women who were made to assume heroic roles: thus Silvia in *El trato de Argel*; Marcella in *Los cautivos de Argel*; Lucinda in *Los esclavos libres*; Camila in *El esclavo de Venecia* and others. The dramatic formula that underpinned these Spanish works included a captured Christian woman; a Muslim (either Turkish or Moorish) ruler who falls in love with her; the woman's rejection of his advances because of her love for a Christian—who is also a captive; the ruler's wife (or close relative) who falls in love with the male Christian captive; and then, in the nick of time, the escape of the captives to Christendom and their happy marriage.[69] In such plays, as also in later novellas, European fiction and Mediterranean reality were far apart: Spanish writers clearly preferred to fantasize about women in captivity, as Heywood also did, than to describe the actual conditions of Spanish women in concubinage. As Spanish writers did not depict the "emotional traumas of Spanish new-Christians,"[70] fearing the impact on their audience, neither did English playwrights present women captives, fearing the traumas that such humiliation could produce in London.

The first information about British women captives in North Africa survives in the record about the June 1631 attack by Algerian privateers under the leadership of the Dutch convert Murad. The pirates attacked Baltimore and hauled off many wives, female servants and daughters: the maid of Old Osborne; "Alexander Pumery's wife"; John Rider's wife; "Mrs. Robert Hunt"; the wife of Abraham Roberts; the wife and daughter of Covent Groffin; the wife, mother and maid of John Harris; the maid of Dermot Meregey; the wife of Richard Meade; the wife and sister of Richard Kerpe; and over thirty more women, excluding children.[71] While men had the agility to flee, women, encumbered with children, were an easy catch. In September 1636, John Dunton reported that after he was enslaved, the Algerian *rais* "Aligolant" commanded him to sail to "ye English Channel for taking of English women being of more worth than other."[72] So desirable did Englishwomen become, and so alert were Britons to their desirability, that in that same year, an outrageous suggestion was made to King Charles I. An anonymous writer wrote that since there were so many male Britons languishing in North African captivity, and since there was no money with which to ransom them, and since there were lots of active prostitutes in England, and since Moors liked Englishwomen—he suggested that one prostitute be exported to North Africa to ransom six captured Englishmen: "harlots and the idle and the lascivious portion of the female sect [sic] should be exchanged with the Turks for their male captives."[73]

Less than a decade later, in 1645, seven Barbary ships landed in Cornwall."[74] A brief description of this attack was written by Nehemiah Wallington: "August 14, 1645.—Letters from Plymouth certify that the Turkish pirates, men of war, landed in Cornwall, about Foy, and that they have taken away two hundred and forty (of English Christians) of the Cornish men, women, and children, amongst which Mr. John Carew his daughter, that was cousin to Sir Alexander Carew that was beheaded, and some gentlewomen and others of note, and have carried them away; a very sad thing."[75] It was indeed sad, because the women were hauled to the slave markets of North Africa where they were sold into private homes and harems and settled themselves, willingly or unwillingly, to the life of captivity. Sad too because these were "gentlewomen" of rank and social stature, possibly royalist in affiliation, whose liberation would not be zealously pursued by a navy that had come under the control of Parliament. Throughout the period under study, ransom was closely tied to royal and political authority: the closer to the corridors of power, the more quickly captives could be ensured of ransom. In the case of these southwestern women, and at a time of national crisis, they were not likely to command immediate attention. But the fact that Barbary corsairs could actually attack the coast was extremely destabilizing. In a gesture of frustration and defiance, and as a result of the repeated Moorish incursions, a parliamentary captain from Cornwall by the name of Anthony Buller decorated his regimental flag with the picture of a frightening, bushy-haired Moor above which he wrote "pro lege et grege," indicating how he was fighting to protect the laws and peoples of England, both against the Moors and against the king.[76] Captivity was destabilizing not only domestic relations but also national politics.

How women fared after their captivity is difficult to gauge since there are no firsthand accounts written by any English woman captive.[77] There was, of course, always the danger of dishonor and rape—something that was quite common in the context of battle (and occurred repeatedly in the context of the Civil Wars in Britain), where the victorious not only asserted their dominance by enslavement of the soldiers but also by the rape of their womenfolk. Piracy at sea carried with it that same danger. In a rousing description of the Barbary pirates' outrages against British captives, an anonymous author addressed the houses of Parliament in 1660: "Above all, is their frequent forcing of Men and boys by their execrable Sodomy, also their inhumane abuses and [f]orce to the Bodies of Women and Girls, frequently attempting Sodomy on them also, some of whom both Males and Females have been so abused as hardly to escape with their Lives; All which Usage is so notoriously known by those who have been redeemed thence, that it needs no proof."[78]

Such outrages must have taken place in the violence of Mediterranean piracy. But, as C. R. Boxer has commented, "the weight of evidence indicates that here [regarding the captivity of women] as elsewhere the Islamic record was clearly better than the Christian. The rape of women was deeply repugnant to the strict rules of tribal warfare." Boxer quotes the observations of a Portuguese soldier who was captured by Algerian corsairs in 1621 and described the segregation and protection of female captives.[79] By the second half of the seventeenth century, Mulay Ismail kept married women with their husbands in quarters exclusively for couples and families. Elizabeth Crisp reported how she posed as a married woman during her Moroccan captivity in 1756 whereby she escaped the seraglio to which she would have been sent had she been single.

In an early modern song of the corsairs, a Saletian privateer boasted of the pleasures that he derived from the captured European women. His words provide a unique description in Arabic of the condition of women after captivity. The poem uses a Marrakeshi tune but refers to Rabat, showing how widely known the song and poem were. The description of the captured women is more imaginary than real, although as the first line indicates, the women were actually given up by the ship commander and crew to the corsairs:

> 10. The Christians surrendered and offered us a present of numerous girls. They recognized their defeat and we captured the beautiful girls.

A notorious practice of sailors and sea captains who carried indentured servants or convicts on their ships was willingly to surrender to privateers all their cargo, including the women, in return for their freedom. (If Voltaire's *Candide* is to be trusted, the practice continued into the mid-eighteenth century.) It is possible that such women, knowing of the horrors that awaited them in America, were not unhappy at the opportunity of relinquishing the religious community that had relinquished them, and submitting to the supposedly infamous Barbary corsairs who were willing to offer them gifts and to welcome them, especially if they were beautiful, into their exotic midst:

> 11. We took the princesses as prize; they swayed their hips as they walked. My friends and companions were happy at the arrival of the beautiful women.
>
> . . .
>
> 18. The beautiful women [*'iljat,* white slaves; sometimes also applied to converts to Islam] smiled happily as they saw the bundles of precious cloth. I became so passionate that I gave names to the beautiful strangers.
>
> 19. I started with Mariam and then I called Fatma and Khadija, whose hair was combed in nutmeg. I distributed all the merchandise—
>
> 20. The precious metal, the gold, the jewels—the beautiful one waddled in them—the silk cloth and brocade of India, cloth for robes.
>
> 21. On surveying the cargo, I gave to the beautiful women all the clothes. I took my pleasure with them, both licitly and illicitly.
>
> 22. The beautiful girl went wild, while the ugly one lay abandoned. God who forgives all, do not abandon your servant who has sinned.[80]

What is striking is the existence in Arabic and Turkish of the feminine form of the word renegade. In English, the term is always masculine, suggesting that converts were always male (and if there were female converts to Islam, they were unimportant). The presence of the word *'iljat* shows that Muslims had extended their vocabulary to accommodate—and recognize—women converts to their faith. Such recognition was signaled by the renaming of women: the European names are forgotten as the women are absorbed into the nomenclature and society of western Morocco.

Captured women had to submit to their fate and endure their new conditions. The chance of escape was nearly nil (especially if the women had children). Sui-

cide or martyrdom was not an option even when women were confronted with
the prospect of being married off to Muslims or included in a royal harem (at
least there are no references to such options—except in Spanish drama). Their
only dubious hope for returning to their country lay with their husbands or
kinsmen raising the required sums of money for ransom. But such ransom was
not always ensured: of all the women who were seized from Baltimore, only two
were ransomed,[81] while the rest, the poorer among them, remained unransomed.
Often, the women had to rely on themselves and await the arrival of compatriot
traders and sea captains in the North African ports. Some of these compatriots
lent the women money with which they bought their freedom—on condition of
repaying the money back (with interest) upon their return to England. "An
acc[oun]t of the Redemption of captives in Argiere bye ye Lord Hodges, 1644"
describes the transactions that were conducted between captives and their compatriots regarding the amounts needed for ransom. "Ann Parsons And her 2
Chylldren" needed about 157 pounds, six shillings and three pence, which she
borrowed from the ship captain. Such borrowing continued until the end of the
seventeenth century. "Ann ffossett" in Algiers borrowed fifteen pounds and fifteen shillings from William Bowtell in order to pay her own ransom; and so did
Judith Johnson, Elizabeth Rose of Brighthemston and Margaret Hoskins.[82] Left
with no other alternative, the women borrowed money, but upon returning to
their communities, they found themselves so impoverished by debt that they had
to beg on the streets to raise the money they owed. In a church account of 1627,
there is a reference to a gift: "Gave to two poore women, prisoners in Turkey iid"
(two pence).[83] In the absence of any other way to gain their freedom, captive
women could not but borrow from their compatriots—and suffer penury upon
return.

In 1637, after John Dunton had succeeded in liberating English and Welsh
men and women, along with a few French, Dutch and Spanish captives, he listed
the "names of the women that were redeemed": Mary Russell, Anne Bedford and
Joan Gillions (London); Jane Dawe (Dorchester); Rebecca Man (Exeter); Grace
Greenefield (Bristol); Grace Marten (Bantrey); Margaret Bowles, Katharine
Richards and Mary Batten (Yohall); and Elizabeth Renordan (Kingsaile). Dunton
did not mention the price of each ransomed woman, only her place of origin,
which, as with most of the men, was the Southwest. A few years later, in 1646,
Edmund Cason listed the names of 256 captives, among whom were 19 women,
including 3 sisters. Two women had their children with them and were priced as
one item: "Mary Weymouth, and her two children, James and Iohn . . . 215
Dollers"; "Bridget Randall and her son of London . . . 225 3/4 Dollers."[84] Although, on some occasions, captured women were separated from their husbands and children (as Cervantes showed in his *El trato de Argel* and De Vega in
Los cautivos de Argel), they were more often not. Englishwomen, and for that
matter European women, too, kept their children. A French account in 1714 tells
of the family of Philip Vivant of Marseilles (wife and five sons) who had been in

captivity for over a quarter of a century; and the family of James Chauve, consisting of his wife, his daughter and her husband. Not only had the families stayed
together, they had grown in number as children reached adulthood and married
from among other captives in the country.[85]

The fact that many of the women in Cason's list were ransomed at a high cost
is significant: it indicates that they had not been rendered unmarriageable[86]—that
their captors were not unwilling to exercise restraint if that restraint could translate into higher ransom prices. In 1670, an English lady and her maid were
brought to Algiers on a captured English ship. Because the lady was the niece of
the consul in Venice, a huge ransom was promptly arranged and paid, whereupon
the lady was released unharmed and safely conducted on an English ship to Italy.
A sailor, John Baltharpe, described the episode:

> One English Lady and her Maid
> Who that same time were sore afraid
> Least that bad usage they should have
> Because that then they were their slave
> But the English Consull did them buy
> And took them from their Custody
> With Honour then he did them treat
> And let them want nothing was fit
> This Lady was to Venice bound,
> Before the Turks they had her found:
> Her Unkle Consull of that place
> Sent a great Ransome for his Neece;
> And to Legorne we then convoy'd
> Both Lady fair, and eke her Maid.[87]

Such treatment was accorded the rich and famous for whom captivity could be
brief and not too uncomfortable. Similarly, a "true list of Captives" mentioned a
certain "Laurnetia Whan" who was captured on 30 July 1671 and released ten
days later; and "Sushena Turk" (was she a "Turk" converted to Christianity?)
who was captured on 8 April 1672 and released eleven days later.[88] Captured
women could even be protected from their captors: the French apostolic vicar in
Algiers was able to prevent the dey from sending a young woman from Majorca
into his harem—something that the dey never forgot.[89] A Briton who lived in
Algiers in the early part of the eighteenth century confirmed that women who
were rich were protected and "well entertained" and quickly ransomed by their
countrymen, but those who were poor and unransomable were sold by the pirates to individual masters, where their "Virtue [was] seldom a Defence against
the Strategems" of their owners.[90] Such women disappeared from the annals of
British history, perhaps married off and integrated into the North African community of Muslims and non-Muslims. Indeed, as a French priest explained, many

captured women were treated "avec les égards dus à leur sexe,"[91] and if they did not convert to Islam, they were married off to captured or free coreligionists and compatriots. Those who converted, wrote the French redemptionist, Father Dan, in 1637, were married to local converts to Islam who "épousent volontiers les femmes renégates que celles de leur pays."[92] Captivity for some women in North Africa did not necessarily lead to violation, but to matrimony.

Nor did it necessarily lead to conversion, because Muslim men could, of course, marry Christian women without forcing them to Islam. Even in the imperial harem in Istanbul, there were women who remained faithful to their Christian faith. But many girls, captured young, would be as ignorant of Christian teaching as their male counterparts and therefore could have converted simply because of the religious environment. Cervantes' depiction of the Christian piety of la gran sultana, Dona Catalina de Oviedo, is exaggerated (that Catalina would have remembered the Christian instruction she received before her capture at the age of six) but still has a kernel of truth: there were Christian (and Jewish) women among the wives and concubines of the rulers of Islam.[93] Lope de Vega commented through one of his characters about some of the Christian women captives who came from poor backgrounds and rose to power after their captivity and admission into the ruling households of North Africa. In Christendom, declaimed Belida, in de Vega's *Los esclavos libres*, they are poor; here (in North Africa), they are queens ("Perras cristianas, villanas, / allá pobres y aquí reinas" [Christian bitches, villains: there poor, and here queens]).[94] These and others were the women who learned how to compromise and through intelligence and charm rose in power. In early modern Morocco, one of the wives of Muhammad al-Sheikh (d. 1557) was a Portuguese, Manza by name. Abdullah al-Ghalib was married to a Spaniard; Mulay al-Mansur married a convert, Lala Jawhar, who gave birth to two of his sons, Zaidan and Muhammad al-Sheikh al-Ma'mun; Zaidan later married a Spaniard from whom he had Muhammad al-Sheikh al-Asghar (d. 1654) who, in turn, married two Spanish women.[95] Usta Murad, the bey of Tunis, admitted into his "House of Pleasure" *(dar nuzhatihi)* twenty-four captured women in one day;[96] while Mulay Ismail owned more than fourteen hundred concubines from England, France, Spain and Portugal, with the highest numbers coming from Spain and Portugal.[97] "His Women," wrote the captive John Whitehead about Ismail, "are of divers Colours, as White, Black, Mulattoes or Copper colour'd."[98]

One of these women, an English captive, was described by Francis Brooks in his account about his captivity in Morocco. Her story is the most detailed about female British captives in the Maghrib, showing the horror of initial captivity but then the advantage that awaited the captive if she learned how to operate in a harem with hundreds of other rivals. This Englishwoman (whose English name has not survived) mastered the rules of the game, rose to power and, most interestingly, retained warm memories of her native people and country—and tried to help them realize their commercial goals. Her master/husband Mulay Ismail was quick to recognize her talents and to encourage her toward his goal of improving relations with the British traders and with Queen Anne.

In 1685, Brooks reported, Moroccan privateers seized four Englishwomen sailing from London to Barbados. Upon discovering that one of the women was a virgin, the *rais* protected her in his cabin until she and the others were brought to Salé and from there taken to Meknes. She was then presented to Mulay Ismail, the "Emperor," who "urged her, tempting her with Promises of great Rewards if she would turn Moor, and lie with him." The girl rejected the advances, where-upon she was beaten until she finally submitted; the ruler then had his "Desire fulfilled."[99]

The information about the girl is significant: she was on her way to Barbados in a very small ship and with no protection. Were she and her mother being sent as indentured servants, or were they vagrants who were to "sell themselves to the Barbadoes," as Jonathan Swift wrote at the beginning of *A Modest Proposal* (1729)? The fact that neither they nor the other women were ransomed is evidence of their poor and menial lot; the fact that neither her name nor that of her companions was mentioned may also suggest unknown parentage. It is quite possible that in the case of this "English" girl, her virginity and perhaps her beauty destined her for Ismail's harem. That she was terrified of Mulay Ismail and rejected him at the outset is understandable; but by bearing him two sons later, one of whom probably was Muhammad al-'Alem, a successor to the throne, she rose in status and reached what was certainly a better life than the brutal conditions on the plantations.

The status this woman attained should not be seen apart from her initial suffering and loss of religion. But as Daniel Goffman has shown in the case of the Ottoman practice of *devsirme*, while captivity forced the women captives into irrevocable changes, it still, as with the system of the *devsirme*, opened up venues of hope and advancement.[100] Instead of the plantations, the women found them-selves, at least some of them, in courts where they were not (always) expected to "discard their birthrights" but indeed, as in this English case, encouraged to maintain contact with former compatriots and country. This "English woman," as she came to be known, she quickly rose to enjoy the unique privilege of accom-panying the Moroccan ruler on his outings—something that no other member of his harem was permitted to do.[101] She was given the name Balqees, the Arabic name for the Queen of Sheba. An anonymous entry refers to a present made by English merchants led by the ambassador Charles Stewart to "Lala Balkies a Renegado Queen, 5 loads of Cloths" and other items (SP 71/16/613). Evidently, the Englishwoman desired (as did others in Morocco) English products, espe-cially English cloth and attire. Balqees dressed in an English style, which is why she was known to be of English origin by the traders. It is possible that she asked for clothes and stylish apparel that she had seen in England—and which she had never worn and could not have dreamed of affording. In the harem, her dreams of English luxury were coming true, and even after nearly a quarter of a century in Morocco, she still desired the goods of her country. But having become old, she did not command the larger presents that other "queens" received. Still, she retained her status, where others would have fallen.

The English sultana enjoyed power, which the merchants hoped she would use to support their commercial and trading interest. Indeed, the chief wives of the sultan were known to yield some power and therefore were recipients, with their children, of gifts from district governors, military commanders and foreign visitors.[102] In regard to Balqees, Mulay Ismail must have encouraged her to initiate contact with Queen Anne in order to advance Anglo-Moroccan trade and diplomatic relations. In a letter of 24 August 1711, Ismail's ambassador in England wrote the following address to the English queen (transmitted by Lord Dartmouth): "I am ordered to present the Love & Esteem of Lella[103] Sultana Odima to your Majesty with great Assurance on Her part to Serve Your Majesty whom she will be glad of Opportunitys to shew the sincerity she desires to contribute all she can to cultivate a good correspondence between your most Serene Majesty & the Empr. My Great Master."[104]

An amazing change of fortunes: from an unknown English migrant or indentured servant, Balqees had risen to become the "great" *(odima)* sultana of Morocco. Now she was intent on showing the queen of Britain how the Britain that had ignored her in the past now needed her goodwill. She wanted to communicate with Queen Anne as an equal and to tell her that she, the drifter whom nobody had bothered to ransom, held the key to commercial enterprise in Morocco. She was, after all, a queen.

Such power irked the French, who realized that their own commercial and diplomatic access to the Moroccan markets was being compromised by this English sultana. Dominick Busnot, a French redemptionist priest who visited Meknes, noted the following: "The next in favour with the King after Sultana Zidana, is an English woman, who was taken, when she was Fifteen Years of Age, and whose Constancy he overcame by causing her to be cruelly Whipp'd, and her Feet to be put into hot Oil to oblige her to turn Mahometan; she is Affable, Courteous, and willing to do a good Turn."[105]

Only to her own people, the priest forgot to add. The priest was rather concerned that a Frenchwoman, the sister of one Philip Vivant, had converted to Islam and had been added to Mulay Ismail's harem without, however, attaining any position of influence. Her other sister, Ismail had given to his son Mulay Zaidan, but she too had remained powerless. Meanwhile, the Englishwoman had become the favorite of the ruler. For, continued the priest, Mulay Ismail usually got rid of his wives when they reached thirty years of age; only Sultana Zidana seemed to have been excluded from that practice, along with "the English Woman, who knows how to keep in her Favour, as well as the King's [and therefore enjoys] more Liberty than the rest, and commonly bears her Company."[106]

The Englishwoman seemed to have had her way with her former country.

Another entry in the State Papers mentions "A Rich Crimson Velvet Chair or sidan for the Darling sultaness a Native of England."[107] The Englishwoman still remembered the sedans of her country, which she had seen but probably never used. Now that she was queen with wealth and authority, she would order a sedan of her own—which the queen of Britain would have to concede. The present was to be taken back by the Moroccan ambassador in London. On 4 June 1713, presents that were to be sent to Morocco with the returning ambassador included a firm confirmation of the expensive gift to the English sultana of Morocco.

Such generosity toward the English sultana was not without its rewards. In 1720, English sailors aboard the ship *Experiment* were captured by Moroccan pirates and hauled off to Meknes. After they were paraded triumphantly into the city, they were about to be tortured or bastinadoed, according to the humor of the ruler, when: "As Fortune would have it, who, amidst her very Persecutions, often Times shews some sort of Indulgence, one of his Favourite Sutlana's, an English Woman, that, by the Means of insupportable Cruelties, was forc'd to embrace Mahometanism, was that very Day brought to Bed of a Son: In Joy for which, he . . . caus'd a certain Distribution of mouldy Rice, brackish Sherbet, and dry'd musty Fish, to be given us, and then left us to our respective Fates at the next Day's Market."[108]

While one Englishwoman was a sultana in Morocco, another Englishwoman rose to power in Algiers. In 1677, the English fleet sailed against Algiers under Commander Narbrough. Eager to assert power, Narbrough captured three Algerian ships as a result of which war broke out between the two countries. The dey, the Turkish representative, was an old man and did not have a stomach for battle, but he was under the complete control of his wife, "a cunning covetous English woman who would sell her soul for a bribe."[109] And sell it she did to the members of the Diwan who used her to overbear her husband into war. Evidently, like some other female captives, this woman became involved in North African affairs and administration. Another Englishwoman married into a distinguished Moroccan family after which her son rose to become the ambassador who was sent to England in 1682. As Colonel Kirke noted from Tangier in December 1681, "The [Moroccan] Embassador appears to bee a person of good temper and understanding, his descent is from one of the most ancient families of Morocco by his father; his mother was, it seems, an English woman."[110] To be a captive woman was not to be helpless or inactive. In 1690, the Spanish delegation that was sent to Meknes to negotiate the release of one hundred Spanish captives was instructed to seek the help of "la cautiva cristiana" at whose residence other delegations had stayed before.[111] Meanwhile, another Spanish woman captive had risen to become the "queen" of Algiers: Dona Ines de las Cisternas. The "histoire veritable" written by one Rousseaux, an "avocat au parlement," told of a Spanish lady, Dona Ines, who was enslaved in Algiers in the 1680s. As a result of her beauty, the ruler, Mezo Morto (reg. 1684–90), fell in love with her and courted her with dignity and chastity until she agreed to marry him and became "La Reine d'Alger." She seems to have lived happily with him and bore him a number of children; but after his death, she returned to Christendom and, as the account concluded, "La Reine & ses enfans sont encor vivant" (the queen and her children are living in Rome).[112] Her half-Algerian, half-Spanish daughter found a suitable husband from among the nobility. At the beginning of the eighteenth century, a Genoese girl was captured, brought to the Husseinite Tunisian bey, converted, and married to him after which she bore him four sons, the eldest of whom succeeded him to power.[113]

In these cases, Christian women attained social status through captivity. They also attained political status as they facilitated exchange and trade, and cemented strategic alliances and commercial agreements between their adopted country and their original homeland. Although their commitment was firm to their new country, they knew, and their husbands/masters knew, too, that they were seen by their former compatriots as still part of European Christendom who could be used, relied on, approached and invoked. Religiously and culturally changed as they were, their compatriots could not but believe that they had continued to retain something of old England or Spain in their hearts—and if not something of their previous Christianity, then a clear memory of their country's customs. A letter by Lady Montague described a Spanish woman who had been captured by an Ottoman admiral who subsequently fell in love with her and married her. Although Lady Montague was convinced that the Spanish woman had acted "wholly on principles of honour," she explained the woman's reasoning after being offered the choice of returning to her people or staying among the "Turks": the captive realized that the "kindest thing [her relatives] could do for her, in her present circumstances, would certainly confine her to a nunnery for the rest of her days." Marrying a Muslim who loved her was clearly a better and a more "honorable" choice.[114]

Alongside these success stories, there were stories of captured women that told of failure and sorrow—women whose names alone have survived, or not even their names. These were women who may never have been ransomed, or were ransomed only after enduring lengthy captivity and tribulation. An English captive in Algiers wrote how the corsairs had destroyed "many of our ships & brought in 100. men & women bound for Virginia."[115] From May 1692 to December 1694, a number of Britons were ransomed from Algiers, including "Elizabeth Bell."[116] On 5 August 1715, "Rebecca and Mary, of Hull" were captured as they were on their way to Leghorn; nothing is reported about them further. On 18 August 1718, "Ann and Mary of Bristol," sailing from St. Tille "with cork for London," were captured and taken to Meknes, but they were fortunate enough to be ransomed within a year.[117] In October 1719, a ten-year-old Irish girl, Mademoiselle de Bourk, whose father was serving the Spanish king, was seized by the "Kabyls" of Algeria, after seeing her mother and brothers drown in a storm.[118] The Kabyls pondered whether to marry her off to one of their princes. Knowing about the strange custom in Christendom where women brought dowries with them to their husbands, they reckoned on gaining wealth. But then, they realized that a better and more secure option was to collect on her ransom. They thus tasked her with writing to the French consul in Algiers and negotiating the payment: she took charge of the negotiations while ceaselessly encouraging her fellow captives in their very difficult conditions. She was ransomed in December and went to Algiers, where she exhibited "a certain Air of Grandure and of a generous Education. She shewed a Firmness of Mind, and had given thereof many Proofs under her Misfortunes."[119] Captivity had matured the little girl beyond her age and forced her to assume responsibility that evidently none in her group was able to assume. In July 1726, Anthony Hatfield, the English consul in Tetuan, reported that an English ship had been brought to Salé, "loaden with woolen manufacture, having 23 men and women on board."[120] On 11 December 1733, it was reported by Captain Cornwall that a Saletian ship had taken "Forty English Seamen, and a Woman"; in a letter sent ten days later, there was no reference to the woman. Had she died, or had she been taken inland by the corsairs?[121]

Perhaps the most despairing story of a woman captive is the one told by Captain Braithwaite in 1729 about an Irishwoman who had been captured, not ransomed (not surprising given her Irishness), and added to Ismail's harem. Unlike the "Darling" sultana or the cunning wife in Algiers, however, she did not "make" it:

> One Mrs. Shaw, an Irishwoman, but now a Moor, came to make Mr. Russel a Visit: Muley Ismael, soon after she was taken, ordered her among the rest of his Concubines; and having an Inclination to lie with her, forced her to turn Moor, for his Conscience would not permit him to lie with a Christian: but soon after having taken a Dislike to her, he gave her to a Soldier, a Renegado Spaniard, who having nothing to maintain her with, the poor Woman was almost naked and starved. She had been a Moor upwards of 9 Years, and when first she came into the Country was very young, and not unhandsome; she had almost forgot her English, and was an Object of great Charity, having a poor Child at her Breast, not above a Fortnight old, and nothing to shift it or provide it withal: Mr. Russel gave her wherewith to clothe her self and her Child, and ordered her to come as often as she could, while we continued at Mequinez.[122]

Here was the first Irish-Moroccan. Probably in her late teens or early twenties, what had remained Irish about her is difficult to identify—except, perhaps, her features. Where did she get the name, Mrs. Shaw, since she had been married to a Spanish convert to Islam? Or was it a name that the English envoy arbitrarily gave to Europeanize her? She had forgotten her English language and her religion, of which she may have known little anyway. It is noteworthy that Braithwaite does not mention that she was to be taken back "home": after all, where was home to such a woman, captured young, acculturated into a Moroccan way of life, having borne a son to a renegade and knowing little of her mother tongue, and nothing about the faith of her unknown fathers.

On 16 August 1747, an Irish regiment crossing from Majorca to Spain was taken by Algerian men-of-war. Among the captured were three ladies (in another report, they were five), one of whom was "formerly Miss Nancy Tichborne, but lately married to one Mr. Reply Captain in the spanish Service. She is about 19 years old much esteem'd for her good sense Virtue and Beauty."[123] They were still in captivity a year and a half later: evidently the money needed to ransom them had not been raised, most certainly because they had been supporters of Bonnie Prince Charles (who was supported by Spain to where they were sailing). Writing on 15 December 1748, Thomas Bolton was pleased that they were "in a very safe condition today in Algiers." Having been captured as a group, the whole Irish Regiment Hibernian had been able to lead their lives without too much harassment. Bolton added that there "are likewise seven or eight Ladies who are the Officer's Wives, all English or Irish; their beauty & distress touches every person in the place in a very sensible manner. Now if any of the Jacobites in England who send over such liberal contributions to Rome, wou'd make a better application of some part of it at Algiers, I shou'd with great pleasure be their Almoner."[124] Again, in the case of women captives, ransom and safety were predicated on their religious or political affiliation. The closer they were to the monarch, the more likely that they would be ransomed—and perhaps more quickly. To be Catholic in the mid-1700s, however, as Bolton clearly suggested, meant that the women could not expect help from London.

Captivity focused British public attention on the issue of miscegenation and interreligious sexuality. After all, if women spent months or years among the "Mahumetans," it was quite likely that they became sexually active, willingly or unwillingly. English sources do not reveal a structural separation between the Muslim man and the Christian woman nor allude to laws that expressly prohibited sexuality and intermarriage—as Edward Coke found out, for instance, between the English and the Jews.[125] The fact that the Maliki school of jurisprudence in North Africa, one of the five major schools of Islam,[126] repeatedly had to prohibit a Muslim from marrying a Christian or a Jewish woman while living away from the "house of Islam" demonstrates that interreligious marriage was frequent. The Islamic reasoning against such marriages was that upon returning to their countries, Muslim captives would leave their children behind to be brought up as "infidels."[127] Qur'anically, however, there was no prohibition against a Muslim man marrying a Christian woman, which is why so many captured women were married to local Muslims.

Interreligious relations may explain the surprisingly high number of plays from the Elizabethan period on that depicted the possible or actual marriage between Turkish or Moorish men and Christian (continental, specifically Catholic Italian and Spanish but also in the Restoration period, English) women. In

Marlowe's *The Jew of Malta* (ca. 1590), Ithamore the Turk talked of marrying Christian Bellamira, while in Thomas Kyd's *Soliman and Perseda*, Lucina married the Turkish general, Brusor, and in *The Merchant of Venice*, Portia might have married "Morocco." In Thomas Dekker's *Lust's Dominion, or The Lascivious Queen* (ca. 1600), Eleazar the Moor was married to the Christian Maria, and in John Mason's *The Turke* (1607), the governor of Florence eagerly offered his daughter Amada in marriage to Mulleasses the Turk. In *The Tempest*, Alonso's daughter, Claribel, was married to the king of Tunis (2.1.67–125),[128] while in *All's Lost by Lust*, the authors depicted the prospect of Christian Jacinta marrying Mully Mumen, a prospect her father was not unwilling to encourage—much as it provoked her own horror: "A Christians armes embrace an infidel!"

If, therefore, the Christian-Islamic confrontation of the Mediterranean Renaissance is to be "gendered," it will show that male domination was associated with the Muslims and female subordination with the Christians.[129] There was no "effeminization" or "neutralization" of Islam since nearly all the actual or fictional cases in English literary sources and documents showed Christian women submitting to Muslim men. Indeed, in one of the most interesting cases of a proposed marriage between an English woman and a Muslim, the latter's dominance was not even contested by the Christian negotiators. In 1614, discussions were held for the marriage of the sultan of Sumatra and the daughter of an English "gentleman of honorable parentage" because it was felt that such a marriage would be "beneficial to the [East India] Company." The matter had to be determined in London since the Englishwoman was going to be sent to live in a non-Christian land. Although some London divines objected to the marriage on the ground that the husband-to-be was a Muslim, the company marshaled its own theologians to prove "the lawfulness of the enterprise . . . by scripture." The marriage never took place, but it is important that an Englishwoman was to be married off to the Muslim in order to secure his commercial goodwill—and merchants, theologians and presumably the girl's parents found the prospect lawful.[130] Throughout, it was clear that the English lady was not going to Sumatra to anglicize or convert the sultan: notwithstanding the fact that she was excellent at English music and needlework, she was going to have to join the ruler's harem, "the rest of the women appertaining to the king," and integrate into her new culture. And when opponents of the marriage warned that the other wives might poison her, her greedy father retorted that if the king of Sumatra "consent it was thought it would prove a very honourable action." The Englishwoman was going to submit to the Muslim man and his world.

Nearly all the Muslim-Christian marriages, potential marriages and sexual affairs in English historical and dramatic sources described Muslim men and Christian women, where the Muslim/male asserted his dominance over the Christian/female. And the situation could not be reversed: no Englishman could take possession of a (free) Muslim woman unless he became a Muslim first and thereby lost his Christianity. Actually, it was not easy for an Englishman to find a Muslim woman: there were no women captives who were brought to England and who became sexually available as Englishwomen were in North Africa—except in Tangier, where captured Moorish women were put to sexual use, as was the case of the women who satisfied the lust of the resident doctor, Dr. Lawrence.[131] But other than in the exceptional case of Tangier, Britons could not break through the barrier of sexual/marriage codes and take possession of a Muslim woman in the lands of Islam. The prohibition in the Qur'an of marriage between Muslim women and non-Muslim men was firmly implemented. When the Great Mogul told Captain William Hawkins in 1608 to marry one of his palace maids in his harem, Hawkins obeyed and married a Christian, the daughter of an Armenian merchant.[132] Similarly Sir Robert Shirley, ambassador to Shah Abbas of Persia, married a Circassian Christian (who, rather curiously, was described on her tombstone in Rome as an Amazon, "Theressia Samposonia Amazonites"); he also had to dress in Muslim clothes, much to the displeasure of King James I.[133] Englishmen and other Europeans in the Islamic world lived by Muslim rules, especially in regard to rules about women.[134]

Perhaps as a result of the strident predominance of Muslim males over Christian females, playwrights stepped forward with their imaginative panaceas. In the same way that the theater confronted the crisis of English or Christian conversion to Islam by presenting negative portraits of renegades and describing the grim punishments they received in this and the future life, so did drama also confront the Muslim male superiority by presenting the conversion of Muslim men and women and their submission in marriage to Christians. Othello was the first Moor on stage to convert and marry a Christian woman, and Lucinda and Zanthia in *The Knight of Malta* were, respectively, the first Turkish and Moorish women to convert and marry Christians. The emphasis, however, in these plays was on the racial rather than the religious difference; there was little if any mention of theology or Christian-Islamic polarization in the plays. In 1621, John Fletcher wrote *The Island Princess*, the first play to show the conversion of a "Moorish" woman to Christianity in order to marry her Portuguese lover. But the play is set in "India," the East Indies, where Muslims had traded and clashed with the Portuguese as of the early sixteenth century.[135] Fletcher described the Moors of the island as pagan worshipers of the sun, the moon and the gods of "maumet," to whom they offered sacrifices of "human blood." As Heywood had islamicized the Moors of Barbary without necessarily knowing much about Islam, so did Fletcher of India; but while Heywood had kept his Muslim protagonists unconverted (until *Part II*), recognizing thereby the forcefulness of Islam, Fletcher converted his "maumet"-worshipping heroine to Christianity. When Quisara asked the Portuguese Armusia to renounce his Christianity in order to marry her, he spurned her and denounced her religion. Vanquished by his passionate defense of Christianity, she renounced her religion and received the blessing of her brother, the king, to marry Armusia. Although the brother did not desert his own worship of "maumet," he showed himself amenable to the Portuguese at the same time as he turned against the Moorish "priest" who had warned him about the consequences of Portuguese colonial designs.[136] Not only did Christianity prevail over Islam, but Portuguese colonization did as well.

This victory of Christianity would be confirmed by Philip Massinger in *The Renegado*, just three years later, where a similar episode is depicted in Tunis: the Christian refuses to convert in order to marry Muslim Donusa, and instead converts her to Christianity.[137] A similar defeat of Islam appeared in "historie." In "An Abridgement of the Historie of the Illustrious Sarra," written sometime between 1660 and 1676, a "Moore daughter by Adoption to Barberouse a Pyrate" is captured by "German Captaines" but is liberated by her lover, Zelim, only for her to be again seized, leaving Zelim for dead. She is taken to the court of King Charles V, who converts her to Christianity. Meanwhile, Zelim is cured by an "old Christian" who "makes him a Christian." Although the text is not clear whether the protagonist had been born Christian and then converted to Islam, it emphasizes that both Sarra and Zelim renounced their Moorishness and became Christian. Sarra, traveling by sea, is captured by Turks and added to the harem of the grand signor. But the "great Sultana" becomes so jealous of her that she arranges her escape after which, and upon embarking at sea, she is captured by Zelim. The two lovers recognize each other, three years after they had been separated, and hasten to Rome where they get married. Christianity defeats Islam and the world of Islam is left behind as the couple presumably live happily ever after in the land of the Cross.[138]

Within a century, the captivity of women became so unthreatening and unreal that a farcical play was finally written about an Englishwoman captive in the seraglio. By the second half of the eighteenth century, both the Turks and the Moors had been militarily contained. A farce about a captured woman reflected the ease with which the topic could now be presented to dramatic audiences from Drury Lane to Covent Garden and from London to Dublin, at the same time that it also provided opportunity to confirm the heroic character of the English, both men and women. Isaac Bickerstaffe's *The Sultan, or a Peep into the Seraglio* describes an Englishwoman who rebels against the strictures of the harem of Suleyman the Magnificent and forces a change in Ottoman history. The woman is audacious and sharp, ridiculing the sultan's eunuchs and heartily drinking wine (but like a good Englishwoman, refusing to smoke); fearlessly, she declares that she is "a free-born woman, prouder of that than all the pomp and splendour eastern monarchs can bestow." She so taunts and resists the mighty sultan that at the end, he gives in to her charm and courage, dismantles his harem, and in an unprecedented move in the history of the Ottoman dynasty, marries her, making her his only consort. It is not surprising that the name of this captive-to-wife is Roxolana: English pride and fantasy could not but replace the historical Ukrainian slave-to-wife Roxolana (d. 1558) with an Englishwoman. For the late-eighteenth-century audiences, only an English captive could have changed Ottoman history.[139]

*   *   *

Sources about the captivity of British women reveal the following pattern. First, some captured British women left their mark on North African history as well as on the history of relations between Britain and Barbary. After all, no Briton rose to a higher position in the Maghrib than the English sultana—not even the son of Samuel Rowley a century before her. Women were traumatized by captivity; but then, they realized, especially the young among them, that among Muslims, they could be fully integrated and would not be excluded because of their skin color or religion. While Moorish women were invariably racialized and degraded in English drama, and while they could never become wives of European men but remained concubines and slaves, British women discovered that Barbary could provide them with opportunity and advancement. For unlike Iberian society, Magharibi society did not establish an intolerant divide between those of "pure" blood and those of tainted blood. Among their Muslim captors, women captives could acquire agency and leave their mark, as did many male captives.

Second, Britons were quite willing to have their female compatriots achieve status in Barbary and thereby facilitate trade and open up venues for commercial cooperation or military negotiations. The number of British women captives was relatively high in the period under study—higher than anywhere else in the world of British economic and imperial expansion, whether in North America or the Far East. It may well be that merchants were pleased to have English and Irish women in the harem in order to tilt the balance against their trading rivals, the French. That those women had been abducted and forced against their will into situations from which they could not escape did not seem to bother the merchants. In this respect, perhaps the most glaring difference that appeared in the treatment of British captives in North Africa related to the national effort (or the lack thereof) to ransom the captives. While some women were ransomed, there are no extant records of petitions by husbands agitating on behalf of their wives, as there were by wives agitating for their husbands. There is more evidence showing the effort to ransom men than to ransom women—suggesting that there was less urgency to ransom a woman than a sailor or a merchant or a minister. Men were revenue generating, women were not; and if the women were captured and did not belong to a rich and well-connected family, then they stood much less of a chance of being ransomed than a man with a nationally needed profession. Perhaps women paid the highest price in the Mediterranean—not only a price for empire, as Linda Colley correctly noted,[140] but indeed, a price for misogyny.

Captivity brought British women in contact with men of different ethnicities, religions and nationalities. As wives, mistresses and concubines, some fared well while others suffered, but all became the first Britons to experience the non-Christian world in its full range of exposures, from the bedroom to the marketplace, and from the mosque to the *hammam*. They lived inside harems and boudoirs, kitchens and maternity wards, and as they assumed their varied functions, they adjusted to new gender roles, eating habits, religious codes and rituals (fast-ing during Ramadan and refraining from their beloved pork), physical hygiene (baths they would have rarely taken back in England), and nonpublic social activities. These women were the first Britons ever in early modern history to be enslaved by the non-Christian Other. Long before British women were hauled off by the American Indians to the "wilde" hinterlands, their predecessors had been paraded in the streets of Algiers and Salé and in the Turks' souk in the old medina of Tunis. Both the captives and the petitioners forced a change in the general perception of women in the first half of the seventeenth century. In the case of the petitioners, the indirect encounter with Barbary through the loss of male bread-winners, as well as the financial, social, and religious consequences that disrupted families and communities, compelled women to enter the public sphere and to coordinate activities with fellow sufferers and with ship owners, sailors and investors concerned about trade and security. It also forced them to canvass politicians and members of Parliament, pound the streets before Whitehall and St. Mary's, and mobilize the first "wifely" movement in British history. In the case of the captives, they inadvertently reminded their kith and kin and traders and ambassadors, back in Britain or in the trading centers of North Africa, of the power and dominance of the Muslim captors—and of the pomp and wealth that some of them attained.

4

Moors in British Captivity

The captivity of male and female Britons and other Europeans was part of the
price of European empire, as Linda Colley has argued: the more the imperialists
reached into other countries and regions, the more danger they faced of being
captured and enslaved by the "natives." The captives were the "underbelly of
British empire"[1] and its commercial and military expansion—which is why British and other European governments prepared lists, memorandums, reports,
depositions, proclamations and other material that described the experiences of
captivity as well as the extent of royal and parliamentary efforts to ensure safety
on the high seas. Governmental as well as ecclesiastical institutions and trading
companies were involved in tracking, counting, negotiating for and ransoming
captives, while princes and monarchs sent their fleets to attack and bombard the
"pirate states" into submission.

Simultaneously, literature played its provocatively imaginative role. In the
early modern period, English, French and Spanish writers described in quasi-
autobiographical accounts as well as in drama and sermon, in verse as in prose,
the brutality and horror of captivity among the Muslim corsairs. Cervantes recounted his personal story in many of his plays and in *Don Quixote*, as María
Antonia Garcés has shown,[2] at the same time as other captives told and retold
their narratives, in every European language, on the page as on the stage. As
Fernand Braudel maintained, European governments encouraged captives and
printers to publish accounts about captivity among Moors and the Turks.[3] And
while Braudel's statement may need to be qualified in the case of early English
accounts,[4] it widely applies to continental texts that created the image of the
Barbary corsairs as rapacious and ruthless pirates. Even after the days of Mediterranean piracy were over, literary critics and historians, missionaries and scholars turned to study the phenomenon of the corsairs and their captives, producing
tome after tome, based exclusively on Euro-Christian sources, that demonized
the corsairs and, by extension, their religion, culture, society, history and civilization.

There is no denying the extensive North African piracy and privateering
against Britons and other Europeans in the early modern period. But finding the
price of the European empires—specifically the British, and, by the same token,
the Spanish, Portuguese and French—chiefly in the suffering of Christian cap-

tives seized by the "natives" is to invoke a Eurocentrism that produces an inaccurate and lopsided view of historical development—and one that, since Braudel's magisterial survey of the Mediterranean, is not defensible. Without taking into account the slave markets in Genoa, Cadiz, Malta, Leghorn, Venice, Naples, Provence, Languedoc, Barcelona, Marseilles, Toulon and Valencia, which specialized in the sale of Muslims, nor the large numbers of English, Dutch and Spanish pirates who operated from North African and Atlantic ports outside the control of the central governments, it is not possible to arrive at a comprehensive overview of early modern Mediterranean piracy. David Brion Davis described, and provided illustrations of, the depredations committed by Muslims and the enslavement and humiliation of Christians and Africans—without situating Muslim actions in the context of European empire and domination.[5] And so did Colley, who followed suit and focused on the violence British captives endured—conveniently forgetting that the English Prize Act, passed in 1708, led to "the highest level of [British] privateering activity"[6]—making Britain the most destabilizing power in the Mediterranean region. To Colley, Davis and others, it was as if the "natives" did not suffer from the wages of imperialism—only the imperialists. But as the white/Christians slaves of the black/Muslim masters paid the price for the "dream of global supremacy" of Britain and other European countries, so, too, did the Muslim/North African captives.

Islamic piracy, enslavement of Europeans and violence against Christians were not sui generis nor were they symptoms of Muslim or native aggression and "terrorism."[7] Such a view can only be upheld if historians are not only selective in their use of the European records of captivity, but more problematically, if they also ignore the records from the Islamic or North African side. True, there are by far more documents recording the history of European captives in Islamdom than of Muslims in Christendom. That is perhaps why it has been easier and more ideologically convenient to focus on European and ignore Muslim suffering. Why Muslims did not leave accounts of their captivity can be credited to many reasons, one of which is the absence of print. Without print, it was not possible to disseminate the numbers, names and dates of captives as in the European tradition, where pamphlets and lists of captives, their places of origin and the ransom prices were repeatedly printed. But in lieu of print, there was a rich oral culture about Magharibi captives that subsequently appeared in written anecdotes, recollections, biographical entries and letters. Cumulatively, this material provides a portrait of the experience of Muslim captives in early modern Christendom—material that does not belong to a distinct genre of writing with its distinct set of conventions, as in the European tradition, nor to a body of macrohistorical documents and treatises. Rather, it appears as subtexts in other texts, intrusions into larger polemics, hagiographies, or histories and religious expositions. But this "meager, scattered, and obscure documentation," as Carlo Ginzburg defines the method of microhistory, "can be put to good use":[8] to provide a panoramic view of the experience of the thousands of Magharibi men and women who were taken captive into Christendom and who, too, paid the price of empire.[9]

In the second half of the fifteenth century, European painters started to include Moors in the nativity scene—modeled on slaves who had been captured in Spain's, Portugal's and Italy's North African incursions. In 1509, Taghri Bardi, the Egyptian ambassador to Venice, paid fifty thousand dinars to the Knights of St. John "to buy" the freedom of Moroccan captives held in Rhodes.[10] From 1495 until 1541, as the Moroccan scholar Ahmad Bu Sharab has shown after studying Inquisition records in Portugal, 9,287 Moroccans were taken captive by the Portuguese alone.[11] Indeed, Moroccan men, women and children became important commodities sought out by the Iberian invaders.[12] In the Spanish attack on Oran in 1509, four thousand Muslims were killed and more than eight thousand taken captive; and in the attack on Tripoli in July of the year after, the Christians took more than fifteen thousand captives. In the "black years" of 1521–22, nearly sixty thousand Moroccans were seized and deported to Europe;[13] and after repulsing Charles V in his attempt on Algiers in 1541, thousands of slaves were liberated, some having originated in "the Maghrib [Morocco], some in Algiers and some in Tunis."[14] The numbers of captives in Spain in the sixteenth century reached one hundred thousand, the vast majority of whom were Muslim.[15] When the Persian ambassador arrived in Leghorn in 1603, he learned that there were five thousand slaves in the city, the majority of whom would have been from North Africa.[16] The adventures of Alonso de Contreras, notwithstanding his bombastic claims, show the extent of European abduction of North African and Levantine Muslims in the early seventeenth century.[17]

That the Barbary corsairs captured thousands of Europeans is not in question; but then, the Europeans captured and enslaved more.[18] That the actions of the Barbary corsairs were motivated by greed and economic need are not in question; but they were also undertaken in retaliation for the violence committed against them by Europeans—government-sponsored acts of empire as well as disparate attacks of pirates and privateers. After Britain was already launched on its imperial project, with its "underbelly" of British captives seized by North African or Indian "natives," even the British trading agent in Algiers, John Morgan, insisted in 1729 that Barbary corsair actions be approached from a comparative European perspective and that if "natives" were to be denounced for capturing Christians, so should Christians be denounced for similar practices: "Have not the Pyrennees their Miquelets, and the Alps their Highlanders? Is not Sardinia and Corsica overrun with Troops of Banditti, even under the Protection of Noblemen? All this is evidently true, and it must be confessed, that with regard to such Practices, Christians too much resemble Barbarians."[19] Morgan concluded that the seizing of European captives and their use as galley slaves was something that the "Barbarians" had learned from the Christians.[20]

Still, as Gonçal López Nadal quoted from Joseph Fontana, "Our history books say, for example, that France took over Algiers to defend itself against the piracy of petty Muslim kings. But they do not tell us that these North African kingdoms were, in their turn, victims of European piracy that prevented them from developing normal trade and forced them into corsairing." Nadal then comments, "It is encouraging to see this deliberate twisting of the popular concepts of piracy and corsairing (contrasting the first as seen from a Christian viewpoint with the second in terms of its consequences for the Islamic world), and refreshing to see the attempt to be beyond the usual tired clichés like 'nest of pirates' and 'corsair republics.'"[21]

Unfortunately, such "refreshing" insights have been ignored by most Anglo-Saxon historians despite the fact that Nadal and other scholars have painstakingly researched both the European and the Islamic side of piracy, and have shown the extent of European enslavement of North African Muslims. Scholars such as Ahmad Bu Sharab, Moulay Belhamissi, Jean-Louis Miege, Salvatore Bono, C. M. Senior and Christopher Lloyd have shown the depredations of European pirates, "terrorists" of the sea,[22] while Lucien Misermont, in a very early study of the French 1683 bombardment of Algiers, showed how unwilling the French had been to return Algerian captives to their country and how much they had provoked the Algerians to declare war on them, which they knew they could win—and which indeed resulted in the destruction of the once-beautiful city.[23] For any study of captives in the early modern period to be comprehensive, account should be taken not just of English sources, but of European and North African sources as well, and not just about European captives but about European captivity of, and violence against, Muslims, too.[24]

What also needs to be recognized in the study of early modern captivity is the nature of captivity and the crucial difference between Muslim captivity of Christians and Christian captivity of Muslims. The North African Arabic sources present a major difference between the practice of captivity *(asr)* and slavery *('ubudiyya)*. The two Arabic terms have been translated by European scholars as "slavery" and have been interchangeably used despite having very different meanings. Although historians of Muslim slavery have examined other terms, such as mamluk, it is important to note that in the Arabic sources of the Maghrib, only *'abd* (slave) and *aseer* (captive) are used.[25] *'Ubudiyya* was practiced by Mediterranean and Atlantic Muslims and Christians against other races such as sub-Saharan Africans or American Indians; and as Christian theologians justified *'ubudiyya* throughout the conquest of the Americas, so did Muslim theologians justify enslaving *'abeed* from the country of the blacks, al-Sudan, to their punctilious rulers. *'Abeed* (pl. of *'abd*) were captives who were to spend the rest of their lives in slavery—as was the case with the Sudanese after their defeat by Mulay al-Mansur in 1591. A century later, after an army was raised of these *'abeed*, known as *'abeed al-Bukhari*, a letter sent by a jurist to Mulay Ismail (1692) stated that "the buying and selling of *'abeed* is religiously sanctioned since God almighty has said that He permits commercial exchange but prohibits usury."[26] Both Muslim and Christian rulers and theologians, along with their

God, had no qualms about the buying and selling of *'abeed,* be it in Africa or America.[27]

Asr, however, was different from *'ubudiyya. Asr* was a slavery that could be prevented or determined by mutual agreement. It was not the one-sided on-slaught on a weaker and more vulnerable race but an exchange and commod-ification of soldiers and sailors, traders and travelers, men and women and chil-dren, for the purposes of gaining ransom payments, exchanging them with captive coreligionists, or utilizing their skills. Throughout the early modern pe-riod, and especially between countries that either traded or fought, *asr* could be controlled, negotiated and bargained for because it pertained to captives who were taken in military or naval encounters between armies or privateers. To use the definition from Alexander H. de Groot (the only historian to recognize the difference), *asr* had the character of a stock exchange, while *'ubudiyya* had the character of a cattle market.[28] The Magharibi always viewed the Europeans within the context of *asr,* where captives could be bargained for and ransomed, sold or bought; they were not *'abeed.*[29] Indeed, the fifteenth-century jurist Ahmad bin Yahya al-Wansharisi had expressly prohibited *'ubudiyya;* a European captive *(aseer)* was always to have the opportunity of returning home.[30]

The Europeans, meanwhile, especially in Iberia and France, swung between the two modes of slavery. Sometimes the Muslim was an *aseer;* at others, espe-cially in the case of those who refused to convert to Christianity, it was *'ubudiyya* from which there was no freedom and in which the captives lost their status as individuals. Moriscos who were captured during an attempted escape to North Africa were consigned with their wives and children to lifelong *'ubudiyya.* And after Charles V decreed that all Muslims in reconquered Spain had to be bap-tized, those who resisted were consigned to the same fate.[31] In the appeal for help the Moriscos sent to the Ottoman ruler in 1501, they specifically indicated that they had become *'abeed.*[32] There was no hope for them—unless the sultan inter-vened militarily, which he did not.

The distinction between *'ubudiyya* and *asr* constitutes the chief difference between Euro-Christian enslavement of Magharibi and Magharibi enslavement of Euro-Christians, and helps further explain why there are by far more writings by and about European *asara* in North Africa than there are about Muslim cap-tives in Christendom: more captives returned from among the Muslims than from among the Christians. And while there were thousands of European cap-tives in North Africa, thousands of them who did not die or convert returned to their countries if their ransoms were paid. But of the tens of thousands of Magharibi who were sold in the European slave markets, few of them returned, and if they were transported to the European plantations in America, then there was not even the hope of return. European captives could always be located and ransomed by their governments—if the governments wanted. The Magharibi had no America to where they could send European slaves forever.

As Europeans feared the Barbary corsairs, so did the Moroccans, Algerians and Tunisians fear the Christian corsairs. Both the European and the Arabic records document the danger of the corsairs of Christendom. Even a small island like Malta, with its zealous knights, was able to seize thousands of Muslims and put them on sale in its very busy slave market. In 1602, the *Discours véritable de la prise de la ville de Mahomette [Hammamet] par les chevaliers de Malte* (Paris, 1602) mentioned 380 Muslim captives who had been seized by the Maltese in Tunis. In the following year, 165 Muslims were seized.[33] In 1607, the Moroccan rebel Ibn Abi Mahali warned that "Malta was between al-Gharb [Maghrib] and Egypt and like a snake, captures pilgrims;"[34] and in 1611, Ahmad bin Qasim's informant reported that there were fifty-five hundred Muslim captives in Malta alone, five hundred of whom were Andalusian or Moriscos and the rest were Turkish and Arab.[35] In 1624, after a sea battle between Maltese and Tunisian ships, the latter released five hundred Muslims from captivity.[36] As Ahmad bin Muhammad al-Maqqari sailed toward Egypt in 1627, he described the terror of the raging sea, but then added another terror: we feared, he recalled, the attack of the enemy, "may God destroy them and relieve the Muslims, especially of cursed Malta; whoever escapes the harm of the Maltese will have received divine help."[37]

If the small island of Malta could pose such danger to the Magharibi, larger and more powerful European countries could be devastating. From the early seventeenth century, the French privateers and pirates became active in Mediterranean seizure of Muslim men and women.[38] On 25 April 1623, the following report was submitted in Arabic by the Algerian dey to his French counterpart:

> During the reign of Husein, Pasha of Algeria, we released over eighty captives without ransom. The captive had attacked us and had been captured with their captain after which they were transferred to Algiers and treated very well in accordance with the honorable word of our sultan. This captain and the rest of the captured infidels were then sent back to you, and after they had been well treated by us, they killed those whom we had sent to you [delegation members] for no reason, and also killed Sinan Agha along with sixty other Muslims. They have done a heinous deed and broken the agreement and were the cause of this abominable deed. That captain of yours has also sent some men in our territories who kidnapped a number of Muslims and enslaved them; he also clashed with some of our ships and sank them, killing all on board.[39]

The French did not just capture Muslims, they also robbed and killed them. In 1640, a number of traders (the signatories were from Tunis, Alexandria, Izmir, Istanbul and Tripoli) complained to the secretary of the navy in France about a French pirate: they had thought Francesco Qrainer (?) a trader since he had gone to Ras al-Teen in Libya with merchandise to "buy and sell," but then he had seized fifty "souls." He freed a few of them after ransom was paid, keeping two women and five boys. The merchants hoped that the French king would act on their behalf because they no longer felt safe in their own land.[40] So widespread and lucrative was the trade in Muslim captives that the French poet Malherbe (1555–1628) celebrated such ongoing enslavement in verse:

Tantot nos navires brave
De la dépouille d'Alger
Viendront les Mores esclaves,
À Marseille decharger.[41]

[Later, our brave ships
from the plundering of Algiers
will come (with) Moorish slaves
to be discharged at Marseilles.]

The "esclaves" were needed for the French galleys, as the English diarist John Evelyn confirmed in his 1644 account. "Their rising forwards," he wrote, "& falling back at their Oare, is a miserable spectacle, and the noyse of their Chaines with the roaring of the beaten Waters has something of strange & fearfull in it, to one unaccostom'd. They are ruld, & chastiz'd with a bullspizle dry'd upon their backs, & soles of their feete upon the least disorder, & without the least humanity."[42]

The suffering of such Magharibi captives and their reaction against European exclusion and expulsion were recognized even by the Europeans themselves. Francis Knight wrote in 1640 that the Algerians had become active in piracy chiefly after the arrival of the Moriscos, who had been banished by "Phillip the third, King of Spaine": for these exiles "increased in ingenuitie of Arts in Fortifications . . . in Arming ships with great allacritie, to doe spoile upon Christians."[43] Corsairing was an act of revenge against Christian societies that had expelled Muslim converts from their homes and lands and later captured them and turned them into 'abeed. In 1684, a French ship seized Algerian captives, which necessitated the visit of an envoy in March 1685. Le Gazette de France reported that Hajj Muhammad Chelebi presented ten Barbary horses to the French king while the envoy's son, pleading with the king for the release of the captives, "se prosterna aux pieds du Roy: qui le reçeut tres favorablement" (prostrated himself at the king's feet, and was received with great favor).[44] But despite throwing himself at the feet of Louis XIV, the Algerian was not able to effect the liberation of his compatriots.[45] A few years later, in December 1691, Mulay Ismail wrote to the French king demanding that an exchange of Muslims be carried out, "tête pour tête" (head for head). He demanded the return of all captives from Salé and Rabat, Tetuan, Fez, Alcazar, and Meknes who had been captured in the last ten years. But the king refused. On 13 August 1693, Ismail complained to the French ambassador in Morocco that the French always wanted to discuss the liberation of their own people and nobody else: "Vous n'êtes venu que pour parler des esclaves François, et non pour autre chose"[46] (you don't come [here] except to talk about French slaves and not about anything else). In May 1698, Hajj Salim al-Qadi and his companions (including four children) presented a deposition to the French authorities. On their way on board a French ship from Alexandria to Sousse, the Tunisians and the Soussans had been attacked by a Maltese ship that took them all captive:

> [The Maltese captain] put us in chains and threw the crew into the sea. . . . We remained four days in irons, threatened by their knives and muskets. Then our captors brought the two ships together and looted our cargo: ten bags of rice, one of couscous, 100 towels, fifty silk handkerchiefs and . . . the captain then took fifty-six riyals and a half from the passengers, and a golden *khilkhal* [anklet/ankle bracelet] from a woman worth fifty riyals. . . . He was then about to throw all of us and the remaining crew [Muslims] into the sea, and sail away. This is what happened to us.[47]

The Case of Britain

As it was not true that there were "no slaves in France,"[48] neither was it true that there were no slaves in Britain. The seventeenth century opened with numerous Moroccan captives in England. In 1598, Queen Elizabeth wrote to Mulay al-Mansur assuring him that she was freeing the Moroccan captives who had sought refuge in England—and who had, she assured him, been well treated.[49] A few years later, negotiations were conducted for the release of other captives, and in one of her last letters in 1603, Queen Elizabeth promised Mulay al-Mansur to free his captured subjects and send back "a vuestras tierras con buen trattamento, como muchas vezes abemos hecho a Moros y a Turcos" (to your lands, with good treatment, as we have done many times the Moors and the Turks).[50] In that year, English piracy and seizure of ships and captives reached such a height that the Venetian ambassador in London declared the English "disturbers of the whole world"; they had grown, he added, "odious to all nations."[51] Robert Daborne's *A Christian Turned Turk* (1609–12) provided a portrait of one of these English-men, John Ward, who turned pirate (and Muslim) in Tunis and prospered by seizing European ships, including those of his former countrymen.[52]

In January 1622, the *muqaddam* (military commander) of Tetuan, Ahmad al-Naqsees, wrote to John Duppa that in the times of Queen Elizabeth, there had been peace between Morocco and the "English nation." But then, a certain English pirate by the name of Touching had begun to haunt the northern Moroccan coast and had captured a Moroccan ship along with all the sailors on board. The *muqaddam* sought the return of the captives, citing "the continuall exclamations of theire wives for the losse and slavery of theire husbands, my sonnes, with the cheefe of his towne."[53] Duppa then continued with one of the saddest of episodes pertaining to captives: after a community of Andalusian exiles had settled in

Tetuan, a relative visited them from Algiers and encouraged them to sell all their property and emigrate with him. They sold their lands and cattle, and as they were sailing to Algiers, they were "taken by our English fleet, who presently pillaged them of all the goods and money they had, not leaving behind them in Tettuan goods or any one of theire kindred [to be] able to releeve them or give them any comfort."[54] The Andalusians, who had been hoping for a new life in Algiers among their Muslim relatives, were now captives among the English *nasara* (Christians).

Two years later, one Mr. Madox of London "sold 150 Moors and Andalusians as slaves."[55] On 12 February 1625, a list was compiled of "the names of the Turks & Moors taken by the English and demanded by ye king and Diwans of Argeir": Hajji Hamed bin Hajji Ibrahim Velendiano from Crete, age 30; Mustafa Cullogli; Hamed Sharif Bilhama; Hamed Cortoby of Cordoba, age 25, captured in Malaga with his daughter Aisha; Hamed bin Gambora, captured in Gibraltar; Abdallah bin Renolt; Massouda, a negress belonging to Thomas Boutten; Ibrahim Tlemsani; Ali Tagarimo, captured in Alicante; Yusuf Tollogly, Tunisian, captured in Calais; "More 9 Turkes & mores in Barnett Seames Custody Dwelling In devonshir neare totnas."[56] These men and women came from all over the Islamic Mediterranean: from the Andalus to Tunis, and from Tlemcen in Algeria to Crete. They had been held among various European nationalities and were then seized by the English. Along with other Muslims, the captives may have been transported to England for purposes of selling them in any of the slave markets around Europe.

By the mid-1620s, Britons had become active in Mediterranean and Atlantic piracy, attacking all nationalities, Moroccan and French, Algerian and Spanish. On 15 October 1624, the pasha of Algiers complained to King James about the seizure of Muslims by his subjects, which forced Algerians to undertake similar deeds: "Some of your Maties Subiects did take some Moores, and Turkes, and now our Captaines did take certaine Englishmen, and sold them, which iff your Matie shall be pleased to send us the Moores, and the turkes, wee shall suddainly and out of hand putt the Christians att Liberty."[57] The pasha told the king to make sure his subjects distinguished between those "who are the Ennemyes and whoe are frinds." Evidently, English pirates were indiscriminate in their attacks, capturing both friend and foe. Three years later, English pirates still did not distinguish between enemy and friend, and the pasha wrote to King Charles complaining how his seamen were breaking the peace treaty negotiated in Constantinople and were pursuing the slave trade; he informed Charles that his subjects had captured some of those English pirates and would keep them in Algiers for eight months until Charles assured him of punishing his piratical subjects.[58] King Charles responded by authorizing the pasha to punish all his subjects who "doe violate or contravene" the agreements reached between the two countries.[59] But such warnings did not reduce piracy: in 1629, the admiralty court directed proceedings "against those who have spoiled ships of Algiers."[60] "These English pirates," spoke Mullisheg in Heywood's *The Fair Maid of the West, Part II,* "Have robb'd us of much treasure" (3.2.89–90).

Hundreds of Muslims were being captured by British seamen as indiscriminately as Britons were being captured by Barbary seamen. While some of the Moroccan captives may have been pirates, others were not and may well have been travelers in the Mediterranean who were unlucky enough to find themselves attacked by any of the European pirates that preyed on the North African shore. Many Moors were captured and imprisoned on false accusations, whereupon embarrassed Barbary and East Levant Company representatives intervened to effect their release. Evidently, it was not always clear to the captors who among the Muslims was the pirate and who was the innocent trader. That is why in two lists of Algerians and Moroccans who were captured on 21 June 1627, there is careful mention of the professional and social background of the captives. The captors wanted to ascertain the identity of their captives:

> The Names of Turkes e Moores belonging to Algeir taken the 21 of June 1627:
>
> 1. Solyman sonne of Mahamet Tailor
>
> 2. Mahamet sonne of Achmet, scriuan
>
> 3. Hagem Hamet sonne of Zeyn Tailor
>
> 4. Causim sonne of Garib shoemaker
>
> 6. Mahamet sonne of Ally mender
>
> 7. Ebrahim sonne of Useph shoemaker
>
> 8. Ally sonne of Usyn Tailor
>
> 9. Sayid sonne of Caussim mender
>
> 10. Useph sonne of Abdalla soldier
>
> 11. Velly soldier of Algeir
>
> 12. Shaban soldier . . .
>
> 13. Ragep of Algeir soldier
>
> 14. Omer sonne of Achmet Tailor
>
> 15. Hadgy musud of Algeir sailor.[61]

The list explains a little about the captives: The first thirteen had been away from Algiers for over a year, and while sailing near the Welsh coast, were run ashore by Captain Hart of Dartmouth, who had then taken their ship and imprisoned them. Since the capture of the ship, thirteen other sailors on board had died. The next three had been slaves at Madwill in Spain and had come to Flushing in the Netherlands: these could well be some of the crew of the bark that William

Draper saw there sometime before giving his deposition on 18 April 1625.[62] The fourteenth and fifteenth individuals had come ashore a "Tartan" at Saltash with five more who had since died. Although there were three soldiers among the captives, the rest belonged to small professions: button maker, tailor, mender, shoemaker and sailor. These men were clearly not dangerous, which may explain why they were permitted to go "wandering and begging about the city of London." As captives in North Africa often begged to collect money for their ransoms, so did these captives.

The other list belonged to Moroccans:

The Names of the Turkes and Moores belonging to Tutuan and Sally in barbary taken the 21 of June 1627:

1. Hamet Reys sonne of Yaah [Yahya?] of Tutan seaman

2. Mahamet sonne of Usin of Tutuan sailor

3. Mahamet sonne of Hussin of Tutuan sailor

4. Mahomet Hogy of Sally scriuan

5. Mahamet sonne of Achmet of Sally Tailor

6. Mussud sonne of Mahamet saylor

7. Abdaraman sonne of Ally Lasis sailor

8. Mahamet sonne of Mahmout: a boye

9. Issa sonne of Ally cooke

10. Abderahman sonne of Syd sailor

11. Mahamet sonne of Hassan sailor

12. Abdalla sonne of Hassan shoemaker

13. Ally sonne of Mahamet sailor

14. Causin sonne of Hamet: buttin maker

15. Umbarac sonne of Ally shippboye

16. Mahamet sonne of Achmet shipboye

17. Casamuch sonne of Useph shipp boye:

18. Hamet sonne of Hussin of Tutuan soldier

He was a slave at Inn [. . . e] was one of those that stole awaye a galley from course e came to flushing.[63]

Muslims had been holding English captives in their ship, but then the latter, "taking their opportunitie surprised them, and brought them into Cornwall, where they were imprisoned." They were kept there for six months. It is unlikely that these prisoners would have been permitted to beg: they may have been viewed as dangerous. But the list interestingly shows a number of boys, a common feature of shipping in the early modern period. Their likely fate would have been similar to British ship boys who were seized by Barbary seamen: conversion and integration. Many Muslim boys, captured by Christian seamen, were converted. In a letter from Winchester on 31 October 1636, Dr. Robert Mason explained that there were "two young Moores not above 13 or 14 yeares of age who some think here in regard to the tenderness of their yeares may be made good Christians." Otherwise, the boys would be condemned along with the other Moors with whom they had been captured, some to be executed in Portsmouth and the rest to be held on the Isle of Wight "in regard to ye frequent allarmes they haue given to these parts."[64]

In 1630, the inhabitants of Salé wrote to King Charles complaining about the depredations committed by the English captain Neaston—and a year later, the Moroccan ruler, Mulay al-Walid, asked Charles I to release all captives back to *bilad al-Islam* (the lands of the Muslims) whether the captives were Moroccan or from other Muslim regions.[65] The letter exists in both Arabic and English. The Arabic is harsh and pointed, the English gentle and courteous. Actually, the English translation puts words in the Moroccan's mouth to make him sound as if he is importuning rather than demanding. The Arabic reads: "Release the [Muslim] captives for the benefit of Islam and do not keep a single Muslim captive, but send them back to the lands of Islam whether they belong to our country or to other countries in the House of Islam. Then we will not keep any captive from the tribes of the English—as long as you keep the promise." Unlike the English version, the Arabic captures the anger, defiance and retaliatory intent of the Magharibi.

King Charles also received a letter from a Moroccan chieftain promising cooperation with him, if he would curb his privateers and ensure the return of Muslim captives to the lands of Islam. The danger of British piracy was spreading throughout the Mediterranean. The letter, which survives unfortunately only in the English translation, provides the voice of a Moroccan chieftain as he discussed the matter of captivity with the king. It shows the anxiety, fear and desperateness with which Moroccans and other Muslims viewed the captivity of their coreligionists by the British. How much of the importuning voice was there in the original version cannot be determined; still, the letter conveys the deep concern among Magharibi for captives in all the lands of the Christians:

In the name of God

Siddi Alli ben muhamed, ben hamed, ben musa. To the high and mightie Prince, Charles, sonne of James of famous memory, king of England— Scotland, Fraunce, and Ireland, wisheth health. Wee haue receiued yor letter for which wee thanke you. The peace betwixt the English and Morres shallbe as in the tyme of Mulley Hamet [Ahmad al-Mansur] and Queen Elizabeth, whereof wee give you full assurance on our part, hoping it shall continue firme on both sides, rather better than before. And your merchants shall haue as they haue had heretofore with us, free trade and commerce, and shall be free as in their owne countrie. And as manie English-men captiues as wee shall heare of in our Countrie or els where lying in our power to release; wee shall by gods assistance send home for their countrie, as wee have done heretofore: hoping you will also haue a caire that as manie Moores as shall flee into your countrie for refuge from Spaine, france or anie other that may liekwise be sent home for their countrie—as wee have now againe done your subiects, before your letters came to our hands, who were cast away by the Cape Blanco, whom as soone as wee heard of wee sent for them, paying for them out of or owne purse: as this your messenger can enforme you. Wee haue written our letter to you in our owne language, and haue caused it to be translated into english. Wee shall be glade to know what thinge is in our countrie may pleasure your Matie: and shall be ready to furnish you, as wee hope you will doe thelike to us with some things wee stand now in need of. Your agent Captaine John Harrison can give you further to understand and so wee commend you to the protection of the onlie one god. Given in this the 5th of September. 1040 [1630][66]

Always threatened by the power of nearby Spain, Sidi Ali was seeking support from England, both militarily and commercially. He was willing to open up his markets for English trade and return all English captives—if King Charles would promise to reciprocate and force his pirates off the seas. Most important, he was hopeful that Muslim captives who fled from Catholic captivity would be helped by the English to return to their lands. After all, despite differences in religion, both Muslim captives and Christian captors shared belief in the same "one god."

Unfortunately, the British privateers were finding in piracy and slavery a lucra-tive enterprise that compensated for economic decline at home and for the loss of markets in a Europe torn by the Thirty Years War. So destabilizing did these pirates become that both King Charles and the representatives of the merchant companies identified them as the casus belli with the Moroccans. John Harrison described the problems he was facing as a result of the activities of the British corsairs. While negotiating with the Moroccans for the safety of British traders, he found that the safety that needed to be negotiated was not only that of the British but of the Moroccans, too. In a letter of 9 October 1631, he complained how a British ship had captured a Saletian ship and sold the sailors "for slaves to the Spaniardes." The culprits, as he noted, were "one Madock maister and Wye merchant." Such a breach of agreement was not only embarrassing, he noted, but dangerous for him as well as for the resident British merchants. He therefore implored the king to write to the king of Spain to release the captives and to have all "the actors in that business . . . committed to prison for their contempt against the Kings proclamation."[67] So apprehensive was Harrison that he wrote another letter a week later (15 October), again blaming his compatriots for the troubles they were causing him and other merchants. He wanted a "milston hanged about their necks and cast into the sea than so manie honest and innocent Christians suffer and lyke to suffer for their saikes."[68] The actions of the pirates were undermining the reputation of the British traders and their king: "It is no merveyle though both Turks and Moores, by their example, slight both His Majestie and our nation." The pirates were giving the Barbary corsairs the justification to attack English and Scottish ships, and to plan in the year after to "threaten the Channell, even our English Channell . . . saying that wee Christians always breake [our word] first."[69] Harrison clearly recognized that when the Barbary corsairs seized British captives, they were not acting out of callous brutality but were delivering a measured retaliation against those who reneged on trading agreements in favor of piracy. Not all the British captives were the "underbelly of empire," suffering and enduring manifold tribulations at the hand of their North African captives; some were pirates and cutthroats, celebrating robbery and brigandage on the high seas.

To aggravate matters, many Barbary corsairs who were captured and taken to England were given the death penalty. Let "your Commissioners know," wrote Robert Mason on 13 October 1636, "that I shall humbly offer it to their Lords consideration whether it be fitt they [captured Moors] should be executed within the Jurisdiction of the Vice-Admiral part of them att Portsmouth & part of them in the Isle of Wight."[70] Meanwhile, and like other pirates, Britons stripped captured ships to their hulls and profited from the sale. An inventory on 10 October 1638 of a North African ship that was captured and taken to London shows the eagerness of the English captors to sell everything they had seized: the "fforemast Rigging," the "Maynemast Rigging," rigging ropes, bowlines, shrouds, "Tye," "One Broaken pott wth a little Tallow in him," "Two Brasse Bares, wth fowre Iron chambers," a sponge, a ladle, eighteen round shot, two longer shot, one old cable and other items. The ship could have been a pirate ship, although it was not heavily armed (only eighteen shots, unless the rest had already been used). Whatever the ship was, the sale of its possessions would bring in a good profit to the captors.[71] The treasure of the Salcombe Bay wreck, consisting of Moroccan jewelry and ingots, may well have been on board an English or Welsh or Cornish pirate ship that sank near the treacherous Salcombe Bay after returning from a season of pillaging the North African shores. The presence of gold earrings with the Moroccan coins (struck between 1594 and 1640), along with copper coins from Friesland, pottery pieces from Germany, and "a merchant's seal of brass or bronze, marked RM," point away from a Moroccan pirate ship and in the direction of a British ship, active in piracy and trade between the European mainland, North Africa and Salcombe Bay in Devon.[72]

Philip Massinger described the treatment of Muslim slaves in *A Very Woman* (1634)—showing it to be quite similar to the treatment of African slaves in America or Christian slaves in North Africa: "Sell the Moors, there," the slave master says, "feel, he's high and lusty, / and of a gamesome nature . . . / Mark but his limbs, that slave will cost ye fourscore. / An easie price, turn him about, and view him" (3.1.49–55).[73] "Of what Religion are they?" continues the buyer about captured Moorish girls. "What you will sir," comes the answer, "So there be meat, and drink in't" (3.1.64–66). Like all captives, the young were easily converted to the religion of their captors. And, in the case of female captives, they were abused sexually. Upon buying a Moorish girl nine years old, the buyer asks,

> Cit. Is she a maid, do'st think?
> Merch. I dare not swear Sir,
> She is nine year old, at ten you shall find few here.[74]

In 1637, the master of an English ship, one Mr. Marriot, captured fifteen Muslims and sold eleven in Spain, making a profit of 101 pounds and nine shillings, of which he was willing to give one-tenth to the king.[75] In 1643, more than one hundred Muslim pilgrims traveling by sea were taken captive, and "God delivered some by ransom and some by proximity" to the shore.[76] So proud were the English about the pillage committed by their compatriots that dramatists did not hesitate to celebrate it in song:

> To Tunis and to Argiers Boyes,
> Great is our want, small be our ioyes;
> Let's then some voyage take in hand
> To get us means by Sea or Land.
> Come follow me my Boyes, come follow me.
> . . . .
> Methinks, my Boyes, I see the store
> Of precious Gems and golden Ore;
> Arabian Silks and Sables pure
> Would make an Haggard stoop to th'lure.
> Come follow me, &c.[77]

There was pride in pillaging Muslim cities full of gems and gold—a pride that was "daily Acted" on the London stage.

In 1662, the French press reported that some English ships had docked in Cartagena with two hundred Algerian captives for sale.[78] Soon after, the "King of Argeirs" wrote to King Charles II: "One of yr ships have taken one of our prize, in which was many of our Peoples, of whome we have had noe tidings [. . .] but of the Captaine who assures us that they were English that tooke him whereupon we have Called the [English] Consull [in Algiers] before us all times, but hietherto never had any satisfaction or word of her [. . .] you are always demanding & putting us in mind of the two Christians, soe on the other side, tis but reason that wee looke after our right alsoe."[79]

As the Algerian complained, the lives and freedom of the English captives were to be cherished and preserved, but not of the Algerians. The tension with Algiers was resolved by a treaty signed on 29 January 1663, which was widely disseminated. The king's purpose in the treaty was to warn not the Algerians but "his

Majesties Subjects" about committing brigandage on the "Turks": evidently, British ships that were hired by Turks and Moors to transport them and their properties were betraying their customers and selling them into Spanish, Italian or Maltese slave markets. The treaty was therefore to assure the Muslims that British commanders would not betray them and would "to the utmost of their power, by fighting or otherwise, preserve and defend them against any whatsoever."[80] Much as the treaty established a mechanism to ensure the safety of the Turks and the Moors and the commitment of their transporters, in 1667, the *agha* of Algiers wrote to the king complaining about "ye Spoils & Dipredeations of late committed upon our good Subjects in their Persons Shipps & Goods by ye Men of War" of England.[81] But the British pirates would not desist: In 1669, "the Bristoll took the 7th of this moneth [September] an Algier bark with 54 persons on board whereof some women & severall children";[82] a short time later, it was reported that "fower" Moors had ended up in the hands of "mr. waren . . . in Ingland."[83] Actually, "A Memoriall of what damage done to the Algerines since the break of the 5th of September, 1669" mentioned the following numbers of North African captives who had been taken off Algerian ships: eleven, fifty-six, twelve, sixteen, twenty, eighteen, and twenty.[84]

By the second half of the seventeenth century, North Africans did not have the kind of naval technology the British and the French possessed, and suffered as a result. In May 1671, the British fleet lay siege to Algiers, destroyed seven ships, took three as prize, and killed "360 of their best Men and upwards." It has pleased God, an anonymous author wrote, to "order it so."[85] Britons were both military and religious conquerors who did not really have to engage the natives or negotiate with them—only force them into obedience or make them face dire consequence. Four years later, on 14 June 1675, Sir John Narbrough was instructed to preserve "to his own use such Turks or Moors as he may happen to take in ships belonging to Tripoli, 'it being likely to turn to better account to the king that they be kept for the service of his own galley at Tangier than sold or otherwise disposed of.'"[86] He was again told that all Turkish and Moorish captives whom he seized in the Mediterranean should be "preserved for His Majties Service for ye Gallies."[87] In July, he chased

> on shore and burnt a Tripoleese ship (once a man-a-war, now a merchantman) out of which he hath taken 98 negroes, men, women, and children and 24 Greeks, The latter whereof he desires directions as to their being made slaves (they pretending themselves Christians) and the former he hath sent to be sold at Malta, his Majesty and my Lords were pleased to approve of his proceedings touching the negroes, and to resolve, in consideration of the Greeks sailing not as passengers but as of the ship's company, and so in hostility with us, as also of their being dwellers in Tripoli and consequently unlikely to be Christians otherwise than in pretence.[88]

In 1679, the governors of Algiers complained to the Dutch about the English, how they had "taken Vessels, and made Slaves of our People."[89] The treaty of 25 November 1680 between Tangier's Colonel Edward Sackville and Muhammad Bin Haddu stipulated that the English could go hunting and fishing wherever and whenever they chose outside the boundaries of the presidio, but if "a Moore should be seene or take within ye aforesaide Limitts . . . shall remaine Captive."[90] In 1681, Mulay Ismail complained to Colonel Kirke that "in the Citie of Tanger there are fortie seven Moorish slaves" whom he was eager to ransom by offering two cows for each captive[91]—an offer the Whitehall Committee of Tangier, safely distant from the difficulties of the British presidio, flatly rejected. We will be, wrote Ismail, "exposed to ye centure of our people, and that it may afford them just occasion of scandal that we have made peace with the English & yet suffer ye Moors to remain slaves even within their own Countrey."[92] When Ismail complained afterward to Kirke that he had found, by reading Christian sources, that the English, being Christians, should not take captives, the Englishman was adamant that Christianity did not prohibit slavery:

> Whereas your Matie says that our Laws permitt us not to make slaves of the Moors, I must assure yr Mtie that we have no Laws that doe forbid it, & since the King my Master buys Slaves whenever he has an occasion for them, yr Mtie will see it is not disagreeable to our constitutions.[93]

In 1682, 250 Algerian captives were sent to Tangier for slave labor there.[94] Only after lengthy negotiations did the Moroccan ambassador to England succeed that same year in securing a promise for the release of some of them. The king "took also resolve to deliver to the Secretary all the Slaves at Tangier that are properly his own, and that all the rest shall be released or removed."[95] On reaching Morocco, the ambassador received 79 Muslims from Tangier,[96] but he later complained to King Charles that there were 5 Muslim captives on an English ship whom he had demanded of the captain. The latter sent him one back, who soon after died, as did the second captive. The ambassador later discovered that 10 captives had already died.[97]

A list of captives in Tangier provides helpful information about the background and status of Muslim slaves. The list was prepared because the Moroccan ruler insisted on the release of his own subjects if British captives were to be released. "How can we with a quiet mind," wrote Mulay Ismail to Kirke, "consent to the going in of a hundred and fiftie Christians to Tanger leaving the building of our house, carried on by the hands of those Slaves, unfinished, and at the same time see four hundred captive Moors working at the gates of Tanger and carrying stone and morter to the Mole."[98] In order to effect the release of the British captives, Colonel Kirke had therefore to buy back the Muslims from their British owners, a task that he found quite difficult.[99] The list identified the captives who had been successfully bought back from their Tangier owners for the purpose of exchange. It is noticeable that the number of captives is by far less than the four hundred whom Ismail had mentioned. Slaves were very likely kept away from the "census" in order for their owners to keep them in their service.

"A list of the Mahumetan Slaves bought on his Maties account of severall Inhabitants in Tanger" presents the following information about forty-three slaves:

	p[ieces] of eight
Norlo	112
Hamet Ali	112
Ali Cason	112 Belonging to
	Daniel Vansesterfleet,
Mahamed Sin	112 James Waring, &
Joseph Ali	112 Robt. Cuthbert
Mesot Mortegett	112
Hamet Benali	112
Jeragile Ali	112
Hamet Genduz	112
Mustafa Mahomet	112
Ali Bensily	112
Baram Ali	100
Mahamed Ali	100
Berecquet Negro	100
Shaban Benkalifa	100
Hamet Bensoliman	112
Bucark Negro	100
Hamet Benhamet	112
Oran Bacicha	150
Mahamed de Shezrell	100 Belonging to
Jetta Secola	100 Robt. Cuthbert
Ali de Santa Cruz	100
Oran de Tunis	100
Hamet de Cabilla	100
Rahall de Birkey	100
Cassim de [?]	100
Aldraman Granado	100 Belonging to
	Capt. Giles
Mahamed Ben Musa	100
Ali Zensana	100
Hamet Caras	100
Hamet Stombly	100
Belle Mahamed de Smyrna	100

Haretta Mahamed	100
Mahamad Bebeck	100 Belonging to Capt. Collier
Mahamad Hessen	100
Hamet Hessen	100
Joseph	100
Oran de Tripoli	100 Belonging to
Absalom de Misery	100 Major Hope
Mahamed de Saley	100
Ali Benhamet	100 Belonging to Capt. Beverley
Hamet de Argier	100
	(Total: 43)[100]

The slaves came from all over the Islamic world: Algiers, Tripoli, Egypt, Salé, Smyrna, Tunis, Santa Cruz and other places. Berbers were included, as well as sub-Saharan Africans ("Negro"). Twenty-eight of the slaves had been bought for 100 pieces of eight; the rest for 112 pieces; only "Oran Baisha" went for 150 pieces because he was a Turkish pasha government official. As in the case of British slaves held by Magharibi captors, these captives "belonged" to specific owners: for them to be released, sale arrangements had to be made with their owners and not just with the political authority.

Along with the devastating captivity and enslavement of Muslims was the bombardment of their cities by the British fleet. And while it is accurate to state, as Linda Colley does, that the British did not always use their superior war technology against the North African coasts, it is important to recognize that the reason was not British fear of repercussions from the Ottoman Empire[101] (the Ottomans would have actually welcomed the bombardment of the Moroccans, especially under the first of the Sa'dian and the first of the Alawite rulers), but rather that France was doing the job for the British. Although the British were rivals of the French, they were not unhappy to see the French bombard North African cities—if only because they hoped to win further the allegiance of the traumatized Muslims who were helpless and defenseless before the new lightweight cannons that had such a long range that no ground fire could reach them.

In 1683, the French fleet attacked Algiers with a technology of bombardment that would devastate the city, irrevocably turn the balance of power against the North Africans, and make Europeans appear so fearsome that only God could defeat them. "O God," wrote the Moroccan traveler Ibn Zakour, who witnessed the attack on Wednesday of Rabee al-Thani in 1094 A.H./April 1683, "deliver us from its [bombardment] evil and remove its terror. O God protect the houses from their [French] earthquakes, and defeat that wicked enemy."[102] On 16 August 1683, the British consul, Paul Rycault, reported the following: "By the best

Computation I can make the French have spent 4000 Bombas out of the 6000: they first brought with them and ye damage to this towne is about 800: houses & shops beat downe besides 4 ships 3 fettezes and one gally sunk, and two half Galleys upon ye Rocks."[103]

"Multitudes of People dayly flocking out to the Gardens," wrote an Englishman in Algiers to his friend in London, "for fear of the Bombs crying out with a General Voice, that the World must needs be now at an end, that never such things as these were seen, that they were not of mans Invention, but sent by the Devil from Hell."[104] Fifty years later, the son of the mufti of the city, Hussein bin Rajab, recalled in his account about Algiers the French destruction of his house, the damage to the city, the flight of merchants and the misery that ensued.[105] The Europeans were not forgotten either, as destroyers or as slave traders.

Two years after Algiers, it was the turn of Tripoli to experience the modernization of European war technology. On 18 June 1685, Sheikh Ahmad bin Muhammad bin Nasir witnessed the French bombardment of Tripoli. His account, which he wrote years later, reflected the Muslim terror and total bewilderment at the new European technologies of war:

> During the Friday evening prayer, the cannons of the infidels (may God destroy them) hurled on us their cannonballs and their bombs. We saw and heard what we have never seen or heard before. At the same time as we saw the lightning of a shot going out of the mouth of the cannon, we saw a red ball, similar to a shooting star, rising into the air. It was immediately followed by another one that rose even higher than the first, and when it fell and touched the ground, it exploded at the point where it fell and broke up into fragments, with a tremendous noise, which deafened the ears. It hit buildings that it destroyed, flat terrains it dug up, high buildings or columns that it flattened, trees it uprooted and set on fire. It happened sometimes that the bomb buried itself in the ground and soon after exploded with a sound more terrifying than any other bomb. . . . One night when the bombardment was intense, the enemy kept on firing on us until the following morning more than one thousand cannonballs, according to a jurist in the city.[106]

In 1687, two English captains bought four hundred Muslim slaves in Venice,[107] and in 1688, a Maltese ship attacked a British ship and captured a number of Libyan travelers and traders, along with their possessions. The pasha complained to King James II about the captives, including "six little Captive beleevers, and two women" and the loss of goods and provisions worth fifty thousand dollars. In order to urge King James toward action, he tried to shame as well as threaten him. In Malta, he wrote, "they have no respect to your Passport, and they have put your Colours the bottome upwards." And if the king failed to redress the injustice, he continued, then he would make sure that British ships would not be safe in all "the Ports belonging to the Countries of Islam," from

Egypt to Constantinople.[108] In 1689, Nathaniel Lodington reported from Tripoli that nine years earlier, "seven moores merchants belonging to this Place" had been seized by Venetian pirates from "a small English Vessell bound from Smirna." It was suspected that the English captain had colluded with the Venetians in the seizure of the Moors.[109] In September 1690, the admiral of the fleet in the Mediterranean was instructed to locate British captives and liberate them by exchanging them with Muslim captives on his or other British ships. And lest the seamen and captains resist such an exchange, they were to be given an allowance equal to the amount of money the Muslim captives would have fetched had they been sold. Evidently, seamen and their captains relied on the sale of Muslims for part of their wages.[110] In 1692, one Hamza Khoja from Tunis arrived in Smirna, whereupon the English consul residing there seized from him all his cargo, to the value of 12,700 dollars. Despite repeated appeals for the return of his possessions, Khoja did not receive justice. Over thirty years later, and unwilling to forget the injustice, he was still hoping for restitution from London: a letter from the Tunisian ruler Hussein bin Ali to King George I reminded the latter of the injustice that awaited rectification.[111] In 1723, Algerian privateers seized three British ships, which the pasha immediately released; but then, continued the pasha in his letter to King George, the British took "many of our Subjects." Some were able to ransom themselves, one "being much tormented, killed himself," but the rest were then sold into Spanish slavery[112].

*   *   *

Throughout the age of European commercial and maritime expansion, the Barbary States were looking toward building fleets that could trade and travel, similar to those in European possession. They so trained their own mariners and seamen, often by learning from European captives and converts, that in the first decades of the seventeenth century, the Magharibi began to show signs of successfully adapting to European seafaring technology. But as they ventured out into the open seas, European ships, from Spain to Malta, and from England to the Papal States, attacked them and carried them into slavery. By the second half of the seventeenth century, the "northern invasion" began to take its toll on the North African populations and economies as the European superpowers prevented the Barbary regions from developing their own merchant fleets and from building the infrastructure of maritime trade and exploration that had made the Europeans rich and dominant. Indeed, the onslaught of the European fleets and pirates on the emergent Magharibi navies, the destruction of fishing and trading vessels by the hundreds, and the capture of the well-trained and well-tried Muslim sailors and sea commanders resulted in the weakening of the commercial and naval strength of the Maghrib and the creation of a "saigne humaine que firent subir a l'économie maghrebine" (a human bloodletting that caused the Maghribi economy to suffer).[113] The depredations the French and the British committed in the Barbary coastal cities, both on the Atlantic and on the Mediterranean shores, along with the captivity of "Moors" and "Turks," resulted in the decay of cities, agriculture and trade and led to a serious decline in the numbers of maritime professionals. As Elroy Martin Corrales confirms, numerous contemporary reports reveal the "grave dommage que l'activité corsaire espagnole avait occasionné à l'économie maritime marocaine"[114] (the grave damage the Spanish corsair activity inflicted on Moroccan maritime economy)—not only Spanish, but British and French, too. This ongoing destruction of Magharibi enterprise was the chief factor that led to the slow death of commerce and the subsequent financial and economic decline of the Maghrib.

So dangerous were the European fleets and so destructive their bombardment that fear of Christian violence, maritime attacks, captivity and terrorization became indelibly marked in Magharibi culture and memory. In many regions, coastal inhabitants deserted their port towns and sought the security of the mountains. "They were not able to defend themselves," wrote a French observer about the Moroccans in 1671, "from the daily visits, which the [Spanish] Brigantines were alwayes making in the Plains: where after they had plundered all they could find, they carried away Prisoners all the Inhabitants into the neighboring Spanish Garrisons, and often into Spain itself, when they caught them."[115] Half a century later, the "northern invaders" were still viewed as harbingers of danger and terror: "the very Women of Sallee and Mamura," reported the English captain John Braithwaite in 1714, "used to frighten their Children, when untoward, by telling them Delgarno [a Spanish sea captain] was coming for them."[116] The Moors, admitted Jean Baptiste, the French redemptionist, "oppose the Descent of any Enemy [on their shores], as taking it for some European Corsair coming to steal away either themselves or their Cattle."[117] From Atlantic Salé to Mediterranean Tunis, from mother to child, there was fear of the Euro-Christians as abductors and pillagers.

In this pillaging, the British played a leading role; this is why they were not forgotten. In the middle of the nineteenth century, the Tunisian traveler Ahmad bin Abi Diyaf (1804–1873) recorded how in "the days of Mustapha Laz [ca. 1665], the ships of the English came to Ghar al-Milh and burnt a ship and bombarded the city towers, whose ruins can still be seen today."[118]

5

From Tangier to Algiers

From the 1650s on, Britain assumed a dominant role in the Mediterranean. Although the seizure of British men and ships by the Barbary States continued, Britain asserted its naval and military presence and changed the course of North African history. In the second half of the seventeenth century, and as a result of maritime victories especially against the Dutch whose shipping rivalry they drastically reduced, Britons developed a sense of imperial glory and destiny. Their riches and ascendancy became evidence of cultural superiority and religious certitude. Having assured themselves that God was English, they now turned to make the world believe that, too, and to bring the natives of the world under the benevolent commercial and military imperium of the worshipers of the English God. In particular, they wanted to make "the Moors before the English bend," as Edmund Waller wrote on 3 June 1665.[1]

This shift in power can best be examined through the new relations that developed with North Africa after the marriage of Charles II to Catherine of Baraganza on 21 May 1662, and Britain's acquisition of the Portuguese garrison of Tangier, an "expensive wedding present," as it proved to be.[2] For the first time, the British found themselves in possession of a colony in the Muslim world, just as the Spaniards and the Portuguese had had for two centuries. For the next twenty years, they would grapple with that colony, unable to formulate a policy that would ensure its success and continuity. In this respect, it was unfortunate that the most direct and cheek-by-jowl encounter Britons had with Muslims in the early modern period took place in a region dominated by slavery and counterslavery, where traders, soldiers, sailors and travelers, both men and women from both sides of the Mediterranean, met each other in the context of religious difference, commercial rivalry, maritime conflict and brutal captivity. It was an encounter that neither Britons nor Magharibi easily forgot.

The Beginnings of Empire, 1662–1680

As soon as Tangier was transferred to King Charles II on 30 January 1662, the question of Britain's role in North Africa immediately came up: how should

Britons approach the new continent, a corner of which they now possessed? With their garrison at a strategic corner, was Tangier to serve as a commercial hub for Euro-African trade, or was it to be a military bridgehead to the colonization of other parts of Africa? If, as Janice E. Thomson observed, "trading companies operated in the [Islamic] East, while the plantation/colonial companies concentrated in the New World," Tangier was geographically and ideologically in the middle between East and West, trade and colonization.[3] Britons fluctuated in their view of Tangier, beginning with imperial hopes—the same kind that had been sounded earlier in the century by Roberts and Harrison—but then settling for trading goals.

At first, Britons treated Tangier in similar fashion to the settlements of North America, which by the Restoration period were consolidating their boundaries, destroying the Indians, establishing economic and commercial cooperation with each other and defining their evangelical role in the "wilderness." Although Tangier was a small city that had been built by the Portuguese, it was immediately declared a bastion that would "enlarge our Dominions in yt sea & advance thereby ye Hon. of o[u]r Crowne," as, on 6 September 1661, King Charles instructed his cousin, Henry Mordaunt, second Earl of Peterborough, who went as Tangier's chief governor. The earl was to govern Tangier "& suburbs thereof, and of all other Citys, Townes, Villages, Forests, Castles & Islands, Landes & Countreyes which now are or which hereafter during this Our Commission shall be delivered or reduced to our Obedience."[4] Tangier was to be the beginning of the British Empire in Africa. King Charles used words very similar to those in the Charter of Virginia, which his grandfather had issued half a century earlier: Tangier was to be turned into a fully fledged settlement with wives joining the two thousand footmen and five hundred cavalrymen that sailed to the garrison. Tangier was to become another Jamestown or Plymouth.

In support of this view, a certain "Mr. James" wrote to "invit people to settle downe upon the coast of barbary I meane Protestants one towne after another beginning from Tanger east but neuer goe further into the country."[5] Such colonization would yield "more then either east or west indies due to theire severall proprietours for it exceeds them both in respect of neernes & a climate our bodys are acquanted with." The English would then be able to conquer Tetuan, "the London of Barbary," and from there continue into North Africa, at the cost of "nothing." They would go into Algeria and reach Tunisia, where the inhabitants, reeling under Turkish bondage, would welcome their arrival as liberators, and "without all Doubt would joyne with us." Westward, the English would occupy Asila and build a fort from which to dominate "above six hundred thousand acres of land" that will be needed to maintain the army, and provide a "secure place to feede all our horses or other Cattle we can steale from the moores." They would then take over the silver mines in that region and turn the native inhabitants into slaves who would produce for them so much silver as "it may Prove better then Potozi."[6] From Tangier, the English could create a new America thereby making France, Italy and Turkey "tremble."

To what extent the author of these goals was familiar with the demography of North Africa—large, urban and highly militarized populations—or its geography is unclear. He could have been echoing the king's words, with some more details drawn from the Spanish experience in America. His and the king's hopes and aspirations were reflected that year in a prose rendering of Thomas Heywood's play, *The Fair Maid of the West*, by "the accurate Pen of I.[John] D. [Dauncey] Gent." The novelization of the play followed Heywood's story line but was even more inventive and elaborate than the original. Gone is the timidity of English Bess and Spencer that had appeared in part 1, during the halcyon days of Anglo-Moroccan coordination. Instead, there is power and assertiveness along with ridiculing contumely for the Moors. When Bess enters the court of Mullisheg, she views herself as an ambassadress for an emergent imperial country; she presents herself in the "most gorgeous feminine Robes, as well for her own pleasure, as to let the Moors have a sight of those beauties which England was enriched." Upon seeing her, the Moroccan Bey *(sic)* falls "down on his knees, and terming her the Goddess of the Sea, made proffer to kisse the hem of her garments, but being raised up by her, and told that she expected no such adoration, but onely came in thither to desire some relief of fresh water, and other necessaries for her Seamen."[7] Bess assumes a prominent role in the court of the Moors, and manages to free "an English Divine" who had "vainly endeavoured to convert the Moores." "Vainly" is an addition in the novel, for now there is no serious interest in converting the Moors, rather in trading with them and consolidating geographical domination. When later, Mullisheg threatens to punish Bess if she does not give up her love for Spencer, she retorts with the well-known English courage and bravado that any English maid, on her own in a foreign land, expresses to the king who holds her life in his hands: "Know base Tyrant, the most fell Tortures that ever barbarous Affrica invented, can no more make us alter our fixt Resolutions."[8] This sentiment may well reflect the expectation and self-assurance of the adventurers and colonists who were sailing to the new enterprise in Tangier.

The instructions that King Charles gave to Peterborough reveal his complete oblivion to the conditions on the ground and the ongoing Moroccan hostility to the Portuguese presidio. They also show his total neglect of logistical and diplomatic difficulties. On 22 March 1662, an army led by a claimant to the Moroccan throne, al-Khadr Ghailan, surrounded Peterborough, who quickly negotiated a truce with him until 22 September. Peterborough knew that Ghailan was leading not desperate natives, but a tightly organized force. While in New England the Indians had been removed and by 1676 their threat eradicated, the Moors around Tangier were militarily powerful, and those with ties to the Ottoman Empire could draw on the might of that empire, which was on the mend under the Korpulu viziers[9] (and currently laying siege to Crete). North Africa was not North America, and the Moors were not the Indians. Peterborough kept the garrison population confined within the walls and sent out feelers to the anti-Ghailan faction under Sidi Abdallah bin Muhammad: since he could not defeat the Moors, he would try to divide them and negotiate separate deals with them. On 12 May 1662, Peterborough received a letter from Abdallah reminding him of a peace treaty the latter had previously negotiated with Admiral Blake. Abdallah beseeched his "deare friende" not to help Ghailan, because only his support for Ghailan had kept the latter "in ye warre against our Castle."[10] Abdallah was willing to cooperate with the Tangier governor because he viewed the British contingent as part of the mosaic of diplomacy and commercial cooperation that constituted the turmoil-ridden Morocco of the 1660s.[11]

On 29 September 1662, the king, not fully aware of developments around Tangier, issued his "Proclamation Declaring His Majesties pleasure to Settle and Establish a Free Port at His City of Tanger in Africa." Having recognized that the bastion could not immediately be the bridgehead of empire, the king assumed a more realistic position and turned the mission of the bastion toward trade. He urged that Tangier become "a good port in the entry of the Mediterranean." It was to be an open port where all nations ("in amity with us") and religions could trade. John Luke, who later served as a chaplain there, supported this view, calling for a very small military contingent to prove that British intentions "were not to make warr wth ye Moors but a peace" that would lead to the increase of trade. He was supported by one Mr. Porey who confirmed the importance of establishing "good correspondency wth ye Moores" since Tangier was "the Metropolitan City." It was important, he added, not to "stir up jealousie & provoke ye people of yt Country to believe yt ye English nation intends to enslave them, & make conquest of their country." There was always the fear that if forts were built and filled with military personnel, the Dutch and French traders would incite the people of the region "to an implacable enmity against ye English Nation."[12]

Regardless of what the Tangier settlers did or did not do, Moroccan enmity was steadily growing. A war of attrition soon followed in which British soldiers were ambushed and killed. In April 1663, King Charles replaced Peterborough with Lord Rutherford, Count Teviot, who began to fortify the garrison. Promptly, Ghailan attacked it, viewing the building of forts on Muslim soil as a violation of the terms of their agreement. An anonymous account about the "Affairs of Tanger" was written later that year, praising Teviot and mocking the primitiveness of the Moors. "One of them," wrote the author, "seeing a Granadoe throwne out of the Fort, presently tooke it up to view what it meant but the shell brake in his hand" and killed him. It was not surprising, therefore, that the "handful of Christians against against [sic] a farr greater number of Infidels" started employing the same methods in finding and killing the Moors as the Spaniards had done in locating Indians: using dogs to sniff out the enemy lurking around the fort.[13] As the Spaniards had defeated the native Indians, so would the English defeat the native Moors. European canines and gun power would inevitably prove victorious.

As soon as the fighting was reported in London, *A Description of Tangier*, along with an account of Ghailan, "the present Usurper of the Kingdome of Fez," was translated from Spanish and published "by Authority"—along with another part, "A Short Narrative of the Proceedings of the English in those parts" under Teviot.[14] The treatise was the most informative and propagandist account about Tangier that had yet appeared in English print. Its purpose was clearly to emphasize the importance of the port city and to silence the voices of those who complained about the venture. The first part, describing Ghailan and his court and "Person," his military forces and administration, was translated from Spanish. In the second part, which described the current situation, the author changed his tone as he relinquished the matter-of-fact descriptions and warned about Ghailan's plans. The Moroccan insurgent, he wrote, possessed a disciplined army of twenty thousand Moors who could march "with [such] order and silence, for forty miles, that they cannot be discovered." Equally ominously for the little garrison was the contact Ghailan was establishing with European powers to help him build a fleet that he could then incorporate into the Ottoman sultan's navy.[15]

Having finished with the military survey, the author turned to the colonial potential of Tangier. The author confirmed how Tangier was the commercial doorway to the rest of Barbary. It was salubrious and abundant in natural resources, the air so temperate that "never any English, Welsh, or Scotch, that were cast upon those coasts, died before they were an hundred years old."[16] The author then listed the mineral resources that were to be found in the kingdom of Fez (in which Tangier was located), such as brass, salt, glass, marble, precious stones and others. The wealth of the land conveniently reminded the author of Old Testament allusions, thereby transforming Morocco into a Promised Land, its brass recalling the blessing of Asher, and its salt, the salt used by Abimelech and Abdamelech—conveniently, because the appeal to the biblical model helped turn the colonial project of expropriation into a religiously sanctioned Christian triumph. Afraid of European imperial greed, the inhabitants, noted the author, had never mentioned the gold and silver in their land, "to avoide the Invasions of other [European] Nations"—very much like the native Indians who also kept quiet before the Spanish conquistadors. The author continued with a list of other natural products such as olive oil, honey, fruit, barley, vines, wood and balm. Tangier and the rest of Morocco, he asserted, were a "Land like Judea,(as it is described Deut. 8.7) A land of brooks of waters, of fountains, and depths, that spring out of valleys and hills."[17] It was a land of promise that the British, the modern Israelites, should not hesitate from seizing. Where other Europeans were merely greedy for quick wealth, the British were fulfilling messianic goals; and where other Europeans plundered the natural resources, the British received them by divine authority. The author's emphasis was both on the military side of affairs and on the prospect of divinely modeled colonization and expansion. The Moors were presented as organized and dangerous, but the land was so attractive and the biblical echoes so strong that Britons were encouraged to think more of the riches that they would gain than the politico-military environment in which the bastion was situated. The God-inspired imperial gaze conveniently ignored the natives and the danger that the natives posed.

But that danger was there, and soon after the publication of the treatise, Count Teviot and 430 soldiers were killed during a foray against Ghailan.[18] An angry publication immediately appeared in London, describing the Moroccans as monsters and serpents, butchers and cannibals. From the objective report about the Ghailan army and its organization in *A Description of Tangier*, the tone now changed into invective and belligerence toward the Moors that would continue in printed material throughout the twenty years of the colony's life. From that year on, the subhumanization and animalization of the Moors would become part of the English discourse. The writers of poetry and doggerel called on England and Scotland to avenge Teviot's death (Teviot was Scottish) and continue to fight and to plant, "and conquerours remain / 'Till Africa be Christian once again."[19] Tangier, according to the author, should serve as the imperial bridgehead for Britons to subdue and convert all of Africa.

In June, King Charles sent Colonel FitzGerald to confront the despair and "désordre" in the garrison. With FitzGerald in charge, the British soldiers regrouped and avenged the killing of Teviot by executing every Moroccan they captured. Slowly thereafter, the garrison inhabitants returned to normal lives, cultivating their gardens, as the French press reported, and developing an infrastructure for a military-cum-trading outpost, similar to what the Spaniards on the Moroccan coasts possessed.[20] The shock of the attack forced a resumption of relations with the other potentates of North Africa, and toward the end of 1664, the commander of the British fleet in the Mediterranean re-signed the peace treaty with Algiers to ensure the safety of the merchant fleet east of Tangier. The treaty demonstrated, wrote the printer in his introduction, the king's desire to improve his subjects' commerce and security. Meanwhile, the Algerians addressed King Charles in the highest honorifics possible: "Umdat al-muluk al-masihiyya wa zubdat al-salateen al-isawiyya mamalik al-inkleez" (the pillar among Christian kings, and the best among the sultans of the followers of Isa [Jesus]—the kingdoms of the English).[21] They also agreed to remove one of the articles in the 1662 agreement dealing with "People belonging to the Dominions of either Party,"[22] thereby giving Britons a monopoly over, and denying themselves the reciprocal right of, trade. Having seen the danger to their commerce and livelihood that the Spanish and the Portuguese presidios in North Africa posed, the Algerians were not sure what position the British would take in the ongoing hostilities between the two sides of the Mediterranean. Maintaining good relations with the new and powerful navy in the Mediterranean was both prudent and necessary.

A clear policy was enunciated for FitzGerald in regard to Tangier. His instructions on 7 June 1664 were to ensure the presence of a strong military force, but not to venture beyond the boundaries of the garrison or to make "inroads into the country." He was to ensure that Tangier was "a free port [with] the administration of justice and the worship of God" and that it was at peace with the Ottoman regencies, but not at the cost of England's "Christian allies and confederates." He was also to "promote all things conducing to the advance of the trade and commerce." As far as King Charles was concerned, Tangier was a trading port the freedom of which, he hoped, would bring revenue to his personal coffers as well as provide a locus for his subjects' Mediterranean trade and naval presence.[23] Since trade could not succeed without military protection, the mart was to be a fort, too, but without an imperial goal. With Parliament not granting him the subsidies that he needed, the king was more eager to generate an income from his colony than to employ it as a spearhead of Christian domination. In the instructions that were given six months later, on 24 February 1665, to Lord Belasyse, "commander-in-chief of the forces in Africa and the Governor of Tangier," who replaced FitzGerald, there was a repetition of the need to ensure free trade, and a warning against cooperating with too many Dutch and French merchants because they could "endanger the safety of the place." The king wanted Tangier to serve British interests against the military designs of the Moors and the commercial maneuverings of the French, whose king was drawing up a grand design for a European Christendom under his control, and against the Dutch, whose commercial fleet was outsailing the British and bringing wealth and affluence to the States General. The king's imperial desire was giving way to commercial realism: military preparedness was for the sole purpose of serving trade.

While sailing past Tangier in 1665, one T. Browne praised the outpost as a "towne of little force and less proffitt, till put into the English hands, now very much mended."[24] Both the conditions inside the bastion and its image among Britons were improving. Indeed, Sir Hugh Cholmeley wrote to the English ambassador in Madrid that there was an abundance of "all sorts of delicacys, and plenty of fresh provisions, as wee hear better and cheaper by much then it is with our neighbours at Cadiz. . . . There is no difference between this place and England."[25] Tangier was becoming comfortable and attractive. In 1666, an anonymous English writer prepared a "History of Morocco" in which he presented a survey of the country from the early sixteenth century until 1666, concluding his treatise with a list of the names of the tribes and the number of their footmen and cavalrymen supporting Ghailan.[26] While there was a growing sense of settlement in Tangier, there was still need for vigilance and for information about past history and current military forces.

At the same time that affairs in Tangier were settling down, London was rising from the devastation of plague and fire, like a "fam'd Emporium," as John Dryden celebrated in *Annus Mirabilis* (1667). Dryden praised his country's maritime empire that extended from "Guinny" to the "Turkish Courts" (821, 823) and hailed the pillaging the British fleet could now undertake: "Our greedy Seamen rummage every hold, / Smile on the booty of each wealthier Chest" (829–30). The reference to the Turkish courts was an allusion to the Barbary Mediterranean. Evidently, now that Britain was in possession of a colony, Dryden was paying attention to Muslim North Africa, and, given Spain's long history in repulsing and colonizing Muslim regions, he was reading about that history as well. His play *An Evening's Love*, which Pepys attended on 12 June 1668 upon its first staging, includes a scene in which English fops in Spain think that they are courting Muslim North African women (3.1). The Spanish Jacinta disguises herself as a Moroccan who had traveled to Spain

> to see some of my Relations who are settled here, and
> turn'd Christians, since the expulsion of my
> Countrymen the Moors.
> Wild. Are you then a Mahometan?
> Jac. A Musullman at your service. (3.1.418–22)

Dryden sustains the Muslim image by using words such as "Alla" and "Mahomet," by joking about the Prophet as a "Cavalier . . . providing so well for us Lovers in the other World, Black Eyes, and Fresh Maidenheads every day," and by invoking the names of Andalusian families—the "Hamets, the Zegrys, and the Bencerrages," and "the Cids and the Bens of the Arabians," famous in Spain's Moorish history (3.1.458–60). By these references to Islam and Muslims, Dryden distinguished the Moors from the Spaniards whom they physically resembled: after all, Jacinta, the Spaniard, had posed as a Moroccan without fear of exposure, for her skin color and beauty as a Spaniard, in the words of one of the English gentlemen, was "much as the Moores left it; not altogether so deep a black as the true Aethiopian: a kind of beautie that is too civil to the lookers on to do them any mischief" (1.2.88–90). For Dryden, the difference with the Moors was not as much "racial" as religious since Christian Spaniards looked very much like "Mahumetan" Moors. Where half a century earlier, the Zanthia of Jacobean drama had been pitch-black and therefore unattractive, now the darksome "Moor" Jacinta is attractive to northern Englishmen.[27]

Meanwhile, inside the Tangier garrison, the situation was as debauched and foppish as the English behavior in the Spanish "Masquerade" in *An Evening's Love*. When Prince James and the lords commissioners listed the instructions for the "Corporation of Tangier" in June 1669, they focused on internal matters of government and security;[28] but two months later, in August 1669, they demanded of the new governor of Tangier to do something about the "Debaucherie, and Dissoluteness" of the soldiers that were negatively impacting trade and commerce.[29] The thousands in the garrison were completely oblivious to anything outside their walls because, with the beginning of the building of the formidable mole (475 yards long and 30 wide), they realized that the sea was to be the world in which they would travel, reconnoiter, chase after wayward ships, and trade.

The residents were not afraid, wrote John Ogilby in 1670, of "what the power of the Moors can or dare do by Land."[30] Actually, they ignored them, as the surviving Colonial Office records of Tangier in those years reveal. There is a complete absence of any references to Moors in the vast piles of documents relating to domestic quarrels, cases of drunkenness, violence, thievery, abuse and fraud. The Tangier settlers lived in a world totally apart from the Moors.

But the ongoing Moroccan dynastic conflicts could not but endanger them. Since Ghailan was increasingly recognized as England's ally in the region, more information was needed about him. In 1669, an account was published in London, about "Tafiletta, the great conqueror and emperor of Barbary," by "one that hath lately been in His Majesties Service in that Country." But the author had not traveled beyond Tangier and had relied instead on French material written by a merchant from Provence who had lived among the "Moores."[31] The author was aware of the difficult situation of the garrison and warned that since signing the treaty with the garrison, Ghailan had lost to his rival, so much so that he had had to flee to Ottoman-dominated Algiers. The author was not hopeful about the immediate future of the garrison: Lord Belasyse had pinned his hopes on Ghailan, only to find that the latter's adversary had won, had gathered around him a large and organized army, and was eying Tangier with dangerous intent.[32] Toward the end of that year, in November, "a Gentleman of the Lord Ambassador Howard's Retinue" published another account in London describing the political and military instability of the country, and providing the first information about coastal and inland Morocco by an Englishman who had actually been there. Emphasizing the barbarity, "horrible Stench," "Negromancy," and anti-Christian sentiment of the natives, the author sought to refute the uncertainty about Tangier and reminded his readers of the "Native Commodities of Africa," and how much the land could furnish the "rest of the World with excellent Productions" were it to fall into "the hands of an ingenious and laborious People."[33] He redirected the imperial gaze to the wealth of the region, and urged the British gazers to be confident in their military might and the natives' barbarity, and thus to conquer and exploit. The line between commerce and conquest was now completely blurred.

With such blurring, the British Mediterranean fleet turned to subdue Algiers since its privateers posed a threat to commercial shipping and to maritime trade by and from Tangier. In June 1669, King Charles sent Sir Thomas Allin to the Mediterranean to "make himself master." There was a long list of demands, which Allin was to present to the Algerians, including a demand for punishing all Algerians who took part in attacks on British ships. He was also to warn them that should they break their treaty with Britain, not only would he "do execution to the Algiers ships in the port," but also alert Tunis and Tripoli to the state of affairs, thereby ensuring their alienation from their North African neighbor.[34] From 5 September to 21 November, Allin besieged and bombarded Algiers, causing extensive damage to the city and to its economy, and demanding at the end a huge bounty that included wheat, "Compass Timber" and "poor jack."[35] The Algerians were forced to sign a treaty that reiterated the articles of the 1664 treaty. But there was an additional article prohibiting them from sailing across Tangier and out toward the Atlantic ports of Morocco[36]—imposing thereby serious restrictions on their commercial activity.

From their base in Tangier, the British had begun their domination of the western Mediterranean. Their sea victory against the most formidable of the regencies, Algiers, reminded Londoners of that part of the world in which compatriots were still taken captive—an issue that was often on the king's and Parliament's agenda, but that had not received significant attention in print since the 1640s. Petitions and appeals had continued to be presented on behalf of captives on the Barbary Coast; and in 1666, an account of the captivity of the Flemish nobleman Emanuel d'Aranda had been translated from French.[37] But with religious and civil liberties so severely restricted by the Great Persecution of Nonconformists, no massive agitation for captives could be organized as had happened in the heady 1630s. Still, the victory over Algiers brought to the fore the question about British captives and their plight in that whole region: how and when were they to be ransomed? As in earlier years, a collection was initiated "towards the relief of captives taken by the Turks and Moors of Barbary."[38] With both the royal coffers and the commercial companies unwilling to dispense the ransom sums, the relatives and kin of captives resorted to the same collections that had been practiced a generation earlier.

To draw further attention to the matter of captivity, a certain A. Roberts published *The Adventures of (Mr T. S.) an English Merchant, Taken Prisoner by the Turks of Argiers*. The account was supposed to have been written by "T. S.," who had been held captive from 1648 to 1652 but died before finishing the account. T. S. described his capture by Algerian pirates, the heroism of the English in fighting off the "Turks," and the cruelty of renegades who were more fierce—even cannibalistic—than the native Muslims. In the first few dozen pages, T. S. proposed to show the "strange Examples of the Proceedings of Providence";[39] the text was to be about Christian endurance—thus the invocation of Job[40]—and about the falsity of Islam. But as he (or perhaps Roberts) continued, T. S. changed his narrative into a story about life in Algeria that provided useful information to traders, travelers, sea commanders and theologians. He wrote about naval defenses and the forts that were strong or weak, the social organization and military preparedness of the Algerians, and the Prophet of "these Heathens." He then told about his "Happy time of . . . slavery" in which he had had numerous sexual escapades with local women. In this respect, T. S. is one of the rare Englishmen to claim affairs with Muslim women. Because he was handsome, women, both married and widowed, were attracted to him. One in particular, he reported, was so courageous in pursuing him that he finally fell in love with her and offered to marry her if she would be willing to escape with him back to

England. Unfortunately, "She had two Children, a Boy and a Girl, that kept her in that place otherwise I think I had then got my Freedom and carryed her away." Later, she gave birth to "a pretty little Girl, somewhat whiter than ordinary; the old Fool [her husband] thought himself to be the Father of it."[41] When other women made themselves available to T. S., he did not decline despite being exhausted, and continued to enjoy the fleshpots of Algiers.

His case may well have been the sole account of sexual liaisons between a Christian man who survives and Muslim women in Barbary. After all, a Christian man caught with a Muslim woman was punished by death.[42] After being sold from one owner to another, the worst being an English renegade, T. S. finally was sold to an "Officer of the Militia" who put him to military use. He traveled with his master around Algeria, fighting and killing and looting Bedouin tribes in the hinterlands where no European had ever been. In the course of describing troop movements and battles, ambushes and maneuvers, T. S. presented a documentary overview of the country—its flora and fauna, its peoples and ethnicities, its mountain ranges and cities. This was the second account about Algeria (after Knight) by an Englishman who had personally lived in the land. Despite confirming the negative stereotypes about the sodomitical and superstitious Muslims of Algiers, T. S. showed that even captives could perform great actions among them. To the reader of the account, captivity did not come across as a disastrous experience; rather, it seemed to open up venues for exploration and heroism. Indeed, T. S. showed how the Restoration captive had become, as Gerald MacLean has so aptly put it, an "ethnographic observer, sex-slave, soldier on the march, war correspondent, big-game hunter, diplomat and political adviser."[43] Furthermore, captivity provided an alternative to the difficult life that T. S. would have led had he stayed in the England of the Civil War and Interregnum, with all the poverty and hunger that people experienced in those years. Finally, after all the difficulties and the excitement, T. S. was released in appreciation of his great English deeds among the North Africans, and he returned to his homeland loaded with gifts from his Turkish master. Perhaps that is the reason why the publisher added a few pages at the end by Richard Norris about the "Tide, and how to turn out of the Streights-Mouth the Wind being Westerly." T. S. provided information about life within Islamic North Africa, and Norris provided directions on how to sail there.[44]

By the time T. S.'s account appeared in print, the British navy under the command of Sir Thomas Allin had completed its operation against Algiers. Although Roberts made no mention of it in his preface, John Baltharpe, a sailor on the fleet that bombarded Algiers, rose to the occasion and composed a poem in which he praised his king and country—and also the fleet commanders and the sailors who had carried out the attack.[45] For him, there was pride and glory in the achievement of the fleet, especially the ship, the *St. David*, which had such firepower that no Moorish or Turkish ship could remotely threaten it. While T. S. had described his eventful and not unhappy life in Algiers, Baltharpe was eager to describe how Algiers had been destroyed—how the *St. David* had wielded death on the "Turks." The British victory sent the poetaster into a celebration of killing:

> It was about the middle of September,
> Dark in the Night, under the Shoar,
> As we lay sculking on our oare,
> New to the Shoar (as he [Algerian ship] came creeping)
> We Boarded him, a Woman weeping
> With a young Child, sate after on,
> The Turks and Moores over board run.
> We went to fishing then for Moores,
> And took them up with blades of Oares;
> The flesh of some, with our Boat-hook,
> We entered, and so up them took.[46]

What Allin had recounted matter-of-factly in his report about the attack, Baltharpe put to meter and rhyme. Allin had mentioned how on 7 September, the *Bristol* had taken "about 56 Moores Men Women & Children."[47] After repeating information about the devastation that the British visited on the Moors, Baltharpe continued by describing the rest of the *St. David* expedition around the Mediterranean, growing more assertive about the naval power of his country and his God. What had begun as a poem celebrating a sea victory soon turned into an anti-Islamic diatribe: Baltharpe taunted "Mahomet" for failing to protect the infidels from the cannons of the Christians. Furthermore, the size of the British fleet assured the author that he did not have to fear the "Pirats of Argeir" any more; rather, he could chase "straight ways after them. [. . .] But way for fear a pace they run."[48] The British were dominating the seas, and although Baltharpe had once been himself captured by the Turks and subjected to enslavement, now it was he and the rest of the crew who were capturing Muslims and selling them in the slave markets of southern Europe. Now it was the British who were fearlessly chasing Algerian and other Barbary ships: "All Turkish Pirats in Argeire, / With our brave Fleet we did not fear."[49]

The Straights Voyage, or St. Davids Poem is the first short epic about the confrontation with Islam in English literature. It is a poor epic, consisting of more doggerel than verse, written as it was by a man without inspiration who apologized for "the dullness of my Pen, and Muse." But Baltharpe had epic pretensions, and in composing *The Straights Voyage* in four parts, he may have been imitating Abraham Cowley's *Davideis* which had appeared in the mid-1650s. Baltharpe appealed sometimes to the "God of Battle" to assist him in his mission, at other time to "my Muse,"[50] and laboriously incorporated disparate classical allusions (Charon and his "Stygeon-Lake").[51] Throughout, he reiterated patriotic feelings, showing how much he wanted to celebrate British heroes in the war against the infidels, thus the effusive praise for Sir John Harman "Commander,

Rere-Admiral," Sir Thomas Allin, Sir Edward Spragg and the sailors, all of whom fought to protect England's trade from the Turks and to magnify England's power in the Islamic world. The poem included much about the difficult conditions of sailors and the plight of their families, but there was also assurance and defiance: the British sailors were ruling the waves and could enter any Muslim harbor, burn its ships and force the liberation of British captives—and then return victoriously home. No previous poem or epic had ever been written about Britain's encounter with Islam, but with Britons now possessing a garrison among the Moors, there was need to show the superiority of Christian society and religion, mariners and sailors, over the "vile" Muslims. After all the setbacks in the previous few years—of plague, fire, Dutch victory in the Thames, royal debauchery and French ascendancy—a patriotic celebration was much appreciated.

North Africa was now on the London map, and readers were eager to learn about that part of the world that was coming under their expanding imperial gaze. George Meriton included a unit on "Barbary" in his *Geographical Description of the World*, intended to provide "Directions for Travellers."[52] Eager to celebrate patriotic pride, John Dryden wrote the first plays on a Moorish theme in the Restoration period. One year after being appointed by Charles II as historiographer royal in 1670, he completed *The Conquest of Granada*, having chosen for his topic the Spanish attack on Granada in 1492 and the defeat and subsequent expulsion of the Moors.[53] That he chose to write about the Moors—and the play is more about the conquered Moors than the conquering Spaniards—suggests public interest in the exotic and the dangerous. Dryden capitalized on this interest: news from Tangier reported rising tension after repeated attacks by Moroccans trying to delay the construction of the mole. A play about Moors, those same Moors who swore by the "holy prophet," was therefore not unsuitable for the times: Part 1 was acted in December 1670, and part 2 in January 1671.

Dryden set the events of the play in Granada of 1492 with obvious parallels to Tangier. As Granada was the last stronghold of Islam in Spain, so was Tangier the first British stronghold in Africa. It was a reversed Granada—a Christian bastion in the midst of a continent of unbelievers into which Britain sought Christian expansion and domination. And as the Spaniards had carried with them into defeated Granada the missionary goal of converting the unbelievers, so were the British hopeful that they would subdue "the Moors in woods and mountains," as part 2 ended propitiously, and "wave our Conqu'ring Crosses in the Aire" (p. 163). The play was an "undisguised celebration of Christian expansionism" not only of Spain into Islamdom, as Khalid Bekkaoui has noted, but of Britons into Tangier and the rest of Africa.[54] For Islam was weak, and the Moors were disunited: after all, it was the dissension between the Abencerrages and the Zegrys, two large Moorish factions, that facilitated the inexorable victory of the Christians.

Half a century after Middleton and Rowley's *All's Lost by Lust* depicted the conquest of Spain by the Moors, Dryden wrote *The Conquest of Granada*, show-ing the reconquest by the Christians. The Jacobean play had been written against the backdrop of piratical incursions and dangerous forays by the Barbary cor-sairs into the English Channel and mainland. It was as if the Moors had then been on the move again trying to conquer Christian territory. Fifty years later, it was the British who were on the move, settling themselves on Muslim soil and begin-ning to challenge the Moors. Dryden portrayed the Moors as evil and depraved, controlled by their lust, ruthless in their pursuit of personal power, and without political or military cohesion. He also changed history and twisted events in his plot to suit his Christian triumphant goal. Although Granada had surrendered to the Spanish forces, he made it fall by assault; and although the original ruler, Boabdelin, had gone into exile, Dryden had him meet his end in battle. Despite writing about a historical Moor, Dryden relied on European sources for the his-tory of Almanzor—specifically, the fictions of Tasso, Calprenede and Homer. The world and history of the Moors were dependent on the needs of the play-wright. With British power at sea, the historiographer royal believed that he had power over history and the telling and possessing of history.[55]

Such imperial ambition, and such inscribing of that ambition onto the theater, was confirmed in the first English text about Morocco that was written by a man who had lived and traveled there. Having served as chaplain to Lord Teviot in Tangier, Lancelot Addison published in 1671, shortly after Baltharpe and Dryden published their works, a historical account of Morocco's "Revolutions" based on conversations with local sheikhs and jurists. It was the first account about that country written by a researcher who had interviewed various people, visited sites and locations, and documented military and political events. Addison recon-structed Moroccan history, accurately, from 1508 and the fall of the Merinid dynasty to his present times. Prominent in the histories and chronologies was the description of the natural abundance of the region: the "pleasant Orchards of Orange, Lemons and Limes, with Gardens yielding plenty and variety of sallad." There were also things rarely to be found in Europe, such as "Tomatos," as well as plants that reminded the traveler of England: the cork trees that were similar to "Scarlet-Oak" and the "Alcarobe" that resembled the "English Bean." There was also grain, wheat, barley, beans and "bread-corn" along with mines of the "best Oars." As for animal life, "Barbary hath variety of all sorts of Beasts, Birds and Serpents; the Land affording Habitations most suitable to such unsociable Beings"—who may well be ruled over and then put to labor.[56] There were riches, natural resources, and an indolent and ignorant population—the ideal combina-tion of reasons for Britain to establish hegemony and conquer the land.[57] While Dryden dramatized the fall of the Moors in Granada, Addison showed the wealth of the Moors in Africa—a wealth that was within British reach.

In the only surviving account by an Englishman inside Tangier between De-cember 1670 and February 1673, *Tangier at High Tide: The Journal of John Luke, 1670–1673*, Luke described how Tangier had been turned into a little

England. As Dryden changed the history of the Moors to suit his London audience, so did the residents of Tangier change its geography to suit their English taste. The settlers built a "Parsons Green," just as they would do in a quaint country village, and gave their forts and natural landmarks British royal names, to ensure the appropriation of the territory. As there was a York river and a James town and a Charles river in North America, so were there York Castle, Henrietta and Charles forts (named after the king's parents), Peterborough Tower, Teviot Hill and Whitby quarry, named after the "little English Hamlet"[58] from where Sir Hugh Cholmeley, chief builder of the mole, came; there were also forts named after Ann, James, Monmouth, Cambridge and Norwood. A church was dedicated to Charles the Martyr, and a school was built for children, along with a public library, a hospital, and a public garden. The residents instituted royalism in North Africa and replicated England's social culture, too: they drank heavily (beer and Rheinish wine), played cards and tables, bowled, listened to viols and lutes, watched English plays (performed by Spanish troupes) and often indulged in sumptuous meals: "extraordinary deal of meat and very good four courses besides the dessert."[59]

Luke's account showed the psychological enclosure of the community and its total indifference to the North African world around it—despite the fact that, as one writer reported on 9 October 1672, the Moroccans were coming into Tangier "with all the freedome imaginable."[60] The Moors simply did not exist, were not seen, nor would they receive description, analysis or even mention. Luke never even mentioned the plague that devastated not only Morocco but also the whole North African region from 1671 to 1672. Instead, he focused on the personal tensions and social pretensions among the inhabitants, described sermons he delivered and attended, and gave a general overview of the state of morality (or the lack thereof) in the presidio. What captured his attention was what was going on inside, not outside, the presidio—chiefly how it was serving as a magnet for women in search of husbands. Luke courted Mrs. Fisher (although he was not intent on marrying her), while Mr. Read "got the maidenheads of all the girls that lived with him."[61] Meanwhile, the same theological anxieties that ministers would have expressed in London churches were voiced in the Tangier church. On 11 December 1670, Luke attended a sermon against "strict Sabbatarians" that was "most unreasonable . . . [since] this place without doubt being inclined rather to too much liberty than an over strictness."[62] Two years later, the minister, Mr. Turner, was still anxious about Sabbatarianism, and on 24 November 1672 he preached about "liberty for the Sabbath day which certainly is noways proper for these loose time."[63] That the sermons were being preached in a presidio situated in North Africa did not impress on Turner the need to provide topics more suitable to the geography and political environment of his congregation. As far as he and his church community were concerned, Tangier was part of Britain, and the anxiety caused by dissenters in the streets and conventicles of London posed the most serious danger to the congregation of Tangier. As for the Moroccans beyond the walls, they were anonymous, dangerous, predatory, deceptive, prone to drunkenness and easily bought off with a present—a pistol, a sword, a few yards of cloth. They were irrelevant and needed to be removed, as the Indians were removed from their New England villages—by burning their food supplies and crops, thereby starving them and forcing them to clear the land for more British settlement. On 23 December 1670, Luke rode "round the lines and discoursing about the Moors and burning their corn."[64] Luke shows how life within the presidio cocooned the consciousness of both individual and community. The outside world of the "Moors" was rarely worthy of record.[65]

Such a complete lack of geohistorical awareness in Tangier was repeated in London, where the Moors were no longer regarded as a people within a specific geography, polity and culture, but as exotic and completely unreal figures to be invented, manipulated, imagined and dramatized on the London stage. In the second "Moor" play of the Restoration period after Dryden's, Elkanah Settle presented in July 1673 his *Empress of Morocco*—a play that showed not only the limited imaginative ability of the author but also his ignorance of the region he was purportedly describing. Where Settle derived the story line of his play is not clear: he claimed in his preface that it was the story that his patron, Henry, Earl of Norwich, had passed on to him after his "honourable Embassy into Africa." But the play reveals traces of Dekker's *Lust's Dominion*, although Settle islamicized the names and relocated events from Spain to Morocco. Settle wanted to include contemporary history, and so he made a few references to the internecine conflict that had been going on in Morocco and which had ended in 1672 with the assumption to the throne of Mulay Ismail. To impress on his audience a sense of realism, he introduced a "Moorish Dance" with an "artificial Palm-tree" along with a "Moorish Priest and two Moorish Women." The engraving of the dance in the printed version of the play shows the figures in "native" costume, with dark features and wild gestures. Settle also referred in the course of the play to the "Seraglio," feebly trying to exhibit his knowledge of "Mahometan" culture, and confirmed the association between the Moors and Islam—thus the various references to the Prophet, "great Prophet" and "his sacred Laws." Settle sustained his Moroccan verisimilitude with references to the Atlas Mountains and his depiction of the violence and evil of the followers of the Prophet: the final act presents a scene of bodies in a dungeon, hanging on a "Wall set with spikes of Iron." The Moors were part of a spectacle of entertainment and horror, presented in labored heroic couplets, to an audience that Settle hoped would appreciate his evocation of the region and its Muslim population.

The play was promptly ridiculed and parodied, and Settle was denounced in an anonymous publication (written by Dryden, Shadwell and John Crowne) for his historical inaccuracy and his total ignorance of the geography and demography of Morocco. *The Notes and Observations on the Empress of Morocco* criticized him for poor versification, implausible characters and, most vehemently, topographical errors: the second act had opened with a vista of a "large River, with a glorious Fleet of Ships, supposed to be the Navy of Muly Hamet" and moored in his city of "Morocco" (Marrakesh)—a city with no such river, as the authors pointed out. Settle was also denounced for his poetic license and unconvincing dramatic "leaps."[66] The region and the history of North Africa were now so well documented, by both English and continental writers, that factual errors such as those committed by Settle were unacceptable. That Dryden, the royal historiographer, had himself falsified history seems to have been forgotten in the attack on Settle. Soon after, Thomas Duffett ridiculed Settle by turning the play into a farce and the protagonists into wenches, apple women, "Morris-dancers, Gypsies, Tinkers, and other Attendants." The farce proved quite successful, especially as it showed the actor William Harris dressed as one of the female characters, Morena, and painted black.[67] Both the play and the farce showed that to the London audience, the Moors were figures to be invented for a merry stage. Imperial desire was giving legitimacy to fantasy.

On 30 January 1674, King Charles issued a proclamation to protect traders from countries against which Britain might declare war. The king was confident about Tangier, which, "through the blessing of God is in a flourishing condition."[68] Although food supplies had declined dramatically in the presidio,[69] there was confidence in London. The assurance of the king was echoed in the journal that the chaplain, Henry Teonge, kept while sailing on the British fleet from 20 May 1675 until 17 November 1676 (he finished writing his account on 25 July 1678). His journal provides the first account by an Englishman for whom the Mediterranean Islamic world had become a locus of enjoyable tourism rather than of dangerous encounter. Teonge is confident and assertive without fear of either the Turks or the Moors; rather, it is they who fear the British ships and fleet. Often, Teonge describes the leisureliness and the comfort of the journey. To amuse himself and his compatriots, he spent much of his time composing poems and ballads, including a "sonnet" about "a bonnie lassie"; he described the varieties of wines he consumed, and composed a poem about the difference between the wines of Zante (Crete) and of Malta. In Malta, a boat brought ladies and gallons of wine to the ship after which the ladies "sang several songs very sweetly: very rich in habit, and very courteous in behaviour."[70] Perhaps most amazing was the assortment of foods, the thirty-three-dish *mezza* he had in Antioch, the fish, fowl, mutton, pork and beef that were delicately prepared for the travelers' pleasure. Teonge's was a cruise trip in the Mediterranean in which the English chaplain found himself in a world of his own, in which he could imagine what he wished and then confirm his inventions by reference to the geography of Ariosto's *Orlando Furioso* and of Sir Philip Sidney's *Arcadia*. The Mediterranean had become a fairyland of desire, and the countries of its basin were places in which to wander, meet other Englishmen (even one from his Cambridge alma mater), examine old houses (in Aleppo) and ride roughshod—"my steed like that of Hudibras for mettle, courage, and colour," he declared, recalling the burlesque poem by Samuel Butler.[71]

As in Luke's account of life inside the presidio, so with the account of life in the open Mediterranean: the Turks and the Moors were rarely mentioned, and when they were, they appeared as frightened seamen and devastated coastal inhabitants. Near Tripoli, wrote Teonge in a triumphant Christian spirit, "they tell us of our ships burning four of their brigantines, and the slaughter of many of the Turks on the shore by our great guns from our ships, which happened a few days before our coming."[72] The British ships stayed there, menacing the people from the safety of their distance and their long-range guns. "The Turks were much alarmed," he wrote (63). A few days later, on 21 September, Teonge wrote: "This morning very early our pinnace chased five of the Tripolines to the mouth of their harbour. . . . In the evening [we drank] to our friends in Florence and Syracuse wine." On the next day, and to "vex the Turks, our ships are all filled with pendants" (66). Two days later, on 24 September, he luxuriated in his country's naval power: "This day we chased a galley of thirty-eight oars many leagues: not finding her to be a prize, we only secured the Captain and the Master for farther trial" (66–67). The British were on the offensive, taking the initiative to dominate the sea and intimidate local populations. Nothing, meanwhile, could intimidate or scare the British. Upon seeing a Turkish ship, they prepared to fight—"Every man in the ship seemed to be very joyfull of an encounter" (85)—and at having occasion to drink, carouse and occasionally to seize or bombard the unnecessary "Turks."

Similar triumph and self-assuredness spilled over from manuscript to the printed page. A propagandist account about the history and evolution of Tangier and its garrison, along with a list of its natural bounties and resources, was published to attract more soldiers, traders and settlers to the city. The author, G[eorge] P[hilips], had arrived there in June 1675 and wrote the account in September. After giving a brief history of the city, showing its classical legacy and thereby assuring future inhabitants that they would be settling in a place exhibiting "Roman Greatness, Ingenuity, Arts, and Architecture,"[73] Philips turned to the beautiful houses ("hardly any without a little Garden") and the natural abundance of the region. Since he was writing to the chancellor of Ireland (there was an Irish regiment stationed in Tangier, whereupon there were later complaints that they spoke "Irish"[74]), he compared and contrasted Tangier with Ireland: the air in Tangier was "exceeding temperate, not so sultry as many times of the day in Ireland, nor so sharp"; the fresh food supplies, however, were as "plentiful and cheap as in Ireland."[75] Meanwhile, and with an eye to potential immigrants from the British mainland, he emphasized Tangier's attractions: Charles Fort was "continually visited like Spring-Garden," and the "House of Pleasure," named White-Hall, was the place where "Ladies, the Officers, and the better sort of people, do refresh and divert themselves with Wine, Fruits, and a very pretty Bowling-Bare."[76] Clearly, British and Irish immigrants could not but find Tangier enticing; after all, it offered all that they had at home.

In describing the natural resources of Tangier, Philips echoed the lists of earlier

English "discoverers" in America. There were "good Pease, Beans, Artichokes, (Asparagus growing wild in the Fields) Strawberries, Lettice, Purslane, Cucumbers, &c. But Melons, so plentiful, so various in the shape and kind, and so delicious, that it cannot be described to understanding and belief." For pages, he listed all the natural riches: "Hens, Chickens, Capons, Geese, and Turkiess are extreamly plentiful, and very good [. . .] the Ducks are certainly the best in the World [. . .] Soles, Gurnets, Mullets, Turbets, Lobsters, Eels, Shrimps, &c."[77] Tangier was another America, ripe for the plucking. And it was an America without the violent Indians. Philips assured his readers that although the garrison soldiers often sortied out to burn the Moors' corn, the Moors never retaliated by poisoning the water that flowed and sustained the garrison because it was a "point of their Law and Religion," he explained, "not to destroy any thing that is made for the natural and necessary use of Mankind." The Moors had a strange religious law that made their enmity not dangerous. Philips turned the Moors into quaint and exotic peoples of a dead past and a historical nowhere. He translated their inscriptions and commented how they were "bare Moorish obsolete Names, at present not known, nor in use"; the only reason he bothered with their monuments, he explained, was to satisfy the reader's curiosity.[78] Philips hoped that the short description of the tour with which he provided his addressee would serve to encourage settlement.

The Barbary Mediterranean was showing weakened "Mahumetans" who were defeated by their own exotic religion as well as by British firepower. Still, the Moors continued to pose danger especially when they captured pious English seamen and tried to force them into conversion. In 1675, John Seller, "Hydrographer to the King," published his *Atlas Maritimus*, with an illustration of three domineering Turks sitting atop two half-naked and tied captives, with one Turk fondling the hair of a captive. Although there is no indication that the captives are British, they are clearly European by their features.[79] Captivity remained the Achilles' heel for a British society that was glorying in its might and imperial desire over Muslims, and the Barbary corsairs continued to destabilize Mediterranean trade and cause merchants to complain, as Samuel Pepys noted in September 1674.[80] Britons seemed not to understand why the Barbary people took them captive—whereupon the Algerians explained that Britons were seized because they reneged on their agreements. Many British sailors, declared the Algerians, were serving on, or transporting goods in, ships belonging to European countries at war with Algeria: their capture was therefore legitimate—a point that even King Charles conceded. And, not too zealous to part with his resources, the king announced that if Britons, serving on "strangers' ships," were captured by the Algerians, they would not be ransomed.[81] Such men had only themselves to blame and should not expect any assistance. A letter sent to Sir John Narbrough in March 1675 confirmed the king's unwillingness to assume responsibility for captives: "what he hath done being more than was ever done by the crown before."[82] Indeed, given the limited resources that were available, Narbrough was informed in May 1675 that the money he had been given for ransoming captives should be used to pay the salaries of the seamen.[83]

Where under Charles I the issue of captives had become explosive and politically destabilizing, under Charles II it was relegated to insignificance, because the number of captives was in the scores not the hundreds; and because the political climate had changed. Not only was there no unified opposition to the king that could use captivity as a rallying cry, but also the kinswomen of captives who had earlier spearheaded calls for redemption had become socially marginalized. Perhaps because of this climate of indifference to captives, a second Restoration captivity account was published, William Okeley's *Eben-Ezer*, again purporting to describe events that had taken place decades earlier (between 11 August 1639 and 30 June 1644). This account, however, was quite different from that of T. S. While the latter had shown captivity as an experience of adventure and excitement, this one showed the danger posed by Muslim brutality and conversionism; and while the former ended on a kind of upbeat note, with T. S. being freed by his captor in appreciation of his English heroism and military effectiveness, William Okeley attempted a dangerous escape and endured much hardship before returning to England. Both accounts were set in the safety of earlier times—the times of the Civil Wars; there was to be no hint of criticizing the king.

Writing in the shadow of the turmoil of the Civil Wars and of the dangers of popery, Okeley was eager to praise the stability of Britain's royal rule while still denouncing the popery he met among captives and redemptors in North Africa, and which he feared in his own country, too. In his account of captivity and escape with his English friends, Okeley challenged the attitude that characterized T. S.'s account, and which he viewed as more fictional than real. He opened by assuring his readers that his description was accurate and unromanticized; he then introduced the religious and patriotic motif that would govern all his account: that "The Christian Religion is surely the most excellent Religion in the World, because it holds the Balance so even between Superiours, and Inferiours."[84] While T. S. had enjoyed his adventure, Okeley had learned from it all about subordination and acceptance of social hierarchy; and while T. S. had been captured on a trading mission, Okeley had been captured while seeking the religious safety of America. Now Okeley felt repentant about his desire to leave his country, for the Englishman possessed all that he needed of faith and ingenuity in his own land and in his own national character. Captivity had shown Okeley how the Protestant had to rely on himself in escaping from Satan as well as from the "Turk." Halfway through the account, therefore, he turned to describe the plans that he and five other compatriots devised for escape, the building of the boat, the secrecy, the perseverance, and finally the sailing away and the dangers at sea, until their arrival in Majorca and the "Providence of God which attended" them back to England. The Moors, Okeley was saying, were defeated by native English intelligence and piety. The Englishman in the Mediterranean was heroic because he had qualities the "Mahometan" lacked.

Okeley's account was published in 1675 and again in 1676 and 1864, evidence of readers' admiration for such a story of heroism. But the anxiety over captivity and the attacks by the corsairs persisted, necessitating new naval action. While it was expensive to undertake such actions, and King Charles preferred to economize, he felt compelled to protect merchants—perhaps recalling how failure to protect traders had won his father many a financially powerful adversary. In a letter sent by the king's Privy Council to Sir John Narbrough, concern over imminent military action was expressed: "from whence charge to his Majesty and loss to his subjects may be found without hopes of much reparation to either."[85] Unfortunately, there was no alternative to war, and the burning of the port of Tripoli by Narbrough in January 1676 showed how devastatingly effective British naval power had become, and how safe sea battles were—for the Britons. In the attack, many Turks and Moors were killed, but not a single sailor among the 157 on board Narbrough's ship was hurt; rather, and after Narbrough had seized five Libyan ships laden with corn, he felt so generous that he distributed 1,956 pieces of eight among his sailors.[86] Such success could not but have been proof of divine assurance, as Narbrough expressed in his notes.[87] Thus the prompt appearance of the account in print, "Published by Authority": it was important to assure the merchants of government intervention on their—and God's—behalf.

Meanwhile, the garrison of Tangier was growing more and more costly to the royal coffers, and both traders and navy officials were learning how much more successful it would be for the British to acquire wealth by trading than by colonizing. While a chaplain like Teonge dreamed of empire, the merchant companies and stockholders dreamed of wealth. Such dreams of lucre encouraged the publication in 1677 of a translation of a French captive's account in Tunis. A Narrative of the Adventures of Lewis Marott showed how after Marott's captivity, the Frenchman returned to Tunis to conduct business with his former captor—and was welcomed by him and offered a "Polacque" (a ship) and a business partnership.[88] Marott took the ship and started trading around the Ottoman-dominated ports of the Islamic Mediterranean, protected by his partner's pass, and soon grew so rich that the Turk gave him the ship as a gift. Meanwhile, letters and information received by King Charles confirmed the desire of merchants to do business in the Mediterranean rather than fight—to "transport shot and masts" to Tunis[89] rather than spend vast sums of money on heavy weapons and on supporting the military garrison in Tangier.

So much did disaffection grow toward the Tangier garrison that calls for abandoning it were raised, even for selling it to the French. As a result, in October 1679, an anonymous writer defended to "a Person of Quality" the benefits of Tangier, showing how the garrison protected trading ships both in the Mediterranean and the Atlantic where England's trade was "equal if not exceeding all other Nations put together." The author pleaded for a stronger military force in the city and hoped that "People of Substance" would be enticed to go and "settle and abide" there.[90] The account was followed by a short section, *The Interest of Tanger,* which renewed the colonial advertisement for people to go and settle there. At present, the author noted, only the "needy and greedy" go there "to fill their Purses, and then to return for England with their Gains." He hoped that laws would be enacted, as they had been in North America, to "encourage sober men to live there." He praised the pleasantness of the city, its wholesome air, "pure and free from all Infection" so much so that the "Moors thereabouts live commonly to a great age." Tangier was more of a spa than a military bastion. It was also the "nearest Plantation that belongs to England" where "Corn, Honey, Cattle, Beef, Sheep, Goats, Camels, Horses, and Buffles" abound. By emphasizing all the amenities of Tangier and its environs, the author explained the real reason why Tangier had not succeeded as a colony. It was not because of its "place, the Air, or Country" but rather because of the "Debaucheries, Profaneness, Irreligion, and Idolatry" that bedeviled it along with the Catholicism to which many Englishmen had succumbed. *The Interest* was an indictment of the immorality of the garrison and its lack of military preparedness and planning. It ended, however, with a solution: Britons should not continue hostilities against the Moors but should venture among them to learn about them and their cultural traditions in order to be able to trade with them. Only after "the Countrey [is] opened for us," would Tangier begin to turn in a profit: indeed, Tangier could become the bridge to the rest of the continent where Britons would be able to "vent all Commodities of Wool which lye upon our hands, amongst the Africans."

The Interest of Tangier fell on deaf ears in a London caught in the hysteria of the Popish Plot, when Titus Oates accused numerous English Catholics of plotting to assassinate the king. The garrison was ignored until the spring of the following year when a dramatic series of events received extensive coverage in the London press. The Moroccans, growing weary with the British unwillingness to discontinue building fortifications, and under the leadership of Mulay Ismail, began a military offensive. In February, the *Currant Intelligencer* reported from Tangier that the Moors were bringing in forces: "What their intentions are is uncertain."[91] Skirmishes and small battles soon followed in which both sides suffered heavy losses. The confrontation left its mark in London because it was seen as the first land war between Britons and Moors, Christians and Muslims.[92] Fighting the infidels in a holy war was not an idea that had been completely removed from English religious fervor. The clashes at the edge of Africa and the struggle of a tiny British bastion against the vast "Mahometan" continent awakened in writers patriotic zeal especially after Britons fell in heroic defense of the bastion. The numerous publications that appeared in that year, describing various stages of the encounter, attest to a wide interest in eyewitness accounts and to a deep-seated desire to valorize British warriors and annihilate the unnamed and unknown Moors.

An Exact Journal of the Siege of Tangier recounted events from 25 March to

19 May 1680. The three anonymous authors of the journal described the siege of Tangier by Moroccan forces, the trench warfare that ensued, the plight of the garrison and the casualties. The situation was dire, and by the end of the account there were desertions and death and a sense of grim despair: "Two Boyes belonging to our Garrison, and a Seaman, went out and turn'd Moors. One of our Men belonging to Henrietta Fort is turn'd Moor, and made Master Gunner. . . . The Moors grow a formidable Enemy, being improved in all the Arts of War, as Mining, Sapeing, Intrenching, Scaling and Battering."[93] A letter written a month later, 25 June, confirmed the conditions in the garrison. Major John White wrote about not having "men nor money to put the town in a posture to resist" the enemy. The Moroccans had grown strong and organized and had "all the skill that any Christians have, and the gunners and engineers that the Great Turk had in the taking of Candy." He pleaded that the information be passed on to the king so that help would be sent in order for the garrison to be able to confront "the great storm the Moors are preparing."[94] William Crooke published *The Moores Baffled*, an account by Lancelot Addison, to emphasize the commercial role of Tangier. Instead of writing about the present conditions in Tangier, Addison recalled the policy that Lord Teviot had pursued two decades earlier. Teviot had realized that he could not be a conqueror in a garrison that was kept on "a niggardly" budget with hungry and unpaid troops.[95] Teviot had thus turned to negotiate with the Moroccans and to assure them that he was not intent on invading their country. He "let them plainly and sincerely know, That the King his Master had not sent him to Conquer, but to Rent their Land: That the chief design of his being sent thither, was . . . to promote such a friendly and safe Traffique, as might conduce to the advantage of both." Teviot had recognized that the goal in Tangier was not colonial but commercial—which is what Crooke also wanted his reader to realize. "Forgive me, Sir," he addressed his imaginary reader, there was need for another Teviot to assure the Moors again "how His Majesty intends nothing but a just, friendly, and lasting Commerce: and that he is so far from taking from them any parcel of their Fields by violence."[96] Such communication was crucial because the Moors, confirmed the deputy governor, Sir Palmes Fairborne, on 3 July, "are no more those silly Moors we had to do with fifteen years ago, but an expert diligent enemy which will require provision accordingly."[97]

In July, there was a turn for the better as soldiers in that "famous Garrison" scored a small victory against the Moroccans. An anonymous chronicler immediately published in London *A True Relation of a Great and Bloody Fight between the English and the Moors before Tangiere,* in which he praised the "Warlike exploits of the Heroick English against the Barbarians." The author reiterated arguments about the importance of Tangier, reminding his readers that the garrison protected shipping against "the Turkish pirates, that so frequently disturb the Trafick in the Mediteranean." He also alerted his countrymen that France and Spain were assisting the Moroccan king, by "Force or Fraud to unite it [Tangier] to his Dominions." Reference to the "Fraud" of the Moorish king was certain to win support for the garrison: a British bastion was under attack by the combined forces of Muslims and European Catholic enemies of Protestantism, but British lieutenants, captains and soldiers—and the author mentioned the names of more than a score of them—were defiantly repulsing the Moors and protecting the nation's Christian interest in Africa.[98] In a short tract, *A Faithful Relation of the Most Remarkable Transactions which have happened at Tangier*, another writer declared that "English Vallour has spread it self into the corners of the yet known World." There was pride in the English (and Irish) soldiers who had fought off the Moors.

Military pride was now dictating the ideology of the conflict with the Moors. Riding the tide of jingoistic celebration, writers described Tangier as recapitulating the English achievement elsewhere in the world, and as establishing a power base in Africa similar to the one in America. In mid-September, the garrison scored another victory, thereby giving occasion for further publications. *A Particular Relation of the Late Success of His Majesties Forces at Tangier against the Moors* reported that the victory was made possible by the arrival of more soldiers and provisions from London. Indeed, the number of men in muster at the end of that month reached 3,605.[99] Unlike the previous tracts, *A Particular Relation* was the first account "Published by [royal] Authority" about developments in Tangier; it bore happy news and vindicated the king's expenditure. Another victory ensued at the end of October, after which *A Particular Narrative of a Great Engagement Between the Garison of Tangier and the Moors* was "Published by Authority" to praise "the great Care, Vigilance and conduct of our late Governour Sir Palmes Fairborne." In this narrative, not only is praise heaped on the "undaunted Courage of the Soldiers," along with the numerous military and naval officers whose names are listed, but also on the sacrifice that the governor made, who lost his life in the course of the battle. In celebration of British heroism, a monument was erected in Westminster Abbey in memory of Sir Palms, "mortally wounded by a shot from the Moors"—the first mention of Moors in that ancient bastion of Anglicanism.

Such was the pride in this victory that John Ross, "an eye Witness," as he described himself on the title page, wrote a tract, *Tangers Rescue* (with a poem at the end), to celebrate the victory, recalling the Roman victory against Hannibal and his "Morish Horse." Britain was the new Rome stretching its empire into Africa and defeating the Moors—the "little Nigroes."[100] With euphoric triumph, Ross unleashed his racist vitriol at the "Nigro" who

feeds upon men, and women, drinks their blood. . . .
They march in clusters, like infection fly
Kill thousands of them yet they multiply.
And yet (like Ireland) I may safely say
No venom breeds in a superfluous way.

While vilifying the Moroccans (and the Irish), the author drew attention to the richness of the land they inhabited:

> fruit, and grass after sweet Summer Showers.
> Their Wax and Honey to all Nations sold;
> Enrich'd with Jewels, and the finest Gold.[101]

Tangier was important because it opened the door to the wealth of the little Nigro who "Fights with the Christians" but can be defeated and subsequently dispossessed by the superior English. Ross presented the conflict as a war between Christendom and Islam, and throughout the treatise, he polarized the "Christians" against the "Mores." For him, the rescue of Tangier was the rescue of Christianity in Africa because the war was a confrontation between the dignified humanity of the European Christians (English and Portuguese) and the subhuman and animal-like creatures of Africa, "like so many Cockatrices Spitting poison from their holes," or like "many Bees," "as poor as the Cercopians that were turned to Froggs." It was not surprising that because the Moors were like animals, the victorious Christians cut off their ears "and hung up and dryed [them] to be Monuments, as Trophees of this famous victory."[102]

Another victory ensued on the third of November, which was reported in *Great and Bloody News From Tangier*. The author waxed lyrical about English prowess and bravery. The Moors had been so thoroughly beaten that they signed on 25 November a humiliating treaty with Colonel Edward Sackvile.[103] Reflecting the joy that the victories generated in the London populace, John Dryden finalized *The Spanish Fryar*, which he had been writing since summer (and which first appeared in print in March 1681).[104] Although the play was intended by Dryden to mitigate the prevailing anti-Catholic feelings in a London still gripped by the hysteria of Titus Oates, he opened it with a scene showing the siege of "Saragossa" by Moors, and the Christians' fear at the approaching battle. Dryden returned in the play to the same period in time in which *The Conquest of Granada* had taken place, but in the first act, he recalled the recent events in Tangier. Using some of the images that had appeared in current publications about the defeat of the Moroccans, Dryden described the Moors laying siege to Saragossa as "Bees . . . arming in their hives" (1.1.48). And as the British forces had chased the Moroccans into their trenches, so did Torrismond (1.1.92); and as the Tangier forces had massacred the Moroccans, so did the Christians in the play slay numberless Moors:

> Their Scouts we kill'ed; then found their Body sleeping:
> And as they lay confus'd, we stumbl'ed o'er 'em;
> And took what Joint cam next: Arms, Heads, or Leggs;
> Somewhat undecently. (1.1.135–37)

And as the British had cut off the ears of the Moors, so did Lorenzo pluck "Jewels, Rings, and bobbing Pearls . . . from Moores ears" (1.1.161–62).

Throughout the first eighteen years of the settlement of Tangier, a momentous change was taking place in Britain in regard to the Moors of North Africa. British naval might translated into complete domination of the venues of trade and transportation and resulted in a national self-image bursting with assertiveness, assuredness and superiority. Inside Tangier, the thousands of settlers lived in complete oblivion of the world around them, except at times of battle. Although they did not expand their trade into the heart of the African continent, as King Charles had once hoped, they believed that they could move laterally and occupy the coastal regions of Mediterranean and Atlantic West Africa, from Santa Cruz to Tunis, expelling thereby the Spanish and the French colonizers, and ensuring themselves of access to vast natural and mineral resources—even more than those they had not found in America. Meanwhile, travelers and traders, sailors and wanderers around the Mediterranean believed themselves invincible because of their superior military technology, their religion and their native English genius. The encounter with the Moors had become completely grounded in colonial desire and religious difference.

The End of British Control of Tangier, 1681–1684

The British victory over the Moors, and the publications that appeared in celebration, encouraged King Charles to demand of the House of Commons financial support for the North African outpost. To bolster his appeal, a letter from an earlier Moroccan sultan to the king's father, Charles I, was published in 1680 to show the kind of cooperation and entente that could be established between England and Morocco. The letter described the request that Mulay Muhammad al-Sheikh al-Asghar had made in November 1637 after King Charles had assisted the Moroccan ruler against rebels in Salé. In the letter, he praised the "great Prophet Christ Jesus . . . as the Lyon of the Tribe of Judah as well as the Lord and giver of peace."[105] He then asked King Charles to join him against Tunis and Algiers, since "the ilands which you governe have bene ever famous for the unconquered strength of there shippeing."[106] The letter was so popular, because of its reverent treatment of King Charles I and its praise of his Christian fortitude, that it was published and copied frequently.[107]

The republication of the letter was clearly intended to show that the Moors could be won over as allies and that Tangier could be preserved. The imperial vision could be sustained—with help from the Moors themselves. The visit of the Moroccan ambassador to London on 29 December 1681, Muhammad bin Haddu, raised expectations of improved relations between Mulay Ismail and King Charles II. Indeed, such were the hopes that a group of Unitarians approached the ambassador with an indictment of Trinitarian Christianity and praise for Islam. They believed that if the Moroccans would see eye to eye with them over matters of religion, there would ensue fruitful cooperation between the two countries. Religion, for the Unitarians, did not have to be a separator, for

they and the Moors were not too dissimilar given their rejection of the doctrine
of the Trinity and the godhood of Jesus:

> Be pleased to observe that all ye Christians through out Persia, Armenia,
> Mesopotamia, those called of S. Thomas, & some Hollanders & Portu-
> gases in Asia, these yt lieu among ye Greecks in Europe, even your neigh-
> bouring Christians in Nubia, all those together, wch farr exceed ye Trinity-
> Asserting Christians, doe maintaine with us that Faith of one Soverain
> God, one onely in Person & Essence. And why should I forget to add you
> Mahumetans who also consent with us in ye Belief & worship of an one
> onely Supreme Deity, to whome be glory for ever, Amen.[108]

There was tremendous excitement at the arrival of the ambassador and his
entourage, and soon, there were even paintings of Haddu—one of him on horse-
back in Hyde Park and another in a frontal traditional pose.[109] A poem reported
the activities of the ambassador, who, in just about a month, had visited the most
notable sites in the metropolis:

> On Candlemas-day there did repair and go
> To White-Hall, the Ambassador of Morocco;
> To see that high and most renowned place,
> And each fine Lord deck'd up with Golden lace.
> From thence he went into Westminster-Hall,
> There to espy and there discover all:
> The Courts of Justice where the Judges sit,
> Men great in wisdome and acute in wit.
> To'th Abby he repairs, and there do see
> Effigies of Nobles sent on Embassie.
> And so to Westminster-School he doth repair,
> To see that place where Learning is most rare.[110]

The poem, published on 10 February 1682, denounced the London rabble that
had "rudely" affronted the ambassador on the streets, especially that he had "out
of love come to us about Tangier." Hopes were high that a peace could be reached
to prevent the further deterioration of Anglo-Moroccan relations. Indeed, affairs
looked so promising that the ambassador felt comfortable about petitioning the
king on behalf of one John Hayward, requesting that the Englishman be appointed to the landwaiter's position.[111] At the same time, Tangier supporters
published the letter from Mulay al-Sheikh al-Asghar as if it were the letter the
ambassador had brought with him to the king. Unfortunately, they failed to omit
the praise the Moroccan ruler had included about "James your Father of Glorious memory"—exposing thereby the anachronism of the letter. Shortly after, the
true letter the ambassador had brought with him was published and included a
postscript demonstrating its authenticity.[112] This letter had a very different tone
from the one that had been sent a half century earlier, for Mulay Ismail was

concerned about the continued construction of battlements and fortifications in the bastion. Although his troops had met with difficulty in the last military confrontation, he knew that the British were far from their supply sources and that they would be willing to compromise.

When ambassadors made a good impression on the society they were visiting, local newspaper reporters, poets and diarists wrote favorably about them. Such writings depended on the personality of the ambassador—whether engaging, articulate or suave—and also on his hosts—how much they were interested in developing relations with the ambassador's king. The balance of power between the countries also played a role, as well as the nature of the negotiations and the demands that ambassador and monarch were making on each other, and most importantly, the diplomatic, commercial or military needs the countries had for each other. Bin Haddu spent six months in England (from 29 December 1681 until 23 July 1682). Upon visiting the University of Cambridge, his secretary, despite being "a mahometan," was awarded a degree, showing the respect with which he (as well as other "ambassadors and foreign princes") was received by the University.[113] Later, he visited the site where the new St. Paul's was rising and "gave 15 guineas to the workmen."[114] The ambassador was clearly not loath to visit churches and seemed to have learned much from his visits about his host country and countrymen. In February, he had gone to the King's chapel where he declared: "We have Beene Towld that the Christians worship a god mad of wood or Stone wch they may throw into the fiarre e see Consumed e this we have believed but I have this day with my Eyes I thank God . . . [I have] seene the Contrary I doe believe the English Nation the best people in Europ."[115] He had learned enough to change his views about the Protestant religion and to take those changes back with him to Morocco. As much as Londoners were learning about Islam from him, so was he learning about Christianity from them.

King Charles wanted to consolidate relations with Morocco in order to secure Tangier. On 13 March 1682, Lord Conway described how eager the king was for the "Morocco Ambassadr" to return to his country to "obtaine the Confirmation of the Articles we desire" of the treaty that was negotiated. As a present and an incentive, the king would send with him three hundred muskets and would release "all the Slaves at Tangeir that are properly his owne, and that all the rest shall be relased or removed as soone as the Articles are confirmed." Meanwhile, the ambassador's assistant, his "bassas" (pasha), was to stay in England until the confirmation of the treaty; indeed, he was welcome to join the king at New Market whereupon the king would rent him a house—although the king preferred that he not join him, in order to economize on expenses.[116] Three days later, Conway confirmed that the king preferred that the ambassador, rather than the convert (from Judaism) Lucas, return to Morocco to see through the confirmation. Meanwhile, a Dutch delegation had arrived in London and had moved into the Moroccan ambassador's residence—simply because it was the house where they had stayed the year before. Sir Winston Churchill had to intervene and make them leave so that the ambassador could return.

The presence of the ambassador in London and his (and his delegation's) extensive interactions with members of the court inspired Elkanah Settle to try his hand at yet another Moor play. Most unfortunately, Settle picked on a theme that could not have been less appropriate and more outdated: the death of England's early ally in Morocco, Ghailan, a man who, ten years earlier, had been defeated by the Alawite dynasty that was ruling Morocco and whom the ambassador served. That Settle entitled the play *The Heir of Morocco* would not have been welcomed by the ambassador, if he had occasion to watch this play (as John Evelyn noted, he attended numerous plays in London). Nor would he have welcomed the praise for "Gayland's Crown" nor the mixing of references to "Gods," "Alla," "Jove," "Pluto" and the "Hell-born Sisters." Perhaps most offensive would have been the numerous allusions to the color black in the play, given that the Moroccan ruler, Mulay Ismail, was himself half-black; the hero, Altomar, is denounced for his "Sooty Soul" and for attempting to paint his "blackness white." Despite its Moroccan associations, the play is set in Algiers just after the 1669 Turkish victory over the Venetians in Crete, and shows the cruelty and despotism of the Muslim ruler, Albuzeidan. With echoes of *Othello*, Settle depicted the love between a military commander and a princess—a love that was subverted by a cruel father. Again, and like Dryden earlier, the playwright misrepresented the historical and religious world of the Moors: although Bin Haddu was creating much excitement at court and in the city, he was not generating interest in accuracy.[117]

Bin Haddu left London on 23 July 1682, and had quite an eventful journey back (see appendix 3). A month later, he reached Tangier, where he presented to Colonel Kirke copies of the treaty that was to be signed by Mulay Ismail. Haddu then wrote a letter to King Charles thanking him for the warm welcome and hospitality he had been shown. But his real purpose was not just to be complimentary; he purported to warn the king about Ismail's intentions. Once the truce was over, he wrote, his master intended to "goe with an Army and place himself against Tanger with mighty forces so as nothing shall be able to oppose him." That army, he continued, would include forces from Algiers that the Ottoman sultan was eager to send against the British outpost, they being "ready at his command for any war against the Christians." Indeed, the Ottoman sultan had derided Ismail for permitting Christians to remain on Muslim soil: "How can you that are the true believers have patience and endure in your countries four Christian Garrisons since you may expel them with so much ease within the space of a day." Furthermore, the powerful tribes of the Moroccan Sus region were in support of Ismail and eager to join in battle against "Tanger and the rest of the Christian Garrisons." Haddu then concluded that, because of the king's love and kindness, "I am willing to give you counsill and acquaint you with all this for it is certain my Master has resolved it and Tanger cannot escape from all these forces when the Peace shall have en end." "Have pity on the city of Tanger," he warned.[118]

The letter was not mere Moroccan hyperbole. For upon leaving England, Haddu had taken with him one thousand guns and fifteen hundred quintals of powder—all bought with the gift of five thousand pieces of eight that Charles had given him. The availability of such weapons and munitions in Moroccan hands meant that the situation in Tangier would become dangerous. Apprehensive, Colonel Kirke sought an audience with Ismail in which he managed to charm him, whereupon Ismail promised to cooperate with him, but only with him: "If you had staid there yourselfe," he assured him in a letter of 27 October 1682, "no Musleman had ever come into it against you."[119] But Kirke had been sent to negotiate not just for Tangier but for the seas around it where English shipping and trade were growing, and Ismail would only participate in such negotiations if King Charles would discuss a peace treaty with him. Where the British monarch wanted peace for his garrison, the Moroccan wanted assurance that the formidable British fleet would not attack Moroccan vessels and coastal harbors—as it had in Algiers and Tripoli in the previous decade. In this respect, Ismail was using Tangier as bait for the British. You can keep Tangier as an open mart for trade, he wrote, on condition that you discontinue military hostilities and threats against Morocco. To demonstrate his sincerity, Ismail promised to send a few lions as a present to the king, in return for which the king would send him a fourth "Coach-Horse" to join the three that he had sent with Haddu as a present, because "a Coach wants four Horses to draw it."[120] A peace treaty would ensure the safety of Tangier and presents for the Moroccan king.

On that same day, 27 October, Ismail wrote an amazing letter to Charles II. It was the first he had written to him since the return of Haddu. Eager to prove his desire for cooperation, he thought that one way in which relations could be smoothed out between the two countries was for the British king to convert to Islam. For Ismail, such a conversion should not be difficult since, as he indicated to the king, Islam recognized the holiness of Jesus, as of other prophets: all that King Charles had to do was to "testifie that our Lord Adam, Noah, Abraham, Moses, Jesus, and all other the Prophets & messengers are seruants of God and his Prophets, and true messengers, let us believe what they haue brought and make no difference between his messengers and testifie that our Lord Mahamed is the last of Prophets and Lord of the Messengers." For Ismail, the conversion of Charles II would resolve the conflict between their two countries. Then, the two people would be able to cooperate since Ismail would not be harassed for permitting infidels on his soil. Having made the offer, Ismail continued with a warning: If the British continued building fortifications, "I will not repose till I have sate down before Tanger and filled it with Moors and reduced it to my possession by the favour of God."[121] Ismail threatened that once in possession of Tangier, he would build a fleet comparable to that of the British king to fight the Christians on the other side of the Mediterranean; he would try to fulfill the age-old dream of all Moroccan rulers for over a century of regaining the lost Andalus. Since King Charles did not respond favorably to the invitation to convert (his reply has not survived), Mulay Ismail complained in a letter to Kirke on 21 February 1683 that the king had written "in terms that wee did not expect from him nor can be applied to us." So he gave up on the king, thinking to co-opt Kirke instead, who seemed helpless in the garrison. Ismail invited him to convert to Islam. "By the Almighty God," he wrote him, "I wish thou wert of my religion for thy discretion courtesie and wisedome has giuen the an entrance into my heart and I never desired any Christian to be of my Religion but thy self."[122] A fortnight later, Ismail wrote an angry and blunt letter to King Charles, opening it with very few of the usual honorific titles that were common in his epistles, and shaming the British king for the inappropriateness and uncouthness of his reply to him.[123]

Meanwhile, inside the garrison, morale was falling quickly, and many British merchants started colluding with the Moroccans. Kirke had complained frequently about Britons selling contraband to the Moroccans "in a season that wee had no peace with them by sea";[124] he had also warned about deserters who converted to Islam and soldiers who sold powder to the Moors.[125] Ismail was still willing to cooperate with Kirke, just because, as he always repeated, he had grown to like him: *al-muhib fi jinabina*, the one who is loved by ourselves, as he addressed him.[126] On 5 July 1683, Ismail wrote another blunt letter to King Charles, "the great one of the Ruum [Qur'anic term for Christians] and the prince [n.b., not king] of the kingdom of the English and the great one of Britain, Saxony, Ireland" in which he informed Charles that another peace treaty had to be signed; without it, continued Ismail, he would not allow the British to keep even a "mustard seed" in Tangier.[127] Ismail did not want the British to leave; he wanted them to stay, but on his own terms.

The days of the garrison were now numbered. As Ismail was writing the above letter, King Charles decided that the bastion should be evacuated and the one-thousand-ton mole, which had taken years and thousands of pounds to build, be demolished. Four months later, in October, Lord Dartmouth, along with Samuel Pepys, arrived in Tangier with their mission to evacuate the inhabitants and destroy the city. What Pepys found was a city rife with debauchery and bribery, with officers, including the governor, Colonel Kirke, indulging in sexual license and corrupt business dealing—and paying little attention to the Moors who dotted the surrounding hills, awaiting the time for attack. Once informed of the king's plans, the British and Portuguese inhabitants in the "Citty of Tangier" seized the opportunity to address a letter in which they bewailed their years in Tangier, which they had hoped would provide a safe home for them and their families. There was a tone of reprimand to the king ("hopes that one day the place might answer all your Majesty's royal cares"), but the writers mollified it by expressing satisfaction at the king's resolution to demolish the mole, "lest falling into the hands of the Moors it might prove fatal to the commerce of Europe."[128] A few days later, another letter by the officers and soldiers in the garrison welcomed the king's move: it was better to withdraw than to await the arrival of the king of Morocco's "royall army into these fields."[129]

Everybody was happy to leave the failed enterprise, but as the colonists departed, they bore with them memories of the North Africa they had occupied for years. Much as they had been separated from the Moroccan-Islamic culture of the region, they had still been influenced by it. When they emptied their church, they took with them all that was inside it, including a "Small Turkey Carpet . . . [and] The Marble with the Arabick Inscription."[130] They would carry with them to Britain the little bits of Arabic Islam they had found. By 5 November, as a poet lamented, all the people had left, ironically carried back to England on board the *St. David*, which had been so celebrated just over a decade earlier as the herald of British domination of the Mediterranean.[131] The destruction of the mole began, and continued for over three months.[132] M. Poseley's words to a friend in London captured the feelings of the evacuees about the Moors whom they viewed as being responsible for their departure: "These Devils like so many Rabbits cover'd in the Sands, or so many Snakes and Poison'd Adders, underneath the long Grass, with their Venomous Darts, spitting Fire at their Mouths, lay in Ambuscade ready to Devour us."[133] The animal imagery that had first been used in 1664 was once again in the fore: hostility to the Moors translated into subhumanization. By 5 March 1684, everybody was gone—leaving behind them ruins and destruction—except for a few coins that the king wanted buried in the site to declare "to succeeding ages that that place was once a member of the British Empire."[134]

Lord Dartmouth tried to paint the defeat in favorable terms. On 5 February 1684, he wrote the following note:

Quitted the Out: Posts with great Safety . . . and (as I hope it will be esteemed) with due honour and Regard to His Majties Service; at Least without allowing the Alcayde any pretense of being sainted for driving the English out of Barbary. . . I believe we parted from them wth a much better esteeme, then the Moores have payd to any Christians that have been withdrawing from any Part of Affrica this many Ages.[135]

But in the eyes of the Moroccans, the British had been defeated. Ahmad bin Abd al-Aziz al-Alawi (d. 1689) noted how his compatriots had repeatedly attacked the outer forts of the British bastion as a result of which the "Christians fled into Tangier and then sent to their leader for help. He sent to them ships which they boarded and sailed away at sea. The mukaddam of the sultan then entered it without any resistance in the [month of] Rabi' of the year 1094."[136]

*   *   *

Tangier proved the site of Britain's first direct encounter with Islam on Muslim ground. The encounter was fraught with difficulties and military challenges, which were reported back to London and other parts of Britain. These difficulties, and the later decline and fall of the colony, forced Britons to redefine their understanding of Moors and "Mahumetans" not just as pirates or traders or ambassadors but also as military adversaries and as national forces confronting them with armies of thousands of fighters. Tangier had precipitated England's first "war" with Muslims in the early modern period—and it was not a war where the English, Scots or Irish were superior, nor where Christianity and whiteness prevailed over "Mahumetanism" and "blackness"—in the way that they had prevailed over the "pagan" American Indians. Tangier had proved that in the regions of Islam, Britons would not be able to found another New England. In captivity writings and drama, as in poems and doggerel, autobiography and official reports, Britons drew the line of separation between themselves as Christians and civilized, and the Moors/Africans as Muslims and uncivilized. In Islam, they located the absolute difference between themselves and the Moors.

The unsuccessful settlement of Tangier had inaugurated the British venture into the Mediterranean. In the eighteenth century, and as naval wars and commercial rivalry raged between Britain and France, the Magharibi seized the opportunity to reassume some of their Mediterranean trade, and during the Napoleonic wars, they sailed and traded without much harassment from European powers. Once the wars were over, however, British, Austrian, French, Maltese, Sicilian and even Russian fleets moved in to remonopolize trade and to drive the Barbary ships out, first from the Atlantic and then from the Mediterranean, bringing to a final end the maritime ventures of the Maghrib.[137] The British subsequently ignored the Moors colonially but not commercially. Although they would become the supreme power dominating Mediterranean trade and finance, Britons did not feel the need to colonize any part of Muslim North Africa again. Only after the French had colonized Algeria in 1830, and Khedivite Egypt had gone bankrupt, did they return in 1881 to the Islamic Mediterranean as "conquerors" and as defenders of the British Empire.

Conclusion

In the seventeenth century, a paradigm shift took place as a result of the political, military and social change that had occurred in Britain. English writings about Barbary corresponded to Britain's transition from a trading to an imperial power, from a country whose merchants peddled their wares to a country with a fleet that could dominate and change the course of events in the region. It was a transition from a society that had to negotiate relations with Islam to one that grew militarily and commercially powerful enough to dominate the Islamic seas.

As Thomas Scanlan correctly notes, the American "native populations" played an important role in the "English attempts to accomplish the task of defining themselves."[1] In this there can be no comparison with the powerful and complex role that the native populations of the Barbary States played in the English attempts to define themselves. But British history has been traditionally written at the price of ignoring the Mediterranean Islamic "periphery" and by focusing exclusively on the Euro-Christian "center" in England and later in the England–New England axis. But the periphery was often as much part of the center as domestic conflicts and internal crises. Indeed, a division between center and periphery is difficult to sustain in the context of Britain's involvement with Barbary; until the middle of the seventeenth century, the Barbary States and the rest of the Islamic Mediterranean were instrumental in refashioning the British self-image and determining historical, political and commercial choices. Whatever measure is used to evaluate relations between Britain and Barbary, the evidence of a "diplomatic" community between them is far more extensive than with Turkey, China, Persia or India—notwithstanding the British ventures into those regions. There were more delegations and embassies to and from Barbary, more travelers and merchants, captives and captors, settlers and migrants, than in any other part of the non-Christian world.

This level of community helps explain the role that Barbary played in Britain's literature of the Golden Age, from Spenser to Dryden, and in the historical and political changes that occurred in that most revolutionary of centuries. No other non-Christian region wielded as much direct influence on English imagination as did Barbary—an influence that informed plays, poems, novels, autobiographies, memoirs, travelogues and histories, in English as well as in translation from French, Spanish and other European languages. Quite direct too was the impact of Barbary captivity on London's population in the 1630s and 1640s. Although the ecclesiastical and parliamentary conflicts with King Charles were the most decisive causes of the Civil Wars, the impact of Barbary captivity was an important factor. In similar fashion, the issue of Barbary captivity played a role in the transformation of female social and even political roles. It was fortunate for kinswomen of captives that as their breadwinners were seized into North Africa, and as they turned to agitate and petition, the civic order was being loosened and was giving way to challenges from women writers and "prophets" and sectarian movements. The emergence of women petitioners coincided not only with Britain's expanding commerce in the Mediterranean but also with the destabilization of patriarchal codes by civil strife and military conflict.

Captivity in Barbary and the cultural and religious repercussions of Muslim ascendancy, as depicted in oral and printed literature, changed the way in which Britons viewed themselves and their most formidable Other, the "Mahometan." The continued captivity of Britons by the Barbary Corsairs, and the twenty-year occupation of Tangier, ensured that there were thousands of Britons who, upon their return from the Mediterranean, had stories about "Moors"—as indeed John Dryden admitted hearing in the preface to *Don Sebastian*. By 1689, the date of the play, Moors and their society, their internecine conflicts and their religious underdevelopment were well known to the English reading public. But to Dryden, such knowledge was irrelevant as he turned, again, to change history and write, as he announced, "pure fiction" about the Moorish past. As in *The Conquest of Granada*, Dryden dramatized in *Don Sebastian* a historical episode—the aftermath of the battle of Alcazar—but invented a new history of the Portuguese. He moved away from historical verisimilitude; the narrative was his, not the Moors,' and he could modify, invent and transform it the way he pleased—and that pleased his audience, too. Poetic license gave him the dramatic power to change past events and to make history subservient to contemporary theatrical need. There was no reality that he could not change because the past belonged to his imagination and memory. The battle of Alcazar that had ended with the defeat and death of the Christian king and the victory of the Moorish king could not be tolerated, and events had to be changed so that they appealed to, and entertained, the audiences. After all, as Dryden proclaimed, "the English will not bear a thorough Tragedy."[2]

But they could bear ridicule of Islam and a negative depiction of Moors and their silly, bloody and lustful culture. For as Britons were now realizing their imperial goal in America (only four years earlier, a book had been written by R. B., "illustrated with maps and pictures," about *The English Empire in America*), they turned to separate themselves from the non-Christian and non-European Moors: Dryden presented his play in December 1689 after the anti-Catholic Glorious Revolution had deprived him of his office and pension.[3] In poverty, religious and political illegitimacy and "bad circumstances," as he wrote in the preface, he turned to do unto Islam what his countrymen were doing unto Catholicism. Himself defeated, he turned to defeat the Muslim Other, employing the same exaggeration and misrepresentation that his countrymen used against Catholics in their libels and satires. In the play, Dryden presented his audience with an Islamic setting where Moors swore by their "Prophet" and their "Law,"

and invoked "Alcoran," "Alchoran" and "Holy Mahomet"—words that constituted about the only knowledge that he showed about Islam in the play. Such
emphasis served to posit Islam as a foil to Christianity—the Catholic Christianity
of his heroic but tragic fighters—and as an expression of an irrational and violent
civilization. The one topic Dryden could ridicule and attack and on which the
British public, both Protestant and Catholic would concur, was Islam.

Where a hundred years earlier, Peele and other Elizabethan playwrights had
emphasized the Negroid features of the Moors, and contrasted them with their
own English/European whiteness, Dryden, along with the other Restoration
playwrights, used the religion of the Moors rather than their race to alterize them
into dangerous Others. After all, when the Spaniard Antonio wore Moorish
clothes, even the mufti was unable to see through his disguise. It was the "genius"
of their religion, he wrote, that made the Moors evil. The Moors, he continued,

> Scarcely want a Guide to move their madness:
> Prompt to rebel on every weak pretence;
> Blustering when courted, crouching when opprest.
> Wise to themselves, and fools to all the World.
> Restless in Change, and perjur'd to a Proverb.
> They love Religion sweeten'd to the sense;
> A good luxurious palatable faith.[4]

To authenticate the Islamic violence and stupidity of the "Affricans," as the
Moors are deliberately called in the play, to emphasize their apartness from Europeans, Dryden introduced widely held information about Morocco and the
Moroccans. The description of the Christian captives in Muslim hands corresponded to what the writings of English captives, and European captives in English translation, had confirmed: how Europeans were sold in slave markets, how
they were treated like animals, how they were made to jump and prance like
horses, how they were poked and slapped around. That the Moorish "Emperor"
in Don Sebastian kept "Lions keen within their Dens" to punish unruly captives
corresponded to Mulay Ismail's keeping of lions in his palaces in Meknes.[5] That
the Emperor's troops were "beleaguering Larache / Yet in the Christians hands"
coincided with the siege of that Spanish presidio by Ismael's forces in 1689 (and
their subsequent victory).[6] Dryden used the Muslims to deride the memory of
the Puritans, a popular analogy in the Restoration. When Mustafa excoriated
the Moorish mob, he identified them with the iconoclastic Puritans who had
demolished "Christian Temples, and [bore] off in triumph the Superstitious Plate
and Pictures, the Ornaments of their wicked Altars, when all rich Moveables
were sentenc'd for idolatrous."[7] The character of Muley-Moluch was evil, Dryden wrote in his preface to the play, because Muley-Moluch reflected the evil of
the present ruler of Morocco, Mulay Ismail.[8] Portuguese soldiers captured in
the battle of Alcazar were brought before Muley-Moluch so he himself could
determine how they would be sacrificed[9]—as Ismail, with his own hands, was

reported to kill his slaves and captives. The sacrifice of soldiers was not a cruel decision of a fictional Moor but part of the religious culture of Islam and a fulfillment of the prophet Muhammad's desire for "Offerings"—as was the case with the rape of Almeyda, which Benducar proclaimed had been made lawful by the Prophet of Islam.[10] Factual information about Morocco was laced with inventions about Islam to produce a fantasia of bigotry about the Moors of alien and monstrous "Affrica."

Like earlier writers, Dryden eagerly highlighted Muslim stupidity: inspired perhaps by T. S. (and Shakespeare's Jewish-Christian marriage in *The Merchant of Venice*), he presented the successful elopement of the Christian captive Antonio with the daughter of the lustful Mufti—who, like other Moorish women in English writings, would renounce her Islam and embrace Christianity. Restoration writers realized that they had to reverse the theme that had dominated Elizabethan and Jacobean drama of the Muslim male (both Turk and Moor) taking possession of the Christian female. After all, in 1682, during Bin Haddu's visit, a Jew-turned-Muslim member of the delegation took an Englishwoman as a wife without provoking any complaint against this Muslim-Christian marriage: "With us [in England]," observed Thomas Rymer, "a Moor might marry some little drab, or Small-coal Wench."[11] On the Restoration stage, therefore, any Moorish woman marrying a Christian was made to renounce her Islam. With the Moors consigned to their mountainous and barbarous regions, with the British having left them after destroying everything they had built on their continent ("demolish and utterly to destroy the said city [of Tangier] and the Mole . . . so as they may be altogether useless, and no pirate or enemy of the Christian faith may at any time hereafter make their abode or retreat there"),[12] Dryden and his London audience could think, imagine, invent and describe the Moors any way they wanted. The Moor was no longer enigmatic, dominant or interesting but was instead a representative of uncivilized and degraded people—which is why his picture was pinned to butts on which London javelin throwers practiced, as John Evelyn noted on 18 December 1685. It was the Moors, wrote Dryden in *Don Sebastian*, not the Europeans, who were now the slaves: "Slaves," declared the renegade, Dorax, "are the growth of Africk, not of Europe"—which is why Moorish history could be "enslaved" by the playwright and why Moorish victories could be reversed, and why Moors themselves could be obliterated or recreated. Neither audience nor playwright viewed Moors any longer as agents in their lives; the Moors who had preoccupied them in Tangier were now a memory, and North Africa was, as Sebastian stated, "a narrow neck of Land for a third World; / To give my loosen'd Subjects room to play"—very much like Tangier to where "loosen'd" Britons had once gone—and from where they had returned.[13]

*   *   *

Don Sebastian was the last major Moor play in the seventeenth century. London society would never again see on stage or the page the excitement and intrigue about the North African Moors that the Elizabethans had witnessed a century earlier. The most impressive and "heroic" Moor, Aphra Behn's Oronooko, would be relocated to America, and completely de-islamized. With their power dominating the seas and the spheres of trade, commerce and diplomacy, Britons no longer even viewed the Moors as historical agents in the Mediterranean but as mere allegories. In the same year in which Dryden's play appeared, a novel was published, *The Amours of the Sultana of Barbary,* where the sultana depicted, as the seventeenth-century hand on the cover of the novel explained, the Duchess of Portsmouth, and "Acmat (the Grand Signior) . . . tall, had a goodly Meen, full of Majesty and Grandeur" was "Charles 2d. K. of England." The parallels continue: Indamora is the sultana who is the Duchess of Portsmouth; Homira is the Duchess of Cleveland; Amurath is the Duke of Marlborough; the "noble Turk" is the Earl of Castelmain and so on. The Moors had become unreal, with no inherent truth: they were distant enough, both geographically and imaginatively, to be invented in any way a novelist or a playwright chose.

Meanwhile, about the only "real" Moors whom Britons were seeing were merchants and traders who sailed into English and Welsh ports, disembarked, wandered about, bought supplies and were accosted by academics eager to perfect their mastery of North African Arabic. In June 1714, Simon Ockley described how, upon coming across terms in Arabic that he could not translate, he would go to London "among merchants yt have been in the Country, & sometimes from the Moors themselves," and query them about enunciation and meaning.[14] More numerously, however, were the Moroccans and other North Africans who arrived to petition for restitution of their property, stolen by French or Maltese pirates while they were sailing on British vessels.[15] The petitioners show how London had become the locus for Magharibi traders and how some of these dispossessed Magharibi were leaving their homes and traveling into the cold North to protest the pirates and privateers who had ruined their lives and livelihoods. Their journeys to England were humiliating and desperate, for they arrived without financial resources (lost to the European attackers), and inevitably had to spend weeks and months before they gained access to the proper authorities—if they did—and presented their petitions. Their poverty, ignorance of the culture, strange looks and overall vulnerability further marginalized them from their hosts. In 1725, there were so many such Magharibi victims of continental piracy that they became quite familiar on London streets, as John Windus observed.[16]

By the time Windus wrote his description of Meknes, Britain ruled the waves, and London was the center of a vast empire of navigation, exchange, barter and communication from the Atlantic and Indian Oceans to the Mediterranean basin. In the ensuing age of empire, Britons no longer treated the Moors as figures of power and authority but relegated them to accounts of captivity or naval reports, with neither drama nor passion, just diplomatic maneuvers, negotiations and the occasional bombardment.[17] Britons no longer expressed any interest in exploring the role of the Moors in their culture and thought. The Moor had moved from a towering figure in the Elizabethan period to a criminal pirate, an obsequious petitioner, a bribable ambassador and a decadent ruler. A century after the first Moors had impressed and intimidated London with their power and exoticism, the "last Moors" sent abject petitions, signifying the demise of Barbary as an inspiration and a challenge.

Appendix 1

AN ACT for the releife of the Captives taken by Turkish Moorish and other Pirates and to prevent the taking of others in time to come.

AN ACT for the releife of the Captives taken by Turkish Moorish and other Pirates and to prevent the taking of others in time to come.

Rot. parl., 16 *Car. p. 2. nu.* 20.

WHEREAS many thousands of your Majesties good and loving subjects with theire Ships and Goods have of late time beene surprised and taken at Sea (as they were in theire lawfull trading) by Turkish Moorish and other Pirats and some of them to free themselves of the cruell and barbarous usage of those Pirats have renounced the Christian Religion and turned Turks and others yet kept in bondage are used with so extreme cruelty as they are in great danger thereby to lose theire lives unlesse they shall alsoe forsake the Christian Religion And diverse of those your subjects kept in bondage (being expert and skilfull Mariners) are usualy imployed at Sea against others your good subjects and prove [very[1]] prejudiciall to them and hurtfull to the trade and merchandise of your Majesties Dominions And whereas aswell your Majesties subjects as Strangers exporting or importing theire goods and merchandize into this Kingdome have ever sithence your Majesties accesse unto this Crowne beene charged with the payment of great sums of money under the name of Custom and that without Consent of Parliament which had they beene legally taken ought to have been chiefly imployed to the safeguard of the Seas and preservation of your good subjects in theire trade of merchandize from the spoile of Pirats and other Sea Robbers but have been exhausted by evil Ministers and not applied to their proper uses so that your Highnes good subjects have beene exposed to the mercilesse cruelty of those Pirats and barbarous infidels And the Commons taking into further consideration your Majesties pressing wants and great occasions of moneys in these times of distemper aswell in the Kingdome of Ireland as other Kingdoms of foreign Princes so that there will be required some further aid to inable your Highnes to effect so great a Worke besides the present Tunnage and Poundage now granted to your Majestie have there-

Recital that many Subjects, expert Seamen, and others, were were detained in Captivity, and forced to renounce the Christian Religion, &c.

and that Money had been since the King's Accession taken from the Subject without consent of Parliament.

Reasons for passing this Act.

fore for this present pressing occasion and for a time hereafter limited taken into theire Resolutions a further way of raising a supply of moneys for the providing and setting forth to the Seas a Navie aswell for the enlargement and deliverance of those poore Captives in Argier and other places if Almightie God shall [so[1]] please to give that blessing unto theire enterprises as alsoe for the preventing of the like future dangers unto your good people theire persons ships and Merchandizes Do therefore pray your Most Excellent Majestie that it may be enacted And be it enacted by authority of this present Parliament That where any Subsidy Custome or other dutie after the nine and twentieth day of September in the yeare One thousand six hundred fourty one and before the foure and twentieth day of June then next following shall be laid or imposed by authority of Parliament upon any Goods Wares or other Merchandize of what nature kinde or qualitie herein mentioned,soever be exported out of or imported into this your Majesties Realme of England or Dominion of Wales that one other sum of One in the hundred according to the rates to be established by Parliament within the time aforesaid over and above the said custome subsidie or dutie so to be laid or imposed to be laid out inshall be raised levied and paid from and after the tenth day of December in the yeare One thousand six hundred fourty one aforesaid of and from all and every such Goods Wares and other Merchandize to be imported into or exported out of this your Majesties and said Realm of England or Dominion of Wales the said summe of one in the hundred to be raised levied and paid for the space of three yeares next after the said tenth day of December and no longer And received and taken by the Lord Maior and Chamberlain of London for the Time being theire Deputies or Deputie and by them the said Lord Maior and Chamberlain of London for the Time being to be layed out payed and imployed for providing and setting out to sea and maintaining of one or more Fleet or Fleets of good and serviceable Ships and other necessaries to be used and imployed for the purposes aforesaid in such sort as by order of a Committee of the House of Lords and a Committee of the House of Commons in Parliament of this your Majesties Realme of England shall be directed And such Lord Maior and Chamberlain of London who shall receive or disburse any the moneys aforesaid shall be accountable and account for all and every theire receipts and disbursements afore mentioned to the said Committee or to such person or persons as the said Committee shall order and appoint

Additional Duty of Customs of One in the Hundred on all Duties to be laid on Goods exported, a herin mentioned, for Three Years, to be received by the Lord Mayor and Chamberlin of London, to be laid out in maintaining a Fleet, under the Direction of a Committee of the Lords and Commons respectively; Lord Mayor, &c. to be accountable to the said Committee.

AND be it alsoe enacted by the authoritie aforesaid that if any Goods Wares or other Merchandize whereof the sum of one in the hundred aforesaid is or shall be due and payable by vertue of this Act shall att any time hereafter be shipped or put into any Boat or other Vessell to the intent to be carried into the parts beyond the Seas or else be brought from the parts beyond the Seas into any part of this your Realm of England or Dominion of Wales by way of Merchandize and unshipped to be laid on land the sume of one in the hundred as aforesaid due or to be due for the same not payed or lawfully tendered and secured to be paid to the Maior and Chamberlain of London for the time being or theire deputy or deputies for the uses aforesaid all the same goods wares and other merchandize whatsoever shall be forfeited and lost the one moity of the rate or value thereof to be to him or them that will seize or sue for the same and the other moytie to be imployed to and for the uses before expressed.

II.
If Goods attempted to be exported or imported, and the said Duty not paid,

the Goods to be forfeited.

AND for the better incouragement of Mariners to undertake the said service and Owners of Ships to let out theire Ships for the said imployment Be it further enacted by the authority aforesaid that if any Ships goods or merchandize of the said Pirats or of the Subjects of any that are or shall be in enmity with your Majestie your heires or successors or the person of any such Pirates shall be taken by the Ships to be imployed in the service before mentioned that one fourth part thereof shall be to the Mariners that shall take the same and one other fourth part to the Owners of the said Ships over and above theire hire and wages and the other two fourth parts to and for such uses as the said Committees shall order and appoint and the overplus of the money to be raised by vertue of this Act and not imployed to and for the service aforementioned (if any shall be) shall alsoe be imployed according to the Order of the same Committees.

III.
Captures from the Pirates how to be divided.

AND be it further declared and enacted by the authority aforesaid that this p'sent Act for the raising of moneys for the setting forth of Ships for the suppressing of Pirates and safety of Merchants shall not hereafter be drawn into example but that your Majesty would in time to come be pleased to intrust such Ministers as may faithfully imploy the moneys raised by Tonnage and Poundage unto the right and proper uses for the guarding of the Seas and safety of Merchants which will advance the honour of your sacred

IV.
This Act not to be drawn into Example.

Majestie abroad and procure the safety peace and happiness of your Highnes loyall and faithfull subjects at home.

Note

1. Interlined on the Roll.

Appendix 2

The Captivity Narrative of John Whitehead

Nothing is known about John Whitehead, but Sir Hans Sloane (1660–1753), to whom Whitehead dedicated his account, was a British collector and physician. After living in London and traveling in France, Sloane worked toward a degree in medicine, which he received in 1683 from the University of Orange in France. He returned to England with a vast collection of plants and other curiosities, and was elected to the Royal Society. In 1687, he went to Jamaica and collected specimens of plants that he catalogued in *Catalogus plantarum quae in insula Jamaica* (1696); and in 1707 he published *A Voyage to the Islands Maderam Barbados, Nieves, S. Christopher's* (1707). In 1693 he became secretary of the Royal Society and began editing its *Philosophical Transactions*. It was in the context of this editorial task that he asked Whitehead to write an account of his captivity, probably urging him to describe all the aspects that would be of interest to his readers. The captivity account became part of the Royal Society archive. Sloane died in January 1753.

> To my most esteemed & very charitable Benefactor M[aste]ᵣ Hans Sloan Doctor of Physick.
>
> S[i]ᵣ
>
> Tho[ugh] none can be more willing than myself with Pleasure to serve you so far as I am able (otherwise I should be most ingreatful on whom you have laid the greatest of obligations, which I shall be ready thankfully to acknowledge on all occasions) yet I am apprehensive, that in my obeying yo[u]ᵣ late commands you will not meet with that satisfaction which I am sorry for: but, as I have in a great measure experienc'd yo[u]ᵣ goodness, I promise to my self your Excuse when you please to consider the heavy Pressures of Servitude which I labour'd under while in Barbary such as Confinement at my Work; Abuses received from a barbarous & inhumane People; the little or no Hope I had of ever seeing Christendom again; and consequently the great Dejection of my Spirits: which you may easily conceive was enough to banish from me all thoughts of making such Observations, and registering Memoires of 'em, as some travelers use to do, for the satisfying of themselves and others. And indeed had I been free from these Miserys, & enjoy'd my Health & Liberty in that Country, I am very sensible of my Insufficiency & want of Capacity to have made such Remarks, as would be worth your Regard. However, to testify my Obedience to your Commands, I shall give you a Relation; tho[ugh] imperfect & weak, of somewhat I have observ'd, as my troubled mind can call things to Remembrance. My Ability to serve you in this Kind is not answerable to my

Good-will: therefore that you may please favourably to accept of the First, for the sake of the Latter, is the humble request of
S[i]ʳ
Yo[u]ʳ most obliged, and most humble servant
John Whitehead

On the first of January 1690/1 I sail'd from the Road of Carrickferyas Supra-cargo on a small vessel bound for the Island Theneviffa; the Master & eight hands more being on Board. We were ten in Company & took our course about the North of Ireland to shun the French Privateers: but tho[ugh] we escap'd them, on the 9th of Feb. following it was our lot (as the most Wise the Divine Providence was pleas'd to order it) to fall into the hands of our greatest Enemys, I mean, those barbarous Infidels the Moors; for partly by reason of bad Weather, and partly though Ignorance & Mistake of the Master, in the Night our ship fell in amongst Banks of Sand on the Barbary shores, against which the surges of the sea breaking rose like Mountains: & had it not been then spring tide (for the Moon chang'd that very night) and just the time of High-Water; we must needs all have perisht: for as we were upon the Banks, sometimes the ship struck; but at last was driven ashore almost to a full-Sea Mark: where she quickly bilged and stranded and had her Deck stav'd down by the seas that wash'd all over her. When the Tide ebb'd from her, we saw the Damage was not to be repaired by us: and tho[ugh] the ship had continu'd sound and tight, when we lookt towards the sea; we saw it was impossible to get her over the Banks & Shallows, which were two miles off shore, against the broken surges of the sea, and far less could our Boat, tho[ugh] it was whole, do us any service: for the Beaches were much alike when the Wind was off shore, as when it blew right in [on the Northside of Cape de Non]. The Place is a Sandy Bay in the Latitude of 28 Degrees and 40 Min. The Land we found to be a Sandy Desert without grass or trees - shrubs enough grow there, and abundances of Prickle Pears (so one of our company called them; having as he said seen several in the West Indies). There are of them small & great, some 18 or 20 Foot in circumference near the ground, and 4 or 5 Foot high: they rise somewhat tapering towards the top, and grow in Clusters like Grapes, or closer, but with this Difference, each Grape of the Cluster is round, but the Particles that compose the Pear-Prickle are long, and have each of 'em a sharp Prickle on the top: they are soft as cowcumbers, and when bruis'd or broken yield a milk that will drop from them of a bitter taste, which 'tis said if it touches the Eyes will make one blind.

There were in this Desert such swarms of Locust, that I could scarce set my boot down without treading on them: in some Places, they were so thick, that they seem'd at a distance to be a pleasant spot of Grass: when they rose together, they made a Shadow on the Ground; as if a cloud had interpos'd betwixt & the Sun. I saw no Beast there but one Anthylop nor Spring nor River except once that two Moors about a Stone's Cast from the sea mark made a Hole in the Sand with their Hands, as deep as they could reach till they came to a white

Clay, whense sprung up immediately as sweet water as ever I drank in my Life, only it was whitish & a little muddy, for we gave it not time to settle.

About 25 miles to the Northward of the Place where the ship was cast away, we were brought among Mountains to a Village of tents all black, made of Goats Hair. The People that dwelt there, had no Corn and consequently not a Bit of Bread to eat: they kept cattle but could not afford themselves any Flesh to eat, at least did not for four days that I was amongst 'em. Their Food besides their Milk, so far as I could perceive; was only Locusts, which when they had catcht & kill'd, they laid on their tents to be dried by the Sun; afterwards they pull'd off Head, Wings, & Legs; and ate the Body alone, which will be about two inches long, & near as much about: they tasted, as seemed to me, somewhat of fishes for I have eaten several of them dried after this Manner; but they have another way of cooking them which my Stomach would not at all approve of: that is, after the Locusts are dried, they pat them into a trough without dismembering them as before; and beat or pound all together very small; then they put them into a Platter of milk stirring all about and so eat it up. They would by no means let us see where they kept their Water, which I suppose was only standing Water in some Hole covered from the Sun for about that time of the year there is sometimes great Rain there. Their Cattle had no Water to drink, but I believe the Showers that happen'd and the Dew that fell in the Night on the Grass refresht them. When their Cattle have eaten all bare round about them, they load their Tents & their Lumber on their Camels (setting their Wives and Children above all, who sit in things like Cradles made of thick sticks) and drive their Cows, Sheep, & Goats before them to another Place, where they pitch their Tents again in a Ring; and make a Hedge of Thorns and Shrubs about all. Their Cattle are brought every Evening into the Middle within the Ring where they are kept till Morning, to save them from being devour'd by Lions that range about in the Night.

From these Tents we were carry'd through the mountains about 35 miles to the North easterly, into a large Plain to a small Fortress called Wadnoon [Wadi Nun], kept by three hundred Souldiers Horse & Foot, who were commanded by an Alcaide: their Wives & Children liv'd with them in the Fort. The Walls of it, as also of the houses within it, were only of Earth, which when moistened a little with Water, is mixt well, & made into a dry sort of Morter: whereof nine or ten inches at a Time is put into Wooden Cases or Boxes and ramm'd close together with Beetles or Rammers of Wood: when the Boxes are full they remove them, and place them again on the top of that they ramm'd in them before. Their Houses are flat rooft, they lay Canes or Bundles of sticks close together over the Timbers; and then Earth on the Canes: when it rain'd their Houses were very leaky for want of Lime there to make good Morter: for which Reason their Walls also soon decay.

They had no other Corn here than Barley, which they ground with Hand-Mills that often made their Meal of Flower very Sandy: they make broad thin Cakes which they bake in an earthen Pan, of the fashion of a frying Pan, set over an easy Fire. All the People that live in Tents, also the poorer sort that live in Towns, make their Bread after this manner throughout all the Emperor of Morocco's Dominions.

We left Wadnoon, and after we had rid about 100 Miles, we came to Taradante [Taroudant] the Metropolis of Sooss [the Sus region], and place of Residence of the Emperor of Morocco's Lieutenant, who Governs all that Country under him. The Governor at that Time was a Bashaw, who since was sent for by the Emperor, & strangled upon Complaint made by the Country of his Avarice & Cruelty; and for not pleasing the Emperor by sending him Presents great enough. As we were Coming to this Place we saw several Towns that had come to Ruine: a Moor of our company (that spoke some few Words of corrupt Spanish, or Lingua franca, as 'tis called) as we pass'd by these depopulated Towns, pointing his Finger to them, told me the Emperor had kill'd most of the People, and that the rest had fled to the Mountains. The Bashaw was then in camp with an Army of 14,000 Men against these Mountaineers, who had got together in a Body of 30000 to defend their Liberty. Since that, as I acquainted you before, the Bashaw was sent for by the Emperor, who sent one of his own Sons in his Place: through whose Clemency & good Government (tho[ugh] a youth not twenty years of age) these People did most of them submit to him: while he was governor he was well belov'd, which made his Father jealous of him, and apprehensive that some time or other he might revolt: therefore he recall'd him, and picking a Quarrel with him, he beat him, and sent another Governor in his Place. In this 100 miles we found the Country but ill watere'd: on the road we met with narrow Ditches fourty or fifty foot long archt to save Rain Water & cover it from the Sun, for the Convenience of Travellers. I do not remember that I saw Wheat growing there (some I am satisfy'd they have notwithstanding) but great Plenty of Barley. I have seen there seven or eight miles in Length, and a mile & a half or two miles over, as near as I could guess, all Barley, as high almost as my Shoulder as I sat on Horseback. The People were then a reaping which was about the middle of March.

Taradante is situate in a pleasant Plain 60 miles to the Eastward of S^t [Santa] Cruz [Agadir], a Sea Port that lys in the Latitude of 30 Deg. Min where the River Sus that passes Taradante falls into the Atlantick Ocean: while I was there I had not Liberty to go out of the Castle till I came away: therefore could see but little of the City within: where view'd at a Distance it seem'd to be a large Place. The Walls are of a good Height, and firm Works made of good Morter, whereof one third part is Lime, & the other two thirds Earth which, when well mixt, and ramm'd or beaten into such Cases as I made mention of before, becomes so hard when thoroughly dry'd, that a Pickax will scarce enter it. As the cases are remov'd, the Work is plaister'd on both sides with a white morter, which does very much beautify it, & also preserve the Walls from Decay. See Fig 1.2.

From Taradante we travell'd twelve Miles North easterly, and came to Atlas Mountains which we crossed to go into the Kingdom of Morocco: in our Way we pass'd some Places of great Danger by reason of the narrowness of the Passages on the tops of Precipices; but our Mules were sure footed.

In nine days after we left Tardante we came to the City of Morocco [Marrakesh], which was also govern'd by a Bashaw: it is wall'd about, and seem'd to be of a great Circumference: we were also confin'd in the Castle there, while we staid so that we had not Liberty to take a view of the City within: that part of it which we past in going to & from the Castle look'd like a decay'd place; the Houses were but thin & scattering; and here & there lay a Dung-hill or heap of Dirt and Rubbish: but I was inform'd it was not so farther into the City. A River passes it which runs away to the Northwestward to the Atlantick Ocean.

After we left the City of Morocco, in three or four days we came to a small Town called Tedla [Kasba Tedla], not wall'd about. 'Tis situate near to, or on the Bank of another River that falls into the same Atlantick Sea at a town called Azamore [Azemmour], three leagues to the East of a Garrison that the Portuguese have on that Coast called Masagan [Mazagan]. There is a Castle on the South side of the River, built lately by the Emperor's Christian Slaves, almost opposite to Tedla. On the Road coming hither we met with Giants Graves (so they were call'd by a Moor, one of our Guard that could speak Spanish) they were of prodigious Length. There was about half a Score of them. One of our Company alighted from his Mule, and measured the longest of them which was five and twenty of his Paces. I found another to be two & twenty of the Mule's Paces that I rode on, for I did not alight. They were all covered with stones to the Length: but it seems there has not been that Care taken to mark the due and proportional Breadth: for by the stones they were but three or four Foot over. The Moor told me that a tooth of one of these Giants did weigh seven pounds; and that they were some of the Aborigines of the Country. In this last 3 or 4 days journey; the Weather being excessive Hot; and neither Spring nor River to be seen above half the Way, (and my self and the rest of the Christians not being able to endure thirst & to satisfy our selves with so little Water as the Moors allow'd either to themselves, or to us of that they carry'd along with them in Leathern Bottles) We were necessitated to drink of any stinking Pool of Rain Water that we could meet with; and then after the Fatigue of our Journey every Day, sleeping in the Night abroad under unwholesome Dews that fell, and sometimes, Rain made us all sick: some of an Ague & Feaver, and some of a Feaver alone: and in this Condition after four Days Journey from Tedla we were brought to Maccaness [Meknes] where the Emperor of Morocco keeps his Court. In eight Days after we came hither Six of our Company dyed: and two more some few Weeks thereafter. My self and other recover'd of that Sickness, after we had labour'd Ten weeks under it in extreme Misery: but the other is since dead. So that of all our Ships Company, I am only through the mercy of God remaining now alive.

Maccanes is divided into two Parts, the Old town & the new. The first is situate on an easy Hill, the Buildings descending from the Top on each side. 'Tis said to be built & wall'd about first by the Portuguese, who once were Masters of a great Part of the Country. The old Walls were thrown down, and new Walls have been rais'd about it within this ten or twelve years. 'Tis thirty miles to the

North of Fess [Fez] and seventy Miles East & by South from Sally [Salé], and lays in the Latitude 33 Deg. 30 Min. A small River runs by the North side of it, which falls into the Atlantick Ocean at Manora, 15 miles to the Eastward of Sally. The Emperor's Palace is seated at the East End of the Town, and is encompassed with a high Wall: The Circumference about three quarters of a Mile, but the Circuit of the old Town and Palace together is about two miles and a half. On the South Side of the Town and Castle or Palace, at a little Distance from them, lys the New Town. To the South Eastward of all are the Emperor's Gardens and his Stables, all wall'd about. The Compass of all together, that is, of the old & new Towns; Palace: Stables, and Gardens is Six or Seven Miles. The Palace is lately built. The Houses within are very high, covered with green tyles, not flat-roof'd, as generally the Houses of the Town are, but sloping, eminent above the Battlements on the Top of the Walls that surround the Palace which afford a hansome Prospect at a Distance. I was never within it but have been inform'd that there are stately Courts in it, of a square figure, set about with Marble Pillars, which support fine painted Works above, and in the Middle of the Courts hansome Marble Fountains, of the Fashion of great Basins, that have Holes in the Bottoms of 'em through which delicate Water does boil up constantly, that is brought by Conduits from it's Spring about three miles. In one of the Courts there are seventy & two Marble Pillars.

The Emperor has about Two hundred Eunuchs that are the inner Guards of his Palace, & of his Women; of whom he has several Hundred and has always a School of young virgins a bringing up for him: from whence he still takes al his Pleasure such as are come to fit years to be his Concubines notwithstanding that he is near Sixty years of Age. His Women are of diverse Colours as White, Black, Mulattos or Copper colour'd of several sorts: His Father was a White; his Mother a Black; and he is Mulatto himself: which Colour is doubtless best liked by him; the Woman that is most in his Favour, and to whom he has given the Title of Sultaness; as also that Son whom he has Nominated to be his Sucessor, being both of his own Colour. His Eunuchs dare suffer no Man to go into the Palace where the Women are but himself. He never permits them to go abroad, but when 'tis his Pleasure to call them out: and then he rides before them with his Launce on his Shoulder: some Hundreds of them following him all in a Croud on foot; and Eunuchs on Horse-back at some distance from them firing their Pieces laden with Ball round about, to give Notice that the Emperor's Women are abroad, at which time all clear the Way: Christians, Jews, and the Moors themselves to shun being seen by the Emperor or his Eunuchs: Such as are at his Works are then also oblig'd to make haste & quit them, & keep themselves out of sight till the Women be past, least they should be shot by the Eunuchs, or Launc'd by the Emperor himself. 'Tis said he had three hundred Children nine or ten years ago.

The Habit of the Men that are of Ability, and do furnish themselves with a compleat suit of Apparel, is after this Manner: the Moor puts on first, Linnen Drawers that reach down to his Feet; then his linnen Shirt which hangs down about the length of his Knees above or on the outside of his Drawers, each sleeve of the Shirt is as large as the Body: above his shirt he wears a colour'd Cloath Wastecoat, not much unlike to the fashion of ours except that it wants Sleevs: yet some do wear them with Sleevs in Winter. On their Heads (which they shave all except one Lock that they leave) they wear red Caps with Silken or Linnen Sashes twisted and roll'd about them. Above their Wastecoat they wear a white Garment about fifteen foot long, and about half so broad made of Wool: which they wrap about their shoulders, and put sometimes over their Heads: the breadth of it hanging down loosely about them to their Shoes. This long Garment is call'd by the Moors a Haig, which is made so fine and thin for summer Wear and is so white, that it looks like Muslin: but for Winter they have of another sort, thick and warm. Sometimes above their Haig they have a short Cloak open before from the Breast downwards, with a Hole in it at the Neck to put their Head through, and a little Hood like a Monk's Cowl hanging down behind between their Shoulders to put upon their Head when they please. They have also a long Cloak of blew Cloath: 'tis wide and large as an English Cloak: but close before, and has a Hole at the Neck and Hood as the short one. They have also a white loose Coat close before, with a Hole at the Neck for their Head to go thorow, and Holes in it for their Arms: above this they ty a Sash about their Middle: This they wear instead of a Wastecoat: 'tis like a wide smock or shift for Women without sleeves: most of all the People of the Country wear such next their Skin: some are made of Leather (for there's not the tenth part of them use linen shirts, and many no Drawers that are of the poorer Sort) their long Blanket they wrap about them above That: and their short Cloak above all when 'tis cold. Or else instead of a short Cloak, such a Coat as the Emperor gives to his Christian Slaves every year: close before with a Hole at the Neck for the Head to go through, and a Hood behind, with short sleeves. (The Seamen go after another fashion, they wear a short Jacket, and long Breeches) Their shoes are almost like Irish Brogues: of one Sole of Neet's leather: the upper leather of Goats skin & lin'd, the outside colour'd yellow, the Lining red. I never saw any wear Boots but the Emperor which were of red Leather [Goats skin] plaited or folded very even, not lengthwise, but cross & round his leg. Wigs, Cravats, or Neck-cloaths, Gloves, Breeches, nor Stockins they wear none.

The Apparel of the Women of that Country does much resemble that of the Ancient Irish the white Women plat their Hair, and the Blacks, (whose Hair is short & curl'd) to be of the Fashion, fasten to their Heads false Plats of black Silk, or Woollen Thred which they turn or ty up after such a manner that the middle of it lys upon their shoulders. Those that are of Fashion lay a square Piece of red or yellow silk on their Heads: one side thereof hanging down over their Shoulders behind: above which they bind about their Temples a piece of white Silk or fine Linnen like a Cravate or Neckcloath, the Ends of it hanging down behind. They wear Neck-laces about their Neck, and broad Silver ornaments about their Wrists and Ancles. Also Drawers of fine Linnen that reach in Folds or Plaits upon their Legs down to their Shoes: above their Drawers their Smock or Shift hangs down, the sleeves of it very large, open & not gathered at the End: as are also the sleeves of the Men's Shirts. Above their Shift they have a Garment fourteen or fifteen foot long, and about half as broad, which they make fast about them much after the Manner as the Irish Women do their Breckams, tying it about their Middle with a Silken Girdle; and keeping it together over their Shoulders, & on their Breast with broad Silver Buckles: and when they go abroad they wear another such long Garment loose about them, which they bring over their Head; both these under & upper Garments are white: and are of the same sort of stuff that the Mens' Haigs are of: the finer sort they wear in Summer: the thicker in Winter. And generally when they go abroad, they ty a piece of Linnen Cloath, about 4 or 5 Inches broad, cross their Mouth & Nose. Their Shoes are made of Goats Leather, colour'd red, very soft and fine. The poorer sort instead of silk bind a nasty woollen Clout about their Heads. They wear no Linnen at all nor any thing on their Bodys, save their Blankets, which are commonly as their Head clouts, dirty & nasty to an abominable degree.

The Emperor has besides White men that are in his Army (as 'tis said) above fourty thousand Blacks, his slaves, which he arms upon Occasion when his Blacks are not in Camp, he keeps them at Work about building or levelling of Ground. The Guard that attends his Person, every day, are all Boys between twelve and twenty years of age, and almost all of 'em, Blacks & Mulattos, Officers Sons. He rides before, and they follow him close all in a Crowd, most commonly on foot, sometimes on Horseback, especially if he goes any considerable way abroad from his Palace: Each of them has his Firelock, which he must constantly keep upon pain of Death as bright as when it first came out of the Gunsmiths Hands. He gives them all Linnen Shirts and Drawers to wear: short Jackets, some sad colour'd & others light which they ty close about them with a Sash: the great Sleeves of their shirts are ty'd together behind to keep their hands from being muffled & incumber'd. They have also large Cloaks (such as were describ'd before in giving account of the Men's Habit) which they wear when 'tis cold or rains.

Tho[ugh] I call only the Blacks his Slaves, (as being brought with his Money; and the Children of such) yet I think they are all so that are in the Country: for by these same Blacs, he keeps the Whites in aw, and enslaves 'em all. His Government is altogether pro suo Arbitrio. His will is Law, which none dares to controul, or resist, or say a Word against: tho[ugh] he be often guilty of the greatest Acts of Injustice & Cruelty in the Accomplishment of it: for a Trifle, a thing of Nothing, he will take away a Man's Life, being ordinarily Executioner himself: and when his Hand is in, the Innocent often perish with the guilty: and some happen to be kill'd for Company, who perhaps were but accidentally on the Place, and whom he could charge with no Faults at all: his Fury sometimes raging so, that it is not over till his Eye is fill'd with a tragical Sight of the Bodys of Slaughter'd Men.

Once of his Concubines, with his and her Child in her Arms, once requesting some thing of him which he deny'd her. She, as he was going from her, thinking him to be out of hearing, gave him a Curse, which he overheard and thereupon immediately caus'd his Eunuchs to pluck the Infant; tho[ugh] innocent and his own, from its Mother's Arms; and to tear it Limb from Limb; and afterwards to strangle her.

He has killed many of his People for not paying, when they were not able, the Taxes he had impos'd upon them. One morning he caus'd above fifty of such miserable Creatures to be slughter'd all together: and then, to excuse his Avarice & Cruelty, gave out, that they did not own God, nor his Prophet, (meaning the Imposter Mahomet) neither did they circumcise: but liv'd, Christian-like, incestuous Lives, the Father defiling his own Daughter, and the Brother his Sister; and that they were not worthy to live on the Earth any longer. If he Spares Life to any such Persons, he condemns them with their Children to labour at his Works so long as they live who must be satisfy'd with such allowance as he is pleas'd to give them to live on.

Many have also died by his own Hands for being absent from their Work, or because he has found somewhat amiss from their Work, or that it has not been carry'd on with Expedition, as he has often only pretended: when he has been in his bloody Humour, He has call'd to the Boys that are of his Guard, for Piece after Piece laden with Powder & Ball and has not left off firing till he has laid a dozen on the Ground himself. When he kills with his Launce, he does often after the same manner satiate his inhumane appetite with the Blood of more than One or Two. He is very dextrous in using the Gun, the Launce, and the Sword; the last of which he uses not but when on Foot; as he does the Launce always on Horse-back. Sometimes he has ordered such as have been Officers & overseers to be made fast to a Mules Tail and dragg'd to death.

In the year 1697 as he was one time in the Fields, playing with, and exercising his Boys he ordered some of them to fire at a Dog that was running by them: and at the same time looking about, he perceiv'd a little Boy behind him; cocking his Piece, with the Muzzle of it, through the Boy's Inadvertency, somewhat towards him: upon which he said to the little Boy, What art thou going to kill me? and immediately imagining some Plot to be among them to take away his Life, he caus'd him, and a great many others that were behind him to be disarm'd. About a dozen of them, besides the little Boy, he kill'd immediately upon the Spot: and the next day commanded near fourty more to be strangled; all of them asserting their Innocence as to what he charg'd them with to the very last.

When he deals this cruelly with his own People as you may perceive by the Particulars I have instanc'd in but now, what usage may his Christian Slaves expect from him!

The Food he allows to them is only a Cake of black Bread every Day, that may weigh about a pound and a half. 'Tis black because made of the rottennest Corn in his Magazine. 'Tis commonly of Barley, sometimes of Wheat: many times it has had such a nauseous smell, that a Man could not endure it at his Nose; and has been so bad; that the Beasts have refus'd to eat it: Their Drink is Water the common Drink of the Country.

Such a Coat as I made mention of before pag. 22 of the coursest sort, that may cost about two shillings, or half a Crown at most (I mean the values of so much in the money of the Country) is all the cloathing that is give[n] to each Captive, for a year.

Their Lodging when I was brought first to Maccaness was under a great Bridge, he had built cross a Valley, between two Hills, strongly archt, the top of it made plain and even with the higher parts of the Hills at each End; along which the Emperor and his Guards us'd to ride in an insulting Manner, as it were trampling on the Christians Heads: but that Place was pull'd down above six years ago, and the Christians were turn'd out in the Winter, to lodge in a great Square Place enclos'd with high Walls: but no Houses provided for them do defend their wearied Bodys in the Night from the violence of the Weather. So that if they had not built little Houses & Hutts for themselves, which they were necessitated to do in the night when they should have slept (for their cruel Master could not allow them Time from his Work to do in the day-time) and had they not also taken Care to get somewhat to lay under them, & to cover them with, they must have lain down on the bare Ground like Beasts without any Cover nearer to them than the Heavens. But the poor Christians joyn & help one another: some that have Supplys from their Friends in Christendom buy what is wanting; and others that have none help build and in time make a shift all to get Holes to creep into. To such a Pass the poor Christians are always brought when their Master is pleas'd to remove them from one Place to an-other.

There are about 1500 Christians of several Nations now in Slavery under the Emperor of Morocco, wiz. about 700 Spaniards, 300 Portuguese, 260 French, and about 220 English: of all whom, there are not 200, (that is not the seventh part of them) that have greater Allowance from him, than the aforesaid Cake of Bread a Day, and a Coat once a year, whether in Time of Health or Sickness; and those few Christians that are allow'd more are such as Smiths, Carpenters, and some that break Stones and burn Lime: the former two have it to encourage such of the Captives as may be of such useful Trades to declare themselves. The others, by reason that their Work requires strength and greatly impairs a Man's Health: The Burners being oblig'd to stand by the Hill in the Night, as well as in the Day, by Turns at the end of each four Hours: for which reason they are allow'd some the value of two pence & some of a Penny a day, which their covetous Task-masters often wrong them of.

The chief Guardian or Goaler of the Christians, who locks them up every night, counts them out in the Morning, as soon as he can see, to the several Drivers or overseers: who carry them to their respective Works, where they are kept labouring till the Stars appear in the Evening: when they are all brought back, and numbered in again to the chief Guardian, as if they were putting so many Cattle into a Pound. Sometimes they can't have leave to go from their Works to drink or fetch a little Water: at some Work they happen sometimes to be detain'd several Hours in the Night, and sometimes all Night, the Work of the following Day exacted of them to the full not withstanding.

The Labour in which the Christians are generally employ'd tends to building of Walls & Houses, & leveling of Ground. Some get stones and make Lime of them: they get the stones after this Manner: The Quarry is commonly on the side of a steep Hill: they dig down in it till they come to the Bottom of the stone which they undermine: when they come near to where the Stone has a Parting from the Bank behind, then it falls, and sometimes surprises both Christians and Moors that be under it, and crushes them to Death. I have seen Stones tumbled down after this Manner so great, that one of them would have made 1000 or 1200 Ton of Lime when broken and burnt. In these large stones they make Holes of a convenient Depth, as the Thickness of the stone may require, by driving down Iron Drills that are 6 or 8 Inches about. The Head of the Drill is capt, and the mouth of it fac'd with steel. One Man holds it, and turns it about at every stroak that a man gives it on the Head with an Iron Sledge. The Hole when made is loaded with Powder, and well ramm'd down; and leaving in the Hole a small Iron Rod, like a thick Wire, that may reach down amongst the Powder, the Mouth of it is stopt close with small Stones and Tarres: Then the Iron Rod is drawn out, and Powder put into its Place for Priming: which when fired bursts the great Stone in Pieces; and these Pieces are again broken with Iron Sledges fac't with Steel till they be so small as that they are fit to be put into the Hill to be burn'd for Lime. Some dig Earth where Ground is to be levell'd, or to mix with Lime for the Walls. Some make Morter. Others carry Earth, Water, Lime, Stones, Morter. Some ramm the Morter into such Boxes or Cases as I mention'd before, & so Build up the Walls. And some drive Wagons that are drawn by Bulls, Six in each Team, and carry Earth Lime Stones etc. I was one of this last Occupation my Self. Sometime all the Christians, Sometimes a part of them are brought to work together at Tweeza, as the Moors call it, which I cannot better explain than by terming it Hurry & Expedition at which Work all are forc't to run with their Baskets full of Earth or Lime on their Heads which when thrown down at the Place appointed, they make what haste they can back for another Load being driven and cruelly beaten, and whipt with thick Cudgels & Whips, forward and backward, by many Drivers that are set over them.

And yet, as the Want of wholesome Food & other Necessarys, Hard Labour, Insultations & Abuses and many bitter & cruel Blows were not Pressures heavy enough to precipitate poor Christians to their untimely Ends, their unreasonable Master will dispatch them out of the World with his own Hands, upon small Occasion. Some he has kill'd for attempting to make their escape and many for a far less Fault for when he pleases he makes the least a Capital Crime: as when their has been some little thing done amiss, or that has not pleas'd him, at the Work. He kill'd seven Christians at one Time for being absent from their Work. He has, without saying a Word, shot a poor man whom he happen'd to surprise asleep at the Work. He has kill'd some of his Waggoners, because that the Waggons being made when the Timber was green, when it come to be dry they shak't loose and some of the Wheels fell down. He has ordered nine & twenty Christians to be thrown down from the top of a Wall [?] Foot high: because he suspected some of them to have kill'd a Mastif Dog that he had from Spain, and could not find out who did it. Some of them were kill'd outright, some were sorely bruis'd; and some had Arms & Legs broken by their Falls: and after that he set his Dogs on one of them that had been thrown down, whom he chiefly suspected to have kill'd the Dog: and stood by till they tore out his Bowels.

At that Time had there been as many more Christians at Work in that Place, they had been all toss'd off the Wall for he ordered his Guards to collar and bring before him all that were there. 'Tis but ordinary with him when perhaps there is but one in the Fault, to knock down or beat all round, with a thick Trunchion; or else to pound them with the But End of his Launce.

His Bashaws and Alcaides are ordered by him to oversee, and carry on his Works: Each of them the particular Work that is committed to his Charge: to mentain which, he grants him the Taxes laid upon such a People, or Part of the Country, as he nominates to him; and gives him also such a Number of Christians as he thinks fit to labour at that Work. Now many times when such a Person that is thus ordered by him to furnish and mentain the Work with all necessarys, does either through Covetousness or Negligence prove Tardy, the Christians are beaten because they did not acquaint him therewith: which if any of them should do, the Moor if he comes off with his Life will be sure to repay: if he don't other Moors will.

Now considering the little care he takes to preserve his Christian Slaves alive, and his Proneness upon the least Occasion to kill them, One would think after all, that he does not value a Christian much: but would let him have his Liberty for a small Ransome: and yet a Captive cannot purchase his Redemption for less than Two Hundred & fifty pounds sterl[ing]. Some have paid fifty; and some one hundred pounds more to have their Freedom.

As the French Spaniards and other Papists call themselves Roman Cathalicks, so the Subjects of the Emperor of Morocco do call themselves Moors: tho[ugh] they be of divers Nations and Colours, viz. Moors or Arabians and Barbarians: these are Whites, another sort of Arabians that are Tawny; Blacks; and that smutty Issue of all degrees between White and Black that proceeds from the Mixture of the Whites with the Blacks, and of either of them with the different sorts of Mulattos; and also from the Mixtures of the several Degrees of Mulattos amongst themselves. The Moors conqur'd the Country and subdu'd the Barbarians who were the first Inhabitants. The Blacks have been, and are still, brought in by the Moors: being sold to them by their own Country People who border on the Emperor's Territorys to the Southward.

There his People, according to their Power, shew no less barbarity and cruelty than himself to the poor Christians. His Sons kill them as he does himself. His Alcaides and overseers do often beat and abuse them, ordering them to be stretcht out by four Men that have each of them hold of a Limb and cruel Blows to be given them, sometimes several Hundreds at a Time, with great Cudgels on the Buttocks, as hard as can be laid on: or else with great Whips that lash all round their Bodys. The Blows make their Skin as black as that of a Negro; & the stripes raise Bumps, and cut the Flesh, and the vulgar generally curse the Christians as they pass by them and teach their little Children to do the like.

When they meet the Christians carrying their Dead to the Grave, their Burrying Place being about four Miles from the Town, they bawl out, Fuel, Fuel [fue él] for Hell, and stone them that carry the Corps. To avoid which Insultations, with leave had from the chief Guardian, the Christians do often carry out their Dead some Hours before Day: tho[ugh] some Places of the Way be very uneven, and in the Winter time so slippery & dirty after Rain, that, being in the Dark, they often times cannot keep their Feet, but fall with the Corps. And were it not that the Christians belong all peculiarly to the Emperor himself, of whom the People stand more in Awe & Dread than they do of God Almighty; there would be no passing for a Christian to & again amongst them, who are the greatest Bigots of all the Mahometans; and the most bitter and (except of the Jews) the most implacable Enemys to Christians. Indeed in the Town of Sally, and some other Sea Ports, they are not so barbarous.

Note

1. On the Northside of Cape de Non.

Appendix 3

"A Voyage into the Mediterranean Seas"

From Edward Dummer (d. 1713), "A Voyage into the Mediterranean Seas" (1685), British Library King's MS 40, fols. 4–6.

Bin Haddu went on board the ship "Woolwich" on 24 July 1682 along with "Cuddam hamett [Muqaddam Hamet], Lucas, and the Interpreter an English Renegado (commonly by the Christians called Jonas, and by the Moors Alcayd Abdalla)." The next day, continued Dummer:

> wee Anchored in Plymouth sound, a Matter (it appear'ed) the Moors expected not or wanted Occasion to quarrell amongst themselves, The Aggressor was Cuddum hamett animated by Lucas against the Ambassadour, The Matter of fact was this.

> Cuddum sends to Capt Holding (then upon the quarter Deck) for Irons for a Man, but not understanding well the Moorish messenger, desired the Renegado to be called, meaning by him to have understood more fully the Message of Cuddum, But Cuddum comes himself to the Capt. and at that same Instant the Renegado also, whome Cuddum seeing, in a very violent transport takes by the Throat saying (in Moorish) Secure the Xian Dog, and therewith laboured to push him downe into the great Cabbin; The Ambassadour and his Men (being upon the Poope) seeing the passage, Some of them Leapt downe and with us that were Xians present, endeavoured to stop his fury, so that Instantly the rest of the Moors from above and those from below were gott to gether, Some with Knives, some with Stilletto's, striking one at another over, and under our Arms, that were Xians promiscuously mixt among them.

> A Symiter was handed to the Ambassadour, he came from the Poope to the Gangway the whole Ships Company was in an Uproar, the Anchor just fallen from the Catt, but the Capt. (the surprize a little past) ordered in a Moment a few lusty fellows upon the Quarter Deck with Cuttlaces Drawn laid hold of Cuddam, bidding one of his owne Moors (who spoke a little English) advise him to retire immediately or he should be cut in pieces, the Moor apprehensive desired the Captaines care of the Renegado (whome he pretended would escape) and went with great quickness and Rage to the great Cabbin where two sentinells were placed upon him.

> The Ambassadour by this time was gotten within the Cuddy Door his appartment for Lucas and Caddum had dismist him of the Great Cabbin in the Downes or he willingly left if for his personall security which in this Action greatly appeared and there disputed with Lucas very Hotly without attempting

violence, at length they drew into the Cuddy; and there argued themselves in some better agreement (but the animosity not to be removed) all became againe outwardly quiet, and that it might continue, soe, The Captaine (an Eye Witness to the Violence) resolves to keep Cuddum strictly confined, till wee should arrive at Tanger;

In this scuffle a few cutt fingers were all the Damage, a Moor laying hold of Cuddum's Stilletto he drew in through his hand and cutt his fingers very much, some others gott hurt, of the like Nature but not so bad, my self was slightly touch't endeavouring to stop the Hand of a Moor sticking with a knife over mine, at another, this was about a quarter of an hours Rage and soe Ended.

Notes

Abbreviations

Add.	Additional Manuscripts
BL	British Library
CLSP	Calendar of Letters and State Papers
CO	Colonial Office (Tangier)
CSP	Calendar of State Papers and Manuscripts
CSPD	Calendar of State Papers, Domestic
CSPF	Calendar of State Papers, Foreign Series
HMSO	His/Her Majesty's Stationery Office, London
PRO	Public Record Office
SP	State Papers, Foreign (Algeria, Morocco and Tunisia)

Introduction

1. Scanlan, *Colonial Writing*, 3.

2. Pagden, *Lords of All the World*, 6.

3. Maley, "'This Sceptred isle,'" 97.

4. Youings, *Raleigh in Exeter 1985*, 19.

5. Elizabeth I, *Collected Works*, 329. As David Armitage succinctly stated in *Literature and Empire*: "The impress of Empire upon English literature in the early-modern period was minimal, and mostly critical where it was discernible at all. . . . Post-colonial studies have generated proto-colonial studies, and recent scholarship has found the literature of the sixteenth and seventeenth centuries to be deeply, because necessarily, inflected by the 'imperial' experiences of racial difference, irreducible 'otherness,' assertions of hierarchy, and national self-determination. However, to apply modern models of the relationship between culture and imperialism to early-modern literature and Empire demands indifference to context and inevitably courts anachronism. It is therefore necessary to be as sceptical about post-Imperial demystifications as it once was about mid-Imperial complacencies" (in Canny, ed., *Origins of Empire*, 102).

6. Greene, "Beyond the Northern Invasion," 47.

7. See Youings, *Raleigh in Exeter*, 39–57.

8. Knapp, *Empire Nowhere*.

9. Cormack, "Britannia Rules," 45–68. Building on Edward Said's *Culture and Imperialism*, Bruce McLeod has correctly argued that "a great deal of national culture during the seventeenth and eighteenth centuries was imbued with a geographical imagination fed by the experience and experiments of colonialism" (*Geography of Empire*, 8).

10. As in Charles Kingsley's *Westward Ho!* (1855).

11. Neville-Sington, "'A very good trumpet,'" 71.

12. Alden T. Vaughan and Virginia Mason Vaughan maintain that "there was a general waning of English commercial interest in Africa" toward the end of the sixteenth century

("Before Othello," 29). I disagree. Until the Great Migration, North Africa was more attractive than North America. See my *Turks, Moors and Englishmen*, introd., chap. 3.

13. PRO, SP 71/13/part 2, 153.

14. Tawit, "Wathaiq Sa'diyya lam tunshar," 52.

15. Quoted in Scanlan, *Colonial Writing*, 34.

16. Hakluyt, *Principal Navigations*, 6:282–83.

17. See my *Turks, Moors and Englishmen*, 61–62; and MacLean, "On Turning Turk."

18. Gustav Unger claims that there was an English "colonial dispute" regarding North Africa ("Portia," 91). While there was commercial activity, there was definitely no colonial activity.

19. Gillies, *Geography of Difference*, 27.

20. Newman, "'And wash the Ethiop white,'" 154.

21. Hornstein, *Restoration Navy*, 2.

22. Corbett, *England*, 1:198.

23. Weiss, "Back from Barbary," 157–58.

24. Colley, *Captives*, Part I.

25. McLeod, *Geography of Empire*, 22.

26. Teonge, *Diary*, 126.

27. I am borrowing the terminology from Niranjana, *Siting Translation*, 23.

28. "Two Turks Men of War lye in this Channel, which we finde contribute much to the security of those Seas at present" *(London Gazette*, 28 May–31 May 1666).

29. Brotton, *Trading Territories*; Brotton, *Renaissance Bazaar*; Goffman, *Ottoman Empire*.

Chapter 1

1. I am following E.A.J. Honigmann (*Othello*, 350), who argues for 1602–3 as the date of the play *Othello*.

2. Vaughan and Vaughan, "Before Othello," 29.

3. Bartels, "Making More," 433–52.

4. Cawley, *Voyagers*.

5. Doran, "Politics," 26.

6. Castries, *Sources inédites d'Angleterre*, 1:358.

7. Heywood, *If you know me not*, 1:300.

8. Saldanha, *Crónica de Almançor*, 150.

9. Wilkins, *Three Miseries of Barbary*, B1v.

10. Saldanha, *Crónica de Almançor*, 152.

11. *CLSP Simancas*, 4:516. He had left Morocco on 2 November 1588 accompanied by Henry Roberts. See also Castries, *Sources inédites d'Angleterre*, 1:513n1; and the account by Roberts in Hakluyt's *Principal Navigations*, 6:426–28.

12. Wernham, "Queen Elizabeth," esp. 2–8.

13. Castries, *Sources inédites d'Angleterre*, 1:513, January 1589.

14. Wernham, *Calendar of State Papers, Foreign, Elizabeth, Jan-July 1589*, 23:125.

15. Castries, *Sources inédites d'Angleterre*, 1:520–21 (quoting the 8 March 1589 memorandum of the ambassador).

16. Peele, *Device of the Pageant*, 209. For a detailed study of Marlowe's treatment of Islam in the context of Anglo-Ottoman relations in the 1580s, see Jonathan Burton,

"Anglo-Ottoman Relations and the Image of the Turk in *Tamburlaine*," *Journal of Medieval and Early Modern Studies*, 30 (2000): 125–157.

17. Chew, *Crescent and Rose*, 526.

18. Braunmuller, *George Peele*, 79. Simon Shepherd, too, identified royal succession as the central concern of the play (*Marlowe*, 146–47).

19. Hyland, "Moors," 96.

20. Peele, *Battle of Alcazar*, 226.

21. Hunter, "Othello and Colour Prejudice," 145. Indeed, at Ipswich in 1589–90, one pound was given to the "Torkey Tumblers"; at Norwich on 22 April 1590, two pounds were distributed in reward to "the Quenes men when the Turke went vpon Robbes at Newhall"; and in the same period a Turk performed with the Queen's players in Coventry" (quoted in Alsop, "Moorish Playing Company," 135). As Alsop notes, "It is apparent that they [Turks] were Moors."

22. Bradley, *Text to Performance*, 130.

23. To argue, as does D'Amico (*English Renaissance Drama*, 81–84), that the good Moor, Abdelmelec, counterbalances the evil Muly Mahamet is to ignore the fact that the former died in the course of the battle, leaving the throne for his brother, the powerful Muly Seth of the play.

24. See the study of the figure of Stuckley in Peele's *Battle of Alcazar*, 247–73.

25. Castries, *Sources inédites d'Angleterre*, 1:519.

26. Ibid., 1:522–23.

27. Wernham, *Expedition*, 177. Letter to Sir Roger Williams to [Walsingham?], 1 June 1589.

28. Castries, *Sources inédites de France, Dynastie Saadienne*, 2:182.

29. *Fugger News-Letters, Second Series*, 188.

30. Wernham, *List and Analysis*, 2:454.

31. *CLSP Simancas, 1587–1603*, 550, 21 July 1589.

32. PRO, SP 102/4/9 (2).

33. Tazi, *Histoire*, 8:154.

34. While Drake himself recognized the impact of al-Mansur's nonaction on the outcome of his mission, a modern historian of the "Portugal Expedition," R. B. Wernham, in a lengthy and detailed examination of the affair ("Queen Elizabeth"), had absolutely nothing to say about the Moroccan factor.

35. *CLSP Simancas*, 4:550.

36. Castries, *Sources inédites d'Angleterre*, 1:536.

37. Jones, "Racial Terms," 64.

38. PRO, SP 12/240/28. *Acts of the Privy Council, July 1621 to May 1623* (London, 1932), 329 and 467.

39. Castries, *Sources inédites d'Angleterre*, 2:89–90.

40. This absence led Castries to speculate that the delegation never left for England (*Sources inédites d'Angleterre*, 2:89n3).

41. Shakespeare, *Merchant of Venice*, ed. Brown.

42. *Fugger News-Letter, Second Series*, 278.

43. Castries, *Sources inédites d'Angleterre*, 2:94, note.

44. Al-Fishtali, *Manahil al-Safa*, 187.

45. Ibid., 197.

46. Burchett, *Complete History*, 360.

47. Castries, *Sources inédites d'Angleterre*, 2:93–94. See also Castries, *Sources inédites de France*, 2:229.

48. Quoted in Fryer, *Staying Power*, 10.

49. Castries, *Sources inédites d'Angleterre*, 2:84.

50. Barthelemy, *Black Face, Maligned Race*, 147.

51. D'Amico, *English Renaissance Drama*, 170.

52. See the discussion of Marx's use of the term and its application to *The Merchant of Venice* in Netzloff, *England's Internal Colonies*, 20–36.

53. For the destabilization the Moor effects in Shakespeare's world, see my and Rudolph Stoeckel's "Europe's Mediterranean Other," 230–52.

54. Metzger, "'Now by My Hood,'" 52–63.

55. *Fugger News-Letters, Second Series*, 295.

56. Regla, *Estudios sobre los moriscos*, 195–218.

57. *CSP Venice, 1592–1603*, 255.

58. Ibid., 9:271.

59. Ibid., 275.

60. Castries, *Sources inédites d'Angleterre*, 2:121.

61. Ibid., 2:145–46.

62. Africanus, *History*, 3:994. See also *The Worlde, or An historicall description*, 202: "Amongst all the potentates of Afrike, I do not thinke that there can any one be found to excelle this prince, either in wealth or power."

63. I am using the edition of *Lust's Dominion* edited by Khalid Bekkaoui, 1.4.

64. BL, Cotton MSS Nero B X1, 78. The letter is also reproduced in Castries, *Sources inédites d'Angleterre*, 2:149–50. The manuscript copy in Cotton is followed by a translation by William Bedwell and an explication of terms such as *sultan, ifranji*, and *al-hamdu-lil-lah*. What is odd is that the date is 20 March 1604—four years after the arrival of the ambassador in London.

65. Castries, *Sources inédites d'Angleterre*, 2:158.

66. PRO, SP 71/12/51.

67. Castries, *Sources inédites d'Angleterre*, 2:157.

68. Ibid., 2:177–79.

69. Karim, *Maghrib*, 219; Tawit, "*Zawaya al-tarikh*," 43.

70. Al-Fishtali, *Manahil*, 49, quoted in Bin Haddah, *al-Maghrib wal-Bab al-Ali*, 113n3.

71. Castries, *Sources inédites d'Angleterre*, 1:394.

72. See letter from Roger Bodenham to Burghley on 12 June 1582, in Castries, *Sources inédites d'Angleterre*, 1:400.

73. Hakluyt, "Second Voyage," 183.

74. Kyd, *The Works of Thomas Kyd*, 1.3.

75. Castries, *Sources inédites d'Angleterre*, 2:144.

76. Africanus, *Geographical Historie*, 387.

77. Castries, *Sources inédites d'Angleterre*, 2:188.

78. Henin, *Wasf al-mamalik al-maghribiyya*, 32.

79. *The Play of Stucley*, in Simpson, *The School of Shakespeare*, line 2192.

80. Castries, *Sources inédites d'Angleterre*, 2:203.

81. Ibid., 2:166.

82. Pianel, "Le Maroc," 517.

83. Castries, *Sources inédites d'Angleterre*, 2:166.

84. Ibid., 2:203.

85. *Rasail Sa'diyya*, National Library of Rabat, MS Kaf 278, fols. 195–98.

86. It was Bernard Harris, "Portrait of a Moor," 89–97, who first made the association.

87. Hall, *Things of Darkness*, 7.

88. Lupton, "Othello Circumcised," 73–89.

89. Loomba, "'Delicious traffick,'" 205.

90. Vickers, *Shakespeare*, 2:29.

91. Loomba, *Shakespeare, Race, and Colonialism*, 95, 97.

92. Vitkus, "Turning Turk in Othello," 145–76.

93. For an early survey of "Shakespeare and the Turk," before the topic became ideologically loaded, see Draper, *Orientalia and Shakespeareana*, chap. 9.

94. Bartels, "Making More," 436.

95. Chew, *Crescent and Rose*, 521n2.

96. Also Paul Robeson, Godfrey Tearle, John Gielgud and James McCracken.

97. See my "Renaissance England," 39–55.

98. Neill, "Mulattos," 369.

99. *CSPD, Edward VI, Mary, Elizabeth I and James I, 1598–1601*, 5:478. As Maria Rosa Menocal has noted, the whole issue of "purity of blood" in Spain developed precisely because there "were no visible racial differences" (*Ornament of the World*, 262).

100. Nichols, *Progresses and Public Processions*, 3:516. See the documents in Castries, *Sources inédites d'Angleterre*, 2:184–85, 189–92.

101. Quoted in Hall, "Colonisation and Miscegenation," 95.

102. Heywood, *The Fair Maid of the West, Parts I and II*.

103. It is unlikely that Heywood knew R. C.'s *A True Historicall discourse of Muley Hamets rising to the three Kingdomes of Moruecos, Fes, and Sus*; evidence in the play points to an Elizabethan rather than a Jacobean timeframe.

104. As Warner G. Rice pointed out, it could have applied to any of three men who went by that name ("Moroccan Episode," 131–40).

105. The first clear English reference to the palace—"a Castle of great fame, for their Globes of pure gold that stand upon the top of it, and weighing 130000. Barbarie Dukets"—appeared in Speed, *A Prospect*, 5–6.

106. Castries, *Sources inédites d'Angleterre*, 2:137.

107. Hoenselaars, *Images of Englishmen*, 225.

108. The only previous transreligious kiss was between the dying Perseda and Sultan Soliman, but it was a kiss of death.

109. See Barthelemy, *Black Face, Maligned Race*, 165, for further discussion of this passage.

110. Howard, "An English Lass," 114.

111. Heywood, *Lust's Dominion*, act 4, scene 3, page 110.

112. For a slightly longer discussion of this topic, see my "Enter Mullisheq." It is important that in the accounts of Elizabethan captivity among Moors, the Moors were not identified by their religion, perhaps because the captives did not know anything about North African "Mahometanism." Although numerous writings had appeared in English translation about the Islam of the Ottomans, the Maghrib had a different cultural expression of Islam—a difference that may well have confused the captives-turned-writers.

113. Middleton, *The Works*, 7:247–49.

114. Beaumont and Fletcher, *The Works*, 5:164, 128.

115. Middleton and Rowley, *The Spanish Gipsie, and All's Lost by Lust.*

116. Shakespeare, *The Tempest*, ed. Vaughan and Vaughan, 48–49, quoting Morton Luce, editor of a 1901 edition of *The Tempest.* It is interesting that when E.A.J. Honigmann wrote about Othello marrying Desdemona and lording "it over Europeans," he compared the audience reaction to such a black Othello to their reaction to Caliban were he "to reappear as Prospero, king of the island" (*Othello*, 29). It is also interesting that at the time of the writing of *The Tempest*, a black man was living in Mildred Poultry (see Knutson, "A Caliban," 110–27).

117. Richard Wilson has decisively shown that the background to the play is the Mediterranean basin ("Voyage to Tunis," 333–57). Jerry Brotton blamed the postcolonialists for downplaying its Mediterranean setting ("Carthage and Tunis," 132–37).

Chapter 2

1. Pagden, *Lords of All the World*; Fuchs, *Mimesis and Empire.*

2. For studies on Barbary captives from Britain and the rest of Europe, see Lane-Poole, *Barbary Corsairs*; Penz, *Captifs français*; Coindreau, *Corsairs de Salé*; Clissold, *Barbary Slaves*; Wolf, *Barbary Coast*; Benassar and Benassar, *Chrétiens d'Allah*; and my introduction to *Piracy, Slavery and Redemption.*

3. Andrews, *Ships, Money and Politics*, 168. In *Merchants and Revolution*, Robert Brenner closely studied the tension and subsequent clash between King Charles I and the City merchant establishment of the Levant and East India companies, but he paid very little attention to the crisis of the captives. Kevin Sharpe in *The Personal Rule of Charles I* also paid little attention to these captives and their political impact. The only historian who has studied the captives and England's Mediterranean involvements is David Delison Hebb in his *Piracy and the English Government.* Both K. R. Andrews and A. Thrush used the findings of Hebb to analyze the background of ship money and the 1637 Salé expedition, but neither linked the crisis of the captives to the advent of the Civil Wars (Thrush, "Naval Finance," 133–62).

4. Beazley, *Voyages and Travels*, 2:178–79.

5. *The Worlde, or An historicall description*, 202 ff.

6. Castries, *Sources inédites d'Angleterre*, 2:222–27.

7. Ortelius, *Theatre of the Whole World*, 115.

8. Wilkins, *Three Miseries of Barbary.*

9. Henin, *Wasf al-mamalik al-maghribiyya.*

10. Grimstone, *Estates*, 1108–37.

11. *A Geographicall and Anthologicall description*, 38–39.

12. Speed, *A Prospect*, 5–6.

13. For the career of John Harrison, see my entry on Harrison in the *New Dictionary of National Biography.*

14. Castries, *Sources inédites d'Angleterre*, 2:573–82.

15. Cenival and Brissac, *Sources inédites*, 3:31–57.

16. Rouard de Card, *Les traités*, 7.

17. Ibid., 7–10, 195 (treaty of 24 September 1631). See also item 11 of the treaty, which gave authority to the French to deny the English access to the region.

18. Heylyn, *Cosmographie*, 34, 36, 37, 45.

19. Cenival and Brissac, *Sources inédites*, 3:549–50.

20. Indeed, as David Loades has shown, by 1635, 44 percent of London's imports came

from the Islamic world, contrasted with only 5 percent from North America (*England's Maritime Empire*, 147).

21. Beaumont, *Knight of the Burning Pestle*.

22. See the letter from Plymouth, 13 August 1625, and the reply by Francis Stewart to Buckingham three days later. Castries, *Sources inédites d'Angleterre*, 2:585–87.

23. Carew, *Letters*, 51.

24. Ibn Abi Dinar, *Kitab al-mu'nis fi akhbar Ifriqiyah wa Tunis*, 192.

25. *The Famovs and Wonderfvll recoverie*, A2.

26. Ibid., A2v.

27. *CSP Venice*, 17:155.

28. *A Relation Strange and True*, B2r-v.

29. Roe, *Negotiations*, 32.

30. PRO, SP 16/2/78.

31. PRO, SP 16/5/24.

32. *CSPD, Charles I, 1625–1626*, 1:81.

33. *Debates of the House of Commons in 1625*, 117.

34. The extent of the impact of the corsairs on western Britain becomes evident when the records for Deptford (*Trinity House of Deptford Transactions*), which include repeated references to captivity, are contrasted to the records of Hull, on the northeastern coast of England, which include only one reference (*First Order Book of the Hull Trinity House*, 71).

35. See the detailed study by Todd Gray, "Turkish Piracy," 159–71.

36. Castries, *Sources inédites d'Angleterre*, 2:565.

37. Ibid., 2:568.

38. Ibid., 2:577.

39. PRO, SP 71/12, 2:159–60.

40. Castries, *Sources inédites d'Angleterre*, 2:595–96.

41. *Acts of the Privy Council, 1623–1625*, 335.

42. In April 1625, the Privy Council looked into the possible "misappropriation of [ransom] money" by one Edward Eastman; in November, Nicholas Leat was accused of mismanagement and it fell upon the Privy Council in the person of the archbishop of Canterbury to examine the bills and accounts. *CSPD, Charles I, 1625–1626*, 1:11; *Acts of the Privy Council, 1625–1626*, 243.

43. PRO, SP 71/1/55.

44. *CSPD, Charles I, 1625–26*, 1:343.

45. *Cobbett's Parliamentary History*, 2:109.

46. Ibid., 174.

47. The Turks, he said, "were still roving in the West, the Dunkerks in the East, the cries came out of all parts. Their losses great, their dangers more, their fears exceeding all. No merchant doth venture on the seas, hardly they thought themselves secure enough on land. It was alleged by some, that as the king's ships were stopped from going to relieve them when it was ordered by the council, so they were then. Though ready on the coasts, or in the harbours near them, where these rogues were most infectious, nothing might be done. Nay in some cases it was proved that the merchants had been taken even in the sight of the king's ships, and that the captain being importuned to relieve them, refused their protection or assistance, and said they were denied it by the instructions which they had" (quoted in Gosse, *History of Piracy*, 137).

48. *Acts of the Privy Council, 1625–1626*, 480.

49. See Supple, *Commercial Crisis*, chap. 3.

50. Cust, "Charles I," 208–36.

51. Anderson, *Historical and Chronological Deduction*, 2:320. See also 333 for reference to another bribe in 1628.

52. Ricard, *Mazagan et le Maroc*, 160.

53. *Fourth Report*, part 1, 14.

54. See the study of these sermons by Todd, "A Captive's Story," 37–56.

55. See my discussion of Byam and the returning captives in *Islam in Britain*, chap. 2.

56. PRO, SP 71/22/673.

57. *Lords Proceedings 1628*, 216, 555, 558, 690.

58. *Commons Debate 1628*, 64.

59. *Cobbett's Parliamentary History*, 2:384.

60. Weiss, "Back from Barbary," 132.

61. Eliot, *Negotium Posterorum*, 4.

62. Wadsworth, *The English Spanish Pilgrime*, 38.

63. BL, Add. MSS 21993, fols. 281–84.

64. For the attack on Baltimore, see *CSP Ireland*, 621–23; and the detailed study by Henry Barnby, "Sack of Baltimore," 101–29.

65. PRO, SP 71/1/151.

66. PRO, SP 71/1/111 r–v.

67. PRO, SP 71/1/130–32 v.

68. Another version of the report to the king, written from memory, as its anonymous author stated, appears in PRO, SP 71/1/100–102.

69. PRO, SP 71/1/162.

70. PRO, SP 71/12/222.

71. *Stuart Royal Proclamations*, 2:418–19.

72. Quoted in Gardiner, *Constitutional Documents*, 37.

73. PRO, SP 16/298/50.

74. *CSPD, Charles I, 1635*, 8:389.

75. PRO, SP 71/12/233.

76. The statement by Sharpe that after 1636, "complaints about pirates appear to be much reduced" ignores numerous reports to the contrary (*Personal Rule*, 596).

77. PRO, SP 16/329/29. See other references to Barbary corsair activities in 1636 in *Fourth Report*, 291; and *First Report*, 346.

78. PRO, SP 71/1/157.

79. PRO, SP 71/1/244.

80. Sharpe, *Personal Rule*, 587.

81. FitzGeffrey, *Compassion towards Captives*, "Preface to the Reader."

82. See *Letter from the King of Morocco, to his Majesty the King of England Charles I*, in which Muhammad al-Sheikh asked Charles for assistance. The letter was published twice in 1680 and 1682. See discussion in chapter 5.

83. Cenival and Brissac, *Sources inédites*, 3:292–94.

84. Ibid., 3:326.

85. *CSPD, Charles I, 1637*, 431.

86. *Arrivall and Intertainements*, 26, 25.

87. Ibid., 26.

88. Hebb suggests that King Charles may have been personally involved in the preparations for the ambassador's procession (*Piracy*, 258–59).

89. See the detailed study of French captivity and redemption by Weiss, "Back from Barbary," specifically chap. 5, "Processions of Redemption."

90. *CSP Venice*, 24:256.

91. *CSPD, Charles I, 1637*, 430, 460.

92. Thomas Wentworth wrote to Archbishop Laud that "this action of Salee is full of honour" because it "should help much towards the ready and cheerful payment of the shipmonies" (quoted by Parker, "Barbary in Early Modern England," 136).

93. D'Avenant, *Dramatic Works*, 2:265, 266, 270.

94. PRO, SP 102/4/6.

95. Cenival and Brissac, *Sources inédites*, 3:333.

96. Ibid., 408–23.

97. *Cobbett's Parliamentary History*, 2:554.

98. Ibid., 575.

99. Powell, *The Navy*, 5.

100. Knight, *Relation of Seaven Yeares Slaverie*, 29.

101. Ibid., 31.

102. Ibid., 52.

103. Ibid., 53.

104. Cenival and Brissac, *Sources inédites*, 3:542–46.

105. Ibid., 3:546.

106. A group of merchants went further in their complaint to the king: although he had levied ship money, he had not been able to prevent the seizure of their ships by "Turkish and Other pirates." That, along with the "multitude of monopolies, patents, and warrants" had led to the decay of trade (*CSPD, Charles I, 1640–41*, 17:94).

107. Ibid., 17:134.

108. *Journals of the House of Commons*, 2:48.

109. Suckling, *Copy of a Letter*, 13.

110. *Manuscripts of the House of Lords, Addenda 1514–1714*, 11:257–59.

111. *Journals of the House of Commons*, 2:152.

112. D'Ewes, *Journal*, 54.

113. *CSPD, Charles I, 1641–43*, 18:119.

114. D'Ewes, *Journal*, 117, 203, 221.

115. See the text and a study of the Grand Remonstrance in Forster, *Debates*, 226–29. See also Gardiner's assessment, *History of England* 10:59–61.

116. D'Ewes, *Journal*, 227.

117. About "renegadoes," see my *Islam in Britain*, chap. 1.

118. "Interlined on the Roll."

119. For the full text, see app. 1.

120. T. M., *A Discovrse of Trade*, 43.

121. Von Ranke, *History of England*, 2:231.

122. D'Ewes, *Journal*, 227.

123. Loades, *England's Maritime Empire*, 157.

124. *Private Journals*, 85; see also 88.

125. Ibid., 144, 169.

126. Brenner, *Merchants and Revolution*, 336.

127. Ibid., 457.

128. Ibid., 560.

129. Ibid., 227.

130. See *His Majesties Declaration to All His Loving Subjects of the 12 of August, 1642* in *Stuart Royal Proclamations*, 2:844n.

131. *Private Journals*, 429.

132. Ibid., 429n.

133. Ibid., 450.

134. Robinson, *Libertas*, 1, 4, 12.

135. *King Charles His Letter to the Great Turk*, A2v.

136. *Report on Franciscan Manuscripts*, 187.

137. *True Newes*, title page, 6.

138. *CSPD, Charles I, 1644*, 19:285.

139. *Journals of the House of Commons*, 3:664; *Acts and Ordinances*, 1:553–54.

140. *Journals of the House of Commons*, 4:196.

141. *An Ordinance of the Lords and Commons, 30 January 1644/45*.

142. *Committee for the Navy and Customs*.

143. *Acts and Ordinances*, 1:610.

144. *Journals of the House of Commons*, 4:196; *Acts and Ordinances*, 1:731.

145. *Acts and Ordinances*, 1:732.

146. *CSP Venice*, 27:209.

147. BL, Add. MSS 4191:20.

148. Cason, *Relation*, 5.

149. *Ibid.*, 6. It is interesting that while the Algerian and Tunisian rulers were willing to view Parliament as the sole power in England, the Moroccan ruler, Mulay al-Sheikh al-Asghar, who still recalled the assistance of Charles to him in 1637, refused.

150. Ibid., 11.

151. Quoted in Manning, *The English People*, 290.

152. Thomas Sweet, *Dear friends*.

153. Ibid.

154. Ibid.

155. Corbett, *England*, 1:226.

156. Ibid., 1:227.

157. *CSPD, Charles I, 1637–38*, 192.

158. Russell, *Parliaments and English Politics*, 2.

Chapter 3

1. N. Williams, *Redcoats and Courtesans*, 50.

2. Ibid., 53–54.

3. Luke, *Tangier at High Tide*, 187.

4. Franklin, *Letter from Tangier*, 2.

5. PRO, SP 71/5/48.

6. PRO, SP 102/1/125.

7. Gerald MacLean's term, in "On Turning Turk," 225.

8. Shepherd, *Amazons and Warrior Women*, 65.

9. Thomas, *Religion*, 163.

10. Higgins, "Reactions of Women," 216.

11. Crawford, "Public Duty," 71.

12. Charlotte F. Otten ignores these petitions and opens her discussion of women's petitions and the selections she edits with the 1642 petition (*English Women's Voices*, 85–94).

13. Stone, *Family, Sex and Marriage*, 225.

14. Fraser, *The Weaker Vessel*, 154.

15. Suzuki, *Subordinate Subjects*, 13.

16. Underdown, *Revel, Riot and Rebellion*, 38.

17. Otten, *English Women's Voices*, 86.

18. Stone, *The Family*, 139

19. Although there can be no certainty about the exact number of wives involved in those petitions, it is only logical that since there were British captives in the thousands, there would be "thousands" of "distressed" wives.

20. Quinn, "Sailors and the Sea," 23.

21. Henderson and McManus, *Half Humankind*, 47–98.

22. Cahn, *Industry of Devotion*, chap. 4.

23. Otten, *English Women's Voices*, 87–88.

24. See *Ordinance of Lords and Commons, For the Apprehending* (9 May 1645).

25. Letter to Sir Dudley Carleton, 12 July 1623, in Chamberlain, *Letters of John Chamberlain*, 2:507.

26. *Acts of the Privy Council of England, 1623–25*, 335.

27. PRO, SP 71/1/492.

28. Hebb, *Piracy*, 198.

29. *CSPD, Charles I, 1625–26*, 1:516.

30. Cenival and Brissac, *Sources inédites*, 3:1–3.

31. George, *First Capitalist Society*, 42; Hill, *Century of Revolution*, 32–33.

32. *Acts of the Privy Council of England, 1625–1626*, 480.

33. *Acts of the Privy Council of England, 1627, Jan.–Aug.*, 251.

34. *Lawes Resolvtions of Womens Rights*, 66.

35. PRO, SP 16/301/66.

36. PRO, SP 16/306/85.

37. See Romack, "Monstrous Births," 220.

38. Cenival and Brissac, *Sources Inedites*, 3:223.

39. Ibid., 3:244.

40. *CSPD, Charles I, 1625–26*, 1:398.

41. Clark, *Working Life*, 122; *True Copie*.

42. Finet, *Ceremonies of Charles I*, 231.

43. PRO, SP 16/391/95.

44. PRO, SP 16/391/96.

45. PRO, SP 16/391/97.

46. Historical Manuscripts Commission. *Report on Manuscripts in Various Collections*, 8:99.

47. PRO, SP 16/391/98.

48 Cenival and Brissac, *Sources Inedites*, 3:400–404.

49. PRO, SP 16/408/118.

50. Crawford, *Women and Religion*, 125.

51. *Discoverie of Six women preachers.*

52. Manning, *Politics, Religion*, 178.

53. For an excellent discussion of women petitioners after 1642, see Suzuki, *Subordinate Subjects*, chap. 4.

54. Ibid., 148.

55. *Journals of the House of Commons*, 2:597.

56. Ibid., 3:55–56.

57. *Acts and Ordinances of the Interregnum, 1642–1660*, 1:134–35.

58. The Moroccan ruler refused to "accept any ransom but a letter from the King of England for their redemption.

59. Cenival and Brissac, *Sources inedites*, 3:559–60.

60. Mack, *Visionary Women*, 123, quoted in Linebaugh and Rediker, *Many-Headed Hydra*, 92.

61. Ibid.

62. PRO, SP 18/36/84.

63. *CSPD, 1652–1653*, 387.

64. *CSPD, 1653–1654*, 59.

65. PRO, SP 71/29/494–95.

66. Barendse, *Arabian Seas*, 96.

67. Weiss states that French captives were "virtually all . . . men" ("Back from Barbary," 39). However, there are numerous allusions to French women captives.

68. Crisp, "Narrative of her Captivity," unpaginated.

69. There were other works, however, that depicted the Muslim ruler's overpowering of a Spanish woman. In 1619, Vicente Espinel's *Vida del escudero Marcos de Obregón* included a story about a Spanish woman married to a Muslim pirate, Mami Reis. In 1622, Lope de Vega wrote his *La desdicha por la honra* in which he told the story of Dona Maria, who was the sultan's favorite wife. And in Maria de Zayas y Sotomayor's "El jvez de su causa," in *Novelas amorosas y ejemplares* (1637), the evil Muslim attempts to rape the virtuous Estela but is prevented; Claudia, her rival for the love of Carlos, yields to the lust of the Muslim prince. Not unexpectedly, the former, who endures her captivity with Christian patience, is returned to her country, while Claudia is executed.

70. Gitlits, "New-Christian Dilemma," 63.

71. *CSP Ireland*, 621–22.

72. PRO, SP 16/332/30 V.

73. Quoted by Todd Gray, "Turkish Piracy and Early Stuart Devon," 166, from PRO, SP 16/311/9.

74. *CSP Venice, 1643–1647*, 27:209.

75. Wallington, *Historical Notices*, 2:266.

76. Young, *English Emblem Tradition*, 183.

77. The first known account was by Elizabeth Crisp, "Narrative of her Captivity."

78. *Case of Many Hundreds of English-Captives*.

79. Boxer, *Mary and Misogyny*, 15.

80. Reproduced in Brunot, *La mer*, 326–27.

81. Appleby, "Women and Piracy," 292.

82. PRO, SP 71/3/368, 373.

83. *Fifth Report*, 574.

84. Dunton, *A True Iournal*, app.; Cason, *Relation*, 23.

85. Busnot, *History*, 138.

86. As Sir Godfrey Fisher has noted, a single or widowed "Christian woman, returning home after, perhaps, years of slavery, might still be regarded as a highly eligible bride" (*Barbary Legend*, 101).

87. Baltharpe, *The Straight Voyage*, 39.

88. BL, Sloane MSS 3511, fol. 137.

89. Misermont, *Double Bombardement*, 64–65.

90. [J. Morgan], *Compleat History*, 225.

91. Quoted in Belhamissi, "Captifs musulmans et chretiens," 57. Similar restraint was exercised on women captives from other European nationalities who were also ransomed at a high price, indicating their "intact" conditions. In August 1621, two Sicilian women, Maria and Vittoria di Costantino, were ransomed for 825 ecus of gold, the highest price paid for any captives in that month (al-Basheer, *Jumhooriyat al-Dayat*, 155).

92. Quoted by Belhamissi, "Captifs musulmans et chrétiens," 57.

93. See the exhaustive study of this play by Ottmar Hegyi, *Cervantes and the Turks*.

94. De Vega, *Los esclavos libres*, in *Obras* 5:404.

95. Shukri, "*Al-Uluj*," 132–33.

96. Al-Masudi, *Al-Khulasa al-naqiyya*, 94.

97. La Véronne, *Vie de Moulay Isma'il*, 96; Koehler, *L'Eglise chrétienne*, 157.

98. John Whitehead, BL, Sloane MSS 90, 13v (reproduced in full in the appendix).

99. Brooks, *Barbarian Cruelty*, 27–34.

100. Goffman, *Ottoman Empire*, 68.

101. Cenival, *Sources inédites de l'histoire du Maroc*, 4:267n.

102. See the references in La Véronne, "Relation d'Andrés Mayo," 88–89.

103. Title for a female member of the royal family.

104. PRO, SP 71/15/343.

105. Busnot, *History*, 50–51.

106. Ibid., 52.

107. PRO, SP 71/15/181.

108. *Description of Slavery*, 4–5. There is unfortunately no reference to this English wife in the Arabic sources of the Maghrib. In Abd al-Karim bin Musa al-Rifi's eighteenth-century biography of Mulay Ismail, *Zahr al-Akkam*, 32–34, there is a listing of all the wives and children of the Moroccan king (of whom there were reputed to be around two thousand). There is no reference to an English wife, although there is a reference to a Christian from Spain (mother of Mulay Ahmad). There is a reference to a convert to Islam who was the mother of Mulay al-Fadil; another reference to Maria, also a convert, and mother of Bin Nasir and al-Mu'tamid; and a reference to the mothers of al-Mu'tassim and Sitt al-Muluk, both converts. Whether the English wife was one of these converts is not stated.

109. Quoted in Playfair, *Scourge of Christendom*, 121.

110. PRO, CO 279/28/360.

111. Palau, "De nuevo," 216.

112. Rousseaux, *Avantures de Dona Ines*, 121.

113. Yousseff, *Mechra el Melki*, sec. 4.

114. Quoted in Chung, "Lady Mary Wortley," 107.

115. PRO, SP 71/2/437.

116. PRO, SP 71/3/614.

117. PRO, SP 71/16/583.

118. Comelin, *Voyage*, chaps. 15–23.

119. Boyde, *Several Voyages to Barbary*, 34; a translation of Comelin.

120. PRO, SP 71/17/67.

121. PRO, SP 71/17/308, 312.

122. Braithwaite, *History of Revolutions*, 191.

123. PRO, SP 71/8/269, 273.

124. PRO, SP 71/8/339.

125. "I find that by the ancient Law of England, that if any Christian man did marry with a woman that was a Jew, or a Christian woman that married with a Jew, it was felony, and the party so offending should be burnt alive" (Coke, *Institute of Laws*, 89).

126. The others being Hanbali, Shafi,' Ja'fari (Shi'te) and Hanafi.

127. Ben Cheneb, "Sur marriage," 69.

128. Oddly, Marjorie Raley considers the marriage as a violation of European "colonial exchange" ("Claribel's Husband," 111).

129. For studies on the gendering of the Christian-Islamic conflict, see Fuchs, "Conquering Islands," 45–63; and the extensive discussion of gender and colonization in Brown, *Good Wives*, chap. 2. See also Hall, *Things of Darkness*, chap. 3; and the essays edited by Hulme and Carr in *Europe and Its Others*, 2:17–33, 46–61. See also Howard, "An English Lass," 101–17; and Jowitt, *Voyage Drama*.

130. *CSP Colonial*, 335, 347.

131. Pepys, *Tangier Papers*, 89–90.

132. Markham, *The Hawkins' Voyages*, 404.

133. Davies, *Elizabethan Errants*, opposite 175.

134. For a glimpse of gender relations in India among expatriates, see Kolff, "La 'nation' chretienne," 7–16.

135. See the discussion by Raman, "Imaginary Islands," 131–61.

136. Fletcher, *Island Princess*, 78 ff.

137. See my discussion of this play and of the stage defeat of Islam in *Islam in Britain*, chap. 2.

138. BL, Add. MSS 32094, fols. 275r–288v.

139. I am grateful to Michael H. Fisher for directing me to this play. See his reference in M. Fisher, *Travels of Dean Mahomet*, 141. Earlier in the century, an anonymous London wit used the same name, Isaac Bickerstaff, to ridicule the astrologer John Partridge. In "The Accomplishments of the First of Mr. Bickerstaff's Predictions," Jonathan Swift joined in ridiculing Partridge and his annual almanac.

140. Colley, *Captives*, 98.

Chapter 4

1. Colley, *Captives*, 4.

2. Garcés, *Cervantes in Algiers*.

3. Braudel, *Mediterranean*, 2:799.

4. See my "English Captivity Accounts," 553–73.

5. D. Davis, "Slavery," 51 ff.

6. J. Thomson, *Mercenaries, Pirates and Sovereigns*, 23.

7. The Barbary corsairs were "the terrorists of their day" (Page, *Lord Minimus*, 182).

See also Colley, *Captives*, 50: "I have already drawn an analogy between early modern perceptions of the Barbary corsairs and Western perceptions of terrorism today." It is interesting that a few years earlier, Janice E. Thomson had described Walter Raleigh's activities as "state-sponsored terrorism" (*Mercenaries, Pirates and Sovereigns*, 23).

8. Ginzburg, *Cheese and Worms*, xvii.

9. I am working on a book with a chapter on Arabic captivity accounts, *Early Modern Europe through Islamic Eyes*.

10. Ibn Iyas, *Bada'i al-Zuhur*, 4:164.

11. Bu Sharab, *Maghariba fi al-Burtughal*, 26–27.

12. Bu Sharab, "Mawarid al-Magharibi al-Muqimeen," 88.

13. Loupias, "Destin et témoignage," 69.

14. Al-Jabri, *Ulama' Jarbah*, 32, note; Basset, *Documents musulmans*, 35.

15. Cited in Larquié, "Les esclaves de Madrid," 47n1.

16. *Don Juan of Persia*, 283.

17. Contreras, *Adventures*.

18. It is difficult to give exact numbers of captives on either side. Robert C. Davis has claimed that between the years 1500 and 1800, one million Europeans were captured by the North Africans (*Christian Slaves, Muslim Masters*). But Gillian Weiss has counted all French captives in that period and has come up with a few thousand; I am in the process of doing the same in English sources and expect that since France's population was nearly four times that of England, the number of British captives will be smaller.

19. Morgan, *A Compleat History*, 251. Morgan was living in North Africa in 1729; his book was not published until 1750.

20. Ibid., 516 ff.

21. López Nadal, "Corsairing," 127.

22. See López Nadal, *El corsarisme mallorquí*; Bu Sharab, *Magharibi fi al-Burtughal*; Bu Sharab, *Watha'iq wa dirasat*, 180 ff; Belhamissi, *Les captifs algériens*; Miege, "Captifs marocains," 165–70; Bono, *Les corsaires en Méditerranée*; Senior, *Nation of Pirates*; and Lloyd, *English Corsairs*.

23. Misermont, *Double bombardement*.

24. An excellent survey of French historiography on captivity appears in Weiss's introduction to "Back from Barbary." Although her focus is on French captives, Weiss states that "France and its allies had been agents as well as objects of the Mediterranean slave system" (9).

25. See the discussion of *'abd* and *mamluk* in Lewis, *Race and Slavery*, 125–26n10. Ronald Segal ignores this crucial distinction in his *Islam's Black Slaves*.

26. Quoted in full in El Fasi, "Biographie de Moulai Ismaïl," 28; see the discussion by Hunwick, "Islamic Law and Polemics," 43–68.

27. See John Evelyn's diary entry on 16 September 1685: King James II decided that "the Negroes in the Plantations should all be baptized, exceedingly declaiming against that impiety of their masters prohibiting it, out of a mistaken opinion that they would be ipso facto free" (*Diary*, ed. Bray, 2:238).

28. De Groot, "Ottoman North Africa," 132.

29. A treaty between a Moroccan prince and Venice in 1508 states that if a Christian slave [aseer] from Badis or its territory escapes to the galleys they (the Venetians) shall return him to his owner. But if they take him to Christian territory and liberate him, then

when they return in another year, one of their number shall be taken, God willing (Wansbrough, "Commercial Treaty," 461).

30. Al-Wansharisi, *al-Mi'yar al-mu'arrab*, 2:198–200.

31. Razzuq, *al-Anadalusiyun wa hijratuhum ila al-Maghrib*, 81–82.

32. Monroe, "Curious Appeal," 291, line 64.

33. Bono, *Les corsairs en Méditerranée*, 174–75 and all of unit 4.

34. Quoted in Qadduri, *Ibn Abi Mahalli*, 83.

35. See Qasim, *Supporter of Religion*, 30.

36. Harvey, "Spanish Interpreter," 78, from the autobiography of Ahmad bin Qasim.

37. Al-Maqqari, *Nafh al-Tib*, 1:40.

38. There are numerous references in Weiss, "Back from Barbary," to French seizure of Muslims.

39. Arqash, *Muqadimmat wa Watha'iq*, 295.

40. Vanan, *Nusus wa Wathaiq*, 142–43.

41. Quoted in Belhamissi, *Les captifs algériens*, 45.

42. Evelyn, *Diary*, ed. de Beer, 2:164–65.

43. Knight, *A Relation of Seaven Yeares Slaverie*, 34. This is actually the thesis of Ellen G. Friedman in her study "North African Piracy," 1–16. See also her *Spanish Captives*.

44. *Le Gazette de France*, 16 March 1685, 143.

45. In August 1690, a French ship captured a Saletian ship carrying one hundred men. Twenty-four were killed and the rest were put to labor on the French fleet.

46. Quoted in Rouard de Card, *Les traités*, 22, 26.

47. Grandchamp, *La France en Tunisie*, 8:568.

48. Quoted in Weiss, "Back from Barbary," 28–29.

49. Castries, *Sources inédites d'Angleterre*, 2:132.

50. Ibid., 2:220.

51. *CSP Venice*, 9:556.

52. See Vitkus, *Three Turk Plays*, for the text of *A Christian Turned Turk*.

53. Castries, *Sources inédites d'Angleterre*, 2:528.

54. Ibid., 2:526.

55. *CSPD, James I, 1623–1625*, 11:430.

56. PRO, SP 71/1/53.

57. PRO, SP 71/1/41.

58. PRO, SP 71/1/55.

59. PRO, SP 71/1/308.

60. Marsden, *Law and Custom*, 1:454–55.

61. PRO, SP 71/1/123.

62. *CSPD, Charles I, 1625*, 1:10.

63. PRO, SP 71/1/124.

64. PRO, SP 16/334/50.

65. PRO, SP 102/2/80.

66. PRO, SP 71/12/179.

67. Cenival and Brissac, *Sources inédites*, 3:159–61

68. Ibid., 3:162.

69. Ibid., 3:164–65.

70. PRO, SP 16/334/130.

71. PRO, SP 16/355/140.

72. Porter and Morison, "Salcombe Bay Treasure," 16–18.

73. Massinger, *Plays and Poems*, vol. 2.

74. *A Very Woman*, 3.1.193–95, cited in Tokson, *Popular Image*, 91.

75. *CSPD, Charles I, 1639*, 14:315–16.

76. Al-Qadiri, *Nashr al-Mathani*, 2:28.

77. *Lady Alimony*, n.p.

78. *Gazette de France*, 11 April 1662, 396.

79. PRO, SP 71/1/part 4, 473. A letter, again from the Algerian dey, to the French king, Louis XIV, makes the same complaint (*Correspondence des deys d'Alger*, 1:50–51). There are many similar letters, 1:123, 142 and passim.

80. Charles II, *Articles of Peace*.

81. PRO, SP 71/1/414.

82. PRO, SP 71/1/part 4, 426.

83. PRO, SP 71/14/37.

84. PRO, SP 71/1/part 4, 466–67; there are numerous copies of this report.

85. *True and Perfect Relation*, 6–7

86. Tanner, *Descriptive Catalogue*, 3:67.

87. PRO, SP 71/22/114r.

88. Tanner, *Descriptive Catalogue*, 4:219 (12 September 1675).

89. *Letter written by Governour of Algier*.

90. BL, Sloane MSS 5105.

91. PRO, CO 279/28/398.

92. PRO, CO 279/28/189.

93. PRO, CO 279/28/80v.

94. *Gazette de France*, 4 February 1682, 112.

95. PRO, SP 29/418/308.

96. PRO, SP 102/4/110.

97. PRO, SP 102/4/112.

98. PRO, CO 279/30/369.

99. 5 September 1682, PRO, CO 279/30/70–72v.

100. PRO, CO 279/30/328.

101. Colley, *Captives*, 66–67.

102. Quoted in Belhamissi, *al-Jazair*, 145.

103. PRO, SP 71/2/1136.

104. *Present State of Algeir*, 2.

105. Delphin, "Histoire des pachas," 212.

106. Bodin, "Bombardement," 206–7.

107. Boyer, "Chiourme turque," 57n4.

108. PRO, SP 71/22/66.

109. PRO, SP 71/22/68r.

110. *CSPD, William III, 1 January–31 December, 1698*, 387.

111. PRO, SP 102/3.

112. PRO, SP 201/1/133 (18 August 1723).

113. J. Mathiex, "Trafic et prix," 163–64.

114. Corrales, "Répercussions," 231.

115. *Relation of a Voyage*, 29–30.

116. Braithwaite, *History of Revolutions*, 344. See also the reference to Delgano in Thomas Pellow's captivity account, Morsy, *Le relation de Thomas Pellow*, 71n12.

117. Boyde, *Several Voyages to Barbary*, 19. Boyde does not mention that he is translating from a French source.

118. Ibn Abi Diyaf, *Ithaf ahl al-zaman*, 2:52.

Chapter 5

1. Waller, "Instructions to a painter."

2. See the chapter on Tangier in N. Williams, *Redcoats and Courtesans*.

3. J. Thomson, *Mercenaries, Pirates, and Sovereigns*, 33.

4. BL, Harley MSS 1592:11; PRO, CO 279/1/25r.

5. BL, Sloane MSS 3509:11v–12r.

6. Ibid., 13v.

7. Dauncey, *The Fair Maid of the West*, Part I, Book II, 64.

8. Ibid., 67 and Part II, Book II, 84.

9. A dynasty of viziers, of Albanian origin, who served the Istanbul court in the second half of the seventeenth century. See Kinross, *The Ottoman Centuries*, chaps. 22–23.

10. BL, Harley MSS 6844:91–94.

11. Weiner, "Anglo-Moroccan Relations," 74.

12. BL, Harley MSS 1592:13–20.

13. "A Short narration of the Affairs of Tanger 1663," BL, Add. MSS 505:100, 105, 103.

14. *Description of Tangier*, 26ff.

15. Ibid., 25.

16. Ibid., 53.

17. Ibid., 55, 59.

18. See the detailed account in Rouard de Card, *La défaite*.

19. *Elegie*.

20. Quoted in Rouard de Card, *La défaite*, 19, 26.

21. PRO, SP 108/1/2.

22. *Articles of Peace between Charles II and Mahomet Bashaw*, art. 7.

23. *CSPD, Charles II, Addenda*, 103–5, 126–30.

24. BL, Sloane MSS 1831:8.

25. *Calendar of Manuscripts of the Marquis of Bath*, 2:149.

26. BL, Sloane MSS 3495.

27. Dryden, *The Works*, vol. 10.

28. PRO, CO 279/12/163–65.

29. PRO, CO 279/12/93.

30. Ogilby, *Africa*, 197. See also 198 for a listing of the bounties of the land.

31. *Short and Strange Relation*.

32. Ibid., 13.

33. *Letter from a Gentleman*, 20, 36.

34. *CSPD, Charles II, October 1668 to December 1669*, 9:385.

35. PRO, SP 29/269/part 1, fol. 286.

36. *Articles of Peace and Commerce*, viii.

37. D'Aranda, *History of Algiers*, describing captivity in 1641–42.

38. Quoted in Colley, *Captives*, 76.

39. Roberts, *Adventures*, 3.

40. Ibid., 13.

41. Ibid., 25.

42. In 1672, John Narbrough reported that a merchant from Messina was judged and burned in Tripoli after "they found a Turke woman in the house" (SP 71/22/71v.). But in 1721, a captive claimed that he had had an affair with a Portuguese woman who was a captive in Meknes. That she had converted to Islam is very likely as she appeared with "a Turbant on her Head, set round at the Bottom with Clasps of Diamonds, and in the Middle stood a Jewel, from whence arose a Heron's Feather" (*Description of Slavery*, 9). See also Boyde, *Several Voyages to Barbary*: Christian captives renounce their religion "either thro' Debauchery, if they have a little Liberty, which is but too frequently the Case" (42).

43. MacLean, *Rise of Oriental Travel*, part 4, 190.

44. For a detailed analysis of T. S.'s account, see MacLean, *Rise of Oriental Travel*, part 4.

45. For the little information about Baltharpe, see the references cited in Baltharpe, *The Straights Voyage*, edited by J. S. Bromley, ix–x.

46. Baltharpe, *The Straights Voyage*, 18.

47. PRO, SP 29/269/part 1, 286.

48. Baltharpe, *The Straights Voyage*, 26.

49. Ibid., 43.

50. Ibid., 87.

51. Ibid., 20.

52. Meriton, *Geographical Description of the World*.

53. Dryden, *The Dramatic Works*, 3:163.

54. Bekkaoui, *Signs of Spectacular Resistance*, 114.

55. See however the argument by Thompson that Dryden's defeat of the Moors implicitly represented "the more immediate defeat of economic rivals, the Dutch" ("Dryden's Conquest," 219).

56. Addison, *A Short Narrative*, 90, 93, 95, 100.

57. In that same year, 1671, a translation from French entitled *The Relation of a Voyage made into Mauritania* also mentioned the natural abundance of the regions (28).

58. Philips, *Present State of Tangier*, 33.

59. Luke, *Tangier at High Tide*, 57 (2 February 1671).

60. BL, Add. MSS 3511:160r.

61. Luke, *Tangier at High Tide*, 145.

62. Ibid., 23.

63. Ibid., 176.

64. Ibid., 32.

65. It is interesting that the anonymous Portuguese author of an account on Tangier in 1672 also felt the same: he praised the toleration of Jews and Catholics in the garrison, but had nothing to say about the Muslims: La Véronne, *Tanger sous l'occupation*.

66. *Notes and Observations*, 5, 17, 35, 65.

67. See the portrait in DiLorenzo, *Three Burlesque Plays*, 6.

68. *By the King. A Proclamation*.

69. BL, Add. 3511:174 ff, shows the decline in supplies from November 1672 to the end of 1673. On 6 September 1673, the following supplies were available: "Biskett" for 16 weeks; beef for 14 weeks; pork for 8 weeks, peas for 2/3 weeks; oatmeal for 12 weeks;

butter and cheese "none." By 31 December 1673, there was biscuit for 4 weeks, and everything else, "none."

70. Teonge, *Diary*, 60.

71. Ibid., 27.

72. Ibid., 62.

73. Philips, *Present State of Tangier*, 51.

74. *Letter from Tangier-Bay*, 8.

75. *Present State of Tangier*, 26.

76. Ibid., 31.

77. Ibid., 15, 16, 20–21, 26,

78. Ibid., 61, 63.

79. Seller, *Atlas Maritimus*, "Mediterranean Sea."

80. Tanner, *Descriptive Catalogue*, 4:65.

81. Ibid., 2:380.

82. Ibid., 3:18.

83. Ibid., 3:49.

84. Okeley, *Eben-Ezer*, A1v. Even in the 1764 reprint, the publisher stated in the preface that his purpose for reproducing the account was to "transmit to Posterity the most remarkable Display of Divine Providence in the happy Deliverance of the Author."

85. Tanner, *Descriptive Catalogue*, 3:38.

86. *A Particular Narrative of Burning of Tripoli*, 3.

87. PRO, SP 71/22/217–19.

88. Marott, *A Narrative*, 76.

89. Tanner, *Descriptive Catalogue*, 4:190.

90. *A Discourse of Tanger*, 19, 28, 33, 34, 35, 40.

91. *The Currant Intelligencer*, 14 February 1679/80.

92. See my discussion of the theme of holy war in English writings in *Turks, Moors, and Englishmen*, chap. 5.

93. *Exact Journal*, 12, 13.

94. *Manuscripts of the Earl of Dartmouth*, 51.

95. Addison, *The Moores Baffled*, 6. The text was published again, "The Second Edition," presumably by Addison in 1685.

96. Ibid., 21, 27.

97. Quoted in Hornstein, *The Restoration Navy*, 157n2.

98. *True Relation of a Great and Bloody Fight*, 1–2.

99. PRO, CO 279/28/230.

100. One contingent in the Moroccan army was made up of descendents of sub-Saharan Africans who had arrived in Morocco a little less than a century earlier.

101. Ross, *Tangers Rescue*, 35.

102. Ibid., 7, 9, 23, 27.

103. "Articles of Truce & Comerce for ye Forme of six months from ye date here of concluded & agreed."

104. Dryden, *The Works*, vol. 14.

105. *Letter sent by the Emperor of Morocco*, 4.

106. See the reproduction and commentary in Cenival and Brissac, *Sources inédites*, 3:357.

107. It appeared in *A Description of Tangier*, 9–10, where it is dated 1633; and in

Addison's *A Short Narrative*, 9–14, where it is dated 1625. There is a manuscript copy of the letter in PRO, SP 71/12/168–69, dated 1628. Cenival and Brissac date it 15 November 1637.

108. Lambeth Palace Library, MSS 673, fol. 4.

109. See the reproduction of the latter portrait on the cover of my *In the Lands of the Christians*.

110. *Congratulatory Poem*, 2.

111. *CSPD, Charles II, January 1st to December 31st, 1682*, 320.

112. "Whereas immediately after the arrival of his Excellency the Ambassador from Fez and Morocco, there was published a letter from the Emperor of Morocco to the King of England; this is to undeceive the reader that that was only a Copy of an old Letter reprinted, sent from one of their former Emperors to King Charles the First of ever blessed memory; and that this is the letter brought by the present Ambassador to his Majesty, whom God long preserve" (*Letter sent by the Emperor of Morocco*).

113. Burnet, *History*, 444.

114. *CSPD, Charles II, January 1st to December 31st, 1682*, 134.

115. PRO, ADM 77/2/no. 10.

116. PRO, SP 29/418/64.

117. *The Heir of Morocco*.

118. PRO, CO 279/30/353r–356v.

119. The letter is quoted and translated in Ockley, *An Account of South-West Barbary*, 135.

120. Ibid., 139.

121. PRO, CO 279/30/239–341v.

122. PRO, CO 279/31/169.

123. PRO, CO 279/31/n.p. The English translation in PRO, CO 279/31/340 ff. ignores the blunt rudeness: "Thy letter came to our hands and we understood the contents of it which want order and wherein there are some expressions which ought not to be."

124. Letter of 30 November 1682, PRO, CO 279/30/238r.

125. 21 March 1683, PRO, CO 279/32/173; 17 May 1683, PRO, CO 273/31/308.

126. Ismail to Kirke, 3 March 1683, PRO, CO 279/33.

127. PRO, SP 102/4/108.

128. *Manuscripts of the Earl of Dartmouth*, 96. Also PRO, CO 279/32/208.

129. *Manuscripts of the Earl of Dartmouth*, 98.

130. PRO, CO 279/32/196r.

131. *Tangier's Lamentation*, 3:473–77.

132. *CSPD, Charles II, October 1, 1683–April 30, 1684*, 98.

133. *Letter from Tangier, to a Friend in London*, 1.

134. Quoted in Corbett, *England*, 2:141.

135. CO 279/33/55.

136. *Al-Anwar al-Hasaniyya*, ed. Abd al-Karim al-Filali (Al-Muhammadiyya, Morocco, 1966), 92.

137. Giuseppe, "Archival Mines."

Conclusion

1. Scanlan, *Colonial Writing*, 3.

2. Dryden, *The Works*, 6:25.

3. For a political reading of this play in the context of Dryden's fall from grace, see Bywaters, *Dryden in Revolutionary England*, chap. 2. See also Moore, "Political Allusions," 36–42, where the author identifies many of the characters in the play with contemporary political and religious figures.

4. Dryden, *The Works*, 6:75.

5. Ibid., 54.

6. Ibid., 76.

7. Ibid., 99.

8. Ibid., 24.

9. Ibid., 35.

10. Ibid., 34 and 67.

11. Thomas Rymer, quoted in Vickers, *Shakespeare*, 2:29.

12. So read the instruction to Dartmouth in July 1683 from King Charles II (Pepys, *Tangier Papers*, 58).

13. Dryden, *The Works*, 6:52.

14. PRO, SP 102/2/179.

15. For a study of Barbary petitioners, see my "The Last Moors," 37–58.

16. Preface to Windus, *A Journey to Mequinez*.

17. For a study of British and French views of Moors in the eighteenth century, see A. Thomson, *Barbary and Enlightenment*.

Bibliography

Manuscripts

British Library (BL)
Additional Manuscripts, 505
Cotton Manuscripts, Nero B.X1
Harley Manuscripts, 1592, 6844
King's Manuscripts, 40
Sloane Manuscripts, 90, 1831, 3509, 5105

Lambeth Palace Library
MS 673

National Library of Rabat
MS Kaf 278

Public Record Office (PRO)
Colonial Office (Tangier) (CO)
State Papers, Foreign (Algeria, Morocco and Tunisia) (SP)

Official Documents

Acts and Ordinances of the Interregnum, 1642–1660. Edited by C. H. Firth and R. S. Rait. 2 vols. London: HMSO, 1911.
Acts of the Privy Council of England, 1617–1619, 1625–1626, 1627, Jan.–Aug.
Calendar of Letters and State Papers, English Affairs, Archives of Simancas, Elizabeth 1587–1603. Edited by Martin A. S. Hume. London: HMSO, 1899. (CLSP Simancas)
Calendar of Manuscripts of the Marquis of Bath. Dublin: HMSO, 1907.
Calendar of State Papers, Colonial Series, East Indies, China and Japan, 1513–1616. (CSP Colonial)
Calendar of State Papers, Domestic. The Reigns of Mary, Elizabeth I and James; Charles I; Commonwealth; Charles II; William III; Anne. (CSPD)
Calendar of State Papers, Foreign Series, of the Reign of Elizabeth [I], January–July 1589. Edited by R. B. Wernery. Vol. 23. London: HMSO, 1964. (CSPF Elizabeth)
Calendar of State Papers and Manuscripts, Venice, 1592–1603. Edited by Horatio F. Brown. London: HMSO, 1897. (CSP Venice)
Calendar of State Papers and Manuscripts, Venice, 1621–1623. Edited by Allen B. Hinds. London: HMSO, 1911. (CSP Venice)
Calendar of State Papers and Manuscripts, Venice, 1643–1647. Edited by Allen B. Hinds. London: HMSO, 1626. (CSP Venice)
Calendar of State Papers Relating to Ireland, Charles I, 1625–1632. Edited by Robert Pentland Mahaffy. London: HMSO, 1900. (CSP Ireland)
Commons Debate 1628. Edited by Mary Frear Keeler et al. New Haven, Conn.: Yale University Press, 1978.
Debates of the House of Commons in 1625. Edited by Samuel Rawson Gardiner. London: Camden Society, 1873.

First Report of the Royal Commission on Historical Manuscripts. London: HMSO, 1870.
Fourth Report of the Royal Commission on Historical Manuscripts. Part 1. London: HMSO, 1874.
Fifth Report of the Royal Commission on Historical Manuscripts. London: HMSO, 1876.
Historical Manuscripts Commission. *Report on Manuscripts in Various Collections.* Vol. 8. London: HMSO, 1914.
Journals of the House of Commons. Compiled by Timothy Cunningham. London, 1785.
Lords Proceedings 1628. Edited by Mary Frear Keeler et al. New Haven, Conn.: Yale University Press, 1983.
Manuscripts of the Earl of Dartmouth: Historical Manuscript Commission, Eleventh Report. Appendix, part 5. London, 1887.
Manuscripts of the House of Lords, Addenda 1514–1714. Edited by Maurice F. Bond. London: HMSO, 1962.
Report on Franciscan Manuscripts Preserved at the Convent, Merchants' Quay, Dublin. Dublin: HMSO, 1906.
Seventh Report of the Royal Commission on Historical Manuscripts. Part 1. London: HMSO, 1879.
Stuart Royal Proclamations. Edited by James F. Larkin. 2 vols. Oxford: Clarendon Press, 1983.

Published Sources

Addison, Lancelot. *The Moores Baffled: Being a Discourse Concerning Tanger, especially when it was under the Earl of Teviot.* London, 1681.
———. *A Short Narrative of the Revolutions of the Kingdoms of Fez and Morocco.* Oxford, 1671.
Africanus, Leo. *A Geographical Historie of Africa.* Translated and collected by John Pory. London, 1600.
———. *The History and Description of Africa.* Translated by John Pory. Edited by Robert Brown. London, 1896.

Alsop, J. D. "A Moorish Playing Company in Elizabethan England." *Notes and Queries* NS 27 (April 1980): 135.
The Amours of the Sultana of Barbary: A Novel in Two Parts. London, 1689.
Anderson, Adam. *An Historical and Chronological Deduction of the Origin of Commerce.* 4 vols. 1801. New York: Augustus M. Kelly, 1967.
Andrews, K. R. *Ships, Money and Politics: Seafaring and Naval Enterprise in the Reign of Charles I.* Cambridge: Cambridge University Press, 1991.
Appleby, John C. "Women and Piracy in Ireland: From Gráinne O'Malley to Anne Bonny." In *Bandits at Sea: A Pirates Reader,* edited by C. R. Pennell, 283–99. New York: New York University Press, 2001.
Armitage, David. *The Ideological Origins of the British Empire.* Cambridge: Cambridge University Press, 2000.
Arqash, Dalinda-al, et al., eds. *Muqadimmat wa Wathaiq fi tarikh al-Maghrib al-Arabi al-Hadith.* Mannouba, Tunisia, 1995.
The Arrivall and Intertainements of the Embassador, Alkaid Jaurar Ben Abdella, with his Associate, Mr. Robert Blake. London, 1637.
Articles of Peace and Commerce, Between the most Serene and Mighty Prince Charles II

. . . *and the Most Illustrious Lords the Bashaw, Dai, Aga and Governours of the Famous City and Kingdom of Algiers.* London, 1671–72.

Articles of Peace between the Most Serene and Mighty Prince Charles II . . . and the Most Excellent Signors, Mahomet Bashaw . . . Fifth of October 1662. London, 1662.

"Articles of Truce & Comerce for ye Forme of six months." British Library, Add. MSS 17021, 49r-52v.

Baltharpe, John. *The Straight Voyage, or, St. Davids Poem.* London, 1671.

Barbeau, Anne T. *The Intellectual Design of John Dryden's Heroic Plays.* New Haven, Conn.: Yale University Press, 1970.

Barendse, R. J. *The Arabian Seas.* London: M. E. Sharpe, 2002.

Barnby, Henry. "The Sack of Baltimore." *Journal of the Cork Historical and Archaeological Society* 74 (1969): 101–29.

Bartels, Emily C. "Making More of the Moor: Aaron, Othello, and Renaissance Refashionings of Race." *Shakespeare Quarterly* 41 (1990): 433–52.

Barthelemy, Anthony Gerard. *Black Face, Maligned Race: The Representation of Blacks in English Drama from Shakespeare to Southerne.* Baton Rouge: Louisiana State University Press, 1987.

Basheer, Tawfeeq al-. *Jumhooriyat al-Dayat fee Tunis, 1591–1675.* Tunis, 1992.

Basset, René. *Documents musulmans sur le siège d'Alger.* Paris: E. Leroux, 1890.

Beaumont, Francis. *The Knight of the Burning Pestle.* In *Elizabethan and Jacobean Comedy: An Anthology,* edited by Robert Ornstein and Hazleton Spencer, 205–45. Boston: D. C. Heath, 1964.

Beaumont and Fletcher. *The Works of Beaumont and Fletcher.* Edited by Alexander Dyce. 11 vols. 1843–47. Freeport, N.Y.: Books for Libraries Press, 1970.

Beazley, C. Raymond, ed. *Voyages and Travels Mainly during the 16th and 17th Centuries.* 2 vols. Westminster: Constable, 1903.

Bekkaoui, Khalid. *Signs of Spectacular Resistance.* Casablanca, 1998.

Belhamissi, Moulay. *Les captifs algériens et l'Europe chrétienne, 1518–1830.* Algiers, 1988.

———. "Captifs musulmans et chrétiens XVI–XVIIIe S.: Le cas des femmes et des enfants." In *Chrétiens et musulmans à l'époque de la renaissance,* edited by Abdeljelil Temimi, 53–65. Zaghouan, Tunisia, 1997.

———. *Al-Jazair min khilal rihlat al-Maghariba fi al-ahd al-Uthmani.* Algiers, 1981.

Benassar, Bartolomé, and Lucile Benassar. *Les chrétiens d'Allah: L'Histoire extraordinaire des renégats, XVIe-XVIIe siècles.* Paris: Perrin, 1989.

Ben Cheneb, Mohammed. "Sur marriage entre musulmane et non-musulmans." *Archives Marocaines* 15 (1908): 55–80.

Bin Haddah, Abd al-Rahim. *Al-Maghrib wal-Bab al-Ali.* Zaghouan, Tunis: Mu'assasat al-Tamimi, 1998.

Bodin, Marcel. "Le bombardement de Tripoli de Barabarie par le maréchal d'Estrées en 1685, raconté par un musulman marocain, témoin oculaire." *Revue Tunisienne* 128 (1918): 204–9.

Bono, Salvatore. *Les corsaires en Méditerranée.* Translated by Ahmed Somaï. Paris: La Porte, 1998.

Boxer, C. R. *Mary and Misogyny: Women in Iberian Expansion Overseas, 1415–1815.* London: Duckworth, 1975.

Boyde, Henry. *Several Voyages to Barbary.* London, 1736.

Boyer, P. "La chiourme turque des galères de France de 1665 à 1687." *Revue de l'Occident Musulman et de la Méditerranée*, 6 (1969): 53–74.

Bradley, David. *From Text to Performance in the Elizabethan Theatre: Preparing the Play for the Stage*. Cambridge: Cambridge University Press, 1992.

Braithwaite, John. *The History of the Revolutions in the Empire of Morocco*. London, 1729.

Braudel, Fernand. *The Mediterranean and the Mediterranean World in the Age of Philip II*. 2 vols. Translated by Siân Reynolds. New York: Harper Colophon Books, 1949.

Braunmuller, A. R. *George Peele*. Boston: Twayne, 1983.

Brenner, Robert. *Merchants and Revolution*. Princeton, N.J.: Princeton University Press, 1992.

Bromley, J.S., ed. *The Straight Voyage or St. Davids Poem*. Oxford: Basil Blackwell, 1959.

Brooks, Francis. *Barbarian Cruelty*. London, 1693.

Brotton, Jerry. "Carthage and Tunis, *The Tempest* and Tapestries." In *The Tempest and its Travels*, edited by Peter Hulme and William H. Sherman, 132–37. Philadelphia: University of Pennsylvania Press, 2000.

———. *The Renaissance Bazaar: From the Silk Road to Michaelangelo*. Oxford: Oxford University Press, 2002.

———. *Trading Territories*. Ithaca, N.Y.: Cornell University Press, 1997.

Brown, Kathleen M. *Good Wives, Nasty Wenches, and Anxious Patriarchs*. Chapel Hill: University of North Carolina Press, 1996.

Brunot, Louis. *La mer dans les traditions et les industries indigènes à Rabat et Salé*. Paris: E. Leroux, 1920.

Burchett, Josiah. *A Complete History of the Most Remarkable Transactions at Sea*. London, 1720.

Burnet, Gilbert. *Burnet's History of His Own Time*. London, 1883.

Burton, Jonathan. "Anglo-Ottoman Relations and the Image of the Turk in *Tamburlaine*," *Journal of Medieval and Early Modern Studies*, 30 (2000): 125–157.

Bu Sharab, Ahmad. *Magharibi fi al-Burtughal*. Rabat, 1996.

———. "Mawarid al-Maghariba al-Muqimeen bi-l-burtughal." *Majalat Kuliyat al-Adab w-al Ulum al-Insaniya* 19 (1994): 87–103.

———. *Watha'iq wa dirasat 'an al-ghazu al-Burtughali wa nataijihi*. Rabat, 1997.

Busnot, Dominick. *The History of the Reign of Muley Ismail*. London, 1715.

Bywaters, David. *Dryden in Revolutionary England*. Berkeley: University of California Press, 1991.

Cahn, Susan. *Industry of Devotion: The Transformation of Women's Work in England, 1500–1660*. New York: Columbia University Press, 1994.

Canny, Nicholas, ed. *The Origins of Empire: British Overseas Enterprise to the Close of the Seventeenth Century*. Oxford: Oxford University Press, 1998.

Carew, George Lord. *Letters from George Lord Carew to Sir Thomas Roe*. Edited by John MacLean. London: Camden Society, 1860.

The Case of Many Hundreds of Poor English-Captives in Algier. London, 1680.

Cason, Edmond. *A Relation of the whole proceedings concerning the Redemption of Captives in Argier and Tunis*. London, 1647.

Castries, Henry de. *Les sources inédites de l'histoire du Maroc, dynastie saadienne. . . archives et bibliothèques de France*. Paris: Ernest Leroux, 1909.

———. *Les sources inédites de l'histoire du Maroc . . . archives et bibliothèques d'Angleterre*. Vols. 1 and 2. Paris: Ernest Leroux, 1918–36.

Cawley, Robert Ralston. *The Voyagers and Elizabethan Drama*. 1938. New York: Kraus, 1966.

Cenival, Pierre de, ed. *Les sources inédites de l'histoire du Maroc, dynastie filalienne. . . archives et bibliothèques de France*. Paris: Paul Geuthner, 1931.

Cenival, Pierre de, and Philipe de Cossé Brissac, eds. *Les sources inédites de l'histoire du Maroc. . . archives et bibliothèques d'Angleterre*. Vol. 3. Paris: Paul Geuthner, 1936.

Chamberlain, John. *The Letters of John Chamberlain*. Edited by Norman Egbert McLure. 2 vols. Philadelphia: American Philosophical Society, 1939.

Chapman, George. *Eastward Ho*. Edited by R. W. Van Fossen. Manchester: Manchester University Press, 1979.

Charles I. *King Charles His Letter to the Great Turk*. London, 1642.

Charles II. *By the King. A Proclamation*. London, 1674.

———. *By the King. A Proclamation Touching the Articles of Peace with Algiers, Tunis, and Tripoli*. London, 1663.

Chew, Samuel C. *The Crescent and the Rose*. 1937. New York: Octagon, 1974.

Chung, Rebecca. "Lady Mary Wortley Montagu." In *Travel Knowledge: European 'Discoveries' in the Early Modern Period*, edited by Ivo Kamps and Jyotsna G. Singh, 97–127. New York: Palgrave, 2001.

Clark, Alice. *Working Life of Women in the Seventeenth Century*. London: G. Routledge, 1919.

Clissold, Stephen. *The Barbary Slaves*. 1977. New York: Barnes and Noble, 1992.

Cobbett's Parliamentary History of England. 36 vols. London: R. Bagshaw, 1806–20.

Coindreau, Roger. *Les corsairs de Salé*. Paris: Société d'Éditions Géographiques, 1948.

Coke, Edward. *The Third Part of the Institutes of the Laws*. London, 1648.

Colley, Linda. *Britons: Forging the Nation, 1707–1837*. New Haven, Conn.: Yale University Press, 1992.

———. *Captives: Britain, Empire and the World, 1600–1850*. New York: Anchor Books, 2002.

———. "Going Native, Telling Tales: Captivity, Collaborations and Empire." *Past and Present* 168 (2000): 170–93.

Comelin, François. *Voyage pour la Redemption des Captifs, aux royaumes d'Alger et de Tunis, fait en 1720*. Paris, 1721.

Committee for the Navy and Customs. *Die Martis 18 Martii, 1644*.

Congratulatory Poem, Dedicated to his Excellency, the Ambassador, from the Emperor of Fez, and Morocco. 10 Feb 1682. London, 1682.

Contreras, Alonso de. *The Adventures of Captain Alonso de Contreras*. Translated and annotated by Philip Dallas. New York: Paragon House, 1989.

Corbett, Julian S. *England in the Mediterranean*. 2 vols. London: Longmans, 1904, reprinted 1987.

Cormack, Lesley B. "Britannia Rules the Waves?: Images of Empire in Elizabethan England." In *Literature, Mapping, and the Politics of Space in Early Modern Britain*, edited by Andrew Gordon and Bernhard Klein, 45–68. Cambridge: Cambridge University Press, 2001.

Corrales, Elroy Martin. "Les répercussions de la course espagnole sur l'économie maritime marocaine (XVIe–XVIIIe siècle)." *Revue Maroc-Europe* 11 (1997–98): 227–48.

Correspondence des deys d'Alger. Edited by Eugène Plantet. Paris: F. Alcan, 1889.

Crawford, Patricia. "Public Duty, Conscience, and Women in Early Modern England." In *Public Duty and Private Conscience in Seventeenth-Century England*, edited by John Morrill et al., 57–76. Oxford: Clarendon Press, 1993.

———. *Women and Religion in England, 1500–1720.* London: Routledge, 1993.

Crisp, Elizabeth. "Journal of a voyage by Sea . . . Narrative of her Captivity in Barbary." MS 170/604. Huntington Library, San Marino, Calif.

The Currant Intelligencer, 1679/80.

Cust, Richard. "Charles I, the Privy Council, and the Forced Loan." *Journal of British Studies* 24 (1985): 208–36.

Daborne, Robert. *A Christian Turn'd Turk.* In *Three Turk Plays from Early Modern England*, edited by Daniel J. Vitkus, 149–241. New York: Columbia University Press, 2000.

D'Amico, Jack. *The Moor in English Renaissance Drama.* Gainesville: University Press of Florida, 1992.

D'Aranda, Emanuel. *The History of Algiers and it's Slavery.* London, 1666.

Dauncey, John. *The Fair Maid of the West.* London, 1662.

Daunton, Martin, and Rich Halpern. *Empire and Others.* Philadelphia: University of Pennsylvania Press, 1999.

D'Avenant, Sir William. *The Dramatic Works of Sir William D'Avenant.* 5 vols. 1872–74. New York: Russell and Russell, 1964.

Davies, D. W. *Elizabethan Errants.* Ithaca, N.Y.: Cornell University Press, 1967.

Davis, David Brion. "Slavery—White, Black, Muslim, Christian." *New York Review of Books,* 5 July 2001, 51–55.

Davis, Robert C. *Christian Slaves, Muslim Masters.* New York: Palgrave, 2003.

Dekker, Thomas. *Lust's Dominion.* Edited by Khalid Bekkaoui. Fez: Sidi Mohammed Ben Abdallah University, 1999.

Delphin, G. "Histoire des pachas d'Alger de 1515 à 1745." *Journal Asiatique* (April–June 1922): 161–33.

A Description of Tangier, the Country and People adjoining. With an Account of the Person and Government of Ghailan. London, 1664.

A Description of the Nature of Slavery Among the Moors and the Cruel Sufferings of those that fall into it. London, 1721.

De Vega, Lope. *Obras de Lope de Vega.* Madrid: Real Academia Española, 1918.

D'Ewes, Sir Simonds. *The Journal of Sir Simonds D'Ewes.* Edited by Willson Havelock Coates. London: Oxford University Press, 1942.

DiLorenzo, Ronald Eugene, ed. *Three Burlesque Plays of Thomas Duffett.* Iowa City: University of Iowa Press, 1972.

A Discourse of Tanger. London, 1680.

Discours veritable de la prise de la ville de Mahomette [Hammamet] par les chevaliers de Malte. Paris, 1602.

A Discoverie of Six women preachers, in Middlesex, Kent, Cambridgeshire, and Salisbury. With a relation of their names, manners, life, and doctrine, pleasant to be read, but horrid to be judged of. London, 1641.

Documents Illustrative of American History, 1606–1863. Edited by Howard W. Preston. New York, 1886.

Dollimore, Jonathan, and Alan Sinfield, eds. *Political Shakespeare*. Ithaca, N.Y.: Cornell University Press, 1994.

Don Juan of Persia, a Shi'ah Catholic, 1560–1604. Translated and edited by G. Lee Strange [Guy Le Strange]. New York: Harper and Brothers, 1926.

Doran, Susan. "The Politics of Renaissance Europe." In *Shakespeare and Renaissance Europe*, edited by Andrew Hadfield and Paul Hammond, 21–52. London: Arden Critical Companions, 2005.

Doyle, Anne T. *Elkanah Settle's The Empress of Morocco and the Controversy Surrounding It: A Critical Edition*. New York: Garland, 1987.

Draper, John W. *Orientalia and Shakespeareana*. New York: Vantage Press, 1977.

Dryden, John. *The Dramatic Works*. Edited by Montague Summers. Vols. 3 and 6. 1932. New York: Gordian Press, 1968.

———. *The Works of John Dryden*. Edited by Vinton Dearing. Vol. 14. Berkeley: University of California Press, 1992.

Dryden, John, John Crowne and Thomas Shadwell. *The Notes and Observations on the Empress of Morocco*. London, 1674.

Dunton, John. *A True Iournal of the Sally Fleet*. London, 1637.

Dutton, Richard, ed. "The Triumphs of Truth." In *Jacobean Civic Pageants*. Ryburn: Keele University Press, 1995.

An Elegie upon the much lamented Death of that Noble, and Valiant Commander; the Right honourable the Earl of Tiveot, Governour of Tangiers, Slain by the Moores. London, 1663.

El Fasi, Muhammad. "Biographie de Moulai Ismaïl." *Hespéris Tamuda* 5 (1962): 5–29.

Eliot, Sir John. *Negotium Posterorum*. Edited by Alexander B. Grosart. London, 1881.

Elizabeth I. *Elizabeth I, Collected Works*. Edited by Leah S. Marcus, Janel Mueller, and Mary Beth Rose. Chicago: University of Chicago Press, 2000.

The English Lovers: Or , A Girle Worth Gold. Both Parts, So often Acted with General Applause; now newly formed into A Romance. London, 1662.

Evelyn, John. *Diary of John Evelyn*. Edited by E. S. de Beer. 6 vols. Oxford: Clarendon Press, 1955.

———. Evelyn, John. *The Diary of John Evelyn*. Edited by William Bray. London: Everyman's Library, 1966. 2 vols.

An Exact Journal of the Siege of Tangier. London, 1680.

A Faithful Relation of the Most Remarkable Transactions which have happened at Tangier. London, 1680.

The Famous and Wonderfull recoverie of a Ship of Bristoll, called the Exchange, from the Turkish pirates of Argier. London, 1622.

Finet, John. *Ceremonies of Charles I: The Note Books of John Finet, 1628–1641*. Edited by Albert J. Loomie. New York: Fordham University Press, 1987.

The First Order Book of the Hull Trinity House, 1632–1665 Edited by F. W. Brooks. London: Printed for the Society, 1942.

Fisher, Michael H., ed. *The Travels of Dean Mahomet*. Berkeley: University of California Press, 1997.

Fisher, Sir Godfrey. *Barbary Legend*. Oxford: Clarendon Press, 1957.

Fishtali, Abu Faris al-. *Manahil al-Safa*. Edited by Abd al-Karim Karim. Rabat, 1972.

FitzGeffry, Charles. *Compassion towards Captives, chiefly towards our Bretheren and Country-men who are in miserable bondage in Barbarie*. Oxford, 1637.

Fletcher, John. *The Island Princess*. London: Nick Hern Books, 2002.

Forster, John. *The Debates on the Grand Remonstrance, November and December, 1641*. London: John Murray, 1860.

Franklin, William. *A Letter from Tangier*. London, 1682.

Fraser, Antonia. *The Weaker Vessel*. New York: Knopf, 1984.

Friedman, Ellen G. "North African Piracy on the Coasts of Spain in the Seventeenth Century: A New Perspective on the Expulsion of the Moriscos." *International History Review* 1 (1979): 1–15.

———. *Spanish Captives in North Africa in the Early Modern Period*. Madison: University of Wisconsin Press, 1983.

Fryer, Peter. *Staying Power: Black People in Britain since 1504*. Atlantic Highlands, N.J.: Humanities Press, 1984.

Fuchs, Barbara. "Conquering Islands: Contextualizing *The Tempest*." *Shakespeare Quarterly* 48 (1997): 45–63.

———. *Mimesis and Empire*. Cambridge: Cambridge University Press, 2001.

Fugger News-Letters, First Series. Edited by Victor von Klarwill. Translated by Pauline de Chary. London: John Lane, 1924.

Fugger News-Letters, Second Series. Edited by Victor von Klarwill. Translated by L.S.R. Byrne. London: John Lane, 1926.

Fuller, Mary C. *Voyages in Print: English Travel to America, 1576–1624*. Cambridge: Cambridge University Press, 1995.

Gardiner, Samuel R. *The Constitutional Documents of the Puritan Revolution, 1628–1660*. Oxford: Clarendon Press, 1889.

———. *History of England from the Accession of James I to the Outbreak of the Civil War, 1603–1642*. 10 vols. London: Longmans, 1884.

Garcés, María Antonia. *Cervantes in Algiers: A Captive's Tale*. Nashville, Tenn.: Vanderbilt University Press, 2002.

Gazette de France, 1682.

A Geographicall and Anthologicall description of all the Empires and Kingdomes, both of Continent and Ilands in this terrestriall Globe. London, 1618.

George, Margaret. *Women in the First Capitalist Society*. Urbana: University of Illinois Press, 1988.

Gillies, John. *Shakespeare and the Geography of Difference*. Cambridge: Cambridge University Press, 1994.

Ginzburg, Carlo. *The Cheese and the Worms*. Translated by John Tedeschi and Anne Tedeschi. London: Penguin Books, 1982.

Gitlits, David M. "The New-Christian Dilemma in Two Plays by Lope de Vega." *Bulletin of the Comediantes* 34 (1982): 63–81.

Goffman, Daniel. *The Ottoman Empire and Early Modern Europe*. Cambridge: Cambridge University Press, 2002.

Gosse, Philip. *The History of Piracy*. 1932. New York: Tudor, 1995.

Grandchamp, Pierre. *La France en Tunisie au debut du XVII siècle*. 10 vols. Tunis: J. Aloccio, 1925.

Gray, Todd. "Turkish Piracy and Early Stuart Devon." *Report and Transactions of the Devonshire Association for the Advacement of Science*. 121 (1989): 159–71.

Great and Bloody News from Tangier, or a full and True Relation of a Great and dreadful fight which happened on the 3d. of this Instant November. London, 1680.

Greene, Molly. "Beyond the Northern Invasion." *Past and Present* 174 (2002): 42–71.

Grimstone, Edward, trans. *The Estates, Empires, and Principallities of the World.* London, 1615.

Groot, Alexander H. de. "Ottoman North Africa and the Dutch Republic in the Seventeenth and Eighteenth Centuries." *Revue de l'Occident Musulman et de la Méditerranée* 39 (1985): 131–47.

Guiseppe, Restifo. "Archival Mines: Maghrib and Great Britain in the Records of Public Records Office F 08: Barbary States." Lecture given 24 March 2001, Zaghouan, Tunisia.

Hakluyt, Richard. *The Principal Navigations, Voyages, Traffiques and Discoveries of the English Nation.* 12 vols. Glasgow: James MacLehose and Sons, 1903–5.

———. "The Second Voyage of Master Laurence Aldersey, to the Cities of Alexandria and Cairo in Egypt, Anno 1586." In *Hakluyt's Voyages*, edited by Richard David. Boston: Houghton Mifflin Company, 1981.

Hall, Kim F. "Colonisation and Miscegenation." In *The Merchant of Venice*, edited by Martin Coyle, 92–117. New York: St. Martin's Press, 1998.

———. *Things of Darkness: Economies of Race and Gender in Early Modern England.* Ithaca, N.Y.: Cornell University Press, 1995.

The Happy Slave, A Novel Translated from the French. London, 1699.

Harakat, Ibrahim. *Al-Siyasah wal-Mujtama'fi al-Asr al-Sa'di.* Casablanca, 1987.

Harris, Bernard. "A Portrait of a Moor." In *Shakespeare Survey*, edited by Allardyce Nicoll, 89–97. Cambridge: Cambridge University Press, 1958.

Harvey, L. P. "The Morisco Who Was Muley Zaidan's Spanish Interpreter." *Miscelánea de Estudios Arabes y Hebraicos* 8 (1959): 67–97.

Haseleton, Richard. *Strange and Wonderfull Things.* London, 1595.

Hebb, David Delison. *Piracy and the English Government, 1616–1642.* Aldershot: Scolar, 1994.

Hegyi, Ottmar. *Cervantes and the Turks: Historical Reality versus Literary Fiction in "La Gran Sultana" and "El amante liberal."* Newark: Juan de la Cuesta, 1992.

Henderson, Katherine Usher, and Barbara F. McManus. *Half Humankind: Contexts and Texts of the Controversy about Women in England, 1540–1640.* Urbana: University of Illinois Press, 1985.

Henin, Jorge de. *Wasf al-Mamalik al-Maghribiyya.* Translated by Abd al-Wahid Akmir. Rabat, 1997.

Heylyn, Peter. *Cosmographie, In Four Bookes.* London, 1652.

Heywood, Thomas. *The Fair Maid of the West, Parts I and II.* Edited by Robert K. Turner Jr. Lincoln: University of Nebraska Press, 1967.

———. *If you know not me you know no body.* In *The Dramatic Works of Thomas Heywood*, vol. 1. New York: Russell and Russell, 1964.

Higgins, Patricia. "The Reactions of Women, with Special Reference to Women Petitioners." In *Politics, Religion and the Civil War*, edited by Brian Manning, 177–222. London: Arnold, 1973.

Hill, Christopher. *The Century of Revolution, 1603–1713.* London: Sphere, 1974.

Hoenselaars, A. J. *Images of Englishmen and Foreigners in the Drama of Shakespeare and His Contemporaries.* London and Toronto: Associated University Presses, 1992.

Honigmann, E.A.J., ed. *Othello*, by William Shakespeare. London: Arden Shakespeare, Third Series, 1997.

Hornstein, Sari R. *The Restoration Navy and English Foreign Trade, 1674–1688.* Aldershot: Scolar Press, 1991.

Howard, Jean E. "An English Lass amid the Moors." In *Women, "Race," and Writing in the Early Modern Period,* edited by Margo Hendricks and Patricia Parker, 101–17. London and New York: Routledge, 1994.

Hulme, Peter, and Helen Carr, eds. *Europe and Its Others.* 2 vols. Colchester: University of Essex, 1985.

Hunter, G. K. "Othello and Colour Prejudice." *Proceedings of the British Academy 53* (1968): 139–63.

Hunwick, John. "Islamic Law and Polemics over Race and Slavery in North and West Africa (16th-19th Century)." In *Slavery in the Islamic Middle East,* edited by Shaun E. Marmon, 43–69. Princeton, N.J.: Markus Wiener, 1999.

Hurewitz, J. C., ed. *The Middle East and North Africa in World Politics.* New Haven, Conn.: Yale University Press, 1975.

Hyland, Peter. "Moors, Villainy and the Battle of Alcazar." *Parergon* 16 (1999): 85–99.

Ibn Abi Dinar. *Kitab al-Mu'nis fi Akhbar Ifriqiyah wa Tunis.* Edited by Muhammad Shammam. Tunis, 1967.

Ibn Abi Diyaf. *Ithaf ahl al-Zaman.* Edited by Muhammad Shammam. Tunis, 1989–90.

Ibn Iyas. *Bada'i al-Zuhur fi Waqai' al-Duhur.* 6 vols. Cairo, 1960.

Jabri, Suleyman bin Ahmad al-Hilati al-. *Ulama' Jarbah.* Edited by Muhammad Quawjah. Beirut, 1998.

Jones, Eldred. *Othello's Countrymen: The African in English Renaissance Drama.* London: Oxford University Press, 1965.

———. "Racial Terms for Africans in Elizabethan Usage." *Review of National Literatures* 3 (1972): 54–89.

Jowitt, Claire. *Voyage Drama and Gender Politics, 1589–1642.* Manchester: Manchester University Press, 2003.

Karim, Abd al-Karim. *Al-Maghrib fi 'ahd al-dawla al-Sa'diyya.* Rabat, 1978.

Kingsly, Charles. *Westward Ho!* London, 1855.

Kinross, Lord [Patrick Balfour]. *The Ottoman Centuries: The Rise and Fall of the Turkish Empire.* New York: Morrow Quill Paperbacks, 1977.

Knapp, Jeffrey. *An Empire Nowhere: England, America, and Literature from "Utopia" to "The Tempest."* Berkeley: University of California Press, 1992.

Knight, Francis. *A Relation of Seaven Yeares Slaverie vnder the Turkes of Argeire, suffered by an English Captive Merchant.* London, 1640.

Knutson, Roslyn L. "A Caliban in St. Mildred Poultry." In *Shakespeare and Cultural Traditions,* edited by Tesuo Kishi, Roger Pringle, and Stanley Wells, 110–27. Newark, N.J.: University of Delaware Press, 1994.

Koehler, Henry. *L'Église chrétienne du Maroc et la mission franciscaine, 1221–1790.* Paris: Societé d'Éditions Franciscaine, 1935.

Kolff, D.H.A. "La 'nation' chretienne à Surate au debut du xviième siècle." In *La femme dans les sociétés coloniales,* 7–16. Provence: Université de Provence, Table Ronde CHEE, CRHSE, IHPOM, 1982.

Kyd, Thomas. *The Tragedye of Soliman and Perseda.* In *The Works of Thomas Kyd,* edited by Frederick S. Boas, 160–229. Oxford: Clarendon Press, 1901.

Lady Alimony; or the Alimony Lady. An Excellent Pleasant New Comedy, duly Authorized, daily Acted, and frequently Followed. London, 1659.

Lane-Poole, Stanley. *The Barbary Corsairs*. New York: Putnam, 1901.

Lapeyre, Henri. *Géographie de l'Espagne morisque*. Paris: SEVPEN, 1959.

Larquié, Cl. "Les esclaves de Madrid à l'époque de la décadence (1650–1700)." *Revue Historique* 224 (1970): 41–74.

La Véronne, Chantal de. "Relation d'Andrés Mayo, captif à Meknes de 1669 à 1723." *Al-Qantara* 9 (1988): 85–101.

———. *Tanger sous l'occupation anglaise, d'après une description anonyme de 1674*. Paris: Paul Geuthner, 1972.

———. *Vie de Moulay Isma'il*. Paris: Paul Geuthner, 1974.

The Lawes Resolutions of Womens Rights: or, The Lawes Provision for Women. London, 1632.

A Letter from a Gentleman of the Lord Ambassador Howard's Retinue to his Friend in London: Dated at Fez, Nov 1. 1669. London, 1670.

A Letter from Tangier, to a Friend in London. Describing the Causes, manner and Time, of the Demolishing of Tangier, November the Fifth, in the year 1683. London, 1683.

A Letter from Tangier-Bay The 17th of May. London. 1680.

A Letter from the King of Morocco, to his Majesty the King of England Charles I, for the reducing of Sally, Argiers, & c. London, 1680.

A Letter sent by the Emperor of Morocco And King of Fez to his Majesty of Great Britain, And delivered by his Ambassador in January 1681. London, 1682.

A Letter written by the Governour of Algier to the States-General of the United Provinces. London, 1679.

Letters from Barbary, 1576–1774. Edited by J.F.P. Hopkins. London: Oxford University Press, 1982.

Lewis, Bernard. *Race and Slavery in the Middle East*. New York and Oxford: Oxford University Press, 1990.

Linebaugh Peter, and Marcus Rediker. *The Many-Headed Hydra*. Boston: Beacon Press, 2000.

Lloyd, Christopher. *English Corsairs on the Barbary Coast*. London: Collins, 1981.

Loades, David. *England's Maritime Empire: Seapower, Commerce and Policy, 1490–1690*. London: Longman, 2000.

Loomba, Ania. "'Delicious traffick': Racial and Religious Difference on Early Modern Stages." In *Shakespeare and Race*, edited by Catherine M. S. Alexander and Stanley Wells, 203–24. Cambridge: Cambridge University Press, 2000.

———. *Shakespeare, Race, and Colonialism*. Oxford: Oxford University Press, 2002.

López Nadal, Gonçal. "Corsairing as a Commercial System: The Edges of Legitimate Trade." In *Bandits at Sea: A Reader*, edited by C. R. Pennell, 125–38. New York: New York University Press, 2001.

———. *El corsarisme mallorquí a la Mediterrània occidental, 1652–1698, un commerç forçat*. Palma de Mallorca, 1986.

Loupias, Bernard. "Destin et témoignage d'un Marocain esclave en Espagne." *Hespéris Tamuda* 17 (1976–77): 69–85.

Luke, John. *Tangier at High Tide: The Journal of John Luke, 1670–1673*. Edited by Helen Andrews Kaufman. Paris: Librarie Minard, 1958.

Lupton, Julia Reinhard. "Othello Circumcised: Shakespeare and the Pauline Discourse of Nations." *Representations* 57 (1997): 73–89.

MacLean, Gerald M. "On Turning Turk, or Trying to: National Identity in Robert

Daborne's A Christian Turn'd Turke." *Explorations in Renaissance Culture* 29 (2003): 225–53.

———. *The Rise of Oriental Travel*. New York: Palgrave, 2004.

Maley, Willy. "'This Sceptred isle': Shakespeare and the British Problem." In *Shakespeare and National Culture*, edited by John J. Joughin, 83–108. Manchester: Manchester University Press, 1997.

Manning, Brian. *The English People and the English Revolution, 1640–1649*. London: Heinemann, 1976.

———, ed. *Politics, Religion and the English Civil War*. London: Arnold, 1973.

Maqqari, Ahmad bin Muhammad. *Nafh al-Tib*. Edited by Ihsan Abbas. Beirut, 1968.

Markham, Clements R., ed. *The Hawkins' Voyages during the Reigns of Henry VIII, Queen Elizabeth, and James I*. New York: Burt Franklin, 1970.

Marlowe, Christopher. *The Complete Plays*. Edited by J. B. Steane. London: Penguin, 1973.

Marott, Lewis. *A Narrative of the Adventures of Lewis Marott, Pilot-Royal of the Galleys of France . . . Translated from the French Copy*. London, 1677.

Marsden, R. G., ed. *Documents Relating to Law and Custom of the Sea*. London: Printed for the Navy Records Society, 1915.

Marston, John. *Wonder of Women, Sophonsiba*. London, 1606.

Martín Casares, Aurelia. *La esclavitud en la Granada del siglo XVI: Género, raza, religión*. Granada: Universidad de Granada, 2000.

Massinger, Philip. *The Plays and Poems of Philip Massinger*. Edited by Philip Edwards and Colin Gibson. 4 vols. Oxford: Clarendon Press, 1976.

Mas'udi, Abu Abdallah al-Baji al-. *Al-Khulasa al-Naqiyya*. Tunis, 1323 H. 1905.

Matar, Nabil. *Early Modern Europe through Islamic Eyes: 1578–1727*. In progress.

———. "English Captivity Accounts in North Africa and the Middle East: 1577–1625." *Renaissance Quarterly* 54 (2001): 553–73.

———. "Enter Mullisheq." *Around the Globe* 27 (2004): 30–31.

———. "Europe's Mediterranean Other: The Moor." And Rudolph Stoeckel. In *The Arden Critical Companions*, edited by Andrew Hadfield and Paul Hammond, 230–52. London: The Arden Shakespeare, 2004.

———, ed. and trans. *In the Lands of the Christians: Arabic Travel Writing in the Seventeenth Century*. New York: Routledge, 2003.

———. Introduction to *Piracy, Slavery and Redemption: English Captivity Narratives in North Africa, 1577–1704*, edited by Daniel Vitkus. Columbia University Press, 2001.

———. *Islam in Britain, 1558–1685*. Cambridge: Cambridge University Press, 1998.

———. "John Harrison." *New Dictionary of National Biography*.

———. "The Last Moors: Maghariba in Britain, 1700–1750." *Journal of Islamic Studies* 14 (2003): 37–58.

———. "Renaissance England and the Turban." In *Images of the Other*, edited by David Blanks. *Cairo Papers in Social Science* 19 (1996): 39–55.

———. *Turks, Moors and Englishmen in the Age of Discovery*. New York: Columbia University Press, 1999.

Mathiex, J. "Trafic et prix de l'homme en Méditerranée." *Annales, Economies, Societies, Civilisation* 9 (1954): 157–64.

McLeod, Bruce. *The Geography of Empire in English Literature, 1580–1745*. Cambridge: Cambridge University Press, 1999.

Menocal, Maria Rosa. *The Ornament of the World.* Boston: Little, Brown, 2002.

Meriton, George. *Geographical Description of the World. With a brief Account of the several Empires, Dominions, and Parts thereof.* 2nd ed. London, 1674.

Metzger, Mary Janelle. "'Now by My Hood, a Gentle and No Jew': Jessica, *The Merchant of Venice,* and the Discourse of Early Modern English Identity." *PMLA* 113 (1998): 52–63.

Middleton, Thomas. *The Works of Thomas Middleton.* Edited by A. H. Bullen. New York: AMS Press, 1964.

Middleton, Thomas, and William Rowley. *The Spanish Gipsie, and All's Lost by Lust.* Edited by Edgar C. Morris. Boston: D. C. Heath, 1908.

Miege, Jean-Louis. "Captifs marocains en Italie XVIIe-XVIIIe siècles." *Revue Maroc-Europe* 11 (1997–98): 165–70.

Misermont, Lucien. *Le double bombardement d'Alger par Duquesne et la mort du consul le Vacher.* Paris: Alphonse Ricard et Fils, 1905.

Monroe, James T. "A Curious Morisco Appeal to the Ottoman Empire." *Al-Andalus* 31 (1966): 281–303.

Moore, Robert. "Political Allusions in Dryden's Later Plays." *PMLA* 72 (1958): 36–42.

The Moores Baffled: Being a Discourse Concerning Tanger, especially when it was under the Earl of Teviot. London, 1681.

Morgan, J. *A Compleat History of the Piratical States . . . By a Gentleman who resided there many Years in a public Character.* London, 1750.

Morsy, Magali. *Le relation de Thomas Pellow.* Paris: Editions Recherche sur les Civilisations, 1983.

Mun, Thomas. *A Discovrse of Trade.* London, 1621.

Neill, Michael. "'Mulattos,' 'Blacks,' and 'Indian Moors': Othello and Early Modern Constructions of Human Difference." *Shakespeare Quarterly* 49 (1998): 361–74.

Netzloff, Mark. *England's Internal Colonies.* Houndsmill, Basingstone: Palgrave Macmillan, 2003.

Neville-Sington, Pamela. "'A very good trumpet': Richard Hakluyt and the Politics of Overseas Expansion." In *Texts and Cultural Change in Early Modern England,* edited by Cedric C. Brown and Arthur F. Marotti, 66–90. New York: St. Martin's Press, 1997.

Newman, Karen. "'And wash the Ethiop white': Femininity and the Monstrous in *Othello*"in *Shakespeare Reproduced.* Edited by Jean E. Howard and Marion F. O'Connor, 143–63. New York and London: Methuen, 1987.

Nichols, John. *The Progresses and Public Processions of Queen Elizabeth.* London, 1823.

Niranjana, Tejaswini. *Siting Translation: History, Poststructuralism, and the Colonial Context.* Berkeley: University of California Press, 1992.

Ockley, Simon. *An Account of South-West Barbary Containing what is most Remarkable in the Territories of the King of Fez and Morocco.* London, 1713.

Ogilby, John. *Africa being accurate description of the region of Aegypt, Barbary, Lybia and Billendulgerid.* London, 1670.

Okeley, William. *Eben-Ezer, : Or , A Small Monument of Great Mercy.* London, 1676.

An Ordinance of the Lords and Commons assembled in Parliament, For the Raising of Moneys for Redemption of Distressed Captives. 1644.

The Ordinance of the Lords and Commons assembled in Parliament, For the Apprehending and bringing to condigne punishment, all such lewd persons as shall steale, sell, buy, inveighel, purloyne, convey, or receive any little Children. And for the strict and diligent search of all Ships and other Vessels on the River, or at the Downes. London, 1645.

Ortelius, Abraham. *An Epitome of the Theatre of the Whole World.* London, 1603.

———. *The Theatre of the Whole World.* London, 1606.

Otten, Charlotte F., ed. *English Women's Voices, 1540–1700.* Miami: Florida International University Press, 1992.

Pagden, Anthony. *Lords of All the World: Ideologies of Empire in Spain, Britain and France, c. 1500–c. 1800.* New Haven, Conn.: Yale University Press, 1995.

Page, Nick. *Lord Minimus.* London: HarperCollins, 2001.

Painter, William. *The Palace of Pleasure.* Edited by Joseph Jacobs. London: D. Nutt, 1890.

Palau, Mariano Arribas. "De nuevo sobre la embajada de al-Gassani." *Al-Qantara* 6 (1985): 199–289.

Parker, Kenneth. "Barbary in Early Modern England, 1550–1685." In *The Movement of People and Ideas between Britain and the Maghreb*, edited by Abdeljelil Temimi and Mohamed Salah Omri, 125–51. Zaghouan, Tunisia, 2003.

A Particular Narrative of a Great Engagement between the Garison of Tangier and the Moors. London, 1680.

A Particular Narrative of the Burning in the Port of Tripoli, Four Men of War, Belonging to those Corsairs. London, 1676.

A Particular Relation of the Late Success of His Majesties Forces at Tangier against the Moors. London, 1680.

Peele, George. *The Battle of Alcazar.* In *The Dramatic Works of George Peele*, edited by John Yoklavich. New Haven, Conn.: Yale University Press, 1961.

———. *The Device of the Pageant Borne before Wolstan Dixi* in *The Life and Minor Works of George Peele* edited by David H. Horne. New Haven, Conn.: Yale University Press, 1952.

Pennell, C. R., ed. *Bandits at Sea: A Pirates Reader.* New York: New York University Press, 2001.

Penz, Charles. *Les captifs français du Maroc au XVIIe siècle (1577–1699).* Rabat: Imprimerie Officielle, 1944.

Pepys, Samuel. *Tangier Papers of Samuel Pepys.* Edited by Edwin Chappell. London: Navy Records Society, 1935.

Philips, George. *The Present State of Tangier: in a Letter to his Grace, the Lord Chancellor of Ireland.* London, 1676.

Pianel, Georges. "Le Maroc à la recherche d'une conquête: L'Espagne ou les indes?" *Hespaeris* 40 (1953): 511–21.

Playfair, R. L. *The Scourge of Christendom.* London, 1884.

Polemon, John. *The Second part of the booke of Battailes.* London, 1587.

Powell, J. R. *The Navy in the English Civil War.* London: Archon Books, 1962.

The Present Danger of Tangier . . . in a letter from Cadiz . . to a friend in England. London, 1679.

The Present State of Algeir: Being a Faithful and True Account of the most Considerable Occurrences That happened in that Place, during the lying of the French Fleet before it. London, 1683.

The Private Journals of the Long Parliament. Edited by Willson H. Coates, Anne Steele Young, and Vernon F. Snow. 3 vols. New Haven, Conn.: Yale University Press, 1982.

A Proclamation Touching the Articles of Peace . . . 29 Jan 1663.

A Prospect for the most famous parts of the World. London, 1646.

Purchas, Samuel. *Pvrchas his Pilgrimage. Or Relations of the world and the Religions Observed in all Ages and Places discouered, from the CREATION unto this PRESENT.* London, 1614.

Qadduri, Abd al-Majid al-. *Ibn Abi Mahalli al-Faqih al-Tha'ir.* Rabat, 1991.

Qadiri, Muhammad ibn Tayyib al-. *Nashr al-Mathani.* Edited by Muhammad Hajji and Ahmad al-Tawfiq. 4 vols. Rabat, 1977.

Qasim, Ahmad bin. *Nasir al-din ala al-qawm al-kafirin.* Translated by P. S. Van Koningsveld, Q. Al-Samarrai, and G. A. Wiegers as *The Supporter of Religion against the Infidels* (Madrid: al-Majlis al-A'la lil-Abhath, 1997).

Quinn, D. B. "Sailors and the Sea." *Shakespeare Survey* 17 (1964): 21–36.

R. B. *The English Empire in America.* London, 1685.

Raley, Marjorie. "Claribel's Husband." In *Race, Ethnicity, and Power in the Renaissance,* edited by Joyce Green MacDonald, 95–120. London: Associated University Presses, 1997.

Raman, Shanker. "Imaginary Islands: Staging the East." *Renaissance Drama* 26 (1995): 131–61.

Rawlins, John. *The Famous and Wonderfull recoverie of a Ship of Bristoll, called the Exchange, from the Turkish pirates of Argier.* London, 1622.

Razzuq, Muhammad. *Al-Andalusiyyun wa hijratuhum ila al-Maghrib.* Al-Dar al-Bayda,' 1998.

Regla, Juan. *Estudios sobre los moriscos.* Valencia: N.p., 1971.

The Relation of a Voyage made into Mauritania. London, 1671.

A Relation Strange and True. London, 1622.

The Return of the Ambassador, from the Emperour of Fez. And Morocco, to his own Countrey, By a person of Quality, 24 July 1682.

Ricard, Robert. *Mazagan et le Maroc sous le règne du Sultan Moulay Zidan (1608–1627).* Paris: P. Geuthner, 1956.

Rice, Warner G. "The Moroccan Episode in Thomas Heywood's 'The Fair Maid of the West.'" *Philological Quarterly* 9 (1930): 131–40.

Rifi, Abd al-Karim bin Musa al-. *Zahr al-Akkam.* Edited by Asia Bina'dada. Rabat, 1992.

Roberts, A. *The Adventures of (Mr T.S.) an English Merchant, Taken Prisoner by the Turks of Argiers.* London, 1671.

Robinson, Henry. *Libertas, or Reliefe to the English Captives in Algier.* London, 1642.

Roe, Sir Thomas. *The Negotiations of Sir Thomas Roe in his Embassy to the Ottoman Porte, from the Year 1621 to 1628 Inclusive.* London, 1740.

Romack, Katherine. "Monstrous Births and the Body Politic: Women's Political Writings and the Strange and Wonderful Travails of Mistris Parliament and Mrs. Rump." In *Debating Gender in Early Modern England, 1500–1700,* edited by Christina Malcolmson and Mihoko Suzuki, 209–31. New York: Palgrave, 2002.

Ross, John. *Tangers Rescue; or, A relation of the late Memorable Passages at Tanger.* London, 1681.

Rouard de Card, E. *La défaite des Anglais à Tanger en 1664.* Paris: A. Pedone, 1912.

———. *Les traités entre la France et le Maroc.* Paris: A. Pedone, 1898.

Rousseaux. *Avantures de Dona Ines de las Cisternas.* Utrecht, 1737.

Routh, E.M.G. *Tangier, England's Lost Atlantic Outpost, 1661–1684.* London: J. Murray, 1912.

Russell, Conrad. *Parliaments and English Politics, 1621–1629.* Oxford: Clarendon Press, 1979.

Said, Edward. *Culture and Imperialism.* New York: Knopf, 1994.

Saldanha, António de. *Crónica de Almançor, Sultã de Marrocos (1578–1603).* Edited by António Dias Farinha. Translated into French by Léon Bourdon. Lisbon: Instituto de Investigação Científica Tropical, 1997.

Scanlan, Thomas. *Colonial Writing and the New World, 1583–1671.* Cambridge: Cambridge University Press, 1999.

Segal, Ronald. *Islam's Black Slaves.* New York: Farrar, Straus and Giroux, 2001.

Seller, John. *Atlas Maritimus, or the Sea-Atlas; Being A Book of Maritime Charts.* London, 1675.

Senior, C. M. *A Nation of Pirates: English Piracy in Its Heyday.* London: David and Charles Newton Abbot, 1976.

Settle, Elkanah. *The Empress of Morocco. A Tragedy with Sculptures.* London, 1673.

———. *The Heir of Morocco, with the Death of Gayland. Acted at the Theatre Royal.* London, 1682.

Shakespeare, William. *The Merchant of Venice.* Edited by John Russell Brown. Arden Shakespeare, Third Series, 2001.

———. *The Riverside Shakespeare.* Edited by G. Blakemore Evans. Boston: Houghton Mifflin Company, 1974.

———. *Othello.* Edited by E.A.J. Honigmann. London: Arden Shakespeare, Third Series, 1997.

———. *The Tempest.* Edited by Virginia Mason Vaughan and Alden T. Vaughan. London: Arden Shakespeare, 1999.

———. *Titus Andronicus.* Edited by Russ McDonald. London: Penguin, 2000.

Sharpe, Kevin. *The Personal Rule of Charles I.* New Haven, Conn.: Yale University Press, 1992.

Sheehan, Bernard W. *Savagism and Civility.* Cambridge: Cambridge University Press, 1980.

Shepherd, Simon. *Amazons and Warrior Women: Varieties of Feminism in Seventeenth-Century Drama.* New York: St. Martin's, 1981.

———. *Marlowe and the Politics of Elizabethan Theatre.* Brighton: Harvester, 1986.

A Short and Strange Relation of some part of the Life of Tafiletta, the Great Conqueror and Emperor of Barbary. London, 1669.

Shukri, Abd al-Rahim. *"Al-Uluj bil-Maghrib khilal al-'Asr al-Saadi."* Doctorat d'Etat, University of Muhammad al-Khamis, Rabat, 1992.

Simpson, Richard, ed. *The Play of Stucley.* In *The School of Shakespeare.* London: Chatto and Windus, 1878.

Speed, John. *A Prospect of the most famous parts of the World.* 1627. London, 1646.

Starr, G. A. "Escape from Barbary: A Seventeenth-Century Genre." *Huntington Library Quarterly* 29 (1965): 35–52.

Stone, Lawrence. *The Family, Sex and Marriage in England, 1500–1800.* Abridged edition. New York: Harper, 1979.

Suckling, John. *The Copy of a Letter written to the Lower House of Parliament touching divers grievances and inconveniences of the state.* London, 1641.

Supple, B. E. *Commercial Crisis and Change in England, 1600–1642.* Cambridge: Cambridge University Press, 1959.

Suzuki, Mihoko. *Subordinate Subjects: Gender, the Political Nation, and Literary Form in England, 1588–1688*. Aldershot: Ashgate, 2003.

Sweet, Thomas. *Dear friends: It is now about six yeares since I was most unfortunately taken by a Turkes man of Warre, on the Coasts of Barbary captive into Argiere*. London, 1647.

T. M. *A Discovrse of Trade*. London, 1621.

Tangier's Lamentation. In *Poems on Affairs of State: Augustan Satirical Verse, 1660–1714*. Edited by Howard H. Schless. New Haven, Conn.: Yale University Press, 1968.

Tanner, J. R., ed. *A Descriptive Catalogue of the Naval Manuscripts in the Pepysian Library*. 4 vols. London: For the Navy Records Society, 1909–23.

Tawit, Muhammad bin. *"Wathaiq Sa'diyya lam tunshar."* *Majalat Tetuan* 4 (1958–59): 49–58.

———. *"Min zawaya al-tarikh al-Maghribi."* *Majallat Tetuan* 8 (1963): 23–165.

Tazi, Abdelhadi. *Histoire diplomatique du Maroc*. 8 vols. Rabat, 1987.

Temimi, Abdeljelil, ed. *Chretiéns et musulmans à l'époque de la renaissance*. Zaghouan, Tunisia, 1997.

Teonge, Henry. *The Diary of Henry Teonge*. Edited by G. E. Manwaring. London: Routledge, 1927.

Thomas, Keith. *Religion and the Decline of Magic*. Harmondsworth: Penguin, 1973.

Thompson, James. "Dryden's *Conquest of Granada* and the Dutch Wars." *Eighteenth Century* 31 (1990): 211–26.

Thomson, Ann. *Barbary and Enlightenment: European Attitudes towards the Maghreb in the 18th Century*. Leiden: Brill, 1989.

Thomson, Janice E. *Mercenaries, Pirates and Sovereigns*. Princeton, N.J.: Princeton University Press, 1994.

Thrush, A. "Naval Finance and the Origins and Development of Ship Money." In *War and Government in Britain, 1598–1650*, edited by Mark Charles Fissel, 133–62. Manchester: Manchester University Press: 1991.

Todd, Margo. "A Captive's Story: Puritans, Pirates and the Drama of Reconciliation." *Seventeenth Century* 12 (1997): 37–56.

Tokson, Elliot H. *The Popular Image of the Black Man in English Drama, 1550–1688*. Boston: G. K. Hall, 1982.

Trinity House of Deptford Transactions, 1609–1635. Edited by G. G. Harris. London: Record Society, 1983.

A True and Perfect Relation of the Happy Successe and Victory Obtained against the Turks of Argiers at Bugia. London, 1671.

A True Copie of the Petition of the Gentlewomen and Tradesmen-Wives, in and about the City of London. London, 1642.

True Newes from our Navie, now at Sea. London, 1642.

A True Relation of a Great and Bloody Fight between the English and the Moors before Tangiere. London, 1680.

Underdown, David. *Revel, Riot and Rebellion*. Oxford: Oxford University Press, 1987.

Unger, Gustav. "Portia and the Prince of Morocco." *Shakespeare Studies* 31 (2003): 89–126.

Vanan, Jamal. *Nusus wa Wathaiq fi Tarikh al-Jazair al-Hadith, 1500–1830*. Algiers, n.d.

Vaughan, Alden T., and Virginia Mason Vaughan. "Before Othello: Elizabethan Representations of Sub-Saharan Africans." *William and Mary Quarterly* 45 (1997): 19–44.

Vickers, Brian, ed. *Shakespeare: The Critical Heritage*. London and Boston: Routledge and Kegan Paul, 1976.

Vitkus, Daniel J., ed. *Three Turk Plays from Early Modern England*. New York: Columbia University Press, 2000.

———. "Turning Turk in Othello: The Conversion and Damnation of the Moor." *Shakespeare Quarterly* 48 (1997): 145–76.

Von Ranke, Leopold. *A History of England Principally in the Seventeenth Century*. 6 vols. 1875. New York: AMS Press, 1966.

Wadsworth, James. *The English Spanish Pilgrime. Or A New Discoverie of Spanish Popery, and Iesviticall Stratagems*. London, 1629.

Waller, Edmund. "Instructions to a painter for the drawing of the posture & progress of His Majesties forces at sea . . . victory obtained over the Dutch June 3, 1665." London, 1666.

Wallington, Nehemiah. *Historical Notices of Events Occurring Chiefly in the Reign of Charles I*. London, 1869.

Wansbrough, John. "A Moroccan Amir's Commercial Treaty with Venice of the Year 913/1508." *Bulletin of the School of Oriental and African Studies* 25 (1966): 449–71.

Wansharisi, Ahmad bin Yahya al-. *Al-Mi'yar al-mu'arrab*. Edited by Muhammad Hajji. Beirut: Dar al-Gharb al-Islami, 1981.

Weiner, Jerome B. "Anglo-Moroccan Relations in the First Decade of the Occupation of Tangier, 1662–1672." *Hespéris Tamuda* 18 (1979): 63–75.

Weiss, Gillian Lee. "Back from Barbary: Captivity, Redemption and French Identity in the Seventeenth- and Eighteenth-Century Mediterranean." PhD diss., Stanford University, 2002.

Wernham, R. B. *The Expedition of Sir John Norris and Sir Frances Drake to Spain and Portugal, 1589*. London: For the Navy Records Society, 1988.

———, ed. *List and Analysis of State Papers Foreign Series Elizabeth I*. London: HMSO, 1969.

———. "Queen Elizabeth and the Portugal Expedition of 1589." *English Historical Review* 64 (1951): 1–26; 194–218.

Wilkins, George. *Three Miseries of Barbary: Plague. Famine. Civill war*. London, 1609.

Williams, Noel T. St. John. *Redcoats and Courtesans: The Birth of the British Army (1660–1690)*. London: Brassey's, 1994.

Williams, Norman Lloyd. *Sir Walter Raleigh*. Harmondsworth: Penguin, 1962.

Wilson, Richard. "Voyage to Tunis: New History and the Old World of *The Tempest*." *ELH* 64 (1997): 333–57.

Windus, John. *A Journey to Mequinez; The Residence of the Present Emperor of Fez and Morocco*. London, 1725.

Wolf, John B. *The Barbary Coast: Algeria under the Turks, 1500 to 1800*. New York and London: W. W. Norton, 1979.

The Worlde, or An historicall description of the most famous kingdomes and commonweales therein. London, 1601.

Youings, Joyce, ed. *Raleigh in Exeter 1985*. Exeter: University of Exeter, 1985.

Young, Alan R., ed. *The English Emblem Tradition*. Toronto: University of Toronto Press, 1995.

Yousseff, Mohammad Seghir ben. *Mechra el Melki: Chronique tunisienne (1705–1771)*. Translated by Victor Serres and Mohammad Lasram. Tunis, n.d.

Index

Nabil Matar is professor of English and head of the Humanities and Communication Department at the Florida Institute of Technology. He is the author of *Islam in Britain, 1558–1685* (1998), *Turks, Moors and Englishmen in the Age of Discovery* (1999), and translator of *In the Lands of the Christians: Arabic Travel Writings in the 17th Century* (2003).

Printed in the United States
151789LV00002B/55/A